W9-CJI-213

Letha A. (Lee) See, PhD, EdM, MSW
Editor

Violence as Seen
Through a Prism of Color

Violence as Seen Through a Prism of Color has been co-published simultaneously as *Journal of Human Behavior in the Social Environment,* Volume 4, Numbers 2/3 and 4 2001.

Pre-publication
REVIEWS,
COMMENTARIES,
EVALUATIONS . . .

"**R**elevant, current, and necessary for those who want to help others in the twenty-first century. . . . Adds an important dimension to educating human services professionals in fields such as corrections, child welfare, and family therapy."

Leon Ginsberg, PhD
Carolina Distinguished Professor
College of Social Work
University of South Carolina
Columbia

The Haworth Social Work Practice Press
An Imprint of The Haworth Press, Inc.

Violence as Seen Through a Prism of Color

Violence as Seen Through a Prism of Color has been co-published simultaneously as *Journal of Human Behavior in the Social Environment,* Volume 4, Numbers 2/3 and 4 2001.

The *Journal of Human Behavior in the Social Environment*™ Monographic "Separates"

Below is a list of "separates," which in serials librarianship means a special issue simultaneously published as a special journal issue or double-issue *and* as a "separate" hardbound monograph. (This is a format which we also call "DocuSerial.")

"Separates" are published because specialized libraries or professionals may wish to purchase a specific thematic issue by itself in a format which can be separately cataloged and shelved, as opposed to purchasing the journal on an on-going basis. Faculty members may also more easily consider a "separate" for classroom adoption.

"Separates" are carefully classified separately with the major book jobbers so that the journal tie-in can be noted on new book order slips to avoid duplicate purchasing.

You may wish to visit Haworth's website at . . .

http://www.HaworthPress.com

. . . to search our online catalog for complete tables of contents of these separates and related publications.

You may also call 1-800-HAWORTH (outside US/Canada: 607-722-5857), or Fax 1-800-895-0582 (outside US/Canada: 607-771-0012), or e-mail at:

getinfo@haworthpressinc.com

Violence as Seen Through a Prism of Color, edited by Letha A. (Lee) See, PhD, EdM, MSW (Vol. 4, 2/3, 4, 2001). *"Incisive and important. . . . A comprehensive analysis of the way violence affects people of color. Offers important insights. . . . Should be consulted by academics, students, policymakers, and members of the public." (Dr. James Midgley, Harry and Riva Specht Professor and Dean, School of Social Welfare, University of California at Berkeley)*

Psychosocial Aspects of the Asian-American Experience: Diversity Within Diversity, edited by Namkee G. Choi, PhD (Vol. 3, No. 3/4, 2000). *Examines the childhood, adolescence, young adult, and aging stages of Asian Americans to help researchers and practioners offer better services to this ethnic group. Representing Chinese, Japanese, Filipinos, Koreans, Asian Indians, Vietnamese, Hmong, Cambodians, and native-born Hawaiians, this helpful book will enable you to offer clients relevant services that are appropriate for your clients' ethnic backgrounds, beliefs, and experiences.*

Voices of First Nations People: Human Services Considerations, edited by Hilary N. Weaver, DSW (Vol. 2, No. 1/2, 1999). *"A must read for anyone interested in gaining an insight into the world of Native Americans. . . . I highly recommend it!" (James Knapp, BS, Executive Director, Native American Community Services of Erie and Niagara Counties, Inc., Buffalo, New York)*

Human Behavior in the Social Environment from an African American Perspective, edited by Letha A. (Lee) See, PhD (Vol. 1, No. 2/3, 1998). *"A book of scholarly, convincing, and relevant chapters that provide an African-American perspective on human behavior and the social environment . . . offer[s] new insights about the impact of race on psychosocial development in American society." (Alphonso W. Haynes, EdD, Professor, School of Social Work, Grand Valley State University, Grand Rapids, Michigan)*

Violence as Seen Through a Prism of Color

Letha A. (Lee) See, PhD, EdM, MSW
Editor

Preface by
Coramae Richey Mann, PhD

Violence as Seen Through a Prism of Color has been co-published simultaneously as *Journal of Human Behavior in the Social Environment,* Volume 4, Numbers 2/3 and 4 2001.

The Haworth Social Work Practice Press
An Imprint of
The Haworth Press, Inc.
New York • London • Oxford

Published by
The Haworth Social Work Practice Press, 10 Alice Street, Binghamton, NY 13904-1580 USA

The Haworth Social Work Practice Press is an imprint of The Haworth Press, Inc., 10 Alice Street, Binghamton, NY 13904-1580 USA.

Violence as Seen Through a Prism of Color has been co-published simultaneously as *Journal of Human Behavior in the Social Environment,* Volume 4, Numbers 2/3 and 4 2001.

The development, preparation, and publication of this work has been undertaken with great care. However, the publisher, employees, editors, and agents of The Haworth Press and all imprints of The Haworth Press, Inc., including The Haworth Medical Press® and Pharmaceutical Products Press®, are not responsible for any errors contained herein or for consequences that may ensue from use of materials or information contained in this work. Opinions expressed by the author(s) are not necessarily those of The Haworth Press, Inc.

Cover design by Thomas J. Mayshock Jr.

Library of Congress Cataloging-in-Publication Data

Violence as seen through a prism of color / Letha A. (Lee) See, editor.
      p. cm.
     "Co-published simultaneously as Journal of human behavior in the social environment, vol. 4, nos. 2/3 and 4, 2001."
     Includes bibliographical references and index.
     ISBN 0-7890-1392-4 (hard : alk. paper)–ISBN 0-7890-1393-2 (softcover : alk. paper)
     1. African Americans–Social conditions–1975- 2. African Americans–Violence against. 3. Violence–United States. 4. United States–Race relations. I. See, Letha A. Lee. II. Journal of human behavior in the social environment. Vol. 4, nos. 2/3, 2001. III. Journal of human behavior in the social environment. Vol. 4, no. 4, 2001.
E185.86 .V54 2001
303.6'089'96073–dc21   2001039663

Indexing, Abstracting & Website/Internet Coverage

This section provides you with a list of major indexing & abstracting services. That is to say, each service began covering this periodical during the year noted in the right column. Most Websites which are listed below have indicated that they will either post, disseminate, compile, archive, cite or alert their own Website users with research-based content from this work. (This list is as current as the copyright date of this publication.)

Abstracting, Website/Indexing Coverage .... Year When Coverage Began

- *BUBL Information Service. An Internet-based Information Service for the UK higher education community. <URL: http://bubl.ac.uk/>* **2000**

- *Cambridge Scientific Abstracts <www.csa.com>* **1998**

- *caredata CD: the social & community care database <www.nisw.org.uk>* **1998**

- *Child Development Abstracts & Bibliography (in print & online)* **1998**

- *CINAHL (Cumulative Index to Nursing & Allied Health Literature), in print, EBSCO, and SilverPlatter, Data-Star, and PaperChase. (Support materials include Subject Heading List, Database Search Guide, and instructional video)* **1998**

- *CNPIEC Reference Guide: Chinese National Directory of Foreign Periodicals* **1998**

- *Criminal Justice Abstracts* **1998**

(continued)

*Special Bibliographic Notes related to special journal issues
(separates) and indexing/abstracting:*

- indexing/abstracting services in this list will also cover material in any "separate" that is co-published simultaneously with Haworth's special thematic journal issue or DocuSerial. Indexing/abstracting usually covers material at the article/chapter level.
- monographic co-editions are intended for either non-subscribers or libraries which intend to purchase a second copy for their circulating collections.
- monographic co-editions are reported to all jobbers/wholesalers/approval plans. The source journal is listed as the "series" to assist the prevention of duplicate purchasing in the same manner utilized for books-in-series.
- to facilitate user/access services all indexing/abstracting services are encouraged to utilize the co-indexing entry note indicated at the bottom of the first page of each article/chapter/contribution.
- this is intended to assist a library user of any reference tool (whether print, electronic, online, or CD-ROM) to locate the monographic version if the library has purchased this version but not a subscription to the source journal.
- individual articles/chapters in any Haworth publication are also available through the Haworth Document Delivery Service (HDDS).

ABOUT THE EDITOR

Letha A. (Lee) See, PhD, EdM, MSW, is Professor in the School of Social Work at the University of Georgia. She received her doctorate from Bryn Mawr College in 1982, and taught there as well as at Lincoln University, Atlanta University, and the University of Arkansas. She has spent many years working in national, state, regional, and local social service agencies, and has served as consultant for major organizations including the U.S. Department of Education. Dr. See is a licensed marriage and family therapist, licensed clinical social worker, registered psychotherapist, social work diplomate, and a member of the Academy of Social Workers. She is listed on the *National Clinical Social Work Roster,* in *Who's Who in the World* (Cambridge, England), and is a member of Delta Sigma Theta Sorority.

Dr. See is active in national and international affairs and has studied, traveled, and lectured in countries including The People's Republic of China, Russia, Australia, Japan, Korea, Costa Rica, Puerto Rico, and Mexico. She has also lectured at Harvard University. She is the author of *Tension and Tangles Between Afro Americans and Southeast Asian Refugees, Human Behavior in the Social Environment from an African American Perspective*, and *Terrorism in Academia* (forthcoming). She has published many articles, monographs, book chapters, and guest editorials. Her research interests are in the areas of refugee resettlement, human behavior, immigration issues, women's studies, social policy, and prison violence.

This book is dedicated to

PROFESSOR JOHN HOPE FRANKLIN

who spent a lifetime helping
Americans understand structural
violence in our social system...

The book is also dedicated to the memory of

DR. ROBERT O. WASHINGTON

who died before he saw in print his excellent
co-authored article written for this book.

Violence as Seen
Through a Prism of Color

CONTENTS

Foreword

A nation founded on violence, fraught with massacres, revolution, wars, and violent land grabs, clearly contains sufficient violent components imbedded deeply in its structure. Not too long after arriving on the American shore, white settlers assaulted and massacred the native Indians who had welcomed and aided the hapless new arrivals. The subsequent violent theft of Indian homelands culminating in the obscene "Trail of Tears" along which thousands of Indians died on the forced, long trek to western "reservations." Their corpses were left where they fell on that atrocious trail, without benefit of burial or proper mourning. Nor could any shame be worse than that associated with the brutal treatment of African slaves who were dragged to this country in chains. Lashings, lynching, beating, maiming and castration were perpetrated against the kidnapped and enslaved Africans. There was no shame. Such violence was considered perfectly normal and culturally correct.

For decades, a variety of academic disciplines attempted to isolate the causes and motivations for human acts of violence against their own kind. For the most part, they were unsuccessful, providing only a few jagged pieces to the enormous puzzle. The primary focus was on the individual and individual acts of violence. As a criminologist, my research interests centered on the etiology of offenses such as rape, assault, homicide, and human rights atrocities. Yet, the notion of violence as a structural entity in this nation was never distant from my theoretical consciousness.

This unique volume creatively assembled by Professor Letha A. (Lee) See, acutely refocuses my attention. It provides reinforcement for the perspective that violence is endemic to the United States. American violence provided the initial threads for the fabric of our society, and thus has existed since its inception. "Violence is as American as cherry pie" are the words of Jamil Al-Amin (H. Rap Brown).

Equally singular is Professor See's selection of primarily African American scholars to introduce their perspectives on violence. Their viewpoints are

[Haworth co-indexing entry note]: "Foreword." Mann, Coramae Richey. Co-published simultaneously in *Journal of Human Behavior in the Social Environment* (The Haworth Social Work Practice Press, an imprint of The Haworth Press, Inc.) Vol. 4, Nos. 2/3, 2001, pp. xiii-xiv; and: *Violence as Seen Through a Prism of Color* (ed: Letha A. (Lee) See) The Haworth Social Work Practice Press, an imprint of The Haworth Press, Inc., 2001, pp. xiii-xiv. Single or multiple copies of this article are available for a fee from The Haworth Document Delivery Service [1-800-342-9678, 9:00 a.m. - 5:00 p.m. (EST). E-mail address: getinfo@haworth pressinc.com].

xiii

most fitting since the accusatory legal finger is most often pointed at African Americans and other people of color.

While previous African American scholars variously reviewed the violence of blacks, most did not make the critical connection between the American social structure and violence, or the crucial nexus between whites and violence in America. In *Black Bourgeoisie*, eminent African American sociologist E. Franklin Frazier's notion of the "inferiority complex" of the black bourgeoisie set an unfortunate theme of lower black self-esteem. After all, one could argue, if the black middle class, with its many advantages, suffers from a collective inferiority complex, surely the black underclass has to be seriously lacking in self-esteem. Today, almost forty years later, this erroneous explanation is still espoused to explain black violence. For decades, similar perspectives of individual pathology dominated causes of black violence. However, black West Indian psychiatrist Frantz Fanon came closer to the target when he wrote of blacks "identifying with" their (white) oppressors. Further, in their book, *Black Rage*, African American psychiatrists William H. Grier and Price M. Cobbs describe the ongoing deleterious effects of slavery and its after effects on blacks oppressed in a white society.

More and more frequently, social scientists seek the causes of violence through examinations of the American social structure. The deterioration of traditional American institutions, such as the family, church, school, and a sense of community, shred those delicate fibers that hold our society together. Denial of participation in the political and economic structures and the concomitant poverty, unemployment, underemployment, public welfare, or lower economic statuses are now scrutinized as possible causes of homicide and other violent crimes. We are drawing closer to a structural explanation for violence in the United States, a fact that makes this important collection of scholarly work both timely and significant.

Coramae Richey Mann, PhD
Professor Emerita
Indiana University
Indiana

Preface

The problem of the twentieth century
is the problem of the color line.

–W.E.B. DuBois, PhD
1903

The marvel of the twenty-first century is that
America will have no color line–the totality
of the population will melt into brown.

–Letha A. (Lee) See, PhD, EdM, MSW
2000

A few months ago, I edited a book and a double volume of journal articles on the subject of *Human Behavior in the Social Environment from an African American Perspective* (See, 1998). The writings were presented in the spirit of furthering an understanding of African American behavior, filling gaps in information, correcting erroneous thinking, and effecting shifts in attention on the maelstrom of social change that is taking place in our society. That work was authored by some of the nation's best known and emerging African American sociologists, educators, theoreticians, and psychotherapists. The central thematic concern of the contributors was to break new ground, unearth new insights, ignite new thinking, and present to their readership a mountain of "stubborn facts" about the black experience, black behavior, behavioral consequences, and the circumstances under which black dissonant behavior occurs. Their writings, which combined empirical evidence with deep thought and painful personal experiences, shed light on the thorny problems associated with African American behavior, and included important insights on black vio-

[Haworth co-indexing entry note]: "Preface." See, Letha A. (Lee). Co-published simultaneously in *Journal of Human Behavior in the Social Environment* (The Haworth Social Work Practice Press, an imprint of The Haworth Press, Inc.) Vol. 4, Nos. 2/3, 2001, pp. xv-xvii; and: *Violence as Seen Through a Prism of Color* (ed: Letha A. (Lee) See) The Haworth Social Work Practice Press, an imprint of The Haworth Press, Inc., 2001, pp. xv-xvii. Single or multiple copies of this article are available for a fee from The Haworth Document Delivery Service [1-800-342-9678, 9:00 a.m. - 5:00 p.m. (EST). E-mail address: getinfo@ haworthpressinc.com].

lence. In general, that work stirred widespread discussion, ongoing debate, and challenged social science professionals to "think about the unthinkable."

With devastating clarity, the African American authors brilliantly argued their points and did not tiptoe around complex mind-boggling issues. They realized that some traditional social scientists would be critical of their work and would need to be dragged kicking and screaming before they would listen to, or read, what African American educators wrote about black behavior. In effect, they correctly reasoned that the "old guard" would resist change and not easily accept 21st century "paradigmatic shifts." Further, they observed that some academicians are slaves to the status quo, and are not committed to discarding the same stale and molded interventions and techniques that have proven ineffective in working with African American and diverse populations that keep pouring into this nation in astronomical numbers. Be that as it may, the work of the contributors had a jarring effect, as the book received responses, which have been overwhelmingly favorable.

And so again, the editors of the *Journal of Human Behavior in the Social Environment* have invited me to oversee a second edited book, *Violence as Seen Through a Prism of Color*, and, simultaneously, a double volume of articles designed to address the subject of structural violence in American society. This is a "hot topic" in scope and content, and my task is significantly more risky. The main problem is that I am a social work educator and psychotherapist who has read about violence, but am not formally trained in terrains such as criminology, law, criminal justice and philosophy–specialty fields that must be tapped in order to present fresh, useful, vigorous, empirically-based and conceptual insights into such a weighty issue. Thus, my first laborious task was to review volumes of literature in prominent journals for recent trends and issues on violence.

Surprisingly, as I began the laborious task of reviewing the social work literature, it soon became clear that writings in the field were far "too thin," too unclear, too hopelessly bland, and too theoretically lacking to properly explore structural violence with all of its complex manifestations. This realization led to my examination of award-winning textbooks on violence in the fields of criminology, law, and criminal justice. For that effort I was richly rewarded. Some writings, however, dealt solely with domestic violence, the characteristics of violent offenders, and looked at criminal law. Other publications concentrated on the history, philosophy, punishment, structure and functioning of the criminal justice system with emphasis on the sociology of violence. A few articles were eloquently conceptualized, while others were so filled with social science and legal jargon until they had a dizzying effect. In sum, the voluminous writings sliced, diced, dissected, pulverized, and pureed violence to its least-common denominator. Surprisingly, with all of their brilliance, most of these analytical expositions gave little more than cursory attention to "structural violence" and "white collar crime."

What worries me is that the United States is spending millions of dollars on crime prevention, violence research, demonstration projects, commissions, consultations, and law enforcement initiatives, seeking to find what personal deficits and pathologies are giving rise to violence in this nation. Yet, few, if any, participants and authorities on crime and violence are stating, unflinchingly, that violence may be a structural problem that sticks like Krazy Glue to every group in society, except those who are viewed as the "fathers of violence"–corporate CEOs, big business tycoons, some politicians, elite groups, and the well-connected. These decision makers, whether intentional or unintentional, frequently impose intense pain on individuals, families and groups, but are rarely pointed to as accusers since their "dirty work" is done with "gloved hands." Therefore, my questions are: Could it be that social work educators and criminologists are researching the wrong subjects, and permitting to escape the world's greatest perpetrators of violence? What would turn up in the literature if there was a paradigmatic shift, and the gigantic sums of money spent on researching individual pathology would be spent researching structural variables? With these questions, I concluded that it would be utterly impossible to correctly examine violence and its devastating "brute force" on African Americans and other groups without placing our entire social system of justice under microscopic scrutiny. And so, in the final analysis, I decided that this volume should exhaustively examine structural violence, as it is practiced in some of America's most revered institutions.

My next question, therefore, was–which group of scholars should be invited to toss out irrelevant issues and uncover the structural violence in our society? The answer was–the contributors would need to be a bright assembly of well educated, articulate, multiracial lawyers, researchers, academics, correctional officials, criminologist and ministers–all with impeccable credentials, and the products of some of the best educational institutions in the United States. The authors selected to help produce this work fill that description.

And so, in this book, cold hard stubborn facts, cases, and circumstances about structural violence in American society are addressed in considerable detail. Again, no words are minced, and there is no skipping around reality through the use of intellectual acrobatics. What is offered is an uncovering of how our social system may be giving rise to uncontrolled violence in the 21st century, and how this structural malady can be halted. The analytical perspectives teased out from this work, hopefully, will set the groundwork for the next stage of work–which will entail the presentation of empirical investigations that will flow from the insights gained from the production of this volume.

Letha A. (Lee) See, PhD, EdM, MSW

Overview

This compendium of scholarly work written under the title, *Violence as Seen Through a Prism of Color* has grown well beyond it's initial conception. Aside from retaining its original purpose of looking at violence from a structural perspective, it also includes state-of-the art information regarding the problems, dilemmas, issues, and experiments associated with violence and aggression in general. From one point of view structural violence refers to oppressive, brutal and reprehensive action imposed upon powerless people by institutions with significant power and control. The action taken by these giant conglomerates may be overt or latent, physical and emotional, and may exhibit scorn and denigration toward disaffected groups.

Most observers of the contemporary scene have observed that violence has no human properties or characteristics, thus its mischief must be carried out in organizations whose directions enact laws, make policies, rules, and regulations. Unfortunately, the shame of these monopolistic entities is their obsession for acquiring more and more power and wealth and prohibiting certain groups from enjoying the fruits of the American dream. For example, the antecedents to domestic violence that frequently occurs in Black, minority and other families may stem from a societal structure, governed by insensitive decision-makers who may deny a Black male or minority breadwinner an opportunity to hold a good job with good pay sufficient to properly care for his family. Thus, the stress and strain (imposed by the system) of being unemployed and unable to fulfill ones family obligation may evoke uncontrolled violent behavior. To put it simply, humans react to stress in different ways. More aptly stated by the Pulitzer Prize winner DuBous (1968), "Human animals are unique, unprecedented, and unrepeatable." Accordingly, how they react to the tense terrain of life in an uncaring social system is inextricably linked with the complex violent nature of man. But what is the nature of man?

[Haworth co-indexing entry note]: "Overview." See, Letha A. (Lee) Co-published simultaneously in *Journal of Human Behavior in the Social Environment* (The Haworth Social Work Practice Press, an imprint of The Haworth Press, Inc.) Vol. 4, Nos. 2/3, 2001, pp. xix-xxv; and: *Violence as Seen Through a Prism of Color* (ed: Letha A. (Lee) See) The Haworth Social Work Practice Press, an imprint of The Haworth Press, Inc., 2001, pp. xix-xxv. Single or multiple copies of this article are available for a fee from The Haworth Document Delivery Service [1-800-342-9678, 9:00 a.m. - 5:00 p.m. (EST). E-mail address: getinfo@haworthpressinc.com].

xix

THE VIOLENT BEHAVIOR OF MAN

The literature reveals that for centuries famous thinkers, activists, and reformers from Plato and Aristotle to Ghandi, Durant, and Martin Luther King have mused over the aggression and violent nature of man.[1] Some thinkers have observed that man has reached for heaven through space crafts, plumbed the ocean depths, searched for the secret of life by uncovering the mystery of man's genetic code and exposing the privacy of that information. Not only has Man formulated a number of lucid explanations about life, he is also currently attempting to understand the mysteries of death. Aside from this, man has made headway in probing for more information about the intrapsychic processes, of human beings–their cultural characteristics and social influences, and other factors of human experience. Yet, with all of this wonderful capability, talent, and creativity, man's inhumanity to man is a puzzling phenomenon that has defied understanding and explanation. Because of the restlessness of humankind and it's propensity for engaging in undesirable patterns of behavior, this notoriously difficult and immensely important question has been posed by some of the world's greatest thinkers: What is the nature of man? Is he innately evil, capricious, violent, and prone to exhibit dark aggressive physical acts and verbal force on his own kind? Or, is he just a little lower than the angels–a dynamic and complex being, with potential for possessing spirituality, otherworldly powers, but is endowed with the roots of evil and calamitous tendencies that simply cannot be overcome? Early literature indicates that scholars have rascalled with these philosophical questions and behavioral concerns, which to date have not been demystified. In searching for answers to these questions, deep thinkers have also asked: Do human beings and by extension organizations engage in flagrant violence in the interest of surviving in a hostile environment? Or, in the scheme of things, are they hopelessly violent and destructive with interest only in amassing wealth. Again, there is no answer to this question.

But an even more puzzling line of questions has recently been dumped into the mix when Mohan (1993) tacitly asked–exactly when did man [and organizations managed by them] become evil and violent? Was it doing the evolution from ape to Homo sapiens, or in the process of social transformation? Once again, no answers or optimistic responses have been presented.

Within the past three decades a third line of queries regarding the nature of man and the violent behavior men exhibit in organizations has been posed by an assembly of gene-centered professionals (sociobiologists). This group has converged on an interactive model of gene-centered co-evolution (Barash, 1977, 1978; Dawkins, 1979b, 1980, 1981; Hines, 1979; Jacob, 1977; Krebs, 1977; West-Eberhard, 1979; Wilson, 1975, 1980). Loosely included in this camp are linguistics, developmental psychologists, human geneticists, clinical psychologists, psychiatrists, population ecologists, and ethnographers. The timbre of their concern is even more troubling as they pose this series of questions: Is there a genetic basis for the violent exhibition of human behavior? And, are human beings selfish organisms, set on destroying everything in their path to assure the continuation of their own kind?

What is vividly articulated in this discussion is that violence whether committed or displayed by the individual or under the banner of organizations is a complex, dark, stubborn, menacingly, ugly, heart-rendering, crushing, physical, and verbal force which transcends all human understanding. It is often perpetrated by human beings who preside over formal organizations and are capable of wrecking nations, societies, groups, individuals reaching down into the gene pool and even destroying the perpetrators themselves. Analyzing violence from a structural perspective then requires going back into history and studying symbols, which were selected by number theorists from ancient Egypt. It meant reviewing the symbols used by the great mathematicians–Euclid, Archimedes, Hippocrates, Thales, and Pythagoras, and it meant carefully noting how these great thinkers made use of geometric designs such as pyramids, cylinders, cones, spheres and prisms to assist in clarifying complex theorems, and mathematical axioms. Finally, due to its unique properties, a prism was selected as the symbol of choice around which an examination of structural violence could be neatly framed. The question then was, why select the prism as a theoretical symbol for conceptualizing structural violence, and exactly what is a prism?

WHAT IS A PRISM?

Prisms are blocks of optical material with flat polished sides arranged at precisely controlled angels to each other. They deflect, deviate, and rotate beams of light as well as disperse their wavelengths (Tissue, 1996). There are many types of prisms, each having its own particular geometry to achieve the reflections necessary to perform a specific imaging task (Tissue, 1996). The Casix Inc. (1998) warns however that, "a selection of the most suitable prism is primarily dependent on the application for which it is to be used."

The question then is: what does an abstract symbol like a prism represent in terms of structural violence? Simply put, if we consider this geometric figure as a lens through which individuals and society reflect their perceptions of their world, we can then examine violence as a two-sided concept that must be viewed from the context of a society that interprets both violence and the individual who experiences it. Thus, in all instances violence against people of color must be, of necessity, interpreted within the context of the person or organization that perpetrate the violence and those who are victims of it. A practical application of prisms used to conceptualize structural violence is offered by Jackson-White (2000), who had this to say:

When violence is seen from a prism of color it is immediately realized that each cultural group has its perceptions and meanings attached to violence drawn from the group's social/societal experience with power, discrimination, and oppression. The more severe the oppression and structural discrimination, the more finite is the meaning of violence. In other words, violence for an African American and/or a Native American could be interpreted as the way one responds to them in a causal interaction. The prism (social system) for these populations will be markedly different from the prism of a Caucasian female who may be a product of privilege.

It follows then, that if one accepts the concept of the prism as a reflector of one's individual experiences, it will be understandable why this symbol is useful for describing how people of color have experienced violence imposed by the structure of this society. To help make the case of how structural violence may be seen from a prism of color the authors approached this issue from multiple perspectives. The articles presented in the first section of this work analyze structural violence in the context of the social, political, and economic changes in our post-modernistic society. Oliver discusses why it is important to consider how cultural racism contributes to the construction of motives in the matter of violence. He examines institutional arrangements and analyzes the justification given by individuals for racial acts committed. These acts include lynching, hate crimes and police violence against African Americans. Using the post-modern deconstruction framework cultural racism is discussed as a factor that contributes to impersonal structural violence, especially in situations involving Black offenders and victims.

Aldridge and Daniels are concerned about violence from a socio-historical perspective. They exhaustively examine the works of great African American thinkers like W. E. B. DuBois, hopeful of finding clues for addressing structural violence which adversely affects so many African Americans and other minority groups.

Few scholars view poverty as violence, and expertly dance around the issue. However, Allen draws from Ghandi's philosophical thinking and makes the case that poverty in a nation as rich and powerful as the United States is indeed violence. She examines how poverty affects the poor and theorizes how many facets of the political economy intercepts in the structure of our society.

See and Kashan tread into deep water as they examine violence in the suites. These authors do not resort to speculation but present cold, hard, stubborn facts, carefully researched about the tremendous profit corporations are amassing by making use of prison labor and using prisoners (mostly black) as human cargo. The authors raise questions about the privatization of prisons, and wonder about the prison industrial complex that is heralded in our society as an innovative enterprise.

See and Isaac are concerned about the violence that is taking place against African Americans employed in major corporations in the United States. Special attention is called to the physical violence these Black professionals are experiencing. More damaging however, is the psychological effects that "Black collar" corporate employees are enduring in their quest to climb the crystal staircase or corporate ladder. Intervention strategies for working more effectively with these professionals are provided.

Section II examines structural violence through prison bars, and through new innovative mechanisms. Johnson, a former prison warden and criminal justice official, provides an up close analysis of the violence in the system. His view is that the disproportionate number of Blacks and minorities in the prison system, sentencing practices, and the part played by the media in stigmatizing prison rehabilitative efforts is an American tragedy.

One of the most gripping readings concerns violence against African American women who are incarcerated or confined in law enforcement custody. Isaac, Lockhart, and Williams contrast two prominent frameworks that attempt to explain this social justice phenomenon. The trio argues that the treatment of Black women in prison seem to represent clear violations of human rights of prisoners.

Horne's article is frightening. In the precise language of an attorney and academician he discusses structural violence which is in the planning stage by "the men of science" and pharmaceutical companies. These entities have hit on a grand scheme which is inching toward human genetic experimentation (eugenics) designed to halt the aggressive behavior of undesirable persons in our society. These proposed biometrics and pharmaceutical approaches will be accomplished by making maximum use of anti-depressant and serotonergic drugs; conducting psychosurgery and drug therapy on five year old children; conducting cingulotomy (a form of lobotomy on prisoners turning them into zombies), and thus following a prescribed Black genocidal path through surgery and chemical castration.

Lee and Leonard's reading (section III) examines patterns of violence associated with the tenure process for the African American professor in traditionally white higher education institutions. In this article, violence is examined in the context of its psychological and demeaning effects. The following dimensions are reviewed: recruitment of African American faculty; the review process for tenure; the politics of tenure; socialization and orientation of faculty; junior faculty as victims and tenure denial. Intervention strategies for addressing the problems of violence in academia are recommended.

Washington and Avant examine some of the sociological dimension of violence in today's society and their connections with violence in schools. The article examines factors associated with an increased risk of violent behavior among school age youth. A basic assumption underlying the paper is that in order to change violent behavior of children, professionals must change the environmental circumstance that influence and contribute to undesirable behavior. Embracing the ecological perspective, the paper argues that schools must improve the equality of person-environment exchanges if they are to be effective in today's society.

Section IV addresses the theory issue of violence in male-female relationships. Alridge and Hemmons have constructed an impressive schematic called (The Lens Model) that has promise of providing a framework for interpreting the nature of conflict. The argument is made that structural variables are responsible for much of the friction that exists between Black males and females.

McNeely, Cook and Torres present compelling arguments that women as well as men are initiating violence in our society. These authors present strong empirical data to substantiate their assertions that domestic violence is not necessarily a masculine form of assaultive behavior. The article is sure to begin a new discussion on domestic violence as a human, and not merely a gender issue.

In Section V, Schiele and Stewart examine from an Afrocentric perspective, the recent, explosive and disturbing increase of white male youth homicide, particularly around school settings. The article analyzes the structure of American society that gives rise to this type aggression and violence. The author's analysis merges three structural cultural factors, which stresses the maintenance of white male privilege.

Brown and Gourdine direct their attention to Black adolescent females who are perpetrators as well as victims of violence. The researchers argue that many Black adolescent girls do not receive institutional support, protection, and nurturing, thus their young lives are constantly in a state of disequilibrium.

Farrell and Johnson discuss selected elements of structural violence. In retrospect, they put the civil disturbance in Los Angeles, California, under a microscope and conclude that lessons were not learned from the ordeal.

See looks at violence in the Black church (Section VI). The paper discusses the structural changes that are presently engulfing Black churches, tilting them in a secular direction. These changes include incoming Federal funding, the sponsorship of social programs, theft, racketeering, fraud, and the lack of power sharing that is afforded women who do most of the work but make few decisions. It is hoped that the exposure of this mayhem will encourage Black churches to revert to their original mission–that of fostering equality, justice, empowering families, and providing spiritual guidance for African Americans.

Letha A. (Lee) See, PhD, EdM, MSW

NOTE

1. The word man in early writings also includes women. This manuscript makes no alteration to that tradition. A debate regarding this usage is beyond the scope of this writing.

REFERENCES

Barash, D. P. (1977) *Sociobiology and behavior*. New York: Elsevier.

_____ (1978). *The Whispering Within*. New York: Harper & Row.

Casix Inc. (1998) *Prisms*.

Dawkins, R. (1979b) Defining sociology. *Nature* 280, 427-428.

Dawkins, R. (1980). Good strategy or evolutionarily stable strategy? In *Sociobiology Beyond Nature/Nurture?* (G. G. Barlow & J. Silverberg (Eds.), pp. 331-367. Boulder Westview Press.

Dawkins, R. (1981) In defense of selfish genes. *Philosophy*, October.

DuBous, R. (1969). *So human an animal*. New York: Charles Scribner & Sons. p. vvi.

Freud, S. (1900). The death instinct. In B. Wolman (Ed.) *Handbook of Clinical Psychology*. New York: McGraw-Hill, Inc. p. 311.

Hines, W.G. & Maynard Smith, J. (1979). Games between relatives. *Journal of Theoretical Biology* 79, 19-30.

Jacob, F. (1977), Evolution and tinkering. *Science* 196, 1161-1166.

Krebs, J. R. (1977). Simplifying sociobiology. *Nature* 267, 869.

Mann, C. R. (1993). *Unequal Justice*: A Question of color. Bloomington, In: Indiana University Press.

Mohan, B. (1999). *Unification of Social Work*. CT: Praeger.

Rose, S. (1978). Pre-Copernican sociobiology? *New Scientist* 80, 45-46

West-Eberhard (1979). Sexual selection, social competition, and evolution. *Proceedings of the American Philosophical Society* 123, 222-234.

Wilson, E. O. (1975). *Sociobiology: The New Synthesis*. Cambridge, Mass.: Harvard University Press.

Wilson, D. S. (1980). *The natural selection of populations and communities*. Menlo Park: Benjamin/Cummings.

Acknowledgments

This was a difficult book to produce as it entered waters where angels would "fear to tread." Clearly, examining the structure of any social system, and exposing the violence in that system, is a "heady" undertaking, and can best be described as the work of a social scientist gone astray. Then, too, proposing solutions or syntheses to the malaise in our society is viewed by some as not only a weighty task, but arrogant as well. So, it took encouragement and support to bring such a project as this to fruition.

At one point during the production of this book, I felt it would never be completed–especially since so many authors experienced unbelievable personal and professional difficulties that rendered them unable to complete their manuscripts in accordance with the time line. So, to maintain the sequence of the chapters, I was faced with a dilemma: Either leave gaps and pores in the manuscript, or assume responsibility for writing the missing narratives. As I worried and fretted over the problem, my dear husband, Colonel Wilburn R. See, "the Colonel"–my best friend, my confidante, and my warrior, commanded me, in military jargon, to "make an estimation of the situation and determine the best course of action to follow." I made that estimation and determined that the best course of action was to stop the complaining and the mourning, shed the victimization mentality, and get busy with the writing.

Not only the Colonel, but also my son, Terry L. See, and my sisters, Doris J. Blaine and Edwina Sanders Lynn, were powerful sources of strength. My sisters, like many strong women, screamed at me when I hit a writer's plateau. Likewise, when my eyes could no longer endure the strain of editing another manuscript, "the sisters" reminded me of my roots, of the strong women in our family, and insisted that I dip into my inner strength and keep moving with the project. Therefore, for their encouragement and love, I thank them from the bottom of my heart.

Sincere thanks is also extended to my wonderful colleagues, Drs. John Wodarski and Marvin Feit, Co-Editors of the *Journal of Human Behavior in the Social Environment,* who kept my spirits high as I missed one deadline after

[Haworth co-indexing entry note]: "Acknowledgments." See, Letha A. (Lee). Co-published simultaneously in *Journal of Human Behavior in the Social Environment* (The Haworth Social Work Practice Press, an imprint of The Haworth Press, Inc.) Vol. 4, Nos. 2/3, 2001, pp. xxvii-xxix; and: *Violence as Seen Through a Prism of Color* (ed: Letha A. (Lee) See) The Haworth Social Work Practice Press, an imprint of The Haworth Press, Inc., 2001, pp. xxvii-xxix. Single or multiple copies of this article are available for a fee from The Haworth Document Delivery Service [1-800-342-9678, 9:00 a.m. - 5:00 p.m. (EST). E-mail address: getinfo@haworthpressinc.com].

another. They constantly reminded me that my previous work, *Human Behavior in the Social Environment from an African American Perspective* was a best seller, and was well received in the social work/social science communities. These editors assured me that the present volume of work represents a new powerful way of thinking about violence and, thus, is an important undertaking that will fill a gaping hole in the literature. Those words gave me strength, and, to both, I extend warm and heartfelt thanks.

I am indebted to my friend and one of my favorite colleagues, Dr. Bruce Thyer, who was always available when I needed a brilliant, thoughtful professional to help shape and hone my ideas. His assistance is gratefully acknowledged. In like manner, a thanks is extended to my colleague and "sister," Dr. Geraldine Jackson-White, who assisted me in unscrambling my thoughts regarding the concept of "prisms." Her precious time and effort is gratefully acknowledged.

Again, I thank the contributors to this book who endured, with good cheer, my compulsion in striving toward perfection. How they endured my constant nagging, prodding, calling, and disturbing their light moments with loved ones and significant others, is beyond even my comprehension. Indeed, all are scholars of the highest caliber who taught me a great deal about violence, and added new dimensions to its study and analysis. Unquestionably, theirs was not an easy task, and I thank each of them for a job well done.

With a great deal of emotion, I wish to thank Dr. Coramae Richey Mann, Professor Emerita and "Mother Superior" in the field of criminology for sharing with me her vast knowledge. Although her eyesight is fading, she still expended much of her remaining vision and wrote the brilliant foreword for this book. Additionally, she offered support, made suggestions, and reminded me that examining violence from structural perspective would represent a powerful addition to the social science literature.

Indeed, I am indebted to my friend and brother, Dr./Attorney R.L. McNeely, Professor at the University of Wisconsin–Milwaukee. Through the years, Dr. McNeely, one of social work's most brilliant scholars, has supported my intellectual efforts, given me wise counsel, and has been a part of my small circle of trusted confidantes. I can never repay him for his wonderful support and caring.

Finally, I want to thank Deena Harvill Pave, Dana Shiree Rochon, and Joy Dunn, my three graduate research assistants at the University of Georgia. These students retrieved countless books, articles, and empirical studies that were valuable in helping me gain a deeper understanding of America's criminal justice system. Thanks is likewise extended to Marguerite Booker and Lisa Conklin, both of whom damaged their eyesight word processing some of the articles in this volume over and over and over, again. It would have been impossible to produce this book and the accompanying journal without the help of the efficient Haworth staff. They were patient and supportive. They posed relevant questions, offered valuable suggestions, and each of them has "eagle eyes." They can spot minor errors that the average mortal would overlook. Special thanks are extended to Thomas J. Mayshock Jr., cover design and Production Editors: Naomi Fanning, Diane Stauffer and Heather Niadna. So, again, I say to all--thanks! thanks! and thanks.

Letha A. (Lee) See, PhD, EdM, MSW

SECTION I:
A NEW LOOK
AT STRUCTURAL VIOLENCE

Cultural Racism and Structural Violence:
Implications for African Americans

William Oliver

SUMMARY. This article discusses why it is important to consider how cultural racism contributes to the construction of motives and justifications among individuals who have committed acts of structural violence, including, lynching, hate crime and police violence against African Americans. Cultural racism is also discussed as a factor that contributes to interpersonal structural violence in situations involving black offenders and victims. *[Article copies available for a fee from The Haworth Document Delivery Service: 1-800-342-9678. E-mail address: <getinfo@haworthpressinc.com> Website: <http://www.HaworthPress.com> © 2001 by The Haworth Press, Inc. All rights reserved.]*

William Oliver, PhD, is Associate Professor of the Criminal Justice Department of Indiana University. He received his PhD in Criminal Justice from the State University of New York (Albany). Dr. Oliver has written widely in the area of criminal justice, and his book, *The Violent Social World of Black Men* has been highly acclaimed in the social science community.

[Haworth co-indexing entry note]: "Cultural Racism and Structural Violence: Implications for African Americans." Oliver, William. Co-published simultaneously in *Journal of Human Behavior in the Social Environment* (The Haworth Social Work Practice Press, an imprint of The Haworth Press, Inc.) Vol. 4, Nos. 2/3, 2001, pp. 1-26; and: *Violence as Seen Through a Prism of Color* (ed: Letha A. (Lee) See) The Haworth Social Work Practice Press, an imprint of The Haworth Press, Inc., 2001, pp. 1-26. Single or multiple copies of this article are available for a fee from The Haworth Document Delivery Service [1-800-342-9678, 9:00 a.m. - 5:00 p.m. (EST). E-mail address: getinfo@haworthpressinc.com].

KEYWORDS. Cultural racism, structural violence, institutional violence, interpersonal violence, lynching, hate crime, police violence

INTRODUCTION

Within the last forty years, the study of violence has evolved as a major concern of social scientists. Indeed, the scope of violence research is very broad, including: war, riots, terrorism, child abuse, partner abuse, hate crime, police violence, and interpersonal and community violence, and police brutality (Graham & Gurr, 1979; Silberman, 1978). As a distinct group, a great deal of attention has been directed toward analysis of violence perpetrated by and against African Americans (Curtis, 1975; Ginzburg, 1988; Hampton, 1987; Oliver, 1998; Wolfgang, 1958). This is partially due to the disproportionate representation of African Americans among victims and perpetrators of interpersonal violence.

For example, in 1998 African Americans represented 13 percent of the general population in the United States (U.S. Bureau of the Census, 1999), yet they accounted for 53 percent of persons arrested for murder, 55 percent arrested for robbery, and 36 percent arrested for aggravated assault (U.S. Department of Justice, 1998). Furthermore, African Americans have higher rates of violent crime victimization than whites across all age and income groups (Bureau of Justice Statistics, 1999). For example, young black males 15-24 years of age have higher homicide death rates than any other race-sex subgroup in the United States. In 1995, the homicide death rate for young black males 15-24 was nearly nine times greater than that of similar aged white males, 123 per 100,000, 14 per 100,000 respectively. For every age range from age 1 to 85, African Americans have higher homicide death rates than white males and females of similar ages (National Center for Health Statistics, 1998).

The primary goal of this paper is to examine how cultural racism functions as a structural factor, that contributes to violent acts, committed against and by African Americans. A major assumption of the argument presented here is that cultural racism is a dimension of racism which is rarely considered among the various structural factors which are generally attributed significance as being positively correlated with violent acts perpetrated by and against African Americans. Finally, strategies will be proposed for addressing the problem.

A THEORETICAL FRAMEWORK FOR ANALYZING CULTURAL RACISM

Currently, there is a sharp division among scholars regarding the use of theory for most discussions–especially for an issue as thought-provoking as cultural racism and structural violence. For some, theory would be little more than a set of working concepts or hypotheses by means of which observations could be classified and ordered. For others a theory is a set of interrelated and structured propositions whose purpose is primarily eminently etiological (Rex & Mason, 1980).

It is clear therefore that we live in an age in which there is a deep mistrust of theories (Gilligan, 1998). In fact, a call to eliminate theories, or at least minimize them (See, 1998) in research, in practice, and in efforts such as an analysis of cultural racisms gaining momentum (Gilligan, 1996; See, 1998). The intellectual arguments regarding the relatively new phenomenon of theory utilization is spirited but is outside the parameters of this paper. Be that as it may, until the intellectuals can provide more compelling evidence on why theory should be ameliorated, eradicated or differentially crafted, we must continue with our traditional use of theory and thus set boundaries for examining violence from the view of cultural racism.

In this paper three overarching theories and perspectives may be useful in providing a causal explanation of cultural racism. These include: general systems theory, (Von Bertalanffy, 1968; Churchman, 1968)–the post-modernist or deconstructionist theory–(Baudrillard, 1991; Best & Kellner, 1997)–and the structural-cultural perspective (Oliver, 1989, in press). Taken together these theoretical formations have considerable utility in a discussion of cultural racism. For example See (1998), argues that "systems theory is basically a mathematical model that emerged from the second law of thermodynamics. . . . The important tenets of the systems perspective is that there must be interaction and interrelatedness if the system is to function without disequilibrium. Systems are regulated through negative and positive feedback, and causal influences are curvilinear. Thus, change in one part of the system cause change in the entirety of the system."

It can be argued therefore that from a systems perspective, if cultural racism is eradicated at the highest level of our social system, it will become non-existent at the lower echelons of society since a change in one part of there system affects the entire system.

Postmodernist or deconstruction theory represents a new theoretical paradigm that is both embraced and condemned. Baudrillard (1991) perhaps the most eloquent high-profile theorist of this perspective, whose works upstages that of Foucault (1980), questions the validity of basic concepts in critical social theory. He attacks Freudo-Marxian theories. In brief he provides an alternative perspective on contemporary society concerning the ways in which signs and images function as mechanisms of control within contemporary culture. The signs and images in the American social system at the highest levels of government have not forcibly condemned cultural racism. Therefore, See (1998), and Jenkins (1983) alluded to the post modernistic perspective with this declaration: " . . . there is a clarion call to "junk" all fallacious and stereotypical theories and research on Black people and start all over again . . . "

The third paradigm that has underpinning for the conceptualization of cultural racism is found in the structural-cultural perspective, which is articulated in the paper.

CULTURAL RACISM DEFINED

Within the social science literature there exists a long history of attributing the high rates of social problems and violent behavior among African Americans to racism. What is unique about this literature, however, is that most discussions limit the definition and examination of racism to its institutional dimensions. That is, in most social science literature, which examines social problems among African Americans, racism is conceptualized as the systematic deprivation of equal access to opportunity (Blauner, 1972; Knowles & Prewitt, 1969; Wilson, 1987). In practice, institutional racism involves denying individuals, based on race, access to the political, educational and economic systems and institutions which are the legitimate means used to earn a living and pursue upward mobility in American society (Knowles & Prewitt, 1969). Consequently, racism is often defined as a major source of structural pressure which leads to high rates of social problems, including: unemployment, poverty, lack of vocational training, substance abuse, property crime and interpersonal violence, (Clark, 1965; Staples and Johnson, 1993). Some violence researchers have also sought to explain various acts of collective or institutional violence (e.g., lynchings, race riots, and police violence) as consequences of racist practices (Graham & Gurr, 1979). In contrast to much of the existing literature which assumes a link between institutional racism and violence, the position argued here is that while it is important to consider how blocked access (structural violence) to opportunity creates social pressure which provides a context and catalyst for the occurrence of violence, the concept institutional racism as it is generally defined does not provide an adequate description of the breath of racism as a social practice. Thus it can be argued that movement toward a comprehensive analysis of the relationship between racism and violence perpetrated against and by African Americans must consider the effects of cultural racism.

The term cultural racism represents a deliberate effort to expand the definitional range of racism as a concept and to acknowledge its complexity as a social practice, which results in numerous adverse consequences for African Americans. Thus the term cultural racism is defined here as the systematic manner in which the white majority has established its primary cultural institutions (e.g., education, mass media and religion) to elevate and glorify European physical characteristics, character and achievement and to denigrate the physical characteristics, character and achievement of nonwhite people (Oliver, in press). Cultural racism is an institutionalized feature of American society. Consequently, it is another manifestation of institutional racism. However, in general usage, the term institutional racism does not connote an emphasis on biased or discriminatory cultural practices. Therefore, for purposes of this discussion, institutional racism has as its primary goal blocking African Americans from equal access to the legitimate opportunity structure; whereas, the primary goal of cultural racism is to diminish the cultural image and integrity of African Americans (Akbar, 1984).

A significant example of cultural racism as a social and institutional practice and an example of structural violence involves the conspicuous absence in most elementary and high school social studies curricula of a substantive discussion of the contributions of Africans and African Americans to the development of human civilization (Ben-Jochannan, 1991). Given the importance of history and social studies as a means by which a society introduces its young people to its celebration story, the conspicuous absence of African Americans in history textbooks reinforces and promotes racist ideology and racial stereotypes (Schafer, 1993). Such practices also distort the history and cultural image of African Americans (Akbar, 1984).

All forms of mass media in America have been involved in perpetrating cultural racism. For example, the early minstrel shows were constructed around the creation of characters and routines in which African Americans were portrayed as ignorant, childlike, promiscuous, foolish and violent (Riggs, 1986). Moreover in the evolution of mass media from minstrel shows, vaudeville, radio, film and television, these media have relentlessly presented content that promotes and justifies racial bias against African Americans. For example, in his interpretive history of blacks in American film, Bogle (1973) found that in the first fifty years of American film, African Americans were primarily portrayed as Toms, coons, tragic mulattoes, nannies, and brutal bucks.

Negative images of African Americans are also promoted in television programs. For example, the overwhelming majority of black actors are employed in comedic roles (Schafer, 1993). Moreover, Lichter and Lichter (1988) found that a third of high school students feel that television entertainment is an accurate representation of real life of African Americans.

The infusion of racial bias and stereotypes related to African Americans was also infused into American society through the creation and dissemination of practical artifacts used in the course of daily routine. For example, there is a long consumer history involving the construction and dissemination of stereotypical black images as a means of advertising and promoting both manufactured goods and services (Goings, 1994). Thus during the post Civil War era well into the twentieth century distorted images of African Americans have been used to sell products and subsequently reinforce racial stereotypes and the racial ordering of society (Goings, 1994).

CONSEQUENCES OF CULTURAL RACISM

Exposure to cultural racism has had a distinct set of consequences for whites and African Americans. A major consequence for whites has been a generalized acceptance of racist folklore and stereotypes as being truthful portrayals of African Americans (Fredrickson, 1971). In a study designed to examine agreement with negative stereotypes about African Americans, the Anti-Defamation League found that 76 percent of a national random sample of white Americans agreed with one or more of the following antiblack stereotypes: "blacks are more prone to violence," "prefer welfare over work," "are less ambitious," and "possess less native intelligence." The study also found that 55 percent of the respondents agreed with two or more stereotypes and nearly 30 percent agreed with four or more (Anti-Defamation League, 1993).

Among African Americans, exposure to cultural racism has contributed to the emergence of a cultural crisis. There are three factors that are characteristic of the African American cultural crisis. First, the loss of historical memory as a result of being subjected to macro-structural and cultural practices in which African Americans have been deliberately disconnected from their history and traditional cultural practices. Second, a lack of appreciation of the physical characteristics and cultural practices unique to Africans and African Americans. And third, a lack of cultural confidence leading to a lack of cultural competence (Karenga, 1982). The lack of cultural confidence diminishes the competence of a people to believe that they can collectively work to achieve broad-based goals that benefit the group.

Pettigrew (1981) for example, has suggested that the majority of white Americans are mentally unhealthy given their tendency to accept many of the racial fictions and myths, which represent the expression, and social practice of cultural racism. Feagin and Vera (1995) agree and suggest that "at an individual level white racism indicates a massive breakdown in empathy across the color line" (p. 174). Wright (1975) has argued that in cases where there is an extreme lack of empathy, whites may experience what he has described as a psychopathic racial personality. Finally, Welsing (1991) has suggested that "white supremacy is in fact like other neurotic drives for superiority or domination and, as a neurotic drive, it is founded upon a deep and pervading sense of inadequacy and inferiority" (p. 4). In sum, racist attitudes and myths are inherent in the structure of this society and therefore represent structural violence against African Americans.

A predominant theme in the scholarship of African American psychologists and psychiatrists is that exposure to racism has distorted the personality and mental health of African Americans (Azibo, 1989; Baldwin, 1984; Clark, 1965; Grier & Cobbs, 1968; Welsing, 1981). Psychiatrists Grier and Cobbs, (1968), for example, argued, based on the treatment issues presented by their patients, that African Americans tended to experience a sense of psychological rage as a consequence of their exposure to racism and inhumane treatment.

Many contemporary African American psychologists and psychiatrists support Baldwin's (1984) observation that "psychological misorientation is the most fundamental psychological disorder in the black personality." According to Baldwin (1984), "psychological misorientation" is a personality disorder that exists among African Americans resulting from intergenerational exposure to social pressures and institutions (e.g., the educational system, mass media, and religion) that promote and disseminate anti-black ideologies, socialization messages, and images. Self-destructive behavior is a common behavioral manifestation of psychological misorientation. Examples of some typical patterns of self-destructive behavior related to psychological misorientation include: defining manhood in terms of toughness or sexual conquest, alcohol abuse, drug abuse, drug trafficking, criminal activity and spending an inordinate amount of time participating in street corner-related activities (Akbar, 1984; Oliver, 1998; Wilson, 1990).

The mental health of African Americans is also negatively affected by what psychiatrist Chester Pierce (1970) has defined as offensive mechanisms. According to Pierce (1970) the term offensive mechanisms refers to "the collective micro-offenses by whites to minimize the social importance of any black or any black achievement so that blacks will see themselves as useless, unloved, unable" (p. 268). Thus, "culture makes offensive mechanisms automatic and perhaps obligatory on the part of whites" (p. 282). There are a broad range of verbal and non-verbal behaviors that whites engage in toward blacks that constitute offensive mechanisms or acts of micro-aggression, including: store clerks who assume that white patrons were first in line; security guards who specifically feel compelled to follow African Americans in stores; being denied front line employment; in interactions with blacks, many whites assume that they are uneducated and raised in the ghetto on welfare; and law enforcement officers, who without probable cause, stop African American motorists for what amounts to "driving while black." In the long-term, that is over the course of one's life-span, exposure to acts of micro-insults and micro-aggression has a negative cumulative effect on the collective mental health of African Americans (Pierce, 1970).

The adverse effect associated with exposure to racism is also reflected in the prevalence of traditionally defined mental illness among African Americans. For example, African American men are hospitalized for psychiatric reasons at a rate 2.8 times higher than white men and African American women at a rate 2.5 times greater than white women (National Institute on Mental Health, 1987). More specifically, African Americans are disproportionately diagnosed as schizophrenic or psychotic and make up a large percentage of people receiving services from public mental health facilities (Singleton-Bowie, 1995).

CULTURAL RACISM AND PATTERNS OF STRUCTURAL VIOLENCE

Structural violence is violence that occurs in the context of establishing, maintaining and extending, reducing or as a consequence of the hierarchal ordering of categories of people in society (Iadicola & Shupe, 1998). For example, acts of violence directed toward African Americans that function to reinforce and promote white hegemony is structural violence. Structural violence can also be interpersonal or institutional violence, depending on the context of the violent event and the specific roles combatants represent in violent encounters. In the discussion which follows below, a description of how several patterns of violence (e.g., lynching, hate crime, racial hoaxes, police brutality and black-on-black violence) perpetrated against and by African Americans are forms of structural violence that are influenced by the adverse effects of cultural racism.

LYNCHING AND HATE CRIME

In contemporary times, the term hate crime has been used to refer to criminal acts motivated by racial bias. However, the peak of hate crimes occurred early in the history of America in the form of lynching during the late 1800s. In the 1924 edition of Criminology, Sutherland (1924) defined lynching as the unlawful assault, killing or both of an accused person by mob action. At the end of the Civil War and beginning with the Reconstruction Era into the mid 1930s, lynching was a common response directed toward African Americans whom southern whites sought to intimidate or punish for violation of the existing racial codes (Russell, 1998). Between 1865 and 1955 an estimated 5,000 lynchings of African Americans occurred (Demaris, 1970).

The beliefs, attitudes, and social practices characteristic of cultural racism were salient in the construction of motives and justifications to lynch African Americans (Ginzburg, 1988). Lynching was clearly a form of structural violence in that there were dramatic increases in lynch mob violence immediately after the end of the Civil War and the subsequent Emancipation of African Americans from slavery. Lynching and other acts of mob violence were a means by which whites fearful of the newly freed slaves could reinforce the racial status quo which existed during the slavery era (Ginzburg, 1988). For example, Richard Maxwell Brown (1979) found that from 1868 through 1871, the Klan engaged in a massive campaign to lynch and intimidate African American men. In his research he recorded over 400 Klan lynchings of African Americans in the South between 1868 and 1871.

As social events lynchings had ritual importance to whites as a means to publicly proclaim one's support of a white superiority status quo. In addition, lynchings provided an opportunity for adults to socialize young whites on how to respond to African Americans who violate rules established by the white majority. For example, Messerschmidt (1997) observed that ". . . the typical lynching became a white community celebration, with men, women and children cheering a mutilation and hanging, burning, or both, at the stake" (p. 32).

Allegations that an African American man had raped a white woman was a common charge directed against black men who were targeted for lynch mob violence (Ginzburg, 1988). During the 1880s through 1900 the majority of lynch victims were charged with alleged sexual offenses (Brundage, 1993). Alleging rape was a certain means of precipitating white mob violence against African American men regardless of whether or not the act actually occurred or the dispute between the white and the African American involved a completely different issue (Brundage, 1993). Given the rigid racial status quo and prohibitions against black male-white female sexual relationships, allegations of rape had significant cultural and structural implications in southern society (Messerschmidt, 1997). Black men who flirted with white women, engaged in consensual sexual relations with white women or raped white women were perceived as having engaged in the ultimate violation of the racial status, that is, attempting to act like a white man.

Ritualized castrations of African American men were a common feature of lynchings motivated by allegations of rape (Ginzburg, 1988). These castrations reflected a deeply ingrained white male obsession with the alleged size of black male penises and a generalized acceptance of racist stereotypes which had been used to construct an image of black men as possessing an animalistic sexuality. Thus on a symbolic level lynchings motivated by allegations of rape provided white men with an opportunity to reinforce the stereotype that African American men were animalistic rapists, and that southern white men were chivalrous and righteous protectors (Dowd Hall, 1983).

The lynching of African Americans is illustrative of what Iadicola and Shupe (1997) refer to as interpersonal structural violence. That is, lynchings were acts of violence generally committed by individuals acting outside of formal institutional authority. However, the primary motivation for committing these acts of violence involved an effort to maintain and reinforce the institutionalized racial status quo (see Figure 1).

HATE CRIME

The term hate crime refers to criminal acts motivated by bias, that is, prejudice against a race, religion, sexual orientation, or ethnicity/national origin, as well as disability (U.S. Department of Justice, 1997). In response to the passage of the Hate Crime Statistics Act of 1990, the U.S. Congress has mandated that the Attorney General designate the FBI's Uniform Crime Reporting Programs to collect national data on hate crime (U.S. Department of Justice, 1997).

During 1997, a total of 8,049 bias-motivated criminal incidents were reported to the FBI by 11,211 law enforcement agencies in 48 states and the District of Columbia (U.S. Department of Justice, 1997b). Racially biased hate crimes are the most common type bias-motivated crime reported to the FBI. For example, of the 8,049 incidents reported in 1997, 4,710 (58%) were motivated by racial bias. African Americans are more likely than any other racial group to be victims of racially biased hate crime. The FBI reports that in 1997 blacks represented 3,951 (65%) of 6,084 victims of racially biased

FIGURE 1. Interpersonal Structural Violence

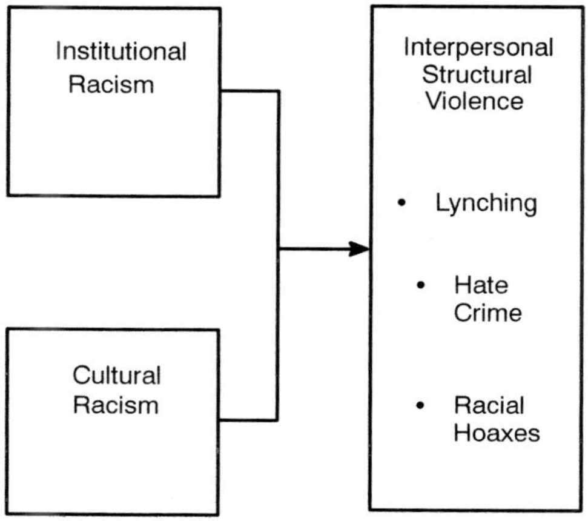

hate crime. In contrast, of the known offenders, 63 percent were white and 19 percent were black (U.S. Department of Justice, 1997).

Many whites prefer to view violent racist acts as the work of marginalized ideologues. However, Feagin and Vera (1995), have suggested that the ritual character of recurring antiblack acts indicate that they have become a traditional part of white communities and of the larger society and thus represents structural violence. Feagin and Vera's (1995) observation is supported by a recent study which found that only 5 percent of hate crimes are committed by individuals who are actively involved in organized groups (Levin & McDevitt, 1993). Moreover, Feagin and Vera (1995) argue that the proliferation of antiblack views is evident in the substantial support that former Klansman David Duke and his protégé Tom Metzger received in their unsuccessful bids for the senate and congress, respectively. For example, Duke, a former grand wizard of a national Klan federation was elected to the Louisiana state legislature and ran a primary campaign for the U.S. senate in which he received a majority of the white votes. Poll results suggest that both Metzger and Duke may not be as far outside the mainstream of white thought as some journalists and moderate politicians have suggested (Feagin & Vera, 1995).

Hate crimes are also being committed by individuals who are members of organized hate groups (Holmes & Holmes, 1994; Levin & McDevitt, 1993). While the majority of hate crimes are committed by individuals who are not active members of hate groups, hate motivated homicides are more likely to involve organized hate groups like the World Church of the Creator or various skinhead factions (Fox & Levin, 2000). Indeed, the number of racially-biased hate groups are increasing in the United States (Levin & McDevitt, 1993; Southern Poverty Law Center, 1999). Over the last decade several white supremacy groups have emerged as the most important in terms of recruitment of new members, and committing violent acts which receive national attention. Included among these groups are (1) the White Aryan Resistance, who has played a major role in recruiting and organizing young white males involved in the skinhead movement; (2) skinheads, especially those groups that have been mentored by the White Aryan Resistance; (3) the World Church of the Creator, a group that advocates race war to advance the interest of the white race; and (4) the Christian Identity Movement. The Christian Identity Movement has developed a religious theology upon which diverse white supremacy groups are uniting. Their theology teaches that whites are the true "chosen people" of God. They believe that whites are naturally superior to other races, and that all people of color are subhuman and more akin to animals than the white race. They also believe that the second coming of Jesus Christ will be preceded by a nationwide race war followed by a communist attack upon the United States. Subsequently, the only survivors will be members of the identity movement (Feagin & Vera; Holmes & Holmes, 1994; Iadicola & Shupe, 1998).

During the 1980s and 1990s, official reports and newspaper accounts of bias-motivated acts of vandalism, arson, intimidation and violence increased dramatically (Levin & McDevitt, 1993; U.S. Department of Justice, 1997). For example (Fox & Levin, 2000), have reported that there appears to be a distinct trend toward the commission of increasingly brutal hate crimes. There are several notorious cases of serious bias-motivated violence which confirm the empirical findings of organizations which systematically monitor hate crime. For example, in 1988, Mulugeta Seraw, an Ethiopian American was beaten and killed in Portland, Oregon by three skinheads who had ties to Tom Metzger's White Aryan Resistance group (Holmes & Holmes, 1994; Feagin & Vera, 1995). In 1989, eighteen year old Yusef Hawkins was chased and shot by a mob of young white males after he wandered into a community in Bensonhurst, Queens, New York looking to purchase a used car which had been advertised in the newspaper. On July 4, 1990 more than thirty white youths attacked a black family with baseball bats as they watched a firework display in Queens, New York (Ladicola & Shupe, 1998). In 1998, James Byrd Jr. was killed after three white men, who had affiliations with an organized hate group, picked him up as he was attempting to hitch a ride home. After being picked up by the men, Byrd was driven to a wooded area where he was stomped and beat and then he was chained to a pickup truck and dragged along a paved road until his head and right shoulder separated from his body (Curry & McCalope, 1999).

The acts of violence described above may be categorized as containing elements of interpersonal violence and structural violence. They are acts of interpersonal violence, in that they are acts of violence that occur between people acting outside the role of agents or representatives, for example, law enforcement (Iadicola & Shupe, 1998). They are also acts of structural violence in that the perpetrators of these racially biased acts of violence are attempting through their actions to promote the superiority of whites and to subordinate African Americans (Iadicola & Shupe, 1998). The motivational catalyst and justification for these acts is rooted in the perpetrators exposure and acceptance of cultural racism (Feagin & Vera, 1995). Perpetrators of hate crimes perceive blacks as less than human, as not worthy of respect, as wanting something for nothing, as contributing to the social and economic deterioration of America generally and to the loss of jobs and status among working-class white men particularly (Feagin & Vera, 1995; Levin & McDevitt, 1993). Their familiarity with racial stereotypes and the cult of racial hate reduces their inhibitions against committing acts of severe violence. Moreover, frustration with the circumstances of their personal lives combined with a racist ideology lead them to seek social esteem by defining themselves as righteous warriors who possess the courage to seek justice for white America (Hamm, 1996).

THE RACIAL HOAX

The racial hoax is another form of structural violence, which has been routinely perpetrated against African Americans. According to Russell (1998), a racial hoax occurs when someone fabricates a crime and blames it on another person because of his race or when an actual crime has been committed and the perpetrator falsely blames someone because of his race. While there is greater awareness and discussion of racial hoaxes today, the racial hoax perpetrated against blacks by whites has a long history. Historically, rape was the most common criminal hoax played upon African American men (Russell, 1998). For example, in 1931 in the case of the Scottsboro Boys, two young white women accused nine "Negro boys" of assaulting and raping them. The women told this story after they had voluntarily rode in a train boxcar with the black boys, who had earlier fought with a group of young white males over who would ride in a covered boxcar. Subsequently, when the train was stopped and the white women were discovered with the black boys, the women panicked and claimed they had been raped. After a speedy trial eight of the nine black boys were sentenced to death.

In contemporary times there have been two racial hoaxes directed against African Americans which represent exemplars of the racial hoax as a form of structural violence influenced by cultural racism. The first of these cases involved Charles Stuart. In November 1989, Stuart reported to police that he and his wife Carol were shot and robbed by a black man as they were returning home from a Lamaze birthing class. Carol Stuart and the unborn child died following the attack. This case received a great deal of media attention given the racial dynamics, that is, an all-American middle-class couple, expecting their first child are shot and robbed by a black man. Subsequently, the wife and child die and the husband is left to recover from his gun shot wound and the loss of his family. The Boston police mounted a massive investigation in the black area where the alleged crime occurred. Many black men were subjected to interrogations, searches and police lineups. Charles Stuart eventually picked a black man named Willie Bennett as the person who attacked him and his family. Upon further investigation of the inconsistencies of Stuart's account and incriminating information from his brother, who Stuart had solicited to kill his wife, Stuart committed suicide (Feagin & Vera, 1995; Russell, 1998).

The other notorious case involving a racial hoax perpetrated against African Americans by a white offender is the Susan Smith case. In October 1994, Susan Smith, a young white South Carolina mother, reported to the police that she had been the victim of a carjacking. The carjacker was described as a young black male, 20 to 30 years old. After gaining control of her car, Smith claimed that the carjacker drove off with her two sons, ages three and fourteen months. In response to the account provided by Smith, a massive statewide search was initiated. Nine days after the search began, Smith confessed that she had murdered her sons by allowing her car to become submerged in a local lake. Her motive for doing so was to make herself more desirable to a man who had broken off a relationship with her because she had minor children (Russell, 1998).

Russell (1998) suggests that racial hoaxes are devised, perpetrated and successful because they tap into widely held fears and stereotypes. That is, the belief that black men are violent is used to shift criminal responsibility from the white offender, the actual offender in the incident, to what Russell (1998) refers to as the fictional "criminal black man." An exaggerated fear of the image of the "criminal black man" persists despite the fact that the majority of whites who experience violent crime victimization are victimized by white offenders (Bureau of Justice Statistics, 1997). For example, in 1998, 84 percent of white murder victims were slain by white offenders (U.S. Department of Justice, 1998).

The racial hoax is a unique type of interpersonal structural violence. Unlike most acts of interpersonal structural violence, the racial hoax is not generally directed toward a specific individual. Rather it is structural violence perpetrated against a distinct racial group. However, it is interpersonal in that the perpetrator of the hoax is not acting as a representative of institutional authority, but is motivated by self interests. A racial hoax may also precipitate acts of institutional structural violence. For example, as in the Stuart case, it is common for law enforcement agencies to engage in overtly aggressive police practices (e.g., searches of homes and vehicles, on the street interrogations of individuals who are of the same sex and race of the alleged offender, and arresting individuals on suspicion of committing a crime). Indeed, encounters between the police and African American males subsequent to the promotion of a racial hoax have a great potential to escalate into violence given the anger of the police and the resentment of those African Americans who feel they have been unfairly targeted by the police because they are black.

POLICE VIOLENCE

Police violence against African Americans may be appropriately classified as institutional violence, structural violence or institutional structural violence. Police violence is institutional violence given that it is violence that occurs by the actions of societal institutions and their agents (Iadicola & Shupe, 1998). When police officers interact with citizens and they initiate necessary, unnecessary or excessive acts of violence against such citizens, their violent actions are governed by the roles they are playing in an institutional context as agents of government. Thus police violence is a form of institutional violence. However, it may also be a form of institutional structural violence, particularly when it is directed against African Americans. That is, police violence against African Americans has historically served the function of maintaining an American racial hierarchy in which the criminal justice system as an institution is used to perpetuate white dominance and black subordination (Higginbotham, 1978; Mauer, 1999; Miller, 1996) (see Figure 2).

There is a lack of adequate national data on police use of force, consequently, researchers must often rely on a variety of city-specific studies in order to discuss the prevalence of its occurrence. What the available data does suggest, however, is that there exists significant racial disparities between whites and African Americans relative to experiencing adverse contacts with the police (Bayley & Mendelsohn, 1968; Kuykendall, 1970). For example, in a recently published national study of police use of force, it was reported that African Americans and Latinos were 70 percent as likely as whites to a have face-to-face contact with the police (Bureau of Justice Statistics, 1997).

A significant source of data on police violence are studies which analyze complaints against the police. In an analysis of complaints against the Los Angeles Police Department (LAPD) from 1987 through mid-1990, it was

FIGURE 2. Institutional Structural Violence

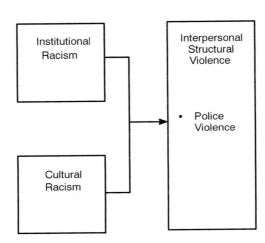

found that African Americans, who constitute 13 percent of Los Angeles' population, filed 41 percent of the complaints. In contrast, Latinos who constitute 40 percent of the population, filed 28 percent of the complaints, and whites who are 37 percent of the population filed 30 percent of the complaints (Rohrlich & Merina, 1991).

Statistics published by the New York City Civilian Complaint Review Board (CCRB) also indicate that African Americans are disproportionately represented among victims of public abuse and violence. For example, in their 1995 bi-annual report the CCRB reported that three quarters (75.9%) of the people who had filed complaints against New York City police officers between January and June of 1995 were African American (50%) and Latino (26%) (Amnesty International, 1996).

Most incidents of police violence are not reported to law enforcement, nor are they brought to the attention of the public through media accounts. However in a content analysis of major national and regional newspapers for the time frame January 1990 through May 1991, Learch (1993) found reports of 130 incidents of serious police brutality against citizens. Her findings revealed that white police officers were centrally involved in 93 percent of the reported cases of police assault and that African Americans or Latinos were the victims in 97 percent of the police assaults reported in the newspapers she examined.

One of the most notorious contemporary cases of police violence was the Rodney King beating which occurred in Los Angeles in March 1991. The facts surrounding the incident suggest that King, an African American male, was severely beaten by the police after he led the police on an eight mile car chase. The police had initially asked King to stop his car after he had been observed speeding. When King finally stopped the vehicle, he was yanked from the car by officers who felt that he was not moving fast enough. Once out of the car he wiggled his butt at a female police officer who had ordered him at gunpoint to lie down on the ground. Finally, he heaved four male officers off of his back when they attempted to handcuff him. Subsequently, he was shot with an electric taser gun, which didn't seem to phase him. When a second electrical shot failed to incapacitate him, King was struck in the face with a police baton. Upon falling to the ground King was severely beaten by several of the twenty-seven police officers who had participated in the car chase. At the criminal trial of the police officers charged with engaging in excessive force, it was revealed through analysis of videotape of the incident that King had received fifty-six blows in eighty-one seconds. The doctors who examined King reported that they found bodily damage: nine skull fractures, a shattered eye socket and cheekbone, a broken leg, a concussion, injuries to both knees, and facial damage (Mydans, 1991).

The four officers who were charged with criminal assault in the Rodney

King incident were subsequently acquitted by an all-white suburban jury. What was unbelievable to many people who had followed the trial was that evidence of guilt appeared to be overwhelming: several officers at the scene testified that the beating was unnecessary and a videotape of the incident was introduced which substantially contradicted the testimony of the accused officers.

The not guilty verdict in the first Rodney King criminal trial is an interesting case study of how the perception of African American men as dangerous criminals pre-conditioned a group of white jurors to disregard overwhelming evidence indicating that the police had engaged in excessive use of force.

The Abner Luima case is another recent incident of police violence against an African American that has received substantial national media attention. In this incident, Luima, a Haitian immigrant was arrested after he had observed a man with blood on his face shouting that he had been hit by the police. In response, Luima claims that he said to the police, . . . "even if somebody do something, the officer want to make an arrest, they are not supposed to hit him, because the person have his rights" (Indianapolis News, 1999). One of the officers who heard Luima's comments said to him, "Stupid nigger, I'm going to teach you a lesson on how to respect cops." Luima was immediately struck in the face with a police radio by the officer and physically assaulted by two other police officers who were present. After the beating, Luima was arrested and taken to a police precinct. At the precinct he was subjected to additional beating which ended when two officers forced him into a bathroom and stuck a police baton in his rectum and then put it into his mouth. The demeaning acts of brutality which were committed in the Luima incident are strikingly reminiscent of many lynchings of African American males committed in the first half of the twentieth century (Ginzburg, 1988; Messerschmidt, 1997).

Finally, one of the most notorious contemporary cases of police violence involves the case of the African immigrant, Amadou Diallo. In 1999, Diallo, an unarmed African was shot at 41 times and hit 19 times. This act of excessive force was precipitated when Diallo reached for and displayed his wallet when he was encountered by four New York City police officers, assigned to the proactive NYPD Street Crime Unit. The Diallo case has generated national debate about aggressive police practices based on the zero tolerance model of policing (Editorial, 1999).

Acts of unnecessary and excessive use of police violence against African Americans can not be fully understood if such acts are narrowly defined as examples of institutional or institutional structural violence. There is a cultural context in which police violence against African Americans is situated. According to Morales (1972), police recruited from the dominant society reflect the values, attitudes and prejudices of the majority community. Moreover, a

California study found that law enforcement officers were primarily recruited from the lower-middle and upper-lower classes; social groups which have been found to manifest high degrees of racial prejudice (Mann, 1993; Swett, 1969). The generalized societal disrespect for African Americans and internalization of antiblack stereotypes are often imported into the police occupational role from the larger society. Thus encounters with African Americans are substantially influenced by racially biased socialization experiences which predate the assumption of the police officer role (Levin & McDevitt, 1993).

For many white police officers conflict-ridden encounters between themselves and African Americans are attributed significant symbolic meaning. Given the pervasiveness of "the violent black man" stereotype, one of the great fears and challenges of police work involves learning how to successfully manage potentially threatening encounters with "the violent black man." These encounters are often characterized by dual tensions, including danger and victory, loss of respect or the acquisition of a valued status among police officer peers, and life or death. Such concerns emerge as a result of police officers familiarity and acceptance of distorted stereotypes of African American men as dangerous because they possess superhuman strength (Skolnick & Fyfe, 1993). Thus, I disagree with those who have suggested that the disproportionate rates of police violence against African Americans are exclusively the result of self-confident overt racism and hatred. Indeed, overt racism and hatred of African Americans is a significant factor leading to the high rates of police violence committed against them. However, I argue from a situational perspective, that as specific police encounters with African American suspects unfold into violent incidents, the primary motivation leading to police violence is white male fear of black males. It is the fear of African American males which leads police officers to respond to the slightest verbal or physical gesture with overt violence. In his classic study of police violence Chevigny (1969) found that the first step in the process leading to excessive force involves a perception by the police of a challenge to authority. In police encounters with African American males, violent actions tend to evolve as a consequence of fear of not being able to successfully meet the stereotypical brute force challenge that the animalistic violent black man represents.

Finally, police violence against African Americans may also be motivated by a conscious desire to reinforce the racial status quo (Myrdal, 1941; Jacobs and O'Brien, 1998). In incidents where this is a salient concern of the police, police officers use violence as a means of teaching the victim a lesson about the importance of knowing and staying in his place (Skolnick & Fyfe, 1993). This concern and motive for police violence against African Americans is indistinguishable from the concerns and motives of white lynch mobs. For example, Messerschmidt (1997) observes: "African American men who engaged in any practice defining a masculinity that indicated that they were acting like a white man became appropriate subjects for white male violence" (p. 27). African American men who challenge police authority by asking why they were stopped or asking for the police officer's badge number or verbally expressing anger about the inconvenience of a stop put themselves at risk for violent retaliation (Russell, 1998).

BLACK ON BLACK VIOLENCE

Given that most acts of interpersonal violence involve an interracial victim-offender relationship pattern (U.S. Department of Justice, 1997a), when these acts occur among African Americans, they are commonly referred to as black on black violence (Oliver, 1998).

Incidents of black on black violence may also be appropriately characterized as a type of institutional structural violence. Iadicola and Shupe (1998) have used the term interpersonal structural violence to refer to incidents in which individuals or groups acting outside of the role of interpersonal agents commit violent acts to maintain, extend or reduce hierarchical structures in society. From this perspective, a typical example of this type of violence is a race riot or other acts of race, gender, ethnic or class violence committed by individuals acting outside of the institutional structure of society. A significant aspect of Iadicola and Shupe's (1998) definition of interpersonal structural violence is that they assume that individuals who commit this type of violence do so as a means of supporting the goals and interests of the dominant institutions in society. With regard to the characterization of black on black violence as a type of interpersonal structural violence, Iadicola and Shupe's (1998) definition has been extended here to also include acts of interpersonal violence which are precipitated by the way in which the American social structure has been organized to have an adverse affect on African Americans (Blauner, 1972). That is, in most instances when African Americans engage in acts of interpersonal structural violence they do not manifest any conscious intent to maintain or extend the racial status quo, even though that is one of the social consequences of the high rates of black on black violence. Black on black violence is a major social problem in the African American community primarily because it occurs disproportionately. For example, African Americans represent 13 percent of the general population, however in 1997 they were over-represented among persons arrested for violent crime: 56 percent of murder arrests, 40 percent of rape arrests, 57 percent of robbery arrests and 37 percent of aggravated assault arrests (U.S. Department of Justice, 1997, 1997a). Moreover, for both African American males and females, 15-24 years of age, homicide is the leading cause of death

(National Center for Health Statistics, 1998). There is no singular cause which explains the disproportionate rates of interpersonal violence among African Americans. Moreover, there is very little consensus among criminologists and other social scientists relative to what causes the high rates of violence among African Americans. Explanations have ranged from institutional racism and economic inequality (Blau & Blau, 1982; Silberman, 1978), the economic transformation of the economy and the emergence of a black underclass (Wilson, 1987), commitment to values and norms which condone violence as a means of resolving disputes (Wolfgang & Ferracuti, 1967), adherence to a southern tradition of violence (Gastil, 1971), the cheapening of black life by the criminal justice system (Hawkins, 1983), racial inequality and displaced aggression (Poussaint, 1983), to street gangs and drug trafficking (Taylor, 1990).

A major limitation of most theoretical explanations of black on black violence is that they fail to consider how exposure to cultural racism contributes to the occurrence of violent behavior among African Americans. While it is important to consider traditional structural factors (e.g., racism, unemployment, poverty, female-headed families, etc.) to determine how strongly these factors may be correlated with violent behavior committed by African Americans, it is also important to note that violent behavior is ultimately a product of how situations or encounters with others are defined (see Figure 3) (Oliver, 1998).

FIGURE 3. Interpersonal Structural Violence Among African Americans

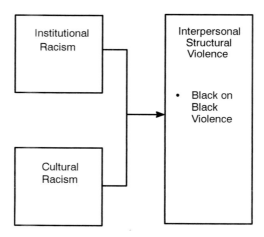

What, therefore, influences how African Americans define situations which they believe require that one resort to violence? I believe that exposure to cultural racism contributes to the existence of a definitional framework which influences how African Americans who are most at risk for engaging in violent behavior define themselves, others, their community and specific encounters. Cultural racism contributes to black on black violence through two distinct pathways (see Figure 3). First, cultural racism is one of several structural pressures–including institutional racism and the race neutral restructuring of the economy–which have contributed to massive social disorganization and social isolation among African Americans who reside in areas characterized by high rates of unemployment, poverty, welfare dependency and female-headed families (Wilson, 1978, 1996). While institutional racism produces social disorganization by denying equal access to the legitimate opportunity structure (Staples & Johnson, 1994), cultural racism leads to social disorganization through the deliberate attack on the cultural integrity and image of African Americans (Akbar, 1984). Racial stereotypes about African Americans (e.g., the view that blacks are lazy, sexually promiscuous, violent, irresponsible and have never made a significant contribution to America or the world) are more likely to resonate with those African Americans who live their lives in communities experiencing concentrated poverty. Thus, the combined effects of institutional racism, cultural racism and the race-neutral restructuring of the economy contribute to the establishment of communities which become fertile fields for the unchecked display of violent behavior. Second, cultural racism influences how all African Americans perceive and define themselves. It is impossible as an African American to be unaware of ones membership in a stigmatized racial group. Moreover, those who are most at risk for participating in violent behavior have had a tendency to accept as valid certain stereotypical images of African Americans (Fishman, 1998). For example, it is not uncommon for African American males who are most at risk for engaging in violent behavior to define manhood in terms of toughness, sexual conquest and thrill-seeking (Anderson, 1999; Oliver, 1998). The inability to achieve manhood through conventional means, leads some African American males to embrace exaggerated and stereotypical images of manhood (Staples, 1982). What is problematic about this however, is that these alternative manhood roles increases one's risk of becoming involved in a violent encounter (Oliver, 1998; Wilson, 1990). For example, it is those African American males who tend to define manhood in terms of toughness, sexual conquest and thrill-seeking that are most likely to spend an inordinate amount of time hanging out on "the streets," using drugs, selling drugs, and committing a host of criminal acts as a means of maintaining a street oriented lifestyle. Indeed, for many of these men their attraction to "the streets" emerges as a consequence of being denied access to the conventional opportunity structure (Anderson, 1999; Oliver, 1998).

RECOMMENDATIONS

All levels of government must take the initiative to form partnerships with educational institutions, the business and faith communities, and civic organizations to eliminate racism. Indeed, a greater awareness of cultural racism as a social practice is a necessary requirement for the establishment and implementation of a comprehensive agenda to prevent various types of structural violence. For example, the elimination of cultural racism must be funded in a manner that is equal to the resources allocated to "the war on drugs." Diversity training must be incorporated as a required component of the K-12 social studies curricula. Early exposure to antiracist education will have long-term benefits for society. Diversity training should also be included as a routine feature of pre-service and in-service training in the work place.

Within the criminal justice system it is critically important that efforts be undertaken to increase the representation of African Americans and other racial minorities in the numerous agencies that are responsible for administering the law. A specific focus of police training should include a workshop which describes how exposure to cultural racism leads to bias in the use of police discretionary authority. Moreover, such workshops should also examine how exposure to cultural racism contributes to the formulation of motives and justifications for various patterns of structural violence.

Finally, laws which prohibit hate crime must be vigorously enforced. In addition, perpetrators of acts of structural violence influenced by cultural racism must be required to participate in violence reduction and diversity awareness programs as a condition of probation, parole or continued employment.

CONCLUSION

The discussion that has been presented above strongly suggest that there are several patterns of structural violence in which the motives and rationalizations of violent offenders are to a degree influenced by their exposure to cultural racism. Consequently, the prevention of structural violence is dependent on proactive public policies and intervention strategies directed toward the elimination of racism in American society.

REFERENCES

Akbar, N. (1984). Chains and images of psychological slavery. Jersey City, NJ: New Mind Productions.

Amnesty International (1996). Police brutality and excessive force in New York City's police department.

Anderson, E. (1999). Code of the streets. New York: W.W. Norton.

Azibo, D. A. (1989). African-centered theses on mental health and a nosology of Black/African personality disorder. *Journal of Black Psychology, 15*, 53-65.

Baldwin, J. A. (1984). African self-consciousness and the mental health of African Americans. Journal of Black Studies 15, 177-194.

Baudrillard, J. (1987c). Modernity Canadian. Journal of Political and Social Theory, Vol. 11, No. 3, pp. 63-73.

Bayley, D. H. & Mendelsohn, H. (1968). Minorities and the police: Confrontation in America. New York: Free Press.

Ben-Jochannan, Y. (1991). Cultural genocide in black and African studies and curriculum. New York: ESA Associates.

Best, S. and Kellner, D. (1991). Postmodern theory. New York: The Guilford Press.

Blau, J. R. & Blau, P. M. (1982). The cost of inequality: Metropolitan structure of violent crime. American Sociological Review, 47, 114-129.

Blauner, R. (1972). Racial oppression in America. New York: Harper-Collins.

Bogle, D. (1973). Toms, coons, mulattos, mammies, and bucks–An interpretive history of Blacks in American films. New York: The Viking Press.

Brown, R. M. (1979). Historical patterns of violence in America. In Graham & Gurr (Eds.), Violence in America.

Brundage, W. F. (1993). Lynching in the new south: Georgia and Virginia, 1880-1930. Chicago: University of Illinois Press.

Bureau of Justice Statistics, (1999). Criminal victimization in the United States, 1998. Washington, DC: U.S. Department of Justice.

Bureau of Justice Statistics, (1997b). Police use of force. Collection of national data. Washington, DC: U.S. Department of Justice.

Chevigny, P. (1969). *Police power: Police abuses in New York City.* New York: Vintage Books.

Churchman, C.W. (1968). The systems approach. New York: Dell.

Clark, K. B. (1965). Dark ghetto. New York: Harper & Row.

Curry, G. E. & McCalope, M. (1999). Reduced to a photo–A family's torment after the tragic dragging death in Jasper, Texas. Emerge, May, 42-47.

Curtis, L. A. (1975). Violence, race and culture. Lexington, MA: Lexington Books.

Davis, M. (1997). The blue wall. Emerge, November, 43-49.

Demaris, O. (1970). America the violent. New York: Cowles Book Company.

Dowd Hall, J. (1983). The mind that burns in each body: Women, rape, and racial violence. In A. Snitlow, C. Stansill & S. Thompson (Eds.), Power of desire: The politics of sexuality. New York: Columbia University Press.

Editorial (1999). The dark side of zero tolerance. Economist 351, 13-15.

Feagin, J. & Vera, H. (1995). White racism: The basics. New York: Routledge.

Fishman, L. T. (1998). Images of crime and punishment–The black bogeyman and white self-righteousness. In C.R. Mann and M. Zatz (Eds.), Images of color, images of crime. Lost Angeles: Roxbury Publishing Company.

Fox, J., & Levin, J. (2000). The will to kill. New York: Allyn and Bacon.

Fredrickson, G. M. (1971). The black image in the white mind. Middletown, CT: Wesleyan University Press.

Gastil, R. (1971). Homicide and a regional culture of violence. American Sociological Review, 36, 412-427.

Gilligan, J. (1996). Violence. New York: Vintage Book Edition.

Ginzburg, R. (1988). 100 years of lynchings. Baltimore, Maryland: Black Classic Press.

Goings, K. W. (1994). Mammy and Uncle Mose–Black collectibles and American stereotyping. Bloomington, IN: Indiana University Press.

Graham, H. D. & Gurr, T. R. (1979). Violence in America: Historical & comparative perspectives. Beverly Hills, CA: Sage Publications.

Grier, W. H. & Cobbs, P. M. (1968) Black rage. New York: Basic Books.

Hamm, M. S. (1993). American skinheads: The criminology and control of hate crime. Westport, CT: Praeger.

Hampton, R. L. (Ed.) (1987). Violence in the black family: Correlates and consequences. Lexington, MA: Lexington Books.

Higginbotham, L. A. (1978). In the matter of color–Race & the American legal process. New York: Oxford University Press.

Holmes, R. M. & Holmes, S. T. (1994). Murder in America. Thousand Oaks, CA: Sage Publications.

Iadicola, P. & Shupe, A. (1997). Violence, inequality and human freedom. Dix Hills, NY: General Hall.

Indianapolis News. (1999). N.Y. Police officer beat and sodomized him, witness claims. May 7.

Jacobs, D., & O'Brien, R.M. (1998). The determinants of deadly force: A structural analysis of police violence. American Journal of Sociology 103, 837-862.

Jenkins, A.H. (1983). The psychology of the African American: The humanistic approach. (2nd ed.). New York: Pergamon Press, Inc.

Karenga, M. (1988). Black studies and the problematic of paradigm–The philosophical dimension. Journal of Black Studies 18, 395-414.

Knowles, L. L. & Prewitt, K. (1968). Institutional racism in America. Englewood Cliffs, NJ: Prentice-Hall.

Kuykendall, J. L. (1970). Police and minority groups: Toward a theory of negative contacts. Police 15, 47-56.

Learch, K. (1993). Current trends in police brutality: Analysis of recent newspaper accounts. Gainesville, FL: Unpublished master's thesis.

Levin, J., & McDevitt, J. (1993). The rising tide of bigotry and bloodshed. New York: Plenum Press.

Lichter, R.S. & Lichter, L.S. (1988). *Television impact in ethnic and racial images.* New York: American Jewish Committee.

Mann, C. R. (1993). Unequal justice–A question of color. Bloomington, IN: Indiana University Press.

Mauer, M. (1999). Race to incarcerate. New York: The New Press.

Messerschmidt, J. W. (1997). Crime as structured action–Gender, race, class and crime in the making. Thousand Oaks, CA: Sage Publications.

Miller, J. (1996). Search and destroy: African American males and the criminal justice system. New York: Cambridge University Press.

Morales, A. (1972). Ando Sangrando (I am bleeding): A study of Mexican American police conflict. LaPuerte, CA.

Myrdal, G. (1941). An American Dilemma. New York: McGraw-Hill.

Mydans, S. (1991). Friends relive night of police beating. New York Times, March 21, p. B1.

National Center for Health Statistics. (1995). Health United States, 1995. Rockville, MD: U.S. Department of Health and Human Services.

National Center for Health Statistics. (1998). Health, United States, 1998. Rockville, Maryland: U.S. Department of Health and Human Services.

National Institute of Mental Health (1987). Mental health, United States, 1987. Washington, DC: U.S. Department of Health and Human Services.

Oliver, W. (1998). The violent social world of black men. San Francisco: Jossey-Bass.

Oliver, W. (2000). The structural-cultural perspective. A theory of black male violence. Forthcoming in Darnell Hawkins (Ed.), Violent crimes: The nexus of race, ethnicity and violence. New York: Cambridge University Press.

Pettigrew, T. (1981). The mental health impact. In B. Bowser & R. G. Hunt (Eds.), Impacts of racism on White Americans. Beverly Hills, CA: Sage Publications.

Pierce, C. (1970). Offensive mechanisms. In F.B. Barbour (Ed.), The black seventies. Boston: Porter Sargent.

Poussaint, A. J. (1983). Black on black homicide: A psycho-political perspective. Victimology 8, 161-169.

Rex, J., & Mason, D. (1986). Theories of race and ethnic relations. New York: Cambridge University Press.

Riggs, M. (1986). Ethnic notions (videorecording). San Francisco: KQED, TV.

Rohrlich, T. & Merina, V. (1991). Racial disparities seen in complaints to LAPD. Los Angeles Times, May 19, p. A1.

Russell, K. (1998). The color of crime. New York: New York University Press.

Schafer, R. J. (1993). Racial and ethnic groups. New York: Harper Collins.

See, L. A. (Lee) (1998). Human behavior theory and the African American experience. *Journal of Human Behavior in the Social Environment* 1, 7-29.

Silberman, C. E. (1978). Criminal violence, Criminal justice. New York: Random House.

Singleton-Bowie, S. M. (1995). The effect of mental health practitioners' racial sensitivity on African Americans' perceptions. Social Work Research 19, 238-245.

Skolnick, J. H. & Fyfe, J. J. (1993). Above the law: Police and the excessive use of force. New York: The Free Press.

Southern Poverty Law Center (1999). The world of the patriots. Intelligence Report (Spring), 10-11.

Swett, D. H. (1969) Cultural bias in the American legal system. *Law and Society Review, 4*, 79-109.

Staples, R. (1982). Black masculinity: The black male role in society. San Francisco: Black Scholar Press.

Staples, R. & L. B. Johnson. (1993). Black families at the crossroads–Challenges and prospects. San Francisco: Jossey Bass Publishers.

Sutherland, E. (1924). Criminology. Philadelphia: Lippincott.

Swett, D. H. (1969). Cultural bias in the American legal system. *Law and Society Review, 4,* 79-109.

Taylor, C. (1990). Dangerous society. Lansing, MI: Michigan State University Press.

U.S. Bureau of the Census. (1999). Statistical abstract of the United States–1997. Washington, DC: Government Printing Office. U.S. Department of Justice. (1998). Crime in the United States. Washington DC: Government Printing Office.

U.S. Department of Justice. (1997). Hate crime statistics–1997. Washington, DC: Government Printing Office.

Von Bertalanffy, L. (1968). General systems theory. New York: Braziller.

Welsing, F. C. (1974). The CRESS theory of color confrontation. Washington, DC: Self Published.

Welsing, F. C. (1981). The concept and color of God and black mental health. Black Books Bulletin 7, 27-29, 35.

Welsing, F. C. (1991). The Cress theory of color confrontation and racism–A psychogenetic theory and world outlook. In F.C. Welsing (Ed.), The Isis paper–The keys to the color. Chicago: The Third World Press.

Wilson, A. (1990). Understanding black adolescent male violence. New York: African World Systems.

Wilson, W. J. (1987). The truly disadvantaged: The inner city, the underclass, and public policy. Chicago. University of Chicago Press.

Wilson, W. J. (1996). When work disappears–The world of the new urban poor. London: Tavistock.

Wolfgang, M. E., & Ferracuti, F. (1967). *The subculture of violence.* London: Tavistock.

Black Violence and Crime
in the 21st Century:
A Socio-Historical Structural Analysis

Derrick P. Alridge
Maurice Daniels

SUMMARY. Although a number of perspectives have been represented as frameworks for analyzing crime and violence perpetuated by
African Americans, no analysis can replace a socio-historical perspective. By carefully studying the works of W.E.B. Du Bois a sharper
analysis of black crime and violence can be clearly delineated. *[Article
copies available for a fee from The Haworth Document Delivery Service:
1-800-342-9678. E-mail address: <getinfo@haworthpressinc.com> Website:
<http://www.HaworthPress.com> © 2001 by The Haworth Press, Inc. All rights
reserved.]*

Derrick P. Alridge, PhD, is an educational historian and Assistant Professor in the
Department of Social Foundations of Education, University of Georgia. He received
his PhD at The Pennsylvania State University in Educational Theory and Policy with
a specialization in American educational history. Dr. Alridge, an expert on W.E.B.
Du Bois, has focused his attention on Du Boisian education, social thought, intellectual history, and policy analysis. He recently assisted in the production of a well-ac-
claimed documentary examining desegregation of the University of Georgia, which
was aired on Georgia Public TV.

Maurice Daniels, EdD, is Associate Professor and Director of the MSW Social
Work Program, University of Georgia. Dr. Daniels received his doctorate from
Indiana University. His major research areas include community organization, civil
rights, and social justice. Dr. Daniel's production of a civil rights documentary which
examines the desegregation of the University of Georgia, aired several times on
Georgia Public Television.

[Haworth co-indexing entry note]: "Black Violence and Crime in the 21st Century: A Socio-Historical
Structural Analysis." Alridge, Derrick P., and Maurice Daniels. Co-published simultaneously in *Journal of
Human Behavior in the Social Environment* (The Haworth Social Work Practice Press, an imprint of The
Haworth Press, Inc.) Vol. 4, Nos. 2/3, 2001, pp. 27-43; and: *Violence as Seen Through a Prism of Color* (ed:
Letha A. (Lee) See) The Haworth Social Work Practice Press, an imprint of The Haworth Press, Inc., 2001,
pp. 27-43. Single or multiple copies of this article are available for a fee from The Haworth Document Delivery
Service [1-800-342-9678, 9:00 a.m. - 5:00 p.m. (EST). E-mail address: getinfo@haworthpressinc.com].

27

KEYWORDS. Violence, crime, socio-historical perspective, structure, "The Philadelphia Negro"

Crime is a phenomenon of organized social life, and is the open rebellion of an individual against his social environment.

–W.E.B. Du Bois, 1899 (p. 235)

INTRODUCTION

During the 1990s, African Americans experienced notable growth in educational attainment, economic mobility, and political power. Due to progressive governmental programs and the acceleration of the black middle class, which emerged from the civil rights revolt, African Americans have collectively amassed more capital than many Third World countries and are receiving respect in social and political arenas (Billingsley, 1992). Despite these modest but significant gains, the problem of violence still persists in black communities. The searching question now posed is: What socio-historical structural factors behind the scenes are influencing this violence? And, why is black crime so prevalent in America's social system? (Beverly, 1998; Schiele, 1998; Snell & Thomas, 1998). In reflecting on the root causes of black crime and violence, and in pondering possible solutions to this mayhem, black scholars are turning to older powerful writings by African American historians and social scientists such as W.E.B. Du Bois and Carter G. Woodson, E. Franklin, Frazier, and St. Claire Drake, to provide insights into present-day problems of black violence and crime.

A review of the growing literature on violence and crime aptly illustrates that the above quartet of pioneering black intellectuals often applied African or African American centered perspectives to the problem of black crime, family disorganization, and other social phenomena in the black community. They astutely recognized that Black-centered theoretical perspectives are necessary in providing an accurate and contextualized analysis of black social conditions, if unbiased research is to be undertaken (See, 1998).

Like the 20th century scholars, some contemporary social scientists are pointing to the importance of designing qualitative and quantitative research studies that employ black-centered perspectives, and black behavior measuring scales, even though they may not be the ultimate choice for exacting modern scientific credibility. For example, See (1999, p. 12) in her book, *Human Behavior in the Social Environment from an African American Perspective* argues convincingly that:

> ... theory must be anchored in an historical understanding of the black experience, and African links to the black family, and black cultural

knowledge. . . . There is a clarion call to "junk" all fallacious and stereotypical theories and research on black people and start over. Obviously, starting over means inviting white, and foreign born researchers to join in formulating valid and reliable theory on the ways African Americans learn, perceive, and develop . . .

In this paper, an application of socio-historical methodology which examines black crime and violence in the United States will be undertaken. Specifically, a delineation of the historical, educational, and economic roots of these maladies will be addressed. Realizing the complexity of the issues, involved a socio-historical approach will help contextualize the problem, crystallize its structural tenets, and provide the groundwork for further explication as we move further into the 21st century. Additionally, the paper will make use of Du Bois' insights and research since his work encapsulates so many facets of the problem of black violence.

A DEFINITION OF VIOLENCE AND CRIME

In this article, a lengthy definition of crime and violence is not undertaken. However, it may be useful to briefly provide clarity to these concepts. With little contrast both terms may be viewed as specific acts that cause pain, and/or death to human beings. Webb (1990, pp. 52-53), in defining violence, says it may be covert, hidden, and clandestine, or it may operate underneath the surface in a disparaging and conspiratorial way. Webb further states:

> To be without hope is violence. To be without love is violence. The deprivation of justice is violence. Ignorance is violence. Unemployment is violence, to be hungry and without shelter is violence. Poverty is violence. To be helpless and misrepresented is violence. To be without liberty and freedom is violence. To be forced to live without human dignity is violence.

From a socio-historical perspective, violence has been infused into the African American experience via the Middle Passage, slavery, Jim Crow, and other forms of institutional racism and discrimination.

Obviously, attempting to define crime is considerably more difficult since it may be applied to behavior or entail a legal description of an act that is fatal or injurious. In the scheme of things, all classes of behavior that are physically or socially injurious or cause death are considered a crime (Sutherland, 1940). It is clear, therefore, that both Webb and Sutherland's definitions of violence and crime are enlightening. Both explanations suggest that the structural manifestation of violent acts have been injurious to African Americans in past years, are still plaguing them today, and must be labeled as crime and violence. How then are these acts to be examined empirically?

SOCIO-HISTORICAL ANALYSIS: BLACK VIOLENCE AND CRIME IN RETROSPECT

Today, social science researchers have become so totally preoccupied in analyzing social problems through the use of Euro-American perspectives and quantitative research methods until a socio-historical methodology is given little more than a courteous nod. Research has been defined as systematic investigation intended to add to available knowledge in a form that is communicable and verifiable. It may embrace both fact finding, to discover answers to applied questions, or general theory building or testing (Zimbalist, 1977). As early as the 1950s, Mencher (1959) discussed the value and need of socio-historical research:

> There is definite need . . . for the development of historical materials in the field of social work research to supply the background for analysis of current studies and trends. . . to gain perspective both on the growth of social work knowledge and on factors influencing the nature of this growth . . . (p. 38)

Therefore, a socio-historical analysis brings an often overlooked dimension to the study of black crime and violence from a structural perspective–giving attention to how these problems will be viewed over time.

To fully comprehend the problem of black violence and crime from a structural or macro perspective, we must first understand the history of African Americans. One commentary is that this population is burdened with past structural problems, and thus are consigned to carry with them a legacy of nearly 250 years of slavery, 100 years of legally enforced segregation, and over two centuries of institutionalized covert and overt racism, discrimination, and prejudice (Gibbs, 1988, p. 17). By ignoring this socio-historical context, and the unbroken campaign of violence that has been subsequently imposed, researchers cannot provide a holistic analysis of the black experience and are merely providing "snapshots" in time. For example, in the May 1998 bulletin of The Office of Juvenile Justice and Delinquency, the authors in chronicling black violence and crime operated from a premise that completely ignored the historical context. They paraded before the reader data attributing the high incidence of black juvenile violence to community (ecological) factors such as living in "poor," socially disorganized neighborhoods (Bulletin of the Office of Juvenile Justice and Delinquency, 1998, p. 2-3).

Unfortunately, the authors failed to draw on historic data in qualifying their arguments regarding the root causes of black violence and crime. Moreover, the analyses were shallow or piecemeal at best, and did not fully synthesize the patterns of behavior being displayed (also, see, See, 1998).

Principally, what is needed in any examination of black violence and crime is a socio-historical analysis from a black-centered context. Brookins and Robinson (1995), provide powerful reasons why a black-centered context is essential in the study of black people by citing the following:

> Among the many challenges African American youth face, internalized oppression or adherence to a suboptimal conceptual framework is potentially the most debilitating in terms of mental health and identity. Consequently, a structured, holistic and deliberate socialization process is needed to equip them with the appropriate psychological and cultural resistance strategies to successfully cope with the inevitable challenges of living in a society that discriminates on the basis of skin color. (p. 172)

The statement of some civil rights activists regarding the significance of a historical perspective is congruent with the keen observations of Brookins and Robinson (1995). Both agree, there is a need for researchers to consider socio-history in examining African Americans as perpetrators of crime and violence. Thus, researchers must direct their intellectual energy in examining white institutional oppression which is framed, tested, directed, and implemented at the highest levels of decision making. Many researchers in earlier years, therefore, screened out causation, and incorrectly attributed black violence and crime to black pathology. Du Bois (1898/2000), in summarizing this problem, wrote:

> Negro problems present themselves to-day after 275 years of evolution. Their existence is plainly manifested by the fact that a definitely segregated mass of eight million of Americans do not wholly share the national life of the people; are not an integral part of the social body . . . (p. 17)

Sadly, the words expounded by this eminent scholar have, to this day, gone unheeded and the issues of black violence and crime, family disorganization, and other problems persist in the 21st century.

W.E.B. DU BOIS ON VIOLENCE AND CRIME IN NEGRO COMMUNITIES

Most well read scholars consider William Edward Burghardt Du Bois, as a giant in the fields of history and sociology. His hardheaded, meticulous and pragmatic studies of the social conditions of African American life have provided scholars and the lay community with a significant body of priceless knowledge relevant to black behavior. After studying at Fisk, Harvard, and the University of Berlin, under a grant from the Slater Fund, and living amongst poor Negro sharecroppers in the mountains of Tennessee, Du Bois was ready for intellectual battle. In Berlin, he studied with some of the world's most renowned thinkers which included Adolph Wagner, Heinrich von Treitschke, and Gustar Schmoler (Barkin, 2000) He later authored an article on societal structure in a journal published by Max Weber (Du Bois, 1906).

In 1896, with a PhD from Harvard, Du Bois accepted an appointment at the University of Pennsylvania where he was an "assistant instructor" in sociology.[1] He recalled that Philadelphia, then, was one of the worse governed of America's cities. During this era, the University of Pennsylvania was interested in the causes of violence and crime in the black community. So, in 1897, he began to conduct a sociological study of every facet of Negro urban life, titled, *The Philadelphia Negro, 1899.*

As a sociologist, Du Bois examined the black family, black labor, black mortality and black crime in the Seventh Ward. He established the city as an ideal laboratory for the analysis of black homicide and his question-driven investigation yielded information on patterns of crime (Du Bois, 1899/1967, 1920). He adopted a loose eclectic methodological approach for examining the social problems of the Negro, but had no structured research prospectus or design. Influenced by his scientific pragmatic approach and personal, racial, and cultural connections with black people, he believed that the "Negro Problem" was the result of historical, social and structural factors that could not be overlooked in research. He stated:

> Of the theory back of the plan of this study of Negroes I neither knew nor cared. I saw only here a chance . . . to study an historical group of black folk and to show exactly what their place was in the community. (Du Bois, 1968, p. 197).

In other words, Du Bois did not limit himself to any dogmatic research design, and permitted his data to make its own statement regarding the social inequality between the races. He went on saying:

> I mapped the district, classifying it by conditions; and compiled two centuries of the history of the Negro in Philadelphia in the Seventh Ward . . . It was a hard job, but I completed it by the Spring of 1898 and published it a year later under the auspices of the University. (p. 198)

Du Bois' work provided a historical, cultural, social, educational, political, economic, and contextualized picture of black social problems. His work responded to racist and revisionist research studies on Negroes that were prevalent at the turn of the 20th century.

For instance, he observed that Negro violence and crime were a major problem in American urban areas and was attributed to structural forces (Du Bois, 1899/1967). It was his feelings that when the United States Supreme Court legitimized and institutionalized the fictional practice of "separate but equal" in the history-shaping case of *Plessy v. Ferguson,* it solidified six decades of unbridled segregation and Jim Crowism in the United States.[2] To him "separate" inevitably implied unequal. This structural decision juxtaposed with cultural survival mechanisms led many black youth to be somewhat cynical of an American meritocracy that supposedly granted economic and social freedom and mobility to all–meaning those with white skin.

Du Bois' work reflects that he was ahead of his time. In fact, his insights relating to black violence and crime are as cogent today as they were at the beginning of the 20th century. In summary, America's macro system has perpetrated violence of immeasurable dimensions, thus a generation of potential contributors to society has been lost. For instance, between 1900 and 1920, more than 1,100 blacks were lynched in the United States (Franklin & Moss, 1988, p. 282; NAACP, 1919), and from 1882 to 1968 that number had swelled to 3,445. In most cases the perpetrators were not brought to justice (Myrdal, 1945; Litwack, 1998). In fact, vigilante hangings were gala events in which white women, children and even grandmothers attended the festivities to observe and enjoy the inhumanity being imposed against African Americans and other people of color (Waskow, 1967; Patterson, 1998).

The blatant violence imposed upon blacks in the South coupled with discrimination and a declining agricultural economy precipitated a mass black migration movement in the decades following World War I. By the 1920s the influx of Negroes into urban cities in the north caused major overcrowding. Along with discrimination in hiring practices, blacks created an even larger underclass similar to the conditions reported by Du Bois in the Seventh Ward of Philadelphia. In addition, mob violence against blacks escalated during the early 1900s and the judicial system around the country solidified a Jim Crow system of apartheid. In every aspect of American life, blacks were at the mercy of an undemocratic system and were excluded from opportunities to compete with whites for social, economic, or political mobility (Berry and Blassingame, 1982).

How, then, do all these atrocities affect an individual psychologically, and what type behavior is exhibited in response to feelings of such psychological pain? Du Bois argued that violence and crime can tear a free society apart, debilitate African Americans psychologically and ultimately erupt into violence of serious proportions (Du Bois, 1899, 1903, 1904). Fanon (1963) was right when he wrote that oppression of any human being eventually causes rage (anger) to build in intensity. This pent-up energy and tension at some point spontaneously explodes, and from the eruption the impulse is there to engage in violent behavior (See, 1998; Freud, 1936, 1948, 1953; Gilligan, 1996). For example, it was not until recently that blacks began to gain a significant semblance of equity with such legislation as the Civil Rights Act of 1964 and the Voting Rights Act of 1965. However, in the midst of these historical leaps, black violence and crime escalated in urban areas such as Chicago, Watts, Detroit, and other cities–not because black people have low cognitive ability and are "inherently violent," as some social scientists would argue, but because they had psychologically reached "a sense of hopelessness, alienation, and frustration" and were prepared to unleash rage which exploded into crime and violence (Gibbs, 1988, p. 19; Akbar, 2000). Further, African Americans were addressing "historical" oppressions in a contemporary era. Such an outburst of violence and retaliation so profoundly surprised white liberals and the Johnson administration that the President appointed a National Advisory Commission on Civil Disorders, referred to as the Kerner Commission (1968), named for its chairman Governor Otto Kerner of Illinois to study the status of blacks in America. The Commission found that historic oppression and intense confrontation has contributed too much of the malaise in black communities and two societies had developed in the United States. The report read:

> What white Americans have never fully understood–but what the Negro can never forget–is that white society is deeply implicated in the ghetto. White institutions created it, white institutions maintained it, and white society condones it. (p. 1)

Just as Du Bois pleaded, almost a century earlier, with the University of Pennsylvania, Columbia University, and Harvard University to broaden the study of "Negro crime and violence" throughout the United States from a structural perspective, his plea went unheeded–as did the 1968 Kerner Commission's stunning report on urban violence of the 1960s (Du Bois, 1968, pp. 201-202; Kerner Report, 1968). In addition, increasing economic poverty within many urban areas, in the midst of national prosperity, caused increased tensions in many African American communities. Even today as Wilson (2000) notes, racial antagonism is exacerbated during slower economic times. As a result, many people become incensed over the policies of a social system that intentionally denied them and several generations of their kin equal access to social and economic opportunities. Predictively, this situation reverberates into the present, but few lay citizens or professionals seem attentive to the impending crisis that is occurring socially, educationally, and economically.

CONTEXT

In order to fully understand the historical and structural problems of violence and crime among African Americans, one must also comprehend the social, educational, and economic contexts. As stated, the sociocultural history of African Americans is important to understanding the contemporary behavior exhibited by this population–especially with regard to between group differences (See, 1998).

In examining social status, Du Bois divided the black population into four classes: (1) the well-to-do, (2) the hardworking laborers who were doing fairly well, (3) the "worthy poor" who were working but merely carving out an existence, and (4) the "submerged tenth" who were merely existing (Du Bois, 1897, 1904; Anderson, 1998, p. 259). One hundred years since Du Bois delineated the social status of blacks, his description continues to reflect an accurate depiction. While there has been some economic growth in black upper class families and the black middle class has grown precipitously, the percentage of black hard working laborers has declined and the percentage of blacks living in poverty is alarming. Not surprisingly, nearly half (42.7) of black youth under 18 live in families that are below the poverty line and these youth are more likely to live in deteriorating neighborhoods with high crime rates (Gibbs, 1988, pp. 4-5; Omi and Winant, 1994). Overall, these situations reflect structural conditions that must be addressed expeditiously as they represent the kind of disorganization and dissonance that generally leads to crime and violence (Gibbs, 1988) (see Table 1).

In turning to the educational context, multiple variables seem to contribute to black crime and violence. Research shows that America's social policies have often led to, and sustained, deplorable conditions for black children such as inferior educational opportunities, poverty, joblessness, and racism. These structural conditions have significantly impacted black family stability and are related to violence in the black community (Billingsley, 1992).

Evidence exists in Du Bois' work (1908, 1912) which suggests that policies contributing to the economic and social de-stabilization of poor blacks, coupled with poor educational opportunities, can account for blacks being unprepared for skilled employment. Also, America's structural policies which can be traced in part to the litigation of *Plessy v. Ferguson* were devastating to African Americans. Thus, many institutions, which had participated in programs to educate blacks, determined that their efforts were contrary to the national policy of racial segregation, and were therefore abandoned (Motley, p. 94). No factor was more blatant and damaging in the first half of the twentieth century (Du Bois' era) than the disparity between the money spent for the education of white children and that spent for the education of black children (Franklin, p. 361; Anderson, 1988; Du Bois, 1935). The racist policies formulated by those in power led to massive under-education of blacks (Comer, 1998, p. 214; Hale, 1994, p. 17).

Although fledgling affirmative action programs were operationalized in the late '60s and '70s to redress the effects of legal segregation and discrimination, by the mid '80s, a more conservative Supreme Court dealt a death knell to many of these programs. Several states, today, including California, led by Ward Connery, anti-affirmative action zealot, passed legislation outlawing affirmative action programs. Recently, Florida under what Dr. Mary Berry refers to as the "snake oil treatment called 'One Florida,'" the final nail was driven into the coffin of affirmative action (Berry, 2000). Thus, many vestiges of race-based social policies continue to exist, and are often exacerbated by present day racial discrimination. There continues to be a disparity in expenditures on education between communities where a majority of African Americans reside and mostly white suburban school districts (Hale, 1994 p. 17; Kozol, 1992).

Ironically, while affirmative action and other programs that resulted from the civil rights movement has had a positive impact on working class and middle-class blacks, the programs had an unanticipated negative effect on poorer blacks. For example, increased economic and housing opportunities led middle-class blacks to move out of more economically diverse traditional black neighborhoods into integrated suburban areas. Often, this exit left poor blacks in substandard neighborhoods with meager educational resources and minimal access to supportive institutions that provided social stability and an unfair criminal justice system (Gibbs, 1988, p. 18; See, Khanshan, 2000). Gibbs concludes that with the increased isolation from the black middle class, poor blacks have fewer positive role models, less access to high quality education, recreation, and cultural facilities, less job opportunities and other vital resources. Black middle class flight to the suburbs not only drained educational resources from black neighborhoods, it also led to the disintegration of important stabilizing forces such as black businesses, political organizations, and social networks. African American children also lost the benefits of these closed environments (Morris, 1999). Moreover, Gibbs asserted that poor black children are now confronted daily with adult role models that are openly involved in drugs, prostitution, gambling, and other forms of criminal behavior.

Du Bois (1910) concluded that the combination of racial discrimination, lack of access to job opportunities, poor educational facilities and opportunities, coupled with a paucity of positive black role models in traditional black communities, has set in motion a sense of hopelessness and social isolation in black low income communities. In sum, this kind of hopelessness and frustration often erupts into urban crime and violence, and can be traced to the structure of this society which has intentionally been stratified by the decision makers who have denied blacks educational and economic opportunities. Du Bois was aware of this, and promoted educational strategies that could address Blacks' social, economic, and political conditions (see Aldridge, 1999).

While historical and social factors played an important role in Du Bois' analysis of black violence and crime, economics and class structures were very important components in his thinking. In The Philadelphia Negro, Du Bois (1899/1967) suggested that racism against blacks was the culmination of class structure and economics that benefited elite groups of whites. By the 1930s, he theorized that the chasm between blacks and poor whites was sustained by a "psychological wage" of whiteness that stopped a unification between the black and working class and resulted in greater economic isolation for the masses of blacks (Du Bois, 1907, 1910, 1911; Jones, 1996, p. 103). During this period Du Bois applied a Marxist perspective to social stratification by connecting this status with their economic plight. Throughout the city of Philadelphia, he discovered that most Negroes were systematically alienated from middle-class life because they were denied jobs that afforded that status. He reasoned that this circumstance was precipitated by the fact that white department store owners, lawyers, and physicians refused to hire black employees fearing that people of color would adversely affect their business. As a result, Negroes were predominate in low skill occupations such as porters and errand boys, servants, and common laborers–positions that froze them in the "blue collar" category.

Bennett (1992) paints an even bolder picture of economic inequality today. She notes that the same occupational policies that "froze" economic progress for blacks during Du Bois' lifetime is continually employed today. In fact, statistical evidence of labor participation actually shows that structural policies are undoubtedly contributing factors to crime and violence. A few of these statistics have been compiled by Bennett (1992) who writes:

The average annual labor participation rate of both black and white men decreased between 1980 and 1992, but the annual labor participation rate of white men (76%) remained higher than that of black men (70%) in 1992 . . . For black and white women, the annual percentage of labor force participation was similar with the greater increase occurring for white women (from 51% to 58%) relative to black women (from 43% to 48%). Thus, the employment trends suggest that although the two groups follow similar trends, the white group experiences greater advantages notwithstanding.

In addition, Bennett (1992) provides data in support of the hypothesis that black people receive less compensation than their white counterparts for work in the same occupation. Thus, Bennett's (1992) data suggest that differential educational levels cannot account for salary differences among black

TABLE 1. Arrests of Black Juveniles in the United States

1995		1997
OFFENSE	PERCENT	PERCENT
Murder/Manslaughter	58%	56.2%
Forcible Rape	45%	39.2%
Robbery	60%	57.8%
Drug Abuse	32%	37.2%
Aggravated Assault	42%	36.4%
Vehicle Theft	38%	40%
Fraud	42%	30.8%
Gambling	77%	62.7%
Disorderly Conduct	35%	36.4%
Vagrancy	35%	48.2%

Sources: Tables constructed by Maurice Daniels and Derrick Alridge from data extracted from *Source Book of Criminal Justice Statistics*, (1998), pp. 342-344; U. S. Department of Juvenile Justice, Office of Juvenile Justice and Delinquency Prevention, (1997).

and white men since, even when their educational levels and occupational choices are controlled, their salaries are not necessarily comparable.

Worse, tied to their economic situation is the Negroes' lack of education during a time when technological and industrial type skills are essential to obtaining a job above the level of manual labor. Jones (1996) is careful to point out that blacks even fare poorly when compared to western and eastern Europeans, mainly because they have been unable to secure an economic niche to secure economic stability. Du Bois (1899/1967) noted that when he began, *The Philadelphia Negro*, the influx of immigrants created vigorous competition between Negroes and immigrants. This conflict resulted in an even lower wage structure, particularly for black males. At the same time, black women were confined primarily to domestic work. Because of a steady work schedule and demand for domestic workers, black women often became the economic foundation of the black family and the community.

While Du Bois was careful not to use the phrase "economics of prejudice" as an excuse for the high level of Negro violence and crime at the turn of the twentieth century, he was clear of its significant role in structurally creating a social climate that manifested such negative behaviors. Similar to the beliefs of his adversary, Booker T. Washington, during the late 1800s, Du Bois believed that if whites practiced goodwill and gave the Negro an opportunity for economic advancement, many African American problems would be eliminated. After his study *The Philadelphia Negro*, however, he began to offer a much more complex explanation regarding the economic plight of African Americans, which, of course, is outside the scope of this discussion.

Shihadeh and Steffensmeir (1996) reveal that while economic depravation does not directly affect high rates of black crime, it does, however, have an indirect affect in terms of increasing family disruptions, which, in turn, elevates the rate of black violence. As a result, they argue that family disruption is the strongest predictor of juvenile violence. The study conducted by Shihadeh, Steffensmeir, and Wilson (1984) echo very similar conclusions that Du Bois drew in (1899) and (1904) when he argued there was a correlation between joblessness and poverty and high rates of black crime and violence.

THE CONTEMPORARY PROBLEM
OF BLACK VIOLENCE AND CRIME:
IMPLICATIONS

While some theorists have argued that cultural factors account for the high incidence of black unemployment and crime research documents that the technology driven economic transition drove millions of black men from stable blue-collar jobs. Today, the high unemployment rate among low-income black men does not allow many black youth to establish intimate contact with a black male employed figure. This joblessness feeds to the crime rate for older black men. Billingsley (1992) posits that this economic transition has been devastating to African American families and has been the major cause of expanding black joblessness, expanding black single-parent families, and an expanding sense of hopelessness. While the benefits to the black community from technological advancements are indisputable and technology has led to advances that range from an increased life span for blacks to reduced black infant mortality, the advancements have also created serious adverse consequences for black families (Billingsley, 1992). Inferior education of blacks, coupled with the advent of an economic transition that required more education and higher skills, has left many blacks jobless, creating dire consequences for their families (Hale, 1994). What, then, does this socio-historical analysis tell us about black violence and crime as we enter the 21st century. Mainly, it affirms that little change has taken place in the fundamental structure of our social system, and the behaviors and attitudes of certain groups remain unchanged.

When Du Bois studied the problem of Negro crime in north Philadelphia from 1897 to 1899, the disproportionate number of Negroes that were arrested for crime and imprisoned in relation to the total population baffled him. For example, he observed that in 1896 Negroes made up four percent of the population but accounted for nine percent of the arrests. In 1899, Negroes represented 33 percent of the prison population while making up only five percent of the general population. Yet, over one hundred years later, Civil Rights leaders and Human Rights advocates are, like Du Bois, alarmed by the number of African Americans who are charged with violence and crime and are imprisoned, while the nation continues to offer excuses for the systemic factors that contribute to this situation.

According to the U.S. Department Office of Juvenile Justice and Delinquency Prevention, black youth are disproportionately cast into the criminal justice system. In 1995, for example, while African Americans made up about 15 percent of the juvenile population, they constituted more than 30 percent of the juvenile arrests for several offenses as seen in Table 1.

The historical, social, and economic contexts of the black experience in the United States cannot be divorced from the research effort if we are to truly understand the problem of black violence and crime from a structural perspective. Clearly, race, economics, public opinion, and politics are factors that contribute to the historical and contemporary problem. But structural factors also explain the disproportionate relationship between black and white crime rates.

CONCLUSION

In this article, attention has been called to the necessity for understanding the socio-history of any groups under study. Further, a warning has been issued delineating the peril in attempting to carry on large scale research studies of an African American problem before an unbiased analysis of the black experience can be drawn. As in Du Bois' day, white social scientists and revisionist historians offered historical observations of what they "believed" were the reasons for black violence and crime. Today, such pseudoscientific research as that authored by professionals who provided genetic and phenotypic explanations for the social problems in the African American community, must be soundly condemned. Black researchers and others interested in debunking such myths must be in the forefront of first providing socio-historical contextualized perspectives, then proceed to engage in rigorous investigations of viable and pragmatic solutions to the problem of black crime and violence.

This new century provides us with new opportunities to use history as a tool for understanding problems such as violence and crime, as well as other social problems that plague our society.

NOTES

1. At the universities where he was employed, Du Bois was at variance with the established academic community. This rift was basically due to his high intellect, acid tongue, aristocratic mannerisms, arrogance, and clothing. When he returned to the U.S. from abroad he sported a beard, leather gloves, a top hat, spats on his shoes,

and carried a cane. This attire was his trademark, but to his detractors it was a "show-off" and an irritant (Peeks, 1971).

2. In 1896, the U.S. Supreme Court santioned segregatoin in the "separate but equal" doctrine set forth in *Plessy v. Ferguson.*

REFERENCES

Akbar, N. (2000). "Foreword." In J. Schiele (Ed.). Human services and the afrocentric paradigm. New York: The Haworth Press, Inc.

Alridge, D. P. (1999) Guiding philosophical principles for a Du Boisian-Based African American educational model. *Journal of Negro Education, 68* (2), 182-199.

Barkin, K.D. (2000). "Berlin Days," 1892-1894: W.E.B. Du Bois and German Political Economy. *Boundary,* 27(2), pp. 80-101.

Bennett, C.E. (1992, March). *The black population in the United States: Population characteristics.* U.S. Dept. of Commerce, Economics and Statistical Administration, Bureau of the Census.

Berry, M.F. (2000, May). Jeb Crow. *In Emerge Magazine.* pp. 56-59.

Berry, M.F. and Blassingame, J. (1982). Drugs and violence in the inner city. In *W.E.B. Du Bois, race, and the city: The Philadelphia Negro and its legacy,* (Eds.), Michael B. Katz and Thomas Sugrue. Philadelphia: University of Pennsylvania Press, (259-277).

Beverly, C. (1998). Black on black crime: Compensation for idiomatic purposelessness. In L. See (ed.). *Human behavior in the social environment from an African American perspective.* Binghamton, NY: The Haworth Press, Inc., (183-203).

Bilchik, Shay (1998). A juvenile justice system for the 21st century, *Juvenile Justice Bulletin.* Washington, D.C.: U.S. Department of Justice, Office of Juvenile Justice and Delinquency Prevention.

Billingsley, Andrew, (1992). *Climbing Jacob's ladder: An enduring legacy of African American families.* New York: Simon and Schuster.

Brookins, C.C. & Robinson, T.L. (1995). Rites-of-passage as resistence to oppression. *Western Journal of Black Studies,* 19(3) 172-180.

Comer, James (1988). *Maggie's American Dream: The life and times of a black family.* New York: New American Library.

Du Bois, W.E.B. (1904). Some notes on Negro Crime; Particularly in Georgia. Atlanta University: Atlanta, GA.

_____. (1906). Die Negerfrage in den Vereinigten Staaten. *Archiv für sozialwissenschaft und sozialpolitik* (Tubingen), 22: 31-79. (This article on "The Negro Question in the U.S." was written at the request of the journal's editor, the renowned Max Weber, who had met Du Bois upon his visit to the United States in 1904.)

_____. (1907). Economic cooperation among Negro Americans, p. 184. Atlanta University: Atlanta, GA.

_____. (1907, February). Negro and socialism. Horizon, 1: 7-8.

_____. (1908). The Negro American family, p. 156. Atlanta University: Atlanta, GA.

_____. (1910, May). The economic aspects of race prejudice. *Editorial Review,* 2: 488-493. (This essay was given as an address at the New York City Republican Club, March 5, 1910, and was printed in pamphlet form that year by that Club.)

_____. (1910). Efforts for social betterment among Negro Americans, p. 136. (See the volume issued in 1898.)

_____. (1911). The Negro race in the United States. In G. Spiller (Ed.), *Papers on inter-racial problems*. London & Boston (published by P.S. King, and by World's Peace Foundation), pp. 348-364. (This is the paper delivered by Du Bois at the Universal Races Congress held in London in July, 1911.)

_____. (1912). The common school and the Negro American, p. 140. (See the volume issued in 1901). Atlanta University: Atlanta, GA.

_____. Speaking before the American Academy of Political and Social Scientists.

_____. Proceedings of the Annual Conferences on the Negro problem. Atlanta University, Atlanta, GA., p. 68.

_____. (1920). *Darkwater, voices from within the veil*. New York: Harcourt, Brace and Howe.

_____. (1935). Does the Negro need separate schools? *Journal of Negro Education*, 4(3) 328-335.

_____. (1963). *An ABC of Color: Selections from over a Half Century of the Writings of W.E.B. Du Bois*. Berlin: Seven Seas, (214). (The selection was made by Du Bois; the book appeared shortly before his death.)

_____. (1963). *Black reconstruction in America: An essay toward a history of the part which Black folk played in the attempt to reconstruct democracy in America, 1860-1880*. New York: Russell & Russell. Originally published in 1935.

_____. (1967). *The Philadelphia Negro: A social study*. New York: Schocken Books. First published in 1899.

_____. (1968). The autobiography of W.E.B. Du Bois: A soliloquy on viewing my life from the last decade of its first century. New York: International Publishers, p. 197. 1997 edition.

Du Bois, W.E.B. (2000). The study of the Negro problems. *The annals of the American academy of political and social science*, 568, March 2000, 13-27. Originally published in 1898.

Fanon, F. (1963). *The wretched of the earth*. New York: Grove Press.

Franklin, J.H. & Moss Jr., A.A. (1988). *From slavery to freedom: A history of Negro Americans*. New York: McGraw-Hill. Sixth edition.

Freud, S. (1936). *The problem of anxiety*. New York: Norton.

_____. (1948). *Collected papers*. London: Hogarth Press.

_____. (1953). *The complete psychological works of Sigmund Freud*. Standard (Ed.). London: Hogarth Press.

Gibbs, Jewelle Taylor. (1988). *Young, black, and male in America: An endangered species*. Massachusetts: Auburn House.

Gilligan, J. (1996). Violence. New York: Vintage Books. (Freud cited). Also see K. Lorenz and N. Tinbergen, (1969), *The study of instinct*. New York: Oxford University Press.

Hale, Janice, 1994, *Unbank the fire: Visions for the education of African American children*. Maryland: Johns Hopkins University Press.

Kerner Report. (1968). Report of the National Advisory Commission on Civil Disorders. U.S. Government Printing Office (p. 1).

Kozol, J. (1991). *Savage inequalities: Children in America's schools.* New York: Harper Perennial.

Mencher, S. (1959). The research method in social work education, Vol. IX of Werner W. Boehm, (Ed.), Social Work Curriculum Study. *Council on Social Work Education.* New York: N.Y. p. 38.

Morris, J.E. (1999). A pillar of strength: An African American school's communal bonds with families and community since Brown. *Urban Education,* 33(5), 584-605.

Motley, C.B. (1998). *Equal justice under law.* New York: Farrar, Straus, and Giroux.

Omi, M. and Winant, H. (1994). *Racial formation in the United States: From the 1960s to the 1990s.* New York: Routledge. Second edition.

Patterson, O. (1998). *Rituals of blood: Consequences of slavery in two American centuries.* Washington, D.C.: Civitas/Counterpoint.

Peeks, E. (1971). *The long struggle for black power.* New York: Charles Scribner's Sons.

Schiele, J. (1998). Cultural alignment, African American male youths, and violent crime. In L. See (Ed.) *Human behavior in the social environment from an African American perspective.* Binghamton, NY: The Haworth Press, Inc., (165-183).

See, Letha A. (Lee). (1998). Human behavior theory and the African American experience. In L. See (Ed.) Human behavior in the social environment from an African American perspective. Binghamton, NY: The Haworth Press, Inc., (7-31).

_____. (1998). *Journal of Human Behavior in the Social Environment.* Volume 1, Numbers 2/3 1998.

Shihadeh, E.S. and Steffensmeir, D.J. (1994). Economic inequality, family disruption, and urban black violence: Cities as units of stratification and social control. Social Forces, vol. 73, (2), pp.729-751.

Snell, C. & Thomas, J. (1998). Young African American males: Promoting psychological and social well being. In L. See (Ed.) *Human behavior in the social environment from an African American perspective.* Binghamton, NY: The Haworth Press, Inc., (125-137).

Sutherland, E. H. (April, 1945). Is "white collar crime" crime? *American Sociological Review,* 10, pp. 132-139.

Waskow, A.I. (1967). *From race riot to sit-in.* New York: Anchor Books.

Webb, W.J. (1990). *Psychotrauma: The human justice crisis.* Ohio: Fairway Press.

Wilson, W.T. (2000). Rsing inequality and the case for coalition politics. *The Annals of the American Academy of Political and Social Science,* 568, March 2000, 568, 78-99.

Zimbalist, S.E. (1977). *Historic themes and landmarks in social welfare research.* New York: Harper and Row.

Poverty as a Form of Violence:
A Structural Perspective

Josephine A. V. Allen

SUMMARY. This paper advances the theory that poverty is one of the deadliest forms of violence. Together, poverty and violence are a potent force that is antithetical to the collective well-being of our society. Existing data reveal that the correlation between poverty and violence is statistically significant. The vast discrepancy between the prosperity of the rich and the profound deprivation of the poor in this country suggest that a structural perspective may be particularly instructive. Poverty as a form of violence will be examined in terms of four interrelated variables and a set of recommendations for change will be proposed. *[Article copies available for a fee from The Haworth Document Delivery Service: 1-800-342-9678. E-mail address: <getinfo@haworthpressinc.com> Website: <http://www.HaworthPress. com> © 2001 by The Haworth Press, Inc. All rights reserved.]*

KEYWORDS. Poverty, violence, collective well-being, political economy, inequality, discrimination

Poverty is the worst form of violence

–Mahatma Gandhi

Josephine A. V. Allen, PhD, is Associate Professor of Policy in the Department of Policy Analysis and Management, College of Human Ecology, Cornell University. She received her PhD from the University of Michigan. Her areas of research include empowerment and family support, family comparative social policy, and the evaluation of social welfare programs. She is the immediate past president of the National Association of Social Workers and has recently completed a term as Vice President for North America of the International Federation of Social Workers.

[Haworth co-indexing entry note]: "Poverty as a Form of Violence: A Structural Perspective." Allen, Josephine A. V. Co-published simultaneously in *Journal of Human Behavior in the Social Environment* (The Haworth Social Work Practice Press, an imprint of The Haworth Press, Inc.) Vol. 4, Nos. 2/3, 2001, pp. 45-59; and: *Violence as Seen Through a Prism of Color* (ed: Letha A. (Lee) See) The Haworth Social Work Practice Press, an imprint of The Haworth Press, Inc., 2001, pp. 45-59. Single or multiple copies of this article are available for a fee from The Haworth Document Delivery Service [1-800-342-9678, 9:00 a.m. - 5:00 p.m. (EST). E-mail address: getinfo@haworthpressinc.com].

45

Violence in the United States is a pattern of behavior that will increasingly shape the daily lives of many Americans as we enter the twenty-first century (Gilligan, 1996; *The New York Times*, March 7, 1995). It is noteworthy that the two forces–violence and poverty, have affected the lives of Americans of every age, every racial and ethnic background, and in every geographic location. However, this impact on the lives of our society's most vulnerable citizens must be examined. Poverty is a social condition that is prevalent in America and is considered by many researchers to be highly correlated with the occurrence of violence (Bailey, 1984; Blau & Blau, 1982). Historically, poverty has been a major feature of public policy debates in the United States. Moreover, at different periods, the poverty debate and its corresponding politics has ushered in numerous federal policies (Harrington, 1962; Piven and Cloward, 1985; Trattner, 1996; Abramovitz, 1996).

Poverty and violence have been inseparably linked, but unevenly addressed in the published literature, and both have been the products of scholars and practitioners alike. This notable gap in the literature however, parallels the equally visible gap caused by the disparity between the enormous wealth of those at the top of the class structure and those at the impoverished bottom of America's socio-economic system. Consequently, the contemporary work of human rights advocates has been to raise the question of human rights violations here in the United States in the context of similar abuses by governments in other parts of the world. For example, in 1990, 52 million (one in five) Americans were recorded in the U.S. Census as living in a poverty area, i.e., a census tract or block numbering area where at least 20% of the residents were poor in 1989 (U.S. Census Bureau, 1995). African Americans are disproportionately poor given their representation in the general population. For example, in 1997, they constituted 12% of the population, but 31% of persons living below the poverty level. Among white Americans the rate of poverty in 1997 was 11% (U. S. Census Bureau, 1998). Racial disparities in poverty are also apparent among children. For example, in 1997, 40% of Black children resided in a household with income below the poverty level, while only 16% of white children lived in such conditions (U.S. Census Bureau, 1998).

Unemployment is another of the more immediate variables contributing to the high rates of poverty among African Americans. What is also being stated here is that four times as many African Americans and three times as many Latinos live within poverty areas as lived outside of them. Thus poverty areas have a different racial and ethnic composition than the rest of the country. For example, in 1997 the Black unemployment rate was more than two times greater (6.5/100,000) than that of whites (2.8/100,000). William Julius Wilson (1996) has suggested that Black male joblessness is a major factor contributing to the emergence of a Black urban underclass. What is problematic about high rates of joblessness among African Americans is that Black men are less likely to marry the mothers of their children if they are unable to secure employment that provides a wage sufficient to maintain a family (Wilson, 1996). Consequently, it is not surprising that nearly half of all Black families are headed by single women. For example, families living in poverty areas are more likely to have a female householder, "woman with no husband present," 29 percent versus 13 percent, and to be less well educated (U.S. Census Bureau, 1995).

The purpose of this paper is to examine from a structural perspective why poverty may be viewed as a form of violence that affects the lives of many Americans. Consideration of the structural relationship between poverty and violence will be presented in four interrelated but distinct sections. First, a discussion of how poverty and violence are related. Second, a discussion of the political economy as a useful theoretical paradigm in conceptualizing poverty as violence. Third, a discussion of several selected societal problems that substantiate the fact that poverty is generally the genesis of much of the violence that we experience as a society. And fourth, a discussion of policy recommendations that are designed to affect change.

POVERTY AND VIOLENCE

Poverty and violence are difficult concepts to address from a conceptual and definitional perspective. Research has shown that our collective tolerance for both is far too high and that the neglect of the poorest among us must be carefully examined (Gilligan,1996). The positive correlation between poverty and violence has been argued very convincingly for many years. Mahatma Gandhi, the great Indian activist, conceptualized poverty as the worst form of violence (Dasgupta, 1968). Gandhi emphasized the need to understand violence in its more passive forms, as discrimination, oppression or exploitation. Conversely, he also emphasized the need to understand poverty in its more physical or active form, as violence. Ghandi stressed that legislative and other actions must be taken to eliminate poverty (violence in its passive form) and to prevent physical acts that can more easily be seen and understood as violence. Indeed the link between the two is everywhere apparent (Dasgupta, 1968). Van Soest (1997) also makes a strong case by linking poverty, violence, and development in her book entitled, *The Global Crisis of Violence*. Expanding the definition of violence from one that concentrates on criminal acts toward people or property to one that includes discrimination, economic inequality and social injustice is important. This concept incorporates a set of cyclical interactions over time. It may include both action and inaction and it may not involve a direct relationship between the victim's, the institution's or the person's responsibility for the injury. All types of violence are equally repugnant (Salmi, 1963). This definition of violence includes harm that is socially sanctioned and avoidable actions that violate one or more human rights or prevent the fulfillment of a basic human need. Violence is seen to occur in three ways: through (1) omission, failing to provide assistance to people in need, (2) as a result of repression, or a violation of civil, political, economic and/or social rights, or through (3) alienation, or severely limiting people's emotional, cultural, or intellectual growth (Dasgupta, 1968).

Applying these definitions of poverty and violence to the United States is instructive. Based on this conceptual framework, poverty may now be defined as any act or condition that causes injury to the health and well-being of others. Thus, the high infant mortality rate in low income communities in the United States, the high rates of homelessness, malnutrition, and unemployment among individuals and families are significant examples of violence in our society in much the same way that assaults, murders or other physical acts of violence are committed in our society.

The United Nations Universal Declaration of Human Rights has been hailed in the United States by poverty policy advocates in their efforts to highlight the plight of poor citizens. Implicit in this declaration of poverty is the notion that income security is a basic need. The speed and rate with which people, living in urban, rural, and increasingly those living in suburban communities, can find themselves without employment, without adequate housing, or suffering from a catastrophic illness is startling. But failing to provide needed services to people given the enormous wealth in the midst of a booming economy is violence–especially when children are involved.

CHILDREN LIVING IN POVERTY

Today's booming economy has failed to reach many children and their families. Children made up 26% of the nation's population in 1997, but 40% of the poor. Almost 1 in 5 children under age 6 (21.6%) lived below the poverty line in 1997 (U.S. Bureau of the Census, 1998). As a consequence of living in impoverished households and in communities in which poverty is common among ones neighbors, poor children are at increased risk of developing a broad range of physical and emotional problems (See, 1998). In addition, children who reside in communities experiencing high rates of poverty are more likely to witness acts of violence and to become victims of violence (Brown and Gourdine, 1999, 2000: Jenkins & Bell, 1997). For example, studies of family violence have found that between 50 and 70% of men who assault their female partners also abuse their children (McKibben and Newberger, 1989). Very disturbing in this regard is the significant correlation between poverty and violence found by researchers at the University of Michigan's Center for Poverty, Risk and Mental Health. "Every day, children living in poverty face increasingly violent and rundown schools and neighborhoods. This violence is not only dangerous for a child's physical health, it is a danger to his/her mental health as well" (Saville, 1997). The Michigan report and findings of other studies as well show that a high density of community poverty is consistently correlated with violence. Amazingly, however, most children growing up in low-income areas are not violent in spite of their surroundings. According to the 1995 Luxembourg Income Study, the United States raises three to eight times more children in poverty than other Western nations and has the largest and fastest growing income gap between the richest five percent and the poorest five percent of its population (Holhut, 1996). Based on his study of violence in America, Holhut (1996) has concluded that, "Drugs, easy access to guns and a violent popular culture are all contributing factors to this nation's high rate of violent crime . . . Nonetheless, poverty remains the most significant factor of all. But it is politically easier to scapegoat teens than to do something about the alarming number of American kids who are growing up in poverty" (p. 2). Gilligan (1996) in his study of violence writes:

> Any approach to a theory of violence needs to begin with a look at the structural violence in this country . . . Focusing merely on those . . . who commit what we define as murder could distract us from examining and learning from those structural causes of violent death that are far more significant from a . . . public health, or human, standpoint. (p. 192)

He further suggests that structural violence is most closely associated with social class in America. That is, those of the lower socio-economic status are more likely to experience higher rates of death and disability than those citizens who are of higher socio-economic status. This class structure is itself a product of the human choices that society makes about how its collective wealth will be distributed. Violence, therefore, of the behavioral variety are deaths and injuries that are caused by specific human acts against other human beings such as homicide, suicide, warfare, and capital punishment. Structural violence, on the other hand, is usually less visible and not as immediate in its impact. The examples offered include the high infant mortality rates in urban inner city communities of color where babies are three times more likely to die before their first birthdays than their more affluent white counterparts. Similarly, the mortality rates for people of color attributable to cancer, hypertension, and diabetes can be prevented in many cases. (Gilligan, 1996: 162). Progressive policy choices and preventive strategies are the types of recommendations that address both poverty and violence. The model in Table 1 illustrates the relationship between poverty and violence and the conditions that occur when a laissez-faire strategy is embraced by the society. It includes factors of inequality, discrimination, and repression as intervening variables that also partially define the victims of these conditions in our complex social system.

POLITICAL ECONOMY AS A THEORETICAL PERSPECTIVE

The political economy perspective is a theoretical framework that is useful in shaping the parameters of this analysis. Political economy, as an analytical perspective, helps us understand how the society's economic, political, and social institutions determine the allocation of scarce economic goods and

TABLE 1. The Relationship Between Poverty and Violence

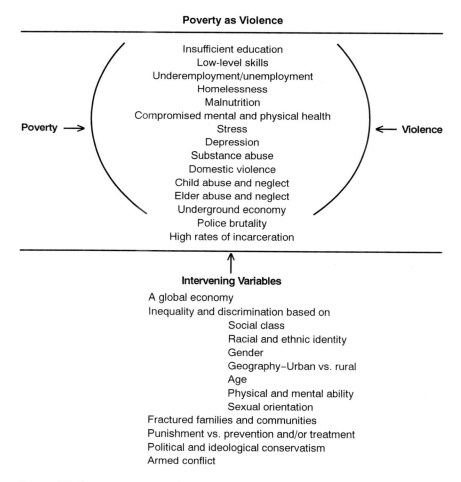

Poverty as Violence

Poverty ⟶

Insufficient education
Low-level skills
Underemployment/unemployment
Homelessness
Malnutrition
Compromised mental and physical health
Stress
Depression
Substance abuse
Domestic violence
Child abuse and neglect
Elder abuse and neglect
Underground economy
Police brutality
High rates of incarceration

⟵ Violence

Intervening Variables

A global economy
Inequality and discrimination based on
        Social class
        Racial and ethnic identity
        Gender
        Geography–Urban vs. rural
        Age
        Physical and mental ability
        Sexual orientation
Fractured families and communities
Punishment vs. prevention and/or treatment
Political and ideological conservatism
Armed conflict

Source: This figure was constructed by Josephine A. V. Allen for the book *Violence as Seen Through a Prism of Color.* Edited by Letha A. (Lee) See. The Haworth Press, Inc.

resources (Heffernan, 1979; Sackery, 1973). This perspective is particularly suited to the current analysis for several reasons. First, it does not attempt to artificially separate political, economic, or the 'social' variables. Secondly, this perspective supports our focus on institutions, i.e., structured relationships, and particularly institutions of power. Thirdly, this perspective emphasizes equality of opportunity as a central normative concern. One of its principle objectives is the explanation of inequality (Allen, 1979; Heffernan, 1979; Sackrey, 1973). Poverty and violence then, are appropriate foci for the political economy perspective (Figure 1) primarily because this model helps to contectualize these conditions that are so prevalent in the United States and in poverty-stricken areas in the global community.

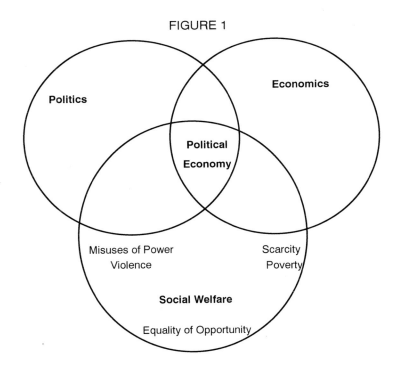

FIGURE 1

Source: This figure was constructed by Josephine A.V. Allen for the book *Violence as Seen Through a Prism of Color*. Edited by Letha A. (Lee) See. The Haworth Press, Inc.

SOME INDICATORS OF POVERTY AS VIOLENCE

Poor Housing

There are a number of indicators of poverty which lead to violence. Housing is one such indicator. As stated, social and economic isolation in American society is perpetuated by the racial discrimination that is so prevalent. In addition, the flight of major corporate and industrial interests to the suburbs or to free trade areas has also contributed to conditions limiting the access of America's poorest citizens to affordable decent, safe and sanitary housing. A review of the literature on public housing reveals that the razing or conversion of traditional high-rise units in urban public housing centers has been the response in many instances to the violence associated with drugs, gangs and other unsafe community conditions in these areas. Furthermore, the dramatic reduction in federal dollars for the maintenance of the nation's public housing stock and the limited investment of public and private dollars in these communities has contributed significantly to the demise of many urban neighborhoods.

There is a significantly large segment of the African American population in this country that is ill-housed in spite of various legislative remedies which purport to address the needs of those Americans living in substandard or dilapidated housing. According to the U.S. Census Bureau (1998), 53% of African Americans pay rent, while only 29% of whites reside in rented housing. The related conditions associated with unequal access to affordable, adequate, and safe housing in safe and nurturing communities include attention to preventive health and mental health care; adequate nutrition; affordable, accessible, and quality childcare; opportunities for education, training, and employment; and accessible public transportation. This strongly suggests that the links between inequality, poverty and violence are strong (U.S. Census Bureau, 1995). Revitalization of the stock of affordable housing has implications for both poverty and violence in these targeted communities. In other words, one way to initiate the transformation of urban poor communities and to increase pride and social organization is by improving the quality of life. Since the 1930s social scientists have documented that poor housing is still one of several factors that is associated with the concentration of delinquency and criminal behavior (Shaw & McKay, 1942). Without a doubt, substandard housing contributes to the overall social disadvantage of African Americans and is a form of structural violence. The reality is that too many African Americans reside in housing that is overcrowded, substandard, and expensive, resulting in widespread despair, hopelessness, anger, and violence. As Forman (1971) points out, the American government must bear a share of the responsibility for creating the present unfortunate housing situation. Moreover, the historical legacy of racial discrimination with respect to blocked access to education, vocational training, and adequate wage employment has implications with respect to violence which is manifested in the form of inadequate housing. Moreover, exclusion of African Americans from certain residential areas because of racial discrimination has contributed to inequities in the quality of housing among Blacks and whites. Residential segregation of African Americans leads directly to social segregation and isolation in schools, churches, hospitals, and in access to public accommodations and recreational facilities. Not only inadequate housing but also inadequate health care represents a form of violence targeting the poor generally and African Americans specificaly.

POVERTY AND HEALTH CARE

It is widely recognized today that good health care is not available equally to all citizens, particularly in the case of African Americans (Harwood, 1981). Major factors contributing to racial disparities are the high risk life-styles associated with poverty. Racial disparities also lead to premature death for many Black citizens. African Americans who are poor are often unable to pay the high cost of adequate health care. Thus, a significant majority of this population die sooner than white Americans. Major causes of death among African Americans are various forms of cancer, hypertension strokes, cirrhosis, Aids, diabetes and homicide–all "black killer diseases" (National Center for Health Statistics, 1998).

Another health problem that is related to poverty and is a catalyst for a host of diseases is stress. Hypertension, stroke, and substance abuse are among several illnesses that are aggravated by stress. African Americans cope with enormous psychological stresses in attempting to live and prosper in a racist society that frequently blocks their progress, thwarts their ambition, and threatens their very survival. Many African Americans feel that the slim chance they had for their children to survive may have been recently eliminated by welfare reform, which significantly affects their access to quality care programs.

POVERTY AND WELFARE REFORM

The Welfare Rights Movement, beginning in the early 1970s and continuing through the contemporary period, was very instrumental in facilitating the empowerment of many Americans with low incomes.[1] With a growing ability to use their voices, and the determination to fight for social justice, came the notion that social well-being, and income maintenance support in particular, are rights. Then in 1996, with the passage of the Personal Responsibility and Work Opportunity Reconciliation Act (PRAWORA), the conception of welfare as a right changed quite dramatically. The 1996 law replaced Aid to Families with Dependent Children (AFDC) with a federal block grant called Temporary Assistance for Needy Families (TANF). This change coupled with globalization problems has raised concern regarding human rights abuses in the U.S. and abroad.

In a recent report from the Urban Institute, it was noted that 20 years ago a divorced or separated mother headed almost all mother-only families. Today, by contrast, almost half of all mother-only families are headed by a woman who has never been married (Sorensen, 1999). The number of children born into unions in which their parents are not married has grown significantly. From the early 1970s until recently, the number of children born each year outside of marriage was quite large; over 1.2 million children were born outside of marriage in 1996. This very high rate has decreased in recent years, however, it is not expected that this overall trend will reverse itself. On the contrary, it is now expected that about one in every three births will be to an unwed mother (Sorensen, 1999). The income options for women and children, as noted above, are very limited.

President Clinton's pledge to "end welfare as we know it" replaced the Aid to Families with Dependent Children (AFDC) program with the Temporary Assistance to Needy Families initiative. This initiative (TANF) is a classic example of violence against the poor. This move has been accompanied by a set of punitive policies and stringent work requirements that have posed a hardship on some poor mothers. These policies call for the imposition of sanctions and time limits, a work requirement even when there are very young children in the home, restrictions on benefit levels as family size increases, as well as significant decreases in the size of the program. There have also been numerous reports of income eligible citizens, refusing to apply for food stamps, Medicaid, child care assistance, housing subsidies, the earned income tax credit, energy assistance, and similar benefits that are needed because of the harsh treatment that was anticipated as well as the social stigma that would be incurred.

The plight of the working poor is exacerbated by employers of largely unskilled workers who pay minimum wages and provide no sustainable benefit packages. In those instances where near minimum wage employment is the sole source of support for a family, poverty continues to overwhelm the life histories and life events of these families. The healthy economy of early 2000 and much of the 1990s has not been significantly different in terms of providing livable wages for most low income citizens. This is true despite the declining welfare rolls and the large number of recipients who have entered the labor force. Families who are current or former welfare recipients also continue to struggle economically in a booming economy (Wilson, 1996). According to Loprest (1999), almost a million fewer people are receiving welfare now than in 1993, a 50 percent decline. Although some of the decline reflects the strong labor market. A study by the Council of Economic Advisers finds that welfare reform accounts for one-third of the reduction in the budget for social programs since 1996. Another clearly related area of concern and point of inquiry is the role played by government in social planning and in the distribution and redistribution of various social, economic and political benefits among the members of society. The disproportionate number of economically vulnerable Americans (children, elders, people with physical or mental challenges) are in grave danger due to the violence of withholding services, and the cutting of needed benefits to the poor–most of whom are people of color. The question that must therefore be asked is–what precipitating factors are giving rise to these punitive attitudes, and violent acts directed against the poor?

INEQUALITY AND DISCRIMINATION

Inequality and discrimination are significant factors facilitating both the development and the perpetuation of poverty. Racism and discrimination based on social class, gender, and geography are also directly linked to institutionalizing the 'poverty as violence' paradigm as an adaptational social context for many of the black urban poor (Anderson, 1999). In a political climate in which the economic hardships of some white Americans are blamed on affirmative action, 'welfare,' multiculturalism, and immigration, it is clear that the poor, immigrants, welfare recipients, people of color, and others who are perceived as being different, are forced to suffer all the more. The National Association of Social Workers' (NASW) annual campaign in 1997 recognized racism as a form of violence. This organization defined violence as crimes that are already punishable, as well as violence done to people by institutions, by a culture of violence, and by limited opportunities. Therefore, during that public service campaign, NASW called for the elimination of racism, the creation of greater economic opportunities, and the prevention of violence (Racial and Ethnic Harmony, 1997).

It is clear that the link between poverty and violence has been characterized by unemployment and underemployment; crime; drive-by shootings; gang activity; the sale and abuse of drugs and alcohol; homicides, other forms of domestic violence; family disruptions caused by the incarceration and disproportionate institutionalization of men and women of color; and police brutality (Decker & VanWinkle, 1996; Mauer, 1999; Oliver, 1998). Violence is part of the fabric of this society–for rich and poor alike. Poverty is another form of the violence that is and has been so much a part of America. Conceptualizing poverty as violence has the advantage of equating two adverse social conditions and focuses our attention on both the importance of, and the prospects for change among African Americans and other impoverished communities within the global society.

CONCLUSIONS AND RECOMMENDATIONS

The claim has not been made that the link between poverty and violence is causal or sequential. Rather, the argument is fundamentally that poverty is itself a form of violence. The two are structurally intertwined and inextricably connected. The social problems referenced in this paper are reflections of poverty and the challenging day to day lives of millions of Americans. Advocacy for the passage of legislation that will redistribute the country's wealth and provide opportunities for all segments of the society is urgently needed. Elimination of the wide disparity in resources among the citizens of this country as well as among citizens of the broader global community is essential. The current economic condition of scarce resources has been associated with violence both historically and in the contemporary period. As conditions of poverty and scarcity reach extreme levels, societies experience greater levels of crime and mass violence (Gilligan, 1996).

If governments are brutal in their methods of governing, they are most often surrounded by equally brutal societies. Throughout the world, scarcity and violence have led to yet more violence and greater scarcity. For societies that are embroiled in successive violent outbursts, the political, social and economic landscapes are bleak. The political economy model emphasizes the reciprocal relationships among social, economic and political well being. We must choose to take action to bring about the kind of change suggested by Gibran.

> Yet unless the exchange be in love and kindly justice, it will but lead some to greed and others to hunger. For the master spirit of the earth shall not sleep peacefully upon the wind till the needs of the least of you are satisfied.

–Kahlil Gibran, *The Prophet*

NOTE

1. Empowerment as defined by the Cornell Empowerment Group is the ability of people lacking equal access to significantly gain and control their lives. It gives rise to mutual respect and caring and encourages the development of a sense of community.

REFERENCES

Abramovitz, M. (1996) *Regulating the Lives of Women*. Rev. Ed., Boston, MA: South End Press.

Allen, J. (1979) *The Political Economy of Housing*. Doctoral Dissertation. Ann Arbor, Michigan: University Microfilms.

Anderson, E. (1999). *Code of the Street*. New York: W. W. Norton.

Anderson, Charles, *The Political Economy of Social Class*. Englewood Cliffs, NJ: Prentice Hall, 1974.

Bailey, W. C. (1984). Poverty, inequality, and city homicide rates: Some not expected findings. *Criminology*, 22, 531-550.

Blau, J. R., & Blau, P. M. (1982). The cost of inequality: metropolitan structure and violent crime. *American Sociological Review*, 47, 114-129.

Block, F., Cloward, R., Ehrenreich, B., and Piven, F. (1987). *The Mean Season*. New York: Pantheon Books.

Bruck. C. (October 9, 1995). The Politics of Perception. *The New Yorker*, pp. 50-76.

Chasin, B.H. (1966). *Casualties of Capitalism: Violence and inequality in the United States*. New York: Monthly Press.

Children's Defense Fund. (1966). *State of America's Children 1996*. Washington, DC: Author.

Cornell Empowerment Group. (1989) *Networking Bulletin: Empowerment and Family Support*, Vol.1, Issue 1.

Dasgupta, S. (1968) Gandhian concept of nonviolence and its relevance today to professional social work. *Indian Journal of Social Work*, 29(2), 113-122.

Dasgupta, S. "Gandhian Concept of Nonviolence and its Relevance Today to Professional Social Work," *Indian Journal of Social Work*, 1968, 29, 113-122.

Decker, S.H., VanWinkle, B. (1996). *Life in the Gang-Family, friends, and violence*. New York: Cambridge University Press.

Gil, D. (1990). *Unraveling social policy: Theory, analysis, and political action towards social equality*. Rochester, VT: Schenkman.

Gilligan, J. (1996). *Violence: Our deadly epidemic and it's causes*. New York. G. P. Putnam.

Ginsberg, L. (1999). *Conservative Social Welfare Policy*. South Carolina. University of South Carolina Press.

Gordon, D. (Ed), (1973) *Problems in Political Economy: An Urban Perspective*, Second Edition, Lexington, MA: D.C. Health Company.

Harrington, M. (1992). *The Other America*. New York: Macmillan.

Harwood, A.C. (1981) *Ethnicity and Medical Care*. Cambridge, MA: Harvard University Press.

Hawkins, D.F. (1990). Explaining the black homicide rate. *Journal of Interpersonal Violence*, 5(2), 151-163.

Heffernan, W. J. (1979). *Introduction to Social Welfare Policy*. Illinois: F.E. Peacock Publishers, Inc.

Hoff, M. (1996). Poverty, environmental decline, and intergroup violence: An exploration of the linkages. In J.S. Ismael (Ed.) *International social welfare in a changing world* (pp. 163-179). Calgary, Canada: Detselig Press.

Holhut, R. (1996). Teen Violence: The Myths and Realities. <*http://www.mdle.com/WrittenWord/rholhut/holhut25.htm*>.

Jenkins, E. J., & Bell, C. C. (1997). Exposure and response to community violence among children and adolescents. In J. D. Osofsky (Ed.), *Children in a Violent Society* (pp. 9-31). New York: The Guilford Press.

Loprest, Pamela, "Long Ride From Welfare To Work," *Washington Post*, Monday, August 30, 1999, Page A19.

Mauer, M. (1999). *Race to Incarcerate*. New York Press: Distributed by W.W. Norton and Company.

McLloyd, V.C. (1990). The impact of economic hardship on black families and children: Psychological distress, parenting, and socio-emotional development. *Child Development*, 61, 311-346.

McKibben, L. and E. Newberger, (1989). "Victimization of mothers of abuse children: A controlled study," *Pediatrics*, 84: 531.

Moch, M., Rosenthal, B., & Goldberg, T. (1995). [Concept paper for curriculum modules, submitted by the New York City NASW Center on Poverty, Violence, and Development to the Violence and Development Project.]

National Center for Health Statistics (1998). Health, United States, 1998. Rockville, Maryland: U.S. Department of Health and Human Services.

New York City NASW Center on Poverty, Violence, and Development. (1994). [Report submitted to the Violence and Development Project]. New York: Author.

New York Times. (7 March 1995). *Crusade Against Poverty*. p.A-16.

Oliver, W. (1998). *The Violent Social World of Black Men*. New York: Lexington Books.

Piven, F. and Richard Cloward (1985). *The New Class War*. Rev. Ed. New York: Pantheon Books.

Piven, Frances S. and Richard Cloward, (1971) Regulating the Poor: The Functions of Social Welfare, New York: Pantheon Books.

Racial and Ethnic Harmony. <*http://www.naswdc.org/P&B/prracial,html*>. 10/1/97.

Sackery, C. (1977) *The Political Economy of Urban Poverty*, New York: W.W. Norton and Company.

Salmi, J. (1993), *Violence and Democratic Society*. London: Zed Books.

Saville, Jamie. "Children's Reasoning About Poverty and Violence." *http://www.research.umich.edu/research_guide/research_news/poverty/viol.html*

Schiller, B.R. (1989). *The economics of poverty and discrimination* (5th ed.). Englewood Cliffs, NJ: Prentice Hall.

See, L.A. (Lee) (1998). Diversity in the Workplace: Issues and Concerns of Africans and Asians. In A. Daly, (Ed). *Workplace Diversity: Issues and Perspectives*. Washington, DC: NASW Press, pp. 354-372.

Shaw, C., & McKay, H. (1942). Juvenile Delinquency and Urban Areas. Chicago: University of Chicago Press.

Sherman, A. (1994). *Wasting America's future: The Children's Defense Fund reports on the costs of child poverty*. Boston: Beacon Press.

Sorensen, E., Mincy, Ronald, and Halpern, Ariel. *Redirecting Welfare Policy Toward Building Strong Families*, No. 3 in Series, "Strengthening Families," <*http://www.urban.org/family/sf_3.html/*>.

Sorensen, Elaine, and Halpern, Ariel. 1999. *"Child Support Enforcement Is Working Better Than We Think."* Washington, D.C.: The Urban Institute. Assessing the New Federalism Policy Brief A-31.

Tessitore, J., & Woolfson, S. (Eds.). (1992) *A global agenda: Issues before the 47th General Assembly of the United Nations.* Lanham, MD: University Press of America.

Trattner, W. (1996). *From Poor Law to Welfare State.* New York: The Free Press.

U.S. Census Bureau (1998). Statistical Abstract of the United States–1998. Washington, DC: Government Printing Office.

U.S. Census Bureau. (1995). *Statistical Brief: Poverty Areas:* June 1995. Washington, DC. *<http://www.census.gov/socdemo/www/povarea.html/>.*

United Nations. (1995e). *Women: Investing in the future* (World Summit for Social Development Issue Paper, Fourth World Conference on Women). New York: United Nations Department of Public Information.

United Nations. (1995d). *Towards full employment.* (World Summit for Social Development Issue Paper, International Labour Organization). New York: United Nations Department of Public Information.

Untied Nations. (1995c). *Shelter, employment and the urban poor* (World Summit for Social Development Issue Paper, United Nations Center for Human Settlements). New York: United Nations Department of Public Information.

Van Soest, D. (1997). *The Global Crisis of Violence.* Washington, DC: NASW Press, Chapter 3.

Wilson, W. J. (1996). When Work Disappears: *The World of the New Urban Poor.* New York: Vintage Books.

Violence in the Suites:
The Corporate Paradigm

Letha A. (Lee) See
Nancy Khashan

SUMMARY. This article examines violence "in the suites" of corporate America. It argues that the magnitude of corporate violence overshadows aggression, and lawbreaking transactions associated with street crime. Specifically, the paper looks at America's Prison Industrial Complex, and privatization as classic examples of the breadth and intensity of corporate malfeasance and structural violence. Suggestions are made on how to humanize the behavior of corporations. *[Article copies available for a fee from The Haworth Document Delivery Service: 1-800-342-9678. E-mail address: <getinfo@haworthpressinc. com> Website: <http://www.HaworthPress.com> © 2001 by The Haworth Press, Inc. All rights reserved.]*

KEYWORDS. Violence, white-collar crime, the Prison Industrial Complex, privatization, sentencing

Letha A. (Lee) See, EdM, MSW, PhD, is Professor in the School of Social Work at the University of Georgia. She received her PhD from Bryn Mawr College, PA in 1982, and taught at Bryn Mawr, Lincoln University, (PA), Atlanta University, and the University of Arkansas. She has spent many years working in national, state, regional and local social service agencies, and has served as a consultant for major organizations including the U.S. Department of Education.

Nancy Khashan, MBA, is Administrative Coordinator for the University of Georgia's School of Social Work Atlanta (Gwinnett Office) located in Lawrenceville, Georgia. She received her bachelor's degree from Brenau University, and her MBA degree from Georgia Perimeter College. She is Adjunct Professor and has expertise in teaching medium and high-level Data Systems.

[Haworth co-indexing entry note]: "Violence in the Suites: The Corporate Paradigm." See, Letha A. (Lee), and Nancy Khashan. Co-published simultaneously in *Journal of Human Behavior in the Social Environment* (The Haworth Social Work Practice Press, an imprint of The Haworth Press, Inc.) Vol. 4, Nos. 2/3, 2001, pp. 61-83; and: *Violence as Seen Through a Prism of Color* (ed: Letha A. (Lee) See) The Haworth Social Work Practice Press, an imprint of The Haworth Press, Inc., 2001, pp. 61-83. Single or multiple copies of this article are available for a fee from The Haworth Document Delivery Service [1-800-342-9678, 9:00 a.m. - 5:00 p.m. (EST). E-mail address: getinfo@haworthpressinc.com].

Although vast amounts of criminological and sociological literature have been compiled on violent crime associated with predatory offenses, serial killing, Mafiosi, murder, rape, and robbery, researchers have not been judicious in studying violence "in the suites" or corporate violence (Finney & Lessieur, 1982; Levi, 1985; Sutherland, 1949). Conversely, they have not burdened themselves by collectively compiling a high quality of empirical knowledge with proper validity and reliability which contributes significantly to an understanding of the causes, origins and antecedents of corporate violence. Crime "in the suites" generally has a sanitized label and is popularly referred to as "high order misdeeds," "upper world crime," "crimes of the powerful," "avocational crime," "economic crime," and "abuse of power." However, Sutherland (1949) originated the label "white collar crime," an ambiguous term which is ideally suited for high level executives who sometimes exhibit endless cruel and abhorrent behavior.

Friedrichs (1996) has observed that traditional criminology has focused on "street crime" not "suite crime," and the emphasis has been largely on "nuts," "sluts," and "perverts," not on corporate executives, politicians, power lawyers, and big business tycoons. Moreover, the public has little knowledge of the enormous financial losses it incurs from corporate crime. In fact, burglary and robbery combined cost the nation about $4 billion, and white-collar fraud, generally committed by educated people of means, costs at least 50 times as much–$200 billion a year. One could argue that indeed, these soaring expenditures devour much of the nation's wealth, impose weighty financial responsibility and extraordinary strain on the federal budget, and pose violence against the people of this nation (Conyers, 1978; Sparks, 1978).

While the FBI places street homicide rate at about 24,000 a year, the Labor Department points out that more than twice that number–56,000 Americans–die every year on jobs in corporate settings, or from malfeasance such as black lung, brown lung, asbestosis and occupationally-induced cancers (Baron, 1993, 1994, 1996, 1997). These callous human violations prompted the moral philosopher C. S. Lewis (1961, p.viii) to disdainfully describe corporate Chief Executives (CEO's) and the organizations over which they preside as follows:

> The greatest evil is not now done in those sordid "dens of crime" that Dickens loved to paint. It is not done even in concentration camps and labor camps. In those we see the final result. But it is conceived and ordered (moved, seconded, carried and minuted) in clean, carpeted, warmed and well-lighted offices, by quiet men with white collars and cut fingernails and smooth-shaven cheeks who do not need to raise their voices. Hence, naturally enough, my symbol for Hell is . . . the offices of a thoroughly nasty business concern.

Friedrich (1996, p. 71) cites several reasons for the failure of researchers to investigate "elite violence": (1) crimes committed in the suites are generally intangible and victims are not directly assaulted; moreover, the violence is indirect; (2) corporate violence usually results from "policies" and "actions" undertaken on behalf of the corporation that expose people to harmful conditions, products, or substances, and rarely is personal animus a part of this equation; (3) the effects of corporate violence are typically far removed from the action that caused the harm, and cannot always be clearly and definitively established; (4) with corporate violence large numbers of individuals act collectively, therefore, no one person is responsible for the ruthless actions that may result in an injury or death; and (5) corporate violence and law breaking virtually by definition are generally motivated not by malice, but by the desire to maximize corporate profits and minimize corporate overhead. Moreover, the violence is a consequence rather than a specifically intended outcome of such motivations.

To stress this point, a number of the nation's renowned educators assert unequivocally that tumultuous corporate violence not only occurs in the suites of Fortune 500 corporations, but also in the nation's highest citadels of learning (Lee & Leonard, 2001). Specifically these scholars observe that leading research universities often operate in ways that are not dissimilar from the management of major corporations. Simply expressed, both have cheated the government in connection with student aid programs, and defrauded their student body for financial gains (Anderson, 1992; Sykes, 1988). Equally shocking, is that some prominent institutions of higher education have been accused of accepting large donations from notorious characters including war criminals, international arms dealers, corporate offenders, insider traders, tax evaders, and the like (Deloughry, 1991; DePalma, 1991; Fendrich, 1992; Friedrich, 1996; Mundy, 1993; Winerip, 1994). The inescapable conclusion reached is that "big money" subsumes science, consequently, research is significantly hampered, and the prevailing funding streams retards the intellectual curiosity of researchers.

Notwithstanding violence in universities and other corporate settings, clearly the evidence shows that crime in the suites is more deadly than crime on the streets. Yet, most citizens, to include some Civil Rights groups (2000), focus their fire, brimstone, and outrage against youth who are described as foul-mouthed, trifling young black males who fight, maim, kill, screw, "play the dozens," and engage in "joinin" (a new form of playing the "dozens"). But, are poor, disadvantaged, low class, inner city, black males the greatest criminals in our social system? Reiman (1990), forcefully argues that it is grossly erroneous to believe that street crime is more ruthless than white collar crime, the difference being that the latter is implacable, subtle, hostile, and has a multitude of protective layers of public relations to provide cover for what See (1998) describes as its "dirty little doings." For example, the recent spate of mergers, takeovers, downsizing, outsourcing, price-fixing, monopolistic practices, consumer deception, embezzlement, and bank fraud do not directly cause physical harm or ruthlessly relieve people of their wallets. Even so, they are acts that still cause immeasurable social and psychological damage (See, 1998). Regrettably, most experts who purport to explain the vicissitudes of psychological criminality are concerned that the human faces of victims of corporate violence do not always burn deep into the corporate consciousness since capitalist profit is their bottom line and, thus, supersedes all other human considerations.

The purpose of this paper is to examine violence in corporate America and the calculus of control that these large formal organizations play in America's social system. Specifically, America's prison system will be examined as a means of exemplifying how corporations take advantage of a captive labor of prisoners (mostly black), in order to accumulate even greater portions of wealth and power. Finally, suggestions will be proposed for humanizing corporations since they are so important to our economy, and contribute so significantly to improving the lives and livelihood of the people in this nation.

TERMINOLOGICAL ISSUES

It is no easy task cutting to the scientific-ideological essence of unscrupulous violence in the suites. Thus, a definition of the term is imperative. Violence is a broad term and refers to acts that may or may not be disabling, or fatal, but may result in harm being directly or indirectly imposed on many groups–notwithstanding their race, religion, origin, and socio-economic status. Although violence and crime are often used interchangeably in the media and in professional literature, there are distinguishing characteristics between the concepts. For example, "violence" in the media generally refers to homicide, or crimes committed by one person against another person or group. Generally, the crime is more sensational, exploitive, afflictional, and is depicted as an act of such magnitude and emotion that it captures the attention, and raises the hackles of the general public (Baron, 1994, 1996, 1997). Contrarily, in the social science literature, the parameters of violence are much more fluid and reflective. Moreover, the meaning of the term may be stretched to describe and analyze infractions by third parties such as white-collar criminals whose greed, and tainted decisions can greatly disenfranchise literally millions of human beings for the sake of accumulating enormous wealth and power. Be that as it may, we must now turn our attention to the mantras of popular wisdom and empirical knowledge to assist in framing the problem of corporate violence.

THEORIES USEFUL FOR EXAMINING VIOLENCE IN THE SUITES

So far a definition of corporate violence has been broadly defined. One implicit explanation presented is that "violence in the suites" refers to crimes committed by corporate executives, big business tycoons, politicians, and the well connected, to name a few, against less powerful persons, groups, or organizations. Yet, there is a need for a sharper theoretical focus and ideological foundation to be brought to bear in guiding our discussion. Although some arguments are advanced that suggest the use of theory is not imperative in advancing ideas, to the contrary others claim that "theoretical" ideas are important pillars to amalgamating ideas from different sources (Thyer, 1999). Still other groups in the literature contend that even practitioners do not always understand the difference between theoretical-empirical, and applied work, theoretical orientations, typologies, and historical analyses. An example of a spirited encounter was the intellectual combat and jousting between the late Donald Creesey (1988) and a pair of Australian scholars Braithwaite & Fisse (1990), regarding the formulation of theory useful in examining corporate crime. Creesey argued, essentially, that it is impossible to formulate a social-psychological theory of corporate crime/violence since corporations are not human beings and have no intellect and no capacity to be guilty of a crime. Contrarily, Braithwaite and Fisse (1990) held, tenaciously, to the position that there is not one scintilla of evidence that corporations should escape charges of misdeeds, and theoretically, it is highly possible for corporations, and even prisons, to be guilty of crime and to suffer from punishment. Although interesting, the essence of that debate which has been referred to as "academic dialectic at its best" transcends the bounds of this writing, but points out the problems involved in establishing a theoretical pecking order in the analysis of crimes in the suites.

It is essential to take notice, however, that theories on violence are formulated by various disciplines. Admittedly, it would stir considerable controversy if one paradigm were employed as "the" model for explaining white collar crime, or "violence in the suites," but if neatly pulled together along with other perspectives, an array of useable frameworks with analytical depth and representative breadth could be useful as seen in Table 1.

In reviewing the theories in Table 1 in concert with more traditional theoretical perspectives, and with what See (1998) refers to as "theory pieces," one may be reasonably certain that an ironclad model could be constructed for setting boundaries for a hearty thoughtful discussion of violence in the suites.

Approximately 30 years ago, a number of theories were compiled which has shown to have wide usage in explaining white collar and other crime. The first in this number was a spiritual explanation or "the devil made me do it" perspective (see Table 1). During the 19th century, Vold and Barnard (1986) advanced a biogenetic explanation which held that criminals looked different from other people, and certainly white collar executives do not look like

TABLE 1. Basic Theoretical Perspectives for Explaining White Collar Crime and Violence in the Suites

Explanation	Tenets of Perspective	Flaws in Perspective
Demonic (Currie, 1968; Quinney, 1980).	• Spiritualistic • Other worldly influences • Causes criminal behavior • Exorcism to exterminate evil spirits	No empirical information
Biogenetic (Vold and Bernard, 1986; Wilson, 1975; Taylor, 1984; Jeffery, 1990)	Criminals are inherently different from most people and look different (body type, brain chemistry). Can be identified by their primitive appearance.	White collar offenders typically do not "look like criminals," jurors may be less likely to impute criminality to them: view too simplistic–no studies
Psychological (Freud, 1923)	Focus is on personality, mental processes, the effects of early childhood trauma, conflict between the desires of individuals, and the needs of civilization. Defects in the super-ego, ego, id.	No systemic study linking white-collar crime to childhood experiences.
Personality (Sutherland, 1949; Coleman et al.; Criddle, 1987)	These criminals are easily frustrated, aloof, quite creative in rationalizing their illegal conduct. They are irresponsible, show lack of dependability, disregard the rules.	The flaws are in the personality construct of the individual.
Sociogenic (Gottfredson and Hirschi, 1990)	Inability to delay gratification, low self-control, power is imported, engage in illegal copying.	Difficult to collect enough relevant data to test the tenets of this model.
Labeling (Becker, Matza, Schur)	Certain behavior is labeled as deviant. It is not the act but social reaction to the act that sticks.	Need empirical verification using prison subjects
Conflict (Dahrendorf Coser)	Focus is on change efforts; both systems and individuals; conflict helps sharpen issues	Need empirical verification using prison subjects.

Note: This table was constructed by Letha A. See (Lee) See, and Nancy Khashan from David O. Friedrich's *Trusted Criminals: White Collar Crime in Contemporary Society.* The Haworth Press, Inc., New York, NY street crime hoodlums. Then, shortly after the turn of the century, Freud (1923) pierced into the intraphysic with his psychodynamic theory and suggested that individuals may commit crimes to bring upon themselves punishment for a preexisting sense of guilt experienced at some points in their life space. During the 1940s, Sutherland (1949) repudiated the psychological level of explanation, and advanced the hypothesis that violence in the suites is learned behavior–no more, no less. An extensive literature review posited that corporations generally recruit people who are predisposed to go along with corporate crime and violence; which is the precise behavioral attributes needed in large formal organizations. Gottfredson and Hirschi (1990) suggested a sociological explanation of white-collar crime. They reported that well educated persons with little self-control may be the perfect candidates for committing white-collar crimes.

Contemporary sociological theorists like Becker (1963) introduced labeling theory. This framework suggests that people label certain behavior as that displayed by a giant corporation as aggressive. Subsequently, it is not the act, but the social reaction to the act that sticks a label on an individual, group, or formal organization. Concomitantly, conflict theorists (Coser, 1956; Dahrendorf, 1957) suggests that conflict elicits disequilibrium and focuses on social change. Hence, in a concentrated effort to alter a system, or a behavior, the variable of conflict is imperative in order to promote growth (see Table 1). For example, the recent Texaco, Coca Cola, Georgia Power and it's parent South Company debacle where black highly competent employees were denied promotion and upward movement in their respective companies is an example of conflict resulting in organizational violence and chaos (Isaac & See, 2001).

In this article an eclectic framework is employed which permits crisscrossing of criminological and sociological perspectives utilized in other fields. To demonstrate the extent of violence some corporations will exact for huge profits, with the blessings of structural forces at the highest levels of government, we look now at corporate involvement in America's prison systems.

AMERICA'S ATTITUDE TOWARD PRISONERS AND THE PRISON SYSTEM

Since the 1980s, the criminal justice system has changed from one of reform and rehabilitation to one of cruelty where insidious draconian measures are being taken to punish perpetrators of crimes (Boldt, 1999; Light, 1999; PLP Pamphlets, 2000). With this mood in the country, few people, corporations, or big business entities are intensely focused on, or care about prisoners, or about the hygienic factors that are associated with the facilities where they are warehoused.

Additionally, the public directs little attention to an increasingly intolerant court system, unfairness and injustice in sentencing practices, and dangerous prison conditions (Bender, 1997). All that is important, and subtly orchestrated by the average person is that criminal justice officials "lock-up criminals, curtail their bad behavior, throw away the key," or proceed expeditiously to "execute the bastards" who committed the crimes, even without ironclad evidence of their guilt (McCloskey, 1996). The 1990s general public is seemingly unforgiving and believe in the Old Testament dictum: "An eye for an eye, and a tooth for a tooth!" These non-ingenious attitudes persist despite the fact that overall adult crime has not increased, although juveniles are committing more violent crimes than in the past (Netherland & Kiefer, 1997). For example, among African Americans 15 to 19 years old, homicide is the leading cause of death (Wodarski and Wodarski, 1993). From 1989 to 1994, the arrest rate for violent crimes (murder, rape, robbery, and assault) rose over 46% among teenagers, compared with 12% among adults. The projection is that by 2005 the number of people ages 14 to 19 will increase by 20% (Fox, 1996).

These attitudes are coupled with more stringent reinforcing slogans, such as "If you commit the crime, you have to do the time." While the public continues with its "heavy-handed," "head in the sand–ostrich mentality," (Abdullah, 1996), little notice is taken of how morally repugnant the criminal justice system is becoming, and how human beings (mainly Blacks and Hispanics), are being unfairly transformed into what has been described as "human slave cargo" who work for the interest of the prison industry (Davidson, 1997).

The question then is what is the phenomenon of the Prison Industrial Complex and how is a (so called), low life prison system of interest to sophisticated executives or the "business elite" who reside in corporate suites? There is an emerging literature that attempts to answer these questions.

THE PRISON INDUSTRIAL COMPLEX

The term Prison Industrial Complex or "prisonization" was borrowed from the final address delivered by President Dwight W. Eisenhower to the nation at the end of his second term of office (1961). He ungraciously warned Congress and the American people that the Military Industrial Complex required close scrutiny since waste, fraud, and abuse can easily creep into an organization and cause untold divisiveness. The President candidly stated that monopoly waste and unaccountability of resources is widespread in the military and scare tactics are often employed to support programs and wrench unnecessary appropriations for "pork" projects. Eisenhower's warning was prophetic as, today, corporations have shifted their attention from the military industrial complex to prison industrialization. This giant adventure is fast becoming an essential component of the U.S. economy, and has as its purpose profit, social control, and an interweaving of private business and government (Johnson, 2000; Goldberg & Evans, 1996).

The Prison Industrial Complex consist of a half million guards, and involves some 10,000 private firms that amass considerable profit from the labor of non-violent offenders (Mauer, 1998). Clearly, this warehousing of Americans is costing taxpayers a fortune. It is preventing the construction of schools and colleges, while this confluence of private companies and entrepreneurs (contractors, educators, food and service providers) accumulate great fortunes off the backs of black prisoners whose voting rights are even taken away (Davis, 1998; Goldberg & Evans, 1996; Netherland & Kiefer, 1997). The sad part of this scenario is that prison guards are paid $51,000 yearly, while teachers are paid on average of $41,000 yearly (Guinier, 2000).

Mauer (1996), one of the most active participants in the *Sentencing Project* compiled a disturbing set of data which provides a profile of young adults who are incarcerated, and therefore will likely become prison laborers for giant corporations.

According to the *Sentencing Project* of the U.S. Department of Justice, the following statistics were compiled:

- Nearly one in three (32%) black males in the age group 20-29 is under some form of criminal justice supervision on any given day–either in prison or jail, or on probation or parole.
- As of 1995, one in fourteen (7%) adult black males is incarcerated in prison or jail on any given day, representing a doubling of this rate since 1985. The current figure for white males is 1%.
- A black male born in 1991 has a 29% chance of spending time in prison at some point in his life. The figure for white males is 4%, and for Hispanics, 16%.
- Hispanics constitute 16% of the prison population nationally, compared to their 9% share of the total population. The Hispanic proportion of the inmate population has risen substantially since 1985, when it constituted 11% of all prisoners.

The number of women in the prison system grew at a much faster rate than for men from 1980 to 1995, increasing by 418%, compared to 236% for men. Black women are incarcerated at seven times the rate of white women (Isaac, Lockhart, & Williams, 2001).

This report, accompanied by data compiled by *The Center on Juvenile and Criminal Justice* on the effects of California's highly praised "three strikes" law, found that African Americans are being incarcerated at a rate of thirteen times that of whites (Johnson, 2001) (see Table 2). The prison industrial complex, then, represents one of the largest profit making ventures for corporations, state agencies, and politicians ever recorded in the history of this country (Bureau of

Justice Statistics, 1994; Federal Bureau of Investigation, 1973-1991). The system that has helped promote this phenomenon is privatization.

PRIVATIZATION

Empirical research concerning correctional privatization has just begun to emerge in the professional literature (Mays, 1966). Already approximately 82 studies have been completed, but many more are in process. Accordingly, the approach in this writing is to take an in-depth look at privatization as a correctional enterprise which seemingly helps big business, politicians, corporations, and the ruling class accumulate wealth and power at the expense of human beings used as slave laborers (Boldt, 1999; Gilmore, 1997). This indepth effort will also serve as "grounding" for research that may be undertaken.

TABLE 2. Disparity Between Prisoners on the Basis of Race

Criminal Injustice: A Study in Black and White

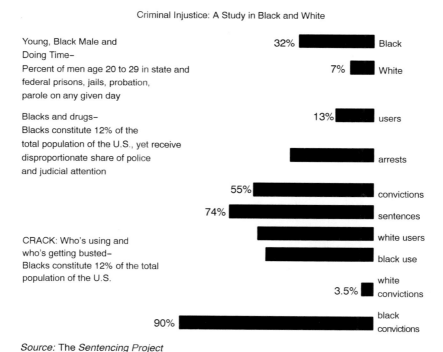

Source: The *Sentencing Project*

Privatization provides service for state correctional systems (Bowditch & Everett, 1985; Camp, 1985; Hutto, 1990). In enlisting corporate correctional service, a contract is tendered whereby a state surrenders all or part of its custodial function to private contractors. These companies, in turn, have the capability for building and managing any penal or correctional systems to include facilities currently operated by the federal government. During the past 20 years, 30 states have contracted private corporations to build and run their prisons and jails, bursting at the seams with poor people who broke the law, mainly for non-violent offenses (Dahl & Glassman, 1991; Goodman & Loveman, 1991).

Private prison management is a corporate enterprise that escalated in the 1980s. There are those who believe that the conservative movement ushered in by the Reagan administration was the catalyst that precipitated privatization. The rhetorical gimmicks of most conservative politicians, fueled by the sustained clamor and relentless "media fright" (about horrible killers, missing children, gangs, bombing, rape, random violence) fed citizen fear and made Privatization an attractive option for many states with budgetary constraints, and with an escalating crime index (see Figure 1).

The call from each President from Reagan to Clinton reiterated a commitment to "get tough on crime and criminals," led to the Violent Crime Control and Law Enforcement Act of 1994 or, as it is better known, the Crime Bill. During Reagan's presidency, there was also a constant drumbeat of "get government off our backs," and "the private sector can do it better, so let them do it." Accordingly, the states adhered to the President's request. We might add, at this juncture, that President Reagan's Commission on Privatization was so pleased with their work until these words were written which elicited thunderous applause from his followers:

> (privatization) may well be seen by future historians as one of the most important developments in American political and economic life of the 20th century. (Ethridge & Marquart, p. 30)

Spurred by Reagan's persuasive and highly inflamed anti-crime rhetoric, the public was galvanized into voting against any candidate running for public office who was perceived as "soft on crime" (Mays & Gray, 1996). Thus, the President's commitment to big business bode well for Privatization.

A second push for Privatization was the Reagan-Bush administration's "War on Drugs" policy. To poor people, particularly African American men and women in urban areas, this initiative was decoded as a "war on poor people" indisputably designed to affect every facet of their lives. Netherland and Kiefer (1997, p. 1) wrote:

> Since the advent of Ronald Reagan's War on Drugs, incarceration has become the answer to the complicated social problem of poverty, racism,

sexual and physical abuse, crime, and drug and alcohol addiction . . . thus with the signal given by the President, sentences handed out for drugs soon filled America's prisons.

In the end, the citizenry was convinced that drug users and distributors should be imprisoned and, by taking this action, communities would benefit.

Community Endorsement of Prisons

It is interesting to note that, in the negotiation process with the states, private contractors give assurance to prison officials and politicians that

FIGURE 1. Crime Clock of 1995

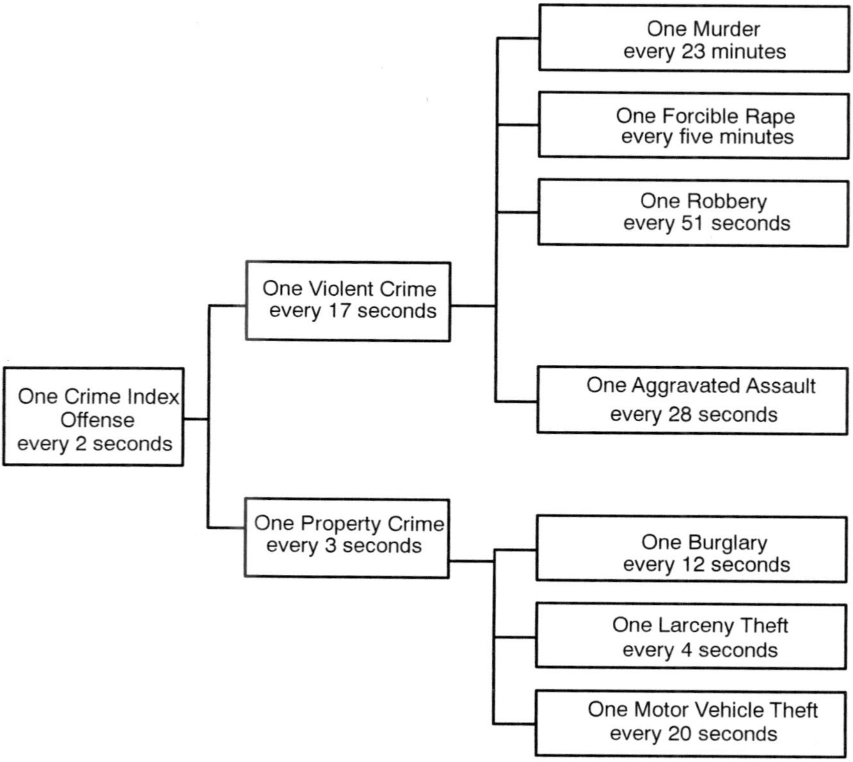

One Crime Index Offense every 2 seconds

One Violent Crime every 17 seconds
- One Murder every 23 minutes
- One Forcible Rape every five minutes
- One Robbery every 51 seconds
- One Aggravated Assault every 28 seconds

One Property Crime every 3 seconds
- One Burglary every 12 seconds
- One Larceny Theft every 4 seconds
- One Motor Vehicle Theft every 20 seconds

Source: Figure adopted from FBI Uniform Crime Report U.S. Dept of Justice, 1994

under their supervision prisons will be expertly managed, and, in addition, the local economy will flourish–especially in depressed areas, and in nearby towns and cities (Evans, 1993). In other words, the argument is advanced that under privatization: (1) a safe, reliable captive labor force that would otherwise be idle and subject to create security problems will be employed; (2) prisoner's wages can help pay for their own upkeep; (3) the public will have safer homes and streets; (4) prisoners will be expected to work eight to nine hours a day, and therefore will be tired and easy to control; and (5) the public has a masochistic fondness for the punishment of prisoners and will vote for politicians who advocate "factories with fences" and "warehouses with walls" (Burger, 1982, 1990; Duncan & Bollard, 1992).

At present, the number of civilian employees coming from local communities working in private penitentiaries alone has risen from 264,000 to 347,000 (Stoker, 1998), but the cost of guards has escalated significantly, and low cost foreign born officers, some of whom are unable to speak English, have been employed to fill the vacancies (Stoker, 1998). Privatization, therefore, has been marketed as a "win-win" for the state, contractors, politicians, the ruling class, citizens, and the entire prison industrial complex, but not to the prisoners themselves who are the losers.

THE IMPRISONMENT
OF NON-VIOLENT OFFENDERS

With regard to loss, at this moment two million people are behind bars in the United States. This represents the highest per capita incarcerated rate in the history of the civilized world (Collins, 1994; Goldberg & Evans, 1998). In 1995 alone, over 150 U.S. prisons were built by private and state industries to accommodate this influx of inmates, and prison building has become an essential component of the U.S. economy. California alone has built in excess of 21 new prisons, added thousands of cells to existing facilities, and increased its inmate population eight fold; which places it as the biggest prison system in the Western industrialized world. In fact, it is bigger than the Federal Bureau of Prisons. Still, predictably, it will run out of room within 18 months (Schlosser, 1998). But, to incarcerate so many people, most of who are poor and minorities, provisions must still be made for their lodging, so a mega construction effort is currently underway.

THE PRISON BUILDING BOOM
AND WALL STREET

Wall Street corporations are actively involved in the new incredible building boom of prison systems in the United States. But, before engaging in this massive financial enterprise, the assurance of profit was determined. For example, a representative from Equitable Securities Corporation studied the prison construction initiative and presented a sophisticated analysis to the company's stockholders who are always eager to amass greater wealth. Not surprisingly, the green light was given to financially invest in the building of America's prisons (Anderson, 1991; Emerge, 1997; Davidson, 1997; Leu, 1985).

It may be surprising to some that Merrill Lynch, Allstate, and Shearson Lehman are a few of the well respected main money lenders for prison construction (see Table 3). These giant financial institutions recognized that prison building is one of the fastest growing industries and one of the best stock performers in the United States (Goldberg & Evans, 1998). Thus, they have thrown caution, ethics, and sensitivity to the wind, and have become "bullish" on the prison industry. Other white-collar investment firms have also become unashamedly involved in prison building and Smith Barney is part owner of a prison in Florida. American Express and General Electric have invested in private prison construction in Oklahoma and Tennessee and Correction Corporation of America (CCA) is one of the largest private prison owners and operates internationally, with more than 48 facilities in 11 states, Puerto Rico, the United Kingdom, and Australia (Mergenhagen, 1996) (see Table 3). The second largest prison owner is Wackenhut Corrections Corporation followed by Dyer (Mergenhagen, 1996; Schlosser, 1998), and all are corporations, which are building and or managing prisons throughout the world.

In interviews held with Civil Rights groups (July, 2000) attention was called to the fact that Fortune 500 and other big corporations are taking advantage of the slave labor of prisoners which pays about $60 for an entire month of nine-hour days. So abhorrent and profound is the prison building phenomena, and the treatment of black and brown criminals until black leaders are shouting "foul" and are declaring that the prison building enterprise, which uses inmate labor to build prisons, represents a conflict of interest.

Some professionals believe that if the public knew that private and state prisons are operating to make profits for corporations, this knowledge would "rattle the national consciousness" and the practice would be ameliorated. Erlich (1995) reports that the U.S. has been lambasting China for its human rights abuses, but is practicing the same oppressive policies. Thus, in this instance, fairness is merely the stuff of scholarly treatises (Amos, 1990).

Erlich (1995) believes that the industrialization of prisons is replacing labor previously performed by union laborers and by Third World Countries, and all laws governing the exportation of prison-made goods are ignored. In fact, in some California prisons huge smokestacks and giant buildings are being constructed, on prison grounds, and throughout the U.S. profit from

TABLE 3. Corporations that Use Prison Labor to Make Products and Provide Services

Name of Corporation	Fortune 500 Rank or State	Revenues $Millions
*All State		29,949
American Cancer Society		Unknown
American Express	73	17,760
AT&T	10	53,261
Badger State Industries (BSI)	Wisconsin	Unknown
*Bank of America Corporation	47	23,585
Bay Networks		Unknown
Bell South	56	20,561
Eddie Bauer		Unknown
Boeing	11	45,800
Pierre Cardin		Unknown
Chatleff Control (Valve Fittings)	Florida	Unknown
Chevron	19	36,376
CMT Blues	San Diego	Unknown
*3 Com		3,147
Compaq Apparel Safety Items		Unknown
Compaq Computers	42	24,584
Correction Corps of America (CCA)		Unknown
Data Processing Accounting Services (DPAS)	San Quentin	Unknown
Dell (Computers)	125	12,327
Dept of Correction's Prison Industries		Unknown
Digital Switch		Unknown
Escod Industries	S. Carolina	Unknown
Exchange Group (Produce "Tickle Me Elmo")	Florida	Unknown
Exmark (Packing for Microsoft)	Washington	Unknown
Florida Citrus Industry	S. Florida	Unknown
*General Electric	125	90,840
Goldman Sachs & Co.		Unknown
*Hewlett Packard		42,895
Honda (Weastec Corporation)	Ohio	Unknown
Honeywell	194	8,028
IBM	6	78,508
*Intel		25,070
Josten's (Graduation caps & gowns)	S. Carolina	Unknown
*JC Penny		30,546
K-Mart		32,183

TABLE 3 (continued)

Name of Corporation	Fortune 500 Rank or State	Revenues $Millions
Lee Jeans		Unknown
Leukemia Society		Unknown
Limousine (Stretch) Companies	Nevada	Unknown
*Lockheed Martin Technologies, Inc. (LTI)	TX, FL	28,069
*Lucent Technologies		26,360
Macy's		Unknown
Matron	SD, OR	Unknown
McDonald's		11,409
MCI Communications	62	19,653
Mecca Seattle Cotton Works		Unknown
Melby Enterprises (Provides prison labor)		Unknown
*Merrill-Lynch		37,731
Microsoft	137	11,358
Morgan Stanley Dean Witter		27,132
Motorola	29	29,794
New Bridge Networks		Unknown
Nike		9,687
Nordstrom	316	4,852
Nortel		Unknown
North American Intercon		Unknown
Northern Telecom Corp. (Canadian Co.)		Unknown
Paine Webber		6,657
Planet Hollywood		Unknown
Prison Realty Trust (ACCA Company)		Unknown
Prudential Health Ins. Co. of America		37,073
RCNA Immigration Telephone System	Arizona	Unknown
Red Cross		Unknown
Redmond Firm		Unknown
Redwood Outdoors		Unknown
Shearson-Lehman Holdings		16,883
Siemens		Unknown
Smith-Barney		Unknown
Spalding		Unknown
Steel Case, Inc. (Furniture)	Michigan	Unknown
Swartz's Welding		Unknown

Name of Corporation	Fortune 500 Rank or State	Revenues $Millions
Target Stores		Unknown
Texas Instruments	148	10,562
Tourist Information Bureau	Iowa	Unknown
Toys "R" Us	143	11,038
Trans Continental World (TWA)		Unknown
UNICOR (A Federal Prison Industry)		Unknown
Union Bay		Unknown
United Van Lines		Unknown
United Vision Group (Eyeglass Manufacturer)	Florida	Unknown
U.S. Military (Battle Dress Uniforms)		Unknown
U.S. Technologies	Texas	Unknown
Utah Asbestos Abatement Contractors Assoc.	Utah	Unknown
Victoria's Secret		Unknown
Wakenhut Corrections Corp. (WCC)		Unknown
Washington Marketing Group (WMG)		Unknown
Weastec Corporation		Unknown

Note: *Denotes company on Fortune 500 list

prison-made goods has skyrocketed from $392 million to 1.31 billion. And "they're not just license plates."

It can be seen, therefore, that indeed there is violence planned and executed in the suites, and black human beings are entering America's prisons and being demoted to slaves whose obligation is to help earn millions of dollars in pure profit for states, politicians, and corporations, much of which is an "under the table" money flow.

THE NEW CORPORATE PRISON WORKFORCE FOR THE 21ST CENTURY

There is no questioning the fact, then, that over 100 corporate firms have found a new lucrative workforce that is making exorbitant amounts of money for corporations that flaunts it's prestige. These corporate giants extend from

AT&T to Avon (see Table 3). Davis (1997) and Stoker (1998) write that "tripling" the prison population (which is contributing to this profit) in fifteen years is unprecedented in a democratic society.

What is fueling growing concern among Civil Rights groups is the "three-strikes" phenomenon, which is the net for capturing prison workers for corporations. Under this legislation passed in March 1994, black men are locked up and consigned to a life of industrial labor in the interest of private businesses. By California's "Three Strikes" and you're out, a life sentence is imposed for a third felony conviction if a previous felony was serious or contained elements of violence. The new felony need not be serious, or violent; and the previous conviction could have occurred in another state or as a juvenile offense if the defendant had been, at the time of the previous offense, sixteen or younger (Shichor, 1996). What underlies this action is that juvenile records can no longer be expunged, and the prison industrial complex will continue to have a steady flow of new workers incoming for the 127 corporations that use prison labor.

The harshest, and most loathsome part of the "three strike" legislation is that 80 percent of the sentence must be served regardless of good behavior or work time credit. Again, due to the troublesome components of the "three strike" initiative blacks and minorities have manifestly come to believe there is a connectedness between industrializing the nation's prison and racial profiling (driving while black/brown). As one would expect the whole concept of racial profiling has become a raw issue. And, the skeptical mind would be prone to believe that profiling Black and Hispanic men, sending them to prison for committing non-violent offenses (like possessing an ounce of crack cocaine) is part of the scorn, denigration, and merciless injustice visited upon blacks in this country. Jerome Miller (1999) of the Detroit Free Press summed up the problem of black men in this way:

> By 2010, a majority of black men ages 18 to 39 will live behind bars . . . In the 1920s and 30s, no more than 20% of the people in prisons were black, including women. Today, 54% of the inmates admitted to federal and state prisons are black. Eventually, Miller says, few people will come into daily contact with black men ages 18-39.

It is readily apparent, moreover, that at the present rate of incarceration, giant corporations will have a captive prison workforce of both black male and female minor offenders for many years to come. Further, black Americans will, as Amos (1990) has noted, "continue to see its collective life ooze away in a genocidal pool of blood."

CONCLUSION

Historically, corporations have made commendable efforts in improving the lives of Americans and they must be given credit for these advancements. They have unlocked many of the mysteries of the universe and transformed scientific discoveries into amazing products that can improve the quality and quantity of life for the people on this continent. By contrast, there is no denying that those who occupy the suites have not always been humane to individuals, and groups like prisoners, and organizations and have engaged in multiple varieties of violence against these disaffected groups. Currently, giant corporations are coming under heavy criticism after enjoying financial gains from exploiting at-risk groups, and are resorting to public relation efforts and the aegis of charity to shore up their altruistic and humanitarianism. All of these actions are for public consumption. For example, after resorting to the exploitation of disaffected groups, these corporations display passion for the oppressed by setting up community projects within their corporation, constructing museums, community buildings, building libraries and giving large sums of money to charity to assist depressed nations, and to help improve the health and lives of poor children. Thus, the power structure catapults into fame. All the while, however, they make certain that ample press coverage is made regarding their charitable contributions. It is recommended that corporations give more financial support to the poor since their profit margins are far beyond an amount that is needed to maintain a competitive edge in the corporate hierarchy and still amass great fortunes.

The following solutions are offered beyond the obvious government intervention to assist in humanizing corporations:

1. One method that is conspicuously absent in the remediation of corporate violence by the powerful ruling class calls for actually employing non-corporate groups to conduct surveys, which would ask corporations how they could become more humane. These data could be used in decision-making.
2. Organizations themselves may consider regulating their own behavior by engaging in a self-study. No studies, reports or statistics can create such a shocking indictment and cause such a swift alteration of behavior than discovering one's own indiscretions. For example, with regard to prison labor corporations, they should examine the abuses constantly reported. Only through education, proper moralistic utilization, ethical codes, and role-playing can a constructive change be realized. Corporations should monitor each other and thus allow for a system of checks and balances to ensure that humanitarian efforts are consistent.
3. A series of assured jobs should be set aside in Fortune 500 companies with expert apprenticeship for ex-convicts for rehabilitative purposes.

This training would give an inmate a second chance, and an opportunity to adapt to the outside world. What better way to ensure that corporate America gives back in a charitable way for the use of cheap prison labor which it is using to amass giant profits.

While corporate violence is the primary focus in this paper, this type of violence is becoming a problem of epidemic proportions for society at a macro level. If we sacrifice our humanitarian issues for the sake of the economy, what can be said for the future of business conduct–and of those who reside in the suites of the United States of America?

REFERENCES

Abdullah. (1996). The Black people's prison survival guide. <http://www.cs.oberlin.edu>.

Anderson, G. (1991). Prisons and money. *America* 64: 516-519.

Anderson, M. (1992). Imposters in the temple. New York: Simon & Schuster.

Bacas, H. (1984). When prisons and profits go together. *National Business* (October): 62-63.

Baron, R.A. (1994). The physical environment of work settings: Effects on task performance, interpersonal relations, and job satisfaction. In B. M. Staw & L. L. Cummings (Eds.), *Research in Organizational Behavior* (Vol. 16, pp. 1-46). Greenwich, CT: JAI Press.

Baron, R.A. & Richardson, D.R. (1994). Human aggression (2nd ed.). New York: Plenum.

Baron, R.A. (1993). Violence in the workplace: A prevention and management guide for business. Ventura, CA: Pathfinder Publishing.

Baron, R.A. & Neuman, J.H. (1996). Workplace violence and workplace aggression: Evidence on their relative frequency and potential causes. *Aggressive Behavior*, 22: 161-173.

Baron, R.A., Neuman, J.H., & Geddes, D. (1997). Workplace aggression–The iceberg beneath the tip of workplace violence: Further evidence on its forms and potential organizational and individual causes. Unpublished manuscript.

Becker, H.S. (1963). *Outsiders: Studies in the sociology of deviance.* New York: Free Press.

Boldt, B. (1999, July). *Coastal post article.* <http://www.coastalpost.com/99/7/8.htm>.

Bowditch, C. & Everett, R.S. (1985). Private prisons: Problems within solutions. Paper presented at the American Society of Criminology.

Braithwaite, J. & Fisse, B. (1990). On the plausibility of corporate crime theory. *Advances in Criminological Theory*, 2: 17.

Bureau of Justice Statistics. (1994). *Prisoners in 1993.* Washington, D.C., U.S. Dept. of Justice.

Burger, W. (1982). More warehouses, or factories with fences? *New England Journal Prison Law*, 111.

_____. (1990). Factories with fences: The prison industries approach to correctional dilemmas. In I.P. Robbins (ed.) *Prisoners and the law*, pp. 2-8. New York: Clark Boardman Company.

Camp, C. & Camp, G. (1985). Correctional privatization in perspective. *The Prison Journal*, 15: 14-31.

Civil Rights Groups. (2000, July). Interviews with Doris Blaine, Edwina Lynn, Kenneth Webb, John Hightower, Myrtle Hightower, Johnnie and Ethel Parks. Chicago, IL.

Collins, C.F. (1997). *The imprisonment of African American women*. North Carolina: McFarland & Company, Inc. Publishers.

Collins, B.R. (1994). The U.S. lock up of prisoners. *Congressional Digest* (June-July), 175.

Conyers, John. (1978). Congressman John Conyers, Testimony: Subcommittee on Crime, *White Collar Crime*. Hedrigs, 21 June, 12 July; 1 December, 1978. U.S. House of Representatives, Committee on the Judiciary. Washington, D.C., 1978, p. 93.

Coser, L. (1956). *The functions of social conflict*. New York: Free Press.

Creesey, D. (1988). The poverty of theory in corporate crime research. *Advances in Criminology Theory*, 1: 31-56.

Dahl, J.G. & Glassman, A.M. (1991). The public sector contracting: The next growth industry for organizational development. *Public Administration Quarterly* 14, (Winter): 483-497.

Dahrendorf, R. (1959). *Class and class conflict in industrial society*. Stanford: Stanford University Press.

Davidson, J. (1997). Caged cargo. *Emerge* (October): 36-46.

Davis, Angela Y. (1998, Fall). What is the prison industrial complex? What does it matter? *Masked racism*. <http://www.arc.org/C-Lines/CLArchives/story1-2-01.html>.

Deloughry, T.J. (1991). Up to 300 institutions may be cut by U.S. from loan programs. *Chronicle of Higher Education* (May 22): A1+.

DePalma, A. (1991). A college acts in desperation and dies playing the lender. *New York Times* (April 17): A1+.

Duncan, I. & Bollard, A. (1992). Corporatization and privatization: Lessons from New Zealand, Auckland: Oxford University Press.

Eisenhower, D.W. (1961). Eisenhower's military industrial complex speech. <http://www.cwrl.utexas.edu/~mcnicholas/E309-Spring98/assign2/GenderFina198/DaveR/eisenhower%27s.html>.

Erlich & Reese. (1995). Prison labor: Workin' for the man. Covert Action Quarterly (Fall).

Ethridge, P. & Marquart, J. (1993). Private prisons in Texas: The new penology for profit. *Justice Quarterly* 10, no. 1 (March): 29-47.

Evans, D.G. (1993). Putting "community" back into community corrections. *Corrections Today* 55: 152-153.

Federal Bureau of Investigation. (1973-1991). Uniform crime reports for the United States. Washington, DC: U.S. Dept. of Justice.

Fendrich, R.P. (1992). Bush's antitrust lawyers attack philanthropy. *Wall Street Journal* (July 27): A13.

Fox, A. (1996) *Trends in Juvenile Violence*. Washington, D.C. Bureau of Justice Statistics.

Friedrichs, D.O. (1996). Trusted criminals. New York: Wadsworth Publishing Company, p. 379.

Goldberg, E. & Evans, L. (1998). *The prison industrial complex.* Global Economy. CA: Berkeley. Prison Activist Resource Center.

Goodman & Loveman. (1991). Does privatization serve the public interest? *Harvard Business Review* (November/December): 26-28, 32, 34, 36, 38.

Gottfredson, M. R. & Hirschi, T. (1990). A general theory of crime. Stanford University Press, Stanford, CA, 4th Ed.

Guinier, L. (2000). Speech delivered at the Democratic National Convention, August, 2000.

Hutto, T.D. (1990). The privatization of prisons. In J. Murphy & J. Dison (eds.) *Are prisons any better?*, 111-127. Newburg Park, CA: Sage Publications.

Isaac, A. & See, L.A. (Lee). (2001). Violence against African Americans in corporate America: In L. See (Ed.) *Violence as Seen Through a Prism of Color.* New York: The Haworth Press, Inc.

Isaac, A., Lockhart, L. & Williams, L. (2001). Violence against African American women in prisons and jails: Who's minding the shop? In L. See (Ed.) *Violence as Seen Through a Prism of Color.* New York: The Haworth Press, Inc.

Johnson, J. (2001). Violence in prison systems. An African American tragedy. In L. See (Ed.) *Violence as Seen Through a Prism of Color.* New York: The Haworth Press, Inc.

Lee, L. & Leonard, C. (2001). Violence in predominantly white institutions of higher education: Tenure and victim blaming. *Journal of Human Behavior in the Social Environment.* Volume 4, Numbers 2/3. 167-186.

Leu, M. (1985). A criminological and sociological approach to theories of and research into economic crimes. In Dan Magnisson, (ed.) Economic Crime: Programs for future research. Stockholm: National Council for Crime Prevention, pp. 32-72.

Lewis, C. S. (1961). The screwtape letter and screwtape purpose. New York: Macmillan, viii.

Light, Julie. (1999, October 28). The prison industry (editorial). <http://www.corpwatch. org/feature/prisons/editorial.html>.

Mauer, M. (1996). The truth about truth in sentencing. *Corrections Today* (February).
_____. (1998). Racial disparities in prison and jail populations. Report to the Council of State Governments. Washington, DC.

McCloskey, J. (1996). The death penalty: A personal view. *Criminal Justice Ethics*, vol. 15, no. 2, 2, 70-75.

Mergenhagan, P. (1996). The prison population bomb. *American Demographics* (February). On-line.

Miller, J. (1999). More black men headed to prison. Detroit: Free Press, 1. <http://www.naawp.net/news/more black men in prison.html>

Mundy, L. (1993). The dirty dozen–academic skankiest funders. *Lingua Franca* (March/April): 1, 24-31.

Netherlands & Kiefer. (1997). The prison industrial complex. <http://proquest.umi.com/pqdwebTS=943376...=1&Dtp=1&Did=000000012757544&Mtd=1&Fmt=3>.

Reiman, J. (1990; 1995) The rich get richer and the poor get prison. Boston, MA: Allyn & Bacon.

Schlosser, E. (1998, December). *The prison industrial complex*. New York: The Atlantic Monthly.

See, Letha A. (1998). Human behavior in the social environment from an African American perspective. New York: The Haworth Press, Inc.

Shichor, D. (1996). *Three strikes and you're out*. Thousand Oaks, CA: Sage.

_____. (1998). Diversity in the workplace: Issues and concerns of Africans and Asians. In A. Daly (Ed.) *Workplace Diversity Issues and Perspectives*. Washington, D.C.: NASW Press, pp. 354-372.

Sparks, R. (1978). Testimony. *Subcommittee on Crimes, White Collar Crime*, p. 146.

Stoker, J. (1998). *From welfare state to prison state*: *Imprisoning the American poor*. New York: Global Policy Forum.

Sutherland, E. H. (1949). White collar crime. New York: Dryden Press, p. 240.

_____. (1956). Critique of the theory. In Albert Cohen, Alfred Lindsey.

Sykes, C. J. (1988). Profscam: Professors and the demise of higher education. Washington, D.C.: Regency Gateway.

Thyer, B.A. (1999). The role of theory in research on social work practice. Keynote address. Ohio State University. 11th National Symposium on Doctoral Research in Social Work.

Vold, G.B., Bernard, T.J., and Snipes, J.B. (1998). *Theoretical criminology*. New York: Oxford Press.

Winerip, M. (1994). Billions for school are lost in fraud, waste and abuse. *New York Times* (February 2): A1+.

Wodarski, J.S. & Wodarski, L.A. (1998). *Preventing Teenage Violence*, NY: Springer Publishing Co.

Violence Against African Americans in Corporate America

Alicia Isaac

Letha A. (Lee) See

SUMMARY. Increasing numbers of African Americans are entering the corporate workplace and becoming vulnerable targets for insidious, devastating and punishing forms of abusive behavior exhibited at all levels in America's corporate structures. This article explores violence against African Americans who are attempting to climb the "crystal staircase" in these formal organizations. A model is proposed to assist black executives survive hostile environments in corporate America and in other settings. *[Article copies available for a fee from The Haworth Document Delivery Service: 1-800-342-9678. E-mail address: <getinfo @haworthpressinc.com> Website: <http://www.HaworthPress.com> © 2001 by The Haworth Press, Inc. All rights reserved.]*

KEYWORDS. Violence, corporate America, power, "crystal staircase," T.E.A.M.S

Alicia Isaac, DPA, currently teaches at Clayton College and State University in Atlanta, Georgia. She recieved her Doctor of Public Administration and MSW degrees from the University of Georgia. She is the President of the A.R. Isaac Group, a consulting firm specializing in policy analysis, program design, implementation and evaluation. Her first book, *The African American Students' Guide to Surviving Graduate School*, published by Sage Publishing Company, is widely used by graduate students. Her second book related to the human potential of surviving traumatic life events is scheduled for completion in summer, 2001.

Letha A. (Lee) See, EdM, MSW, PhD, is Professor in the School of Social Work at the University of Georgia. She received her PhD from Bryn Mawr College, PA and taught at Bryn Mawr, Lincoln University, (PA), Atlanta University, and the University of Arkansas.

[Haworth co-indexing entry note]: "Violence Against African Americans in Corporate America." Isaac, Alicia, and Letha A. (Lee) See. Co-published simultaneously in *Journal of Human Behavior in the Social Environment* (The Haworth Social Work Practice Press, an imprint of The Haworth Press, Inc.) Vol. 4, Nos. 2/3, 2001, pp. 85-104; and: *Violence as Seen Through a Prism of Color* (ed: Letha A. (Lee) See) The Haworth Social Work Practice Press, an imprint of The Haworth Press, Inc., 2001, pp. 85-104. Single or multiple copies of this article are available for a fee from The Haworth Document Delivery Service [1-800-342-9678, 9:00 a.m. - 5:00 p.m. (EST). E-mail address: getinfo@haworthpressinc.com].

INTRODUCTION

As the nation moves into the new cybercentury, concern is mounting regarding the alarming number of firings, resignations, injuries, homicides, accidental deaths, and other forms of personal and structural violence that affect African American (black) executives in corporate and business settings (Castillo, 1994a; Collins & Cox, 1987). Each year, in diverse industrial work places where a number of black executives are employed, more than 6,000 persons die of injuries, an estimated 50,000 die of illnesses caused by chemical exposure, and 6 million suffer from stress and emotional overload (Backman, 1994; BLS, 1995; Duncan, 1995; Windau & Toscano, 1994; U.S. Department of Health and Human Services, 1993). Equally as troublesome, non-fatal fatalities for all age groups cost the economy more than $110 billion a year, and the projection is that these numbers will markedly increase during the 21st century (Castillo, 1994b). In spite of widespread denial, Taylor (1996) charges that "there are racism and discrimination in the boardrooms of most big corporations." Thus, the evidence suggests that corporate violence may be a homicidal risk, a feared environmental factor, and a psychological nightmare for African American executives in general, and for the public at large (BLS, 1994a, b, c, d, 1995; Duncan, 1995; Mulhern, 1998).

Currently, the vivid image formed by the general public of corporate violence is not infractions directed toward black executives, but of disgruntled renegade employees or clients with a willful disregard for life "shooting-up" an executive suite, and reeking havoc throughout the workplace (Fox, 1994; Kelleher, 1996; McCune, 1994; Smith, 1993). An example of such violence is the episode at the Day Traders Corporation located in Atlanta, Georgia, where Mark O. Barton killed 9 people, wounded 13 others, then killed himself (Atlanta Constitution, July 30, 1999). Similarly, Bryan Uyesugi used a 9mm handgun to kill seven men at a Xerox copying repair center (his workplace) in Honolulu, Hawaii (Essayan & Cart, 1999). Although startling, these infinitesimal occurrences hardly tell the whole story of the insidious, pervasive, punishing, and abusing violence that is levied against African American men and women executives in corporate settings. Even more troubling is that violence against black executives' surfaces through overt racism, oppression, depersonalization, alienation, and sometimes death (Daly, 1990, 1994).

A current review of the evidence shows overwhelmingly that the violence experienced by black executives seldom receives more than scant coverage in the press and in textbooks. In all fairness, however, of late a few writings on this issue have begun to appear. All in all, the best available reports addressing corporate violence against black corporate managers have been published in magazine outlets such as Emerge, Essence, Savvy, and Black Enterprise. Almost two decades ago, Savvy caught the public's attention when it chronicled the suicide of Leanita McClain, a brilliant, young black journalist/executive, and former wife of Pulitzer Prize Columnist, Clarence Page. Sadly, she escaped the stresses and strains associated with corporate "hardball" when she made the decision to parachute out of the corporate war zone, take her own life, and forever rest in peace (Savvy, 1984). In March 1998, the public was again reminded of the devastation of corporate violence when Essence reported the suicide of business executive Diana Green (March 1998). This cautionary tale of the rise, fall, and suicide of this Pittsburgh business executive revealed the isolation and loneliness that may await those black executives who make it to the top of the corporate ladder without adequate emotional support (Essence, May 2000, p. 228).

These stories disturb a growing number of exceptionally talented, young black corporate professionals (paragons of integrity), who do not like what they see happening systemically in corporate workplaces. Behind the scenes, they are profoundly disillusioned and discretely discuss with their colleagues' problems, their gross discontent, feelings, and anxieties (See, 2000). They proclaim their disappointments of the racist practices unquestionably exhibited in so much of corporate America, which is impeding their upward mobility. And yet, the failure of these executives to expose what See (2000) describes as corporate America's "dirty little doings," is not buoyed by optimism, but is based on fear of jeopardizing, derailing, and ruining their own careers. And does anyone question the reason for fear on the part of young black professionals of confronting corporate America decision makers on the part of these young professionals with impeccable credentials, given the extraordinary power of these organizations? For example, Exxon, the third largest Fortune 500 Corporation in the United States with revenue of $122,379 million yearly, is a powerful and venerable institution. Likewise, Texaco, with 19,000 U.S. employees, and with $36 billion in annual revenues and net profits of $607 million, is awesome. In fact, some corporations have budgets and payrolls, which, with their customers, affect a greater number of people than most of the ninety-odd sovereign countries of the world. According to Sarangi (1999), if the combined revenues of two auto corporations, Ford and General Motors, are considered, their revenues would exceed the combined GNP of sub-Saharan Africa. Overall, not counting banking and financial institutions, fifty-one of the largest one hundred economies in the world are corporations. Likewise, the top three hundred firms in the United States account for 25% of the world's productive assets (p. 2). Clearly, any corporation with this level of influence, power, wealth, and control could literally destroy a single employee or a small fragmented group of employees in any workplace–especially budding, young African American executives.

The purpose of this article is to examine the phenomenon of corporate violence as it relates to African American male and female executives. Specifically, the article will examine how corporate violence injures these executives emotionally and organizationally, and paralyzes brilliant careers that could flourish in less stressful settings. Experiences articulated in therapy sessions with the authors are used to exemplify the depth and intensity of corporate violence. The framework of an innovative 21st century model will be introduced to enable black executives to cope effectively in hostile environments presided over by corporate magistrates who do not view themselves as racists. It should be noted that implicit in this writing is that corporations are on par with the federal government. Hence, any action taken in a corporate setting is considered a structural action in American society.

It must be acknowledged, however, that not all corporations have resorted to blatant violence against African American executives. In fact, some have provided extraordinary opportunities and supported their Black upward movement. More often, however, many have crafted only "paper remedies" (Detroit News, November 16, 1997), and have taken advantage of the decreasing emphasis of affirmative action policies to block career advancement opportunities. In this recasting, the "bad actions of the many affect the good efforts of the few."

CORPORATE VIOLENCE: A WORKING DEFINITION

A difficult task faced by social scientists is defining violence logically, yet in a way that it can be properly studied. From a definitional point of view, corporate violence is described as malicious acts planned and designed with a clearly defined goal–to generate profit, despite the detriment to organizational members. Some indicators of corporate violence include hostile takeovers of companies, espionage, downsizing, workplace murder, coercion, sabotage of property and products, embezzlement, blackmail, product liability, environmental assault, and large scale malpractice (Friedrich, 1996). In other words, corporate violence is defined as acts without institutional integrity and transgressions imposed on living beings.

Specifically, interpersonal corporate violence involves actually doing harm or inflicting injury to persons where the harm may have psychological consequences and damage to another individual's psychic well-being. For black executives employed in narrow-minded corporate workplaces, interpersonal violence is manifested in the form of coercion, forced conflictual decision-making, name-calling, harassment, racial slurs in cyberspace communications, humiliation and desertion (Sarangi, 1999). It may also include spreading malicious rumors about colleagues or disparaging them to others (Mokhiber, 1988; Mokhiber, 1996; White, 1996). The spectrum of corporate violence in many respects, parallels domestic violence since in both cases the dissonant, or toxic acts, thrive on power and control. Inherent in both forms of violence is an impressive exterior facade. But, as we will later see, tucked away beneath the facade is the experience of severe pain and humiliation.

SOCIAL LEARNING THEORY:
A FRAMEWORK FOR EXAMINING CORPORATE VIOLENCE

There are many different theoretical frameworks on violence that could help explain the problems black professionals encounter in the nation's corporate suites. In this article, social learning theory is a useful framework offered for consideration.

In her book, Human Behavior in the Social Environment from an African American Perspective, See (1998) engaged in an in-depth discussion of the two grand theories–the psychodynamic and behavioral paradigms. She suggests that "theory pieces" can form powerful eclectic formulations in analyzing behavioral phenomenon and can thus provide richness and context to an examination of a specific problem. Bandura (1969), a social learning theorist who is viewed interchangeably with the traditional behaviorist, has conducted a number of research studies which delineates a major premise of social learning theory: the identification and replication of conditions under which certain responses are likely to obtain desired goals. His work reflects how habits (learned activities) can be acquired and reinforced through rewards and consequences. In this discussion, how has corporate America learned to use violence as a means of obtaining its goals and why do African American executives endure such depersonalization? Bandura asserts that there are three origins of aggression: (1) observational learning, (2) reinforced performance, and (3) structural determinates. Observational learning involves closely witnessing the actions of others in a sub-system as they exhibit oppressive behavioral patterns toward subordinates. This authentication involves observing the reaction of those who are being oppressed in order to determine the degree of assertion the victim expends in fighting back, or the pacifism the victim displays. Reinforced performance entails repeatedly testing units of behavior to determine if the same responses to oppressive behavior will occur over time. Finally, structural determinates set the stage for assessing whether the behavior exhibited should be rewarded or punished.

Building on Bandura's work, Dutton (1998) concluded that violent habits have three aspects or components that fuel their existence. First, there must be the "originator"–the person or event that plants the idea of violence and submission into the head of followers. Secondly, there is the "instigator" who assesses the need for the results that the violence brings and triggers the violence, and thirdly, the "regulator" keeps the violence alive by providing the appropriate amounts of pain, coercion, or misinformation. Typically, the organization as granting authority gives its agents permission to engage in these roles by the very nature and structure of the organization itself. Most of corporate America is still very hierarchical, dominated by white males, and structurally exclusive except in positions where blacks have acquired real power. Dutton's work, therefore, gives clarity to the social learning paradigm and elevates it as a robust model for analyzing what happens to black executives employed in corporate America.

PERSONAL AND ORGANIZATIONAL VIOLENCE DIRECTED TOWARDS AFRICAN AMERICAN EXECUTIVES

The literature suggests that some corporate executives who are originators of violence do their homework. In the suites, they make sport out of belittling blacks by calling them "black jelly beans" who "stick to the bottom of the bag," (Wheeler, 1996). They then attempt to conceal evidence of race discrimination (Donovan, 1997; Roberts vs. Texaco, 1996; Mokhiber, 1996; Wheeler, 1996). In board rooms, the "big cheeses" exhaustively study the behavior of blacks along with their speech, voice, posture, eating protocol, mannerisms, hair, and dress (observe if they wear blue and gray power suits). In terms of homework, they know where black executives live, and what kind of cars they drive–all of which provides even more leverage in the violence game. Referable to lifestyle, they know that African American executives are so financially invested in moving into the "upper class" that they cannot afford to walk away from high paid employment (Brenner & Fernsten, 1984). At this moment, the entrenched "good ole boys" know that in the year 2000 blacks were projected to earn an income of almost $600 billion–and would spend $25.2 billion on wearing apparel, $21 billion on new and used vehicles, and $7.4 billion on personal care products and services (University of Georgia School of Business, 1999). Corporations seem to sense precisely when African American executives can be personally victimized and when they will have no recourse but to accept victimization status in silence. Corporate management knows that as long as the corporation and/or big business firms dangle "carrots" (requisite symbols of success), such as expensive homes, luxury cars, credit cards, easy access to loan acquisitions, huge offices, and generous compensations, black executives have a high tolerance for accepting victimization status (Bush, 1977; Isaac, 1999). Ostensibly, corporations like Texaco (Roberts vs. Texaco, 1997) wait patiently for black executives to fall into the "corporate trap," where there is no escape latch or outlet. The corporate decision-makers know when black executives are rendered powerless to change the circumstances of their employment, and they understand fully that locating an alternative work-site that provides the perks offered by their corporations will be difficult. Taken together, the evidence suggest that many corporate executives wait and feel confident that, in due course, the black executive will show a high level of compliance and will become the "house nigger" of the corporation (Isaac, 1999; Moskowitz, 1996; Sampson, 1996).

The works of Lee and Leonard (1999) have brilliantly articulated the kind of humiliation and degradation that is involved when black professionals accept condescending roles in academia–a pseudo corporate enterprise. Their insights hold true for other organizations as well. In fact, whites describe blacks that tolerate disrespectful roles as "corporate politicians" and "team players," contrarily blacks label the role players as "head niggers in charge." Within the narrow bounds of classification in many organizations, African American executives are forced to remain compliant if they plan to remain with the organization for the entirety of their careers (Taylor, 1982).

Essentially, in the corporate world, some African American executives are typecast as "informants," "rubber stamps," "Uncle Toms," "difficult," and "Affirmative Action Babies" (Carter, 1991). However, in very high levels of these organizations, they are described as "two-faced executioners (often used to deliver the killing blow to other blacks)," "nice Negroes (they are not like the other ones)," "black jelly beans" and "the company's showpiece (the one displayed to exhibit the diversity of the corporate structure–if he could make it, so could these other people, if they had worked hard)" (Isaac, 1999; Graham, 1995). Even after being forced to play these self-defacing games, a sizeable number of African American executives, like good soldiers, still provide dedicated service to the corporation. The puzzle for social scientists is how corporations can present to the world such an impressive exterior package bounded by diversity, while inside that package they are imposing such severe pain, humiliation, and violence to employees, including African American executives.

In a therapy session with several clients employed in the corporate world, it was learned that most black mid-level managers actually have little familiarity with the corporate climate, governance, regulations, rules, and tools of the organization (Pritchard & Karasich, 1973). Secondarily, they fail to understand that their period of probation far exceeds that of their white counterparts, and thirdly, blacks have only a scant awareness that messages are transmitted in the suites, signifying that notwithstanding their executives' status, they will basically remain as marginal players in the organization (Texaco Debacle, 1997; Mfume, 1996).

The literature reveals that during the probationary periods for black executives, there is a concomitant period of internalization of the corporate culture. During this learning cycle, African American executives must struggle to hold onto their acquired identity while at the same time seeking acceptability in the corporate world (See, 2000). Unfortunately, it is during this period that coded messages are transmitted to a select group of high-level insiders, referred to by Terry (1973) as the "White Male Club," which are not complimentary of the performance of African American executives.

The "White Male Club" is not a club in the classic sense of the word, but a loose confederate of white men ascribed as society's decision makers. The first criteria for gaining membership in the Club is that one must adhere to one or a combination of criteria: (1) membership is presupposed for white males at birth, (2) members must be committed to technological superiority and dominance on the world scene, (3) members must profess a conservative ideology, (4) members must pledge to uphold the rules of the club and the status quo, and (5) members must let it be known that the club is selective, so minorities and women need not apply. If needed to accomplish the Club's own ends however, both minorities and women may be recruited but are relegated to secondary status and exploited for club purposes (Terry, 1973). Within the past three decades, however, the explosion of technology, global inter-connects and sophisticated communication systems have been astonishingly frightening to the club. Moreover, of necessity, membership in the White Male Club has been extended, and a few minorities and technocrats from the "wrong side of the social system" have gained entry. But even with the expansion and inclusion of alien groups, the number of African Americans to fully break into this elite group is still "few and far between." Clearly, personal and organizational violence in the corporate workplace is a problem for black executives, and is the source of significant emotional strain.

THE EMOTIONAL STRESS EXPERIENCED BY AFRICAN AMERICANS IN THE CORPORATE WORKPLACE

A select group of researchers have written eloquently about the psychological strain anxiety, trauma, and depression that is experienced by new black executives who seek to blend into the corporate culture and acquire group identity and acceptance (McCall, 1994; Nelson, 1993). The literature reveals that during their neophyte period of employment in the sanctuary of the suites, new black executives are sometimes treated as stupid, incompetent, and lazy (McCall, 1994; Texaco, Inc., 94 Civ 2015). Some have been mocked and described as "not good enough" for the rigors of the corporation and should be pushed outside the group (Mfume on Texaco Debacle, 1986). A series of classic studies have been conducted that express the importance of acceptance into group life. For example, Crowne and Marlowe's (1964) work looked at the need for social approval, and Homans (1974) looked at the individual's position within a group's social status system. Deutsch and Gerald's (1955) investigation largely reports on how individuals go along with the group norms largely out of a desire to be accepted by the group (Sherif, 1935). Reisman, Glazer, and Denny (1950) argued in their classic study, *The Lonely Crowd* (1957), that group acceptance is more important than being right. Moreover, for African American executives in the corporate environment being alone is painful, so they often opt to conform to the norms of the organization rather than remain in isolation.

Without a doubt, conformity, which is important in the corporate world, has come to be defined in social-psychology research as yielding to group expectations or definitions of a situation. By conformity, sanctions, rewards and punishments are imposed by the group if the individual is not a team player. Kelman, 1963, in his seminal work made a rather critical distinction among three different types of conformity–compliance, external factor, and internalization. Compliance involves acquiescence to group demands not because noncompliance could result in punishment or loss of reward, but because it helps maintain equilibrium. Conformity involves an external factor and identification with another person or group. Here, the individual goes along with another or adopts an idea or behavioral pattern because he or she desires to be like others in the group rather than for a reward. Kelman's third mode of conformity, internalization, occurs when the individual accepts an action and makes it part of his or her own value system. In this model, the individual actually believes it is the correct and appropriate way things should be done. Kelman's conformity models can be used to account for the stress and trauma African Americans feel when they are left out of the "loop" in the corporate work site.

In a brief interview with a corporate executive, he discussed some of the outrageous and scurrilous factors that frustrate African American executives. He explained:

> At the same time I was striving to hold onto my ties in my black community, I was trying to "make it" in the new corporate environment. I was straddling two worlds–the white corporate world characterized by "gold-plated hostility," and the black world, my primary source of support, comfort and spiritual nurturing. (See, 2000)

Another executive confided that:

> You have no idea how much guilt is involved in transforming from "not being black" to "being black," it is literally draining. You constantly feel pulled in one direction then in the next. Then it all happened–my emotions exploded and I directed my rage against myself. First, I became depressed, I started drinking, I became very ill because I didn't eat, and then my girl friend left me. I had fights at the bar where I drank, withdrew from my friends, and finally tried to take my own life. (See, 2000)

These testimonies, presented in therapeutic sessions, exemplify the heavy burdens that frequently propel black corporate executives to make critical choices–start mounting the "crystal staircase," or leave the corporate work place in search for less stressful employment.

THE CRYSTAL STAIRCASE PHENOMENON

A new phenomenon presently emerging in the corporate literature, is referred to as the "crystal staircase." It is described by Hayes (1997, p. 232) in these words:

> Some say the route to the upper climbs of corporate America is along a crystal stair–a path filled with bountiful salaries, chauffeured cars and other lavish appointments. But missing from the fairy tale are the jagged edges beneath the beautiful, multifaceted façade. And for all of its inviting color, reflection and abundance of light, there is very little heat. But for African Americans, there is often no wizard, Prince Charming or fairy godmother to help ease the way. It can be a lonely, cold ascent taken by an African American executive, who inevitably may be stopped at the glass ceiling.

The crystal staircase is an important analogy as it seeks to describe the journey up the corporate ladder for black executives. This journey is torturous and challenges the endurance of young black executives aspiring to become high level decision-makers. According to African American executives in therapy sessions, what is misleading is the violent tactics, which are employed by corporations to halt the forward movement of African American executives. Clearly their statements suggest that corporations employ luxurious recruiting measures and lucrative bonuses to attract blacks into their organization. They give the impression that equality is widespread in the corporate structure, while it actually operates within the "good ole' boy network" (Hayes, 1998). Sometimes, clients in therapy explain that corporations may label bright young African Americans coming into the organization as "senior-level management prospects," and provide them with high levels of exposure. Accordingly, these actions often cause divisiveness among black and white colleagues and triggers high expectations for the freshman executive. This is a successful tactical maneuver and a violent tool to impose on any human being (Jones, 1973).

Some clients believe that African American executives must pay a high price if they expect to reach the final landing on the crystal staircase. The first casualties are often black women who have been heavily concentrated in expendable staff positions. The next groups scheduled for extinction are young black and white females followed by black male executives. One client said at first, corporations heap praise on their new African American executives, but shortly thereafter start demanding that they place the organization above everything in their life space. In other words, black executives must, like white executives, be willing to lie, cheat, steal, and, in some instances, take a prison rap for the organization. Reports are that, in some corporate structures, CEO's jokingly assert that their organizational chart has space for a Vice President for Prison Service.

Another client said, America's top black female executives may exude the highest level of corporate savvy to the world, and they may indeed meet the rigors of their jobs and be held as compatible with their white male senior managers and staff. Often the "dirty little secret" is that a number of these black female CEO's, like their "white sisters," have "slept" with their bosses in exchange for a position at the apex of power in the organization (Sullivan, 1989; Wright, Wesley-King, & Berg, 1985).

On the first rung of this "crystal staircase," young black high achievers have frequently found themselves accepting social invitations, being forced to ignore embarrassing racial slurs, "nigger jokes," and laughing with frozen smiles when comments are not funny. They endure these pressures for fear of being labeled "overly sensitive." So, they settle for being the "one good black that everyone likes" (See, 2000).

Clearly, climbing the crystal staircase is somewhat analogous to the glass ceiling–the distinct difference being that the latter is profoundly more pliable and has the potential to keep shifting upward. For example, when there is progress that allows African American executives to become upwardly mobile, the ceiling likewise moves upward limiting their aspirations and momentum, especially in "old guard" companies (Hayes, 1997, p. 132).

In essence, if an African American executive could reach the ceiling more quickly, there may be an increased perception of security and fewer opportunities for set-ups and overt racial discrimination to creep into the process. Without that sense of climax, the crystal staircase symbolizes a tedious, arduous, and continuously pressure laden game which must be mastered, if one is to survive in corporate America.

Although a few African Americans have gained scattered footholds on the crystal staircase, a safe landing still remains an exclusively white preserve. A study by the Federal Glass Ceiling Commission (1995) reported that blacks held just 0.6% of senior executive posts, so the climb is almost negligible. In sum, the crystal staircase, which leads to the glass ceiling, is a phenomenon in which African Americans have not yet fully understood how to negotiate, yet this understanding is important to their survival in corporate America.

A MODEL FOR AFRICAN AMERICAN SURVIVAL IN ASCENDING THE CRYSTAL STAIRCASE

Few models, with theoretical grounding have been constructed that are sufficiently robust to assist African American executives climb the crystal staircase that has been constructed in the corporate workplace. Obviously, the first question to be grappled with is delineating what is meant by the currently fashionable, albeit ambiguous, term "model." Joseph Schumpter and Max Weber defined a model as a procedure of abstract theoretical construction that alone renders possible the rational understanding of the human world (Arrow, 1956; Beshers, 1957. A model, in this discussion, is a clearly formulated pictorial diagram that charts a pathway to a higher goal (Meadows, 1957; Morgan & McNeil, 1997).

Indeed, it should be emphasized that most intervention strategies employed in the corporate workplace have centered around Employee Assistance Programs (EAP), diversity training, and crisis modalities for individuals and families. While each of these intervention techniques has brilliance, they are far too timid to render assistance in helping African American executives move up the crystal staircase. Corporations generally pay large sums of money for cultural diversity, team building, and conflict resolution training. Yet, when the outcome of the training is examined, the available evidence shows that it provides little help in solving intergroup conflict that can derail and ruin the careers of young blacks. Neither does it address structural problems such as racism, sexism, and ageism faced by African Americans and other disaffected groups in the organization. To exemplify this point, Pasternak (1994) analyzed a study sponsored by the Hoescht Celanese Textile Fibers Group for the National Organization for the Professional Advancement of Black Chemists and Chemical Engineers. In his analysis, he described the difference in what corporate groups felt were the measures employed to improve conditions and counter an environment for violence, and what members of disenfranchised groups felt about the effort. (The shocking response is seen in Table 1.)

Given the disparity in the extent of initiatives corporate players felt they have undertaken to promote a humanistic environment and how those efforts are viewed by disaffected workers, it is obvious there is a need for the construction of a new model.

T.E.A.M.S.:
A PROPOSED MODEL
FOR ASSISTING BLACK EXECUTIVES
CLIMB THE CRYSTAL STAIRCASE

T.E.A.M.S., an acronym for Technology, Education, Access, Mentoring, and Support, is a dynamic, generic strengths-based system which focuses on the strongest attributes of individuals and groups (Chapin, 1995, 1998; Saleeby, 1992; Sullivan, 1992). It is a structural "solution-based" framework that provides a support to African American executives during the process of planning their careers in a specific organization. T.E.A.M.S. offers collaboration, therapeutic intervention, education, mentoring, and broad scale support.

TABLE 1. Difference in the Feeling of Senior Management and Disenfranchised Groups Regarding Efforts to Improve Environmental Conditions

Management's Perception of Effort	Percent
✓ Involved in mentoring disenfranchised employees	94%
✓ Provided leadership training	89%
✓ Changed and expanded hiring practices	61%
✓ Provided diversity training	61%
✓ Empowered all employees	60%
✓ Promoted and accelerated career development (fast tracker) opportunities	58%
Disaffected Group's Response to Management's Effort	Percent
✓ Nothing had been done	87%
✓ Management had created a number of powerless diversity councils	56%
✓ Same select employees promoted over and over	52%
✓ Group encouraged to go back to school for advanced degrees without providing on-job job application	52%

Table constructed by Isaac and See from Pasternak's Study, 1994.
Constructed for The Haworth Press, Inc., 2000.

It is somewhat analogous to the highly acclaimed "gaming" program sponsored by McDonald's, Inc. which has been so successful in helping African Americans climb the crystal staircase. T.E.A.M.S. is a sophisticated, diverse approach that includes an eclectic model that draws upon linking black corporate executives throughout the world. It is a tool, a means not an end in itself, and its merit is to provide a safe environment for black executives to reflect seriously on how to move upward in their respective work sites, and to collectively figure out how to reach their objective.

T.E.A.M.S. is not an inexpensive model, as it employs the services of a multi-disciplinary team of highly educated consultants, such as professors, attorneys, clergy, educators, social work practitioners, and psychologists–all of whom are knowledgeable about human behavior, formal organizations, and education (Adult Learning Specialists). An abbreviated narration of the T.E.AM.S. program follows.

AN INTERVENTION STRATEGY USEFUL
IN CLIMBING THE CRYSTAL STAIRCASE

Technology

The first module of T.E.A.M.S. concerns technology (T). Since the wave of the future is communication driven, technology can be put into place for Trans-Atlantic and Pacific usage through the medium of the World Wide Web. This initiative can assist African American executives in warding off violent corporate retaliation by becoming a part of a world wide survival group. For the first few years of its existence, the T.E.A.M.S. structure must remain informal with only an ad hoc structure operating. Keeping the organization informal helps to eliminate the "jockeying for power" which can overshadow the original mission of learning how to climb the crystal staircase with ease.

The first order of the T.E.A.M.S. initiative is to call a meeting of all black executives who are part of the Fortune 500 corporations. At this meeting, it must be made as clear as possible that its purpose is to assist black executives survive in a hostile environment. From that core group, an ad hoc committee should be selected that will be responsible for the logistics involved in the selection of T.E.A.M.S. consultants. The black ad hoc executives will be responsible for formulating unambiguous goals, and for informing corporate CEO's of this new strength paradigm. The task of the ad hoc committee is to provide information about T.E.A.M.S.–making sure they understand this is not a union initiative. Black ad-hoc executives are to urge CEO's to support their effort. A concise framework for the utilization of the technology module is as follows:

- An ad hoc committee will energize black executives by posting announcements on the Internet to black corporate executives throughout the world.
- Fortune 500 black executives will present to their CEO's "white papers" which delineates violent acts that have been imposed on African Americans seeking to move up the crystal staircase. They solicit CEO endorsement and support by pointing out that the corporation will "do well by doing good."
- Conduct research and list the names of black executives who have been fired, demoted, or transferred by specific corporations. Specifically call attention to those executives who registered no grievance against violent assaults hurled against them, fearful that their careers would be affected. Technology is then used to assist in locating these employees to help salvage their careers if such an effort is possible.
- Use technology to prepare a Question-Answer "talking-point" manual delineating acts of violence that have been reported by African American executives.

Education

Education (E), is the second module in the T.E.A.M.S. model designed to assist African American executives climb the crystal staircase. A key assumption is that black executives have expertise in management systems, marketing, and finance–skills that drive the corporate world so these must be utilized to help save their careers. In the education module, black executives are taught to "survive and thrive." Professionals who are experts on race relations will teach black executives how to engage in career planning, skill development, and good old-fashioned "corporate politicking." The "surviving" and "thriving" curriculum will be dynamic, intensive, theoretically based, and will fold in cultural diversity training. In time, it will be offered to all multi-cultured groups in the corporation. African Americans who have achieved success will be called upon to share with their junior colleagues some of the joys and sorrows they experienced in navigating the crystal staircase (Hayes, 1998).

Access

Access (A) is a module designed to prevent African American executives from slipping on the crystal staircase. Much of what continues to hamper African American executives is an information "black-out." Not only are black executives left out of the loop in the communication arena, but they fail to communicate with each other (American and Anderson, 1996). T.E.A.M.S. professionals will teach black executives how to gain information through unobtrusive measures–all of which can yield priceless results. Additionally, they will be taught how to bond with each other–an attribute that assisted blacks in throwing off the bonds of slavery at an earlier period.

Mentoring

Mentoring (M), the fourth module in the T.E.A.M.S. model, is designed to assist black executives to accomplish corporate mobility. Some advocates argue that the "good ole boy" network often feels uncomfortable mentoring African Americans, therefore, blacks must find their own mentors. Through cyberspace, T.E.A.M.S. members will have an opportunity to search for mentors (former black executives) nationally and internationally. The worldwide mentoring connection is a powerful, strategic maneuver that can assist black executives in unifying their positions in the corporation. It establishes worldwide political clout, and helps develop a potent support system, which includes informing black executives of job openings in other corporations located in the U.S. and abroad.

In the T.E.A.M.S. model, talented black professors who have attended some of the finest business institutions in the nation will be called upon to serve as "invisible mentors." Likewise, black social scientists and clergy, experts in human behavior, will be called upon to assist black executives in analyzing and interpreting the behavior of corporate officials who must determine the fate of their careers.

Support

Support (S) is the last, and one of the most important modules in the T.E.A.M.S. model. Traditionally, African Americans have not totally supported each other. In fact, some have undercut the effectiveness of those who assumed leadership roles. This type of action can be problematic and can doom the entire T.E.A.M.S. strategy. Further, it can disrupt individual careers and hamper all black executives from successfully climbing the crystal staircase. It should be remembered that organizations tend to "pluck off" solo dissenting voices one at a time. However, it is highly unlikely that the corporation would displace its entire cadre of black executives. Some firm commitment must be made by black executives that if one T.E.A.M.S. executive is unfairly treated (and this can be documented), the T.E.A.M.S. network will spin into action and respond appropriately.

The T.E.A.M.S. model is not one that can be initiated without proper training conducted by those who developed the program, or by others who have been trained to implement it. Ongoing research is being initiated to test the efficiency and effectiveness of each module in T.E.A.M.S. as an intervention vehicle. Likewise, research can predict the degree to which this model can provide support to black corporate executives throughout the world. Finally, an evaluation initiative designed to measure how well T.E.A.M.S. can succeed is being developed.

CONCLUSION

Our discussion has shown that African American executives are gradually gaining visibility in the management structure of corporate America. However, they continue to encounter insidious, pervasive, punitive and violent pressures designed to stymie progress as they navigate their forward momentum. Seemingly, a crystal staircase has been erected that threatens to crack under their weight if corporate norms are not honored. Until recently, no African Americans were appointed CEO's of Fortune 500 corporations–which is the clearest indication of the existence of the crystal staircase.

In this article, the skeleton of a new model tailored for African American executives called T.E.A.M.S. is introduced. This is an innovative, worldwide framework, which is grounded in the theoretical "strengths perspective."

This model folds cultural diversity, team building and corporate training into a broader context. Through T.E.A.M.S. a cadre of high level professionals (ministers, professors, attorneys, psychologists, social workers, and other professionals) will assist in empowering black executives and addressing the violence they are currently experiencing. The T.E.A.M.S. model has significant utility, and will not only be priceless to black executives, but will also assist in empowering the corporation.

It must be duly noted that white executives often encounter many of the same problems experienced by black executives, however the focus here is on violence against black executives. Research should be conducted in an effort to further explore factors associated with violence against all groups in corporate America, which will, in the end, strengthen the corporation.

REFERENCES

Backman, R. (1994, July 15). Violence and theft in the workplace. U.S. Department of Justice, Bureau of Justice Statistics.

Bandura, A. (1969). *Principles of behavior modification.* New York: Holt, Rinehart, and Winston.

Bennett, D.H. (1999, July 30). Shooting rampage: The gunman Barton: Big smile, quiet guy, shady past. Atlanta Journal and Constitution, B4.

Beshers, James M. (1957). Models and theory construction. American Sociological Review, Vol. XXII, 32-38.

BLS. (1994a). Annual survey of occupational injuries and illnesses. Washington, DC: U.S. Department of Labor, Bureau of Labor Statistics. Unpublished database.

BLS. (1994b). National census of fatal occupational injuries, 1993. Washington, DC: U.S. Department of Labor, Bureau of Labor Statistics, BLS News, USDL-94-384.

BLS. (1994c). Violence in the workplace comes under closer scrutiny. Issues in labor statistics. Washington, DC: U.S. Department of Labor, Bureau of Labor Statistics, Summary 94-10.

BLS. (1994d). Work injuries and illnesses by selected characteristics, 1992. Washington, DC: U.S. Department of Labor, Bureau of Labor Statistics.

BLS. (1995). National census of fatal occupational injuries, 1994. Washington, DC: U.S. Department of Labor, BLS News, USDL-95-288.

Brenner, O. and Fernsten, J. (1984). Racial differences in perceived job fulfillment of white-collar workers. Perceptual and Motor Skills, 58: 643-646.

Bush, J. (1977). The minority administrator: Implications for social work education. *Journal of Education for Social Work*, 13: 15-22.

Cain, J.D. (2000, May). The stories you couldn't forget. Essence.

Campbell, B.M. (1984). To be black, gifted, and alone. Savvy.

Carter, S. (1991) *Reflections of an Affirmative Action baby.* N.Y. Basic Books.

Castillo, D.N. (1994a). Nonfatal violence in the workplace: Directions for future research. In questions and answers in lethal and non-lethal violence. Proceedings of the Third Annual Workshop of the Homicide Research Working Group. Washington, DC: National Institute of Justice.

Castillo, D.N. and Jenkins, E.L. (1994). Industries and occupations at high risk for work-related homicide. *Journal of Occupational Medicine* 36: 125-132.

Collins, J.J. and Cox, B.G. (1987). Job activities and personal crime victimization implications for theory. *Social Science Review* 16: 345-360.

Crowne, D.P. and Marlowe, D. (1964). The approval motive. New York: John Wiley.

Daly, A. (1990). Perception of influence and job satisfaction. Unpublished manuscript, School of Social Work, Rutgers University. New Brunswick, NJ.

Daly, A. (1994). African American and white managers: A comparison in one age. *Journal of Community Practice* 1 (1), 57-79.

Davis, J., Honchar, P.A., and Suarez, L. (1987). Fatal occupational injuries of women, Texas 1975-1984. *American Journal of Public Health* 77: 1524-1527.

Deutsch, M..and Gerard, H. (1955). A study of normative and informational social influences upon individual judgement. *Journal of Abnormal and Social Psychology*, 51: 629-636.

Donavan, K. (1997, February 10). Big blue faces a bias change. *The Natural Law Journal*, 107.

Duncan, T. S. (1995, April). Death in the office–Workplace homicides. Law Enforcement Bulletin 64, no. 4, 20-25.

Essoyans, S. & Cart, J. (1999) Seven Slain in Honolulu office; co-worker held. *Los Angeles Times*, p. A12.

FBI. (1994). Uniform crime reports for the United States, 1993. Washington, DC; U.S. Department of Justice, Federal Bureau of Investigation.

Friedrich, D. (1996). Trusted criminals. New York: Wadsworth Publishers, 70-83.

Graham, O. (1995). Head nigger in charge. *Business and Society Review* 94, 43-51.

Hayes, C. (1997). Soul management. Black Enterprise 28 (4), 129-134.

Hayes, C. (1998). Life atop the crystal stair. Black Enterprise 28 (7), 107-114.

Homans, G.C. (1958). Social behavior as exchange. *American Journal of Sociology* 09: 597-606. Also see Social behavior in its elementary forms. New York: Harcourt Brace Jovanovich.

Isaac, A. (1999). Lecture on corporate violence. University of Georgia, School of Social Work. Fall.

Jones, E. (1973). What is it like to be a black manager? *Harvard Business Review*, 51: 108-116.

Kelleher, M.D. (1996). New arenas for violence: Occupational homicide in the American workplace. Westport, CT: Praeger.

Kelman, H.C. (1963) The role of the group in the induction of therapeutic change. *International Journal of Group Psychotherapy*, 13, 339-342.

McCune, J. (1994). Companies grapple with workplace violence. *Management Review*, 3: 52.

Meadows, P. (1951). Models, systems, and science. *American Sociological Review*, Vol.22, 3-9.

Mfume, K. (1997). Statement regarding Texaco. NAACP ISSUES. <www.naacp.org/ president/releases/archives/1996/texaco 2htm.>

Mokhiber, R. (1988) Corporate Crime and Violence. San Francisco, CA: Sierra Books.

Mokhiber, R. (1996). The worst ten corporations of 1996: Texaco shame. *Multinational Monitor's Corporation Rap Sheet*. Vol. 17, Number 12.

Morgan, G. & McNeil E. (1977). Models: From Max Weber to general systems analysis. *Introduction to Sociology*. University of Arkansas. Also see, Arrow, J. (1956) Mathematics Models in the Social Sciences. General Systems Yearbook of the Society for Advancement of General Systems Theory. (Eds.) Ludwig Von Bertlanoffy & Anatol Rapport, Vol. 1, 29-47.

Moskowitz, M. (1996, December 2). This one mean company. *The New York Times*. Also see Sampson, A. (1975). The seven sisters.

Mulhern, J. (1998). Public citizen's congress watch legislation council. Washington, D.C. (202) 546-4996.

Nelson, Jill. (1995). Volunteer slavery. Chicago: The Hable Press, Inc.

Pasternak, C. (1994). Study of the professional advancement of black chemists and chemical engineers. Hoescht Celanese Textile Fibers Group.

Pritchard, R. & Karasick, B. (1973). The effects of organizational climate on managerial job performance and job satisfaction. *Organizational Behavior and Human Performance*, 9, 110-119.

Report on a black pattern of spending. (1999). University of Georgia, School of Business. Fall.

Riesman, D., Glazer, N., & Denny, R. (1950). *The lonely crowd*. New Haven. Yale University Press.

Sampson, A. (1975). *The seven sisters: The great oil companies and the world they made*. Great Britain: Hodder & Stoughton.

Sarangi, S. Corporate Violence in Bhopal. Paper presented at International Conference on Preventing Violence. Mumbia, India.

See, Letha A. (Lee). (2000). Interviews with clients X and Y regarding treatment in the corporate workplace.

Sherif, M. (1935). A study of some social factors in perception. *Archival Psychologia* 27, No. 187:1-60.

Smiley, T. (1996). Hard left. New York: Anchor Books.

Smith, E. (1997). Playing the corporate race card. *Black Enterprise*, 27 (6), 19-22.

Smith, S.L. (1993, October). Violence in the workplace: A cry for help. *Occupational Hazards*, 1.

Sullivan, T. (1989). Women and minority workers in the new economy. *Work and Occupations*, 16: 393-415.

Taylor, A. (1982, December 6). The myth of the black executive. Time, 53.

Terry, R. (1973). The white male club. Neely, Campbell, Gibb, Terry and Associates. 18263 Ohio Avenue, Detroit Mi 48221.

Texaco, Inc. 94 civ. 2015 (Roberts vs. Texaco).

Texaco, Inc. 94 (civ. 2015, Violation of 704(a) of Title VII, 42 U.S.C. 20002-3.

U.S. Department of Health and Human Services (USHHS). (1993, August). Fatal injuries to minorities in the United States, 1980-1989: A decade of surveillance. USHHS/National Office of Occupational Health and Safety, xii.

Weathers, D.M. (1998, March). Death of a superwoman. *Essence*.

Welsing, F.C. (1991). *The Isis papers: The keys to colors*. Chicago: Third World Press.

Wheeler, T. (1996). Texaco boycott targets big oil racism. *People's Weekly World*. 235 W. 23rd Street, NY, NY 10011.

White, Jack (Nov. 18, 1996). "Texaco's white-color bigots." *Time*; Chicago; Vol. 148, Issue 23.

Windau, J. and Toscano, G. (1994). Murder Inc.–Homicide in the American workplace. *Business and Society Review*, no. 89, 58.

Wright, R., Wesley-King, S., & Berg, W.E. (1985). Job satisfaction in the workplace: A study of black females in management positions. *Journal of Social Service Research*, 8 (3), 65-79.

SECTION II:
VIOLENCE AS SEEN
THROUGH PRISON BARS

Violence in Prison Systems:
An African American Tragedy

Jerry G. Johnson

SUMMARY. This article speaks to several dimensions of the correctional enterprise and discusses violence from the perspective of an administrator who has viewed the criminal justice system "up close and personal." The author argues that the system is in a perilous quagmire and many problems that affect blacks and minorities are structurally rooted. These include: (1) violence against black males in the criminal justice system, (2) sentencing for drug use, (3) mistreatment of blacks, violence in prison systems, and (4) the news media, to name a few. Suggestions are offered on how to humanize the criminal justice system which has been labeled by countries throughout the world as "America the Violent." *[Article copies available for a fee from The Haworth Document*

Jerry G. Johnson, MA, received his master's degree in Human Relations from the University of Oklahoma and has attended, and conducted many high-level seminars where complex problems associated with corrections were addressed. He began his career with the Oklahoma corrections system in 1972, and served as an Inmate Release Counselor, Chief Counselor Training Specialist; Deputy Warden, Warden, and Deputy Director of all state programs and services to name a few. Presently, he serves as a consultant for various correctional systems throughout the United States, and is an Adjunct Professor of Criminal Justice at Rose State College, Midwest City, Oklahoma.

The author wishes to express his gratitude to Deena Harvill Pave, graduate student, University of Georgia, for her excellent technical assistance in the production of this writing.

[Haworth co-indexing entry note]: "Violence in Prison Systems: An African American Tragedy." Johnson, Jerry G. Co-published simultaneously in *Journal of Human Behavior in the Social Environment* (The Haworth Social Work Practice Press, an imprint of The Haworth Press, Inc.) Vol. 4, Nos. 2/3, 2001, pp. 105-128; and: *Violence as Seen Through a Prism of Color* (ed: Letha A. (Lee) See) The Haworth Social Work Practice Press, an imprint of The Haworth Press, Inc., 2001, pp. 105-128. Single or multiple copies of this article are available for a fee from The Haworth Document Delivery Service [1-800-342-9678, 9:00 a.m. - 5:00 p.m. (EST). E-mail address: getinfo@haworthpressinc.com].

105

Delivery Service: 1-800-342-9678. E-mail address: <getinfo@haworthpressinc. com> Website: <http://www.HaworthPress.com> © 2001 by The Haworth Press, Inc. All rights reserved.]

KEYWORDS. Violence, criminal justice, African American, tragedy, labeling, racial profiling (driving while black/brown), Prison Industrial Complex

Much has been written by well-meaning sociologists, criminologists and independent observers about the criminal justice system as a mirror in which a whole society can see the darker outlines of its face (Reiman, 1995, p. 1). Today, what is seen in that mirror is a dark-lined face and a white pair of eyes frowning at African Americans, Hispanics, and other powerless groups. The striking image in the mirror is a face that has declared corrosive warfare on most minorities, especially those caught up in America's criminal justice system.

Shelly (1981) has observed that throughout the western world persons who break laws are appropriately apprehended, punished, or sanctioned in order to reduce the threat of crime. But in the United States where crimes are committed every hour of the day and an imprisonment and electrocution binge is in progress, a disproportionate number of poor people–most with black faces–are caught in a societal maze, and locked up for non-violent crimes (see Figure 1). This miscarriage of social justice has caused 20% of the nation's death penalty advocates to push for re-evaluating our prison and capital punishment practices which Jesse Jackson and Civil Rights groups describe as "state supported murder" (Cole, 1992; Forer, 1994; Frazier, 1995; Friedman, 1993; Henderson, 1994).

To make the point more vivid, in 1994, blacks made up 35 percent of the 91,621 federal prison inmates and 43 percent of the nearly 1.2 million inmates in state and local prisons and jails (Emerge, 194, p. 58). At year-end 1998 the total number of prisoners under the jurisdiction of federal, state, and all other adult correctional authorities was 1,302,019 (47% of which were black). Today the total number of prisoners has swelled to well over 2 million (Department of Justice statistics, 1999). Overall the prison population grew 4.8 percent since the 1980s–a growth rate that was slightly less than the average annual population growth of 6.7 percent. Since 1990, relative to the number of U.S. residents, the rate of incarceration in prisons at year-end 1998 was 461 sentenced inmates per 100,000 residents–up from 292 in 1990 (Bureau of Justice Statistics, 1999). On December 31, 1998, 1 in every 113 men, and 1 in every 1,754 women were sentenced prisoners under the jurisdiction of some correctional authority. For blacks, 1 in 3 (32%) compared to 1 in 15 white males and 1 in 8 young Hispanic males, is under some type of correctional control. This soaring rate of imprisonment of minorities has led

FIGURE 1. Crime Clock of 1995

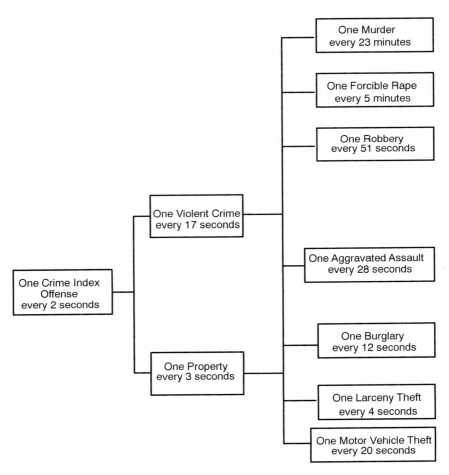

Source: Figure adopted from FBI Uniform Crime Report

Laura Murphy, Director of the American Civil Liberties Union, to call racial bias in the criminal justice system "the new frontier" of civil rights (Horne, 1996, p. 10). In further regard to race, put another way, 1 in 180 white men are in prison, as compared to 1 in 20 black men.

Contrary to popular belief, many African American officials in the hierarchy of the criminal justice system are disturbed by the gripping statistics cited above. In discussions with these committed professionals, they express concern about the "color of justice." Essentially, their disappointment is based on the fact that their lifetime has been spent responding to the universe of violence committed in all groups. They lament the fact that there is more incarceration of the poor and the powerless than occurred in earlier years. Some insist they have literally put their lives and careers in jeopardy attempting to humanize prison systems, yet all of their efforts seem to represent a colossal failure. Still others are pained upon observing that the experience of discrimination and incurable racism is an all too familiar occurrence, and the disbursement of justice is not always fair to people of color, even by those who are sworn to serve the public without malice. All this said, it has been clear to me as a criminal justice official that something is undoubtedly amiss in America's system of justice that so easily charge people of color with violence and institutionalize them for non-violent crimes. Marable (1984), May (1972), Wellman (1977), and Wilson (1990), maintain in essence, that phantom explanations and hypotheses regarding causal factors for black violence (unemployment, lack of education, lack of job skills, broken homes, and drug addiction) are exaggerated, and do not tell the whole story as racism and white supremacy must be factored into the equation. Regrettably, rather than abating, the problem of what Mann (1993) refers to as "unequal justice" systemic unfairness seems to be escalating exponentially and a sense of powerlessness is being expressed by blacks and minorities with every passing year (Selke, 1993).

The purpose of this article is to provide, from the viewpoint of a criminal justice official, an objective, dispassionate and introspective analysis of troubling issues besetting America's present system of justice. Frank and direct insights into "the good, the bad, and the ugly" of the prison environment will be shared from the vantage point of a participant observer who has interfaced with many prisoners inside prison walls. The challenge of this paper is to illuminate, clarify, and amplify troublesome issues regarding violence that are occurring at the structural level. Hopefully, this "inside" view will serve as a template for professionals and the general public, and will assist both in formulating a better understanding of the problems in our nation's criminal justice systems. Among the issues that will be discussed are: black males and violence, arrests, sentencing, imprisonment slave labor politics and the news media.

Finally, suggestions will be offered on how to humanize the tragic criminal justice system, while at the same time making certain that perpetrators pay for their poor behavioral choices and personal indiscretions.

VIOLENCE AGAINST BLACKS:
AN AMERICAN TRAGEDY

One of the greatest difficulties in any discussion referring to violence is framing a definition of the problem. Although at present violence is a well-developed concept in most social science literature, the term still evokes differing points of view. In the past, an infinite number of debates have taken place and varied opinions offered in an attempt to define, describe, enumerate, and categorize the concept of violence, in our crimogenic society (Wilson, 1990). Similarly, many definitions have been advanced regarding the general concept of violence. The difficulty lies in deciding which definitions to accept and which experts seem the most credible. For example, H. Rap Brown (Jamil Abdullah Al-Amin) (1997), a civil rights activist of the 1960s said, "Violence is as American as apple pie" (p. 295). In like manner, Supreme Court Justice William O. Douglas (1997) had this to say about violence:

> The use of violence as an instrument of persuasion is therefore inviting and seems to the discontented to be the only effective protest. Violence has no constitutional sanction; and every government from the beginning has moved against it. But where grievances pile high and most of the elected spokesmen represent the establishment, violence may be the only effective response. (pp. 295-296)

Webb (1990), a minister and professional social service practitioner, provides brilliant and insightful thinking in his definition of violence when he wrote these words:

> To be without hope is violence. To be without love is violence. The deprivation of justice is violence. Ignorance is violence. Unemployment is violence. To be hungry and without shelter is violence. Poverty is violence. To be helpless and misrepresented is violence. To be without liberty and freedom is violence. To be forced to live without human dignity is violence. (pp. 52-53)

But of course Martin Luther King, Jr. (1997) summed up the concept of violence in his utterance of these words:

> The ultimate weakness of violence is that it is a descending spiral, begetting the very thing it seeks to destroy. Instead of diminishing evil, it multiplies it. (p. 296)

Today, Dr. King's words are prophetic, as the ultimate violence of taking the life of another person (without being absolutely certain that the accused committed the crime), and warehousing millions of prisoners (mostly black and Hispanic) for non-violent crimes is not diminishing evil but perpetrating it. Indeed, the failure of prison officials to re-visit this practice is a tragedy that will cause citizens to lose faith in the system of justice and in the end resort to extreme correctional measures.

The word tragedy in the title of this article was carefully chosen because of the symmetry of meaning to the discussion at hand. This concept was derived from the Latin word *tragos* meaning "goat" + *aeidein* meaning "to sing." Together the translated words mean "goat song." Legend has it that in ancient Greece goats made lonesome, pitiful mourning sounds which were precursors of death before their slaughter (Altin, 2000). Shakespeare adopted the powerful word "tragedy" to describe his dramatic plays, which usually ended in disastrous events, terror, calamity and death to all of the main characters.

Using the word tragedy to describe African Americans' plight in the criminal justice system therefore, seems fitting–especially since this group anticipates suffering and physical and psychological death often as a result of committing low-level crimes, when they enter America's prisons. It follows then that African Americans, like the mythical goats of ancient Greece, seem to understand that once an individual is consigned to the criminal justice system he/she will be locked into a den of horror where few second chances are offered, and where there is faint chance of ever returning to a normal life.

With a basic understanding of the concepts in this writing, we move now to an examination of an overall theoretical formulation that may be employed to frame our discussion. Although there is current controversy regarding the necessity for employing theory and many social scientists have abandoned it in favor of more fashionable reimbursable techniques (Hudson, 2000), still this author feels theory gives coherence to a discussion. The view held here is that theory is not a dry academic exercise, but rather a framework that helps one properly craft a discussion such as violence.

A THEORETICAL FRAMEWORK
FOR CONCEPTUALIZING CRIME AND VIOLENCE

In the criminal justice system, social science professionals who have not been closely involved in theory building are often as puzzled as the general public in trying to determine why heinous crimes are committed in our society. Given the significant increase in the number of blacks entering the criminal justice system for multiple offenses, administrators are asking prisoners these questions: what are the causes of the non-violent behavior that resulted in your imprisonment, and what type punishment did you expect? The various responses show that black prisoners feel they were unjustly imprisoned. Along that line, Niehoff (1999) notes, "we have exiled, imprisoned, burned, maimed, shot, hanged, and electrocuted violent people, yet the killers keep coming back." Unfortunately, there are few research studies that can conclusively enlighten us on the puzzling questions regarding prison justice, and even fewer can provide a boundary for studying this violence.

In examining the criminal justice system there are a range of theories that may be useful. However, one that has special utility in this article/chapter is the labeling approach to crime.

LABELING THEORY

Labeling theory is instructive in examining the criminal justice system as it assists us in understanding the pitfalls of classifying people, and the subsequent treatment of them as representatives of a particular category rather than as individuals (Compton, 1999). The consequences of this behavior have been documented in a body of sociological literature on labeling and deviance (Becker, 1963; Lemert, 1967; McCall & Simmons, 1966; Platt, 1977; Rubington & Weinberg, 1968; Schur, 1973; Tannenbaum, 1951). Compton (1999) has stated that labeling or classification distorts individuals' differences. Further, once labeled deviant, individuals may find that they encounter responses determined by the label rather than by their particular characteristics. This attitude sets into motion a "self-fulfilling prophecy" in which individuals become what the label suggests they are (Merton, 1968). Reviewing cohort and other studies, Shireman and Reamer (1986) raise the possibility that the juvenile justice system may unwittingly promote crime by its labeling practices. What we see in the prison justice system is a disproportionate number of blacks being consigned to the system, since they have been labeled as deviant.

Labeling theory is a conceptual formulation that has encountered significant changes, gone through several stages of development, and endured well-deserved criticism. The theory emerged as researchers such as Becker (1963) examined the concept of stigmatism, social pathology, and social disorganization. Labeling theory basically involves how society condemns rule-breaking behavior that is contrary to the standards of conduct laid down by those with power, control and influence. In applying this theory the emphasis shifts from the individual deviator to the reaction of society. In other words when the behavior of an individual is incongruent with the rules, norms, laws and customs established by society then that person is deemed deviant (Becker, 1963).

In the course of vilification the deviant is sometimes labeled as "insane," "crazy," "an addict," and even "a killer." When African Americans are imprisoned they are generally labeled by correctional institutions, sometimes assigned nicknames, are often treated as objects, and stripped of all vestiges of dignity. Essentially, they are treated as if their lives were not their own and as if there is no inherent linkage between individuals and their environment. The downside of labeling people is that it increases the likelihood that others may begin responding to them as representatives of a given category and the person will develop that self-image. These attitudes and behaviors have been thoroughly documented by Becker (1963), Lemert (1967), Platt (1977), Rubington and Weinberg (1968), Schur (1973), Simmons (1969), and Tannenbaum (1951). Reports indicate that inmates who refuse to follow the rules of oppressive prison institutions are labeled as deviant and are severely punished. Not only are the offenders physically punished but also their actions are called to the attention of other prisoners by those with power to control the total environment. It can be seen therefore, that labeling which was meant as a form of punishment may unwittingly promote chaos, conflict, and the urge to commit more crime to maintain the image.

It is important to note here that there are valid criticisms of labeling theory. First, it tends to overemphasize the importance of official labeling. In other words, the instances discussed above are not general rules, but rather exceptions to the rules, since no one will react to being labeled in the same way. Secondly, labeling theory unfairly portrays persons as a deviant. Third, labeling is a primary technique of social control. And finally, persons labeled are affected by those who view them as deviants. It is clear then that labeling behavior sometimes gives rise to unintended consequences.

PSYCHOANALYTIC THEORY

In an examination of the multiple theories found in books on theoretical criminology, it is observed that few provide a "goodness of fit" in a discussion of macro variables that may cause crime. However, the psychoanalytic perspective has what See (1998) describes as "theory pieces" that may be useful in shedding minute rays of light on the causation of individual violent behavior. Psychoanalysis is a biological model, so in employing "pieces" of this paradigm special care must be employed since Freud's work did not discuss criminal behavior to any great extent, nor was it totally subjected to empirical investigation (See, 1998). Be that as it may, the psychodynamic perspective suggests that criminal and delinquent behavior is attributed to disturbances or malfunctions in the ego or superego configuration. Freudians would argue that undeveloped egos, delinquency, and criminality are primary expressions of an unregulated id. More specifically, children who feel unloved fail to form the kind of attachments necessary to foster the proper development of the super ego. Thus, the punishing of others by resorting to a variety of crimes removes guilty feelings and tends to restore a proper balance of good against evil (Vold, Bernard & Snipes, 1998).

What has changed appreciably in recent years that can be explained by the psychodynamic paradigm is the age composition and developmental tasks of youths caught in the criminal justice system–particularly since the 1980s when there was a substantial and disturbing increase in the murder rate of young black males. The murder rate for 14 to 17 year old black males for example has moved from 32 per 100,000 in 1984, to 118 per 100,000 in 1991. According to a 1995 study by the U.S. Justice Department's Office of Juvenile Justice and Delinquency Prevention, although African Americans make up only 12.7% of the nation's youth population, they make up 26% of juvenile arrests, 32% of delinquency referrals to juvenile court, and 52% of those transferred to adult criminal court after judicial hearings (Valentine, 1998).

It may be concluded therefore, that in this paper theory pieces from the psychoanalytic paradigm coupled with theory pieces from social behaviorism and other paradigms are frameworks that will be utilized in an effort to bind together our discussion of structural violence.

ARRESTS IN THE CRIMINAL JUSTICE SYSTEM

Infractions that take place in the criminal justice system are becoming more serious with the passing of years. For example, in state prisons after arrests are made if there is no racial bias, predictably the make-up of the prison population should at least roughly reflect the racial disparity in arrest rates. If 3 times as many African Americans are arrested for less serious crimes, then there should be roughly 3 times as many African Americans per capita in prison for those crimes. But the racial difference among African Americans and whites in prison is overwhelmingly wider than the general arrest rates and thus suggests there is no absence of racial bias (see Table 1). Today, there are 7 African Americans to each white in prison, and the question remains why? Also on any given day in Washington, D.C., African American men from the ages of 18 to 35 are under arrest or under some form of court supervision (Davidson, 1997, p. 36).

Another question posed is: Is there actually racial bias in the arrest rates in the criminal justice system, and is something else going on in America's prisons? According to Steven Donziger (1996), and from my experience as a professional, one way to determine if racial bias has contributed to the minority rate of arrest and imprisonment is to look at the crime rates of African Americans. If blacks are imprisoned in higher proportions to the crime rate, it suggests that they may be treated more harshly by the system. Since crime for all criminals is based on arrest rates. This assessment discounts racial bias that may have occurred before the arrest (some people are arrested because of

TABLE 1. Arrest Rates by Race (1990)

Crimes	Black Share of All Arrests	Disproportion of Black Arrests
Robbery	61.2%	5.1
Murder and Manslaughter	54.7%	4.5
Gambling	47.5%	3.9
Rape	43.2%	3.6
Receiving Stolen Property	41.2%	3.4
Vagrancy	40.8%	3.4
Drug Violations	40.7%	3.4
Weapons Possession	39.8%	3.3
Prostitution	38.9%	3.2
Motor Vehicle Theft	38.4%	3.2
Aggravated Assault	38.4%	3.2
Forgery and Counterfeiting	34.0%	2.8
Disorderly Conduct	32.4%	2.7
Embezzlement	32.1%	2.7
Domestic Violence	30.3%	2.5
Burglary	30.1%	2.5
Vandalism	22.6%	1.9
Curfew and Loitering	17.7%	1.5
Driving While Intoxicated	8.7%	0.9

Source: Constructed by Jerry G. Johnson from data compiled by Andrew Hacker, 1992, for *Violence as Seen Through a Prism of Color*. Edited by L. See, 2001.

a racist police officer, not because they committed a crime). In sum, it is questionable whether arrest records are the best indicators of actual crime rates, or whether arrest records are a good frame of reference for measuring racial bias for each subsequent stage in the criminal process. The evidence from personal observation, and from the literature suggests that as blacks work their way through the criminal justice system from arrest to punishment, they encounter harsher treatment than whites. This is called the "cumulative" effect of racial discrimination. For instance, if there is racial discrimination when a person is arrested, it can result in a harsher assessment of the offense. This in turn can result in a more severe charge, and thus have an extended impact throughout the legal process. This "cumulative" effect does not show up in all jurisdictions, but is a general pattern that is practiced in almost every criminal justice system throughout the United States.

In searching for an explanation to the disparities and cumulative effects in the criminal justice system, the irrefutable evidence reveals that minorities and whites live in completely different worlds when it comes to race and criminal justice. First, arrest data indicate that African Americans commit more crime than whites relative to the population. Second, there are so many more African Americans than whites in our prisons that the difference cannot be explained by higher crime among blacks. Moreover, racial discrimination has to be at work in the system's structure, and it penalizes African Americans at almost every juncture in the system. Finally, whether the cause is higher crime, discrimination, or both, this country is on the verge of a social catastrophe because of the sheer number of African Americans behind bars–numbers that continue rising with breathtaking speed and frightening implications.

To make the point even more strongly, criminologist Elliott Currie (1985) studied two neighborhoods with roughly the same population and the same name, Highland Park. The first Highland Park was a wealthy suburb of Chicago. The second was an impoverished community in Detroit that was largely populated by minorities. In the wealthy Highland Park there were no murders, no robberies and only one rape. In the low-income Highland Park in the same year, there were 27 murders, 55 rapes and 796 robberies. Studies conclusively demonstrate that economic inequality affects not only the extent of crime, but its seriousness as well. Although deluged with facts and figures it is interesting to note that no study has demonstrated conclusively that poverty itself accounts for the racial disparities in imprisonment, but the available evidence seems to point in that direction.

Is it any wonder then that I, along with other officials find our prisons filled with angry young black men who have lost hope and have forged an incarcerated world modified after a "free society" which is based upon violence, power, control, intimidation, and the quest for economic superiority?

SENTENCING IN THE CRIMINAL JUSTICE SYSTEM

A factor that has contributed significantly to the increase in the incarceration of African Americans for violent offenses is the sentencing process. It is widely believed and frequently stated by young black males interviewed in prison, that the "system" has been, and remains, racially discriminatory (e.g., Clark, 1970; Sutherland & Cressey, 1970) (see Tables 2, 3). Subsequently, some believe that since the fertility rates of white Americans are gradually declining, there is a structural conspiracy to warehouse as many black males

TABLE 2. Discrimination in the U.S. Criminal Justice System

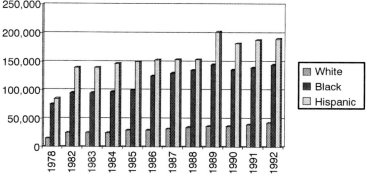

Note: This table shows the number of Blacks and Hispanics incarceratd as compared to the number of Whites.

Sources. Bureau of Justice Statistics, Corrections Compendium, University of Michigan Documents Center "Crime and Race Statistics Page," and *The Sentencing Project*.

as possible–particularly those in their childbearing years (16-46), through the action of racial profiling (driving while black/brown) and subsequently, imprisonment. With reference to general sentencing, the most frequently cited evidence for this assertion is indicated by Gary Fleck (1981), Florida State University, who has compiled research showing more severe sentencing of African American criminal defendants than white defendants–especially in the imposition of the death penalty. There have been at least sixty empirical studies of adult criminal sentencing published that refer to race, and basically all provide strong evidence of racial bias (Overby, 1971).

Some researchers have suggested that racial discrimination accounts for the difference in longer imprisonment sentences between black and white defendants. This is largely due to the fact that African Americans lag behind whites by almost every social and economic measure, and poor blacks are unable to afford expensive counsel. For example, in 1992, 46 percent of black children were born to parents who lived in poverty, compared to only 16 percent of white children. However, with no financial resources for counsel, sentences meted out to African Americans cannot be properly contested.

When the crime bill was enacted in 1994, the Congressional Black Caucus (CBC), backed by civil rights groups, threatened the bill if "racial injustice" protection against discrimination in death sentencing were not included. Luckily, this language found its way into the legislation.

SENTENCING FOR DRUG USE

According to Diana Gordon (1994), the polls consistently show that citizens believe that African Americans are more likely to commit drug crimes than whites, and therefore deserve longer sentences (see Table 4). Associated with those drug crimes are the violent crimes of robbery and assault to obtain the drugs. Unquestionably, this consensus has significantly impacted the rate of incarceration of blacks for violent offenses. Despite the lack of reliable

TABLE 3. Racism in the Criminal Justice System

The key findings of (a report released by the Sentencing Project in October 1995) are the following:

- Almost one in three (32.2%) young black men in the age group 20-29 is under criminal justice supervision on any given day–in prison or jail, on probation or parole.

- The cost of criminal justice control for the 827,440 young African American males in prison is about $6 billion a year.

- In recent years, African American women have experienced the greatest increase in criminal justice supervision of all demographic groups, with their rate of criminal ju tice supervision rising by 78% from 1989-94.

- Drug policies constitute the single most significant factor contributing to the rise in criminal justice populations in recent years, with the number of incarcerated drug offenders having risen by 510% from 1983 to 1993. The number of Black (non-Hispanic) women incarcerated in state prisons for drug offenses increased more than eight-fold–828%–from 1986 to 1991.

- While African American arrest rates for violent crime–45% of arrests nationally–are disproportionate to their share of the population, this proportion has not changed significantly for twenty years. For drug offenses, though the African American proportion of arrests increased from 24% in 1980 to 39% in 1993, well above the African American proportion of drug users nationally.

- African Americans and Hispanics constitute almost 90% of offenders sentenced to state prison for drug possession.

Source: Marc Mauer and Tracey Huling, *The Sentencing Project*, October 1995.

TABLE 4. Sentences to State Prison for Drug Possession, 1992

Racial/Ethnic Group	% of Total Drug Sentences
African American	73.7%
Hispanic	16.0%
Total African American and Hispanic	89.7%

Source: Table constructed by Jerry G. Johnson based on data retrieved in the literature.

data to confirm their assumptions, there are those who would contend that African Americans are arrested in larger numbers because of their higher rates of drug use, possession, and sales (see Figure 2). However annual surveys of the National Institute on Drug Abuse (NIDA) reveal that African Americans comprise only 13% of monthly drug users, compared to the 1993 arrest proportion of 39%. Even if we only consider arrests for drug possession, which should be reflective in the data, African Americans still constitute 34.7% of such arrests. It must be noted that the NIDA surveys do not include institutionalized persons, homeless people not living in a shelter, and people with less stable residence. Therefore, low-income African Americans may be undercounted in the surveys.

Drug use as a tool for increasing the rate of incarceration of minorities in our prison system is not a new phenomenon. The first drug prohibition law was also enacted in an atmosphere of hostility to Chinese immigrant laborers no longer needed to build railroads. It was enforced, as the police chief put it, "to keep them [the Chinese] from opening places where whites might resort to smoking opium." Whether or not the "war on drugs" was consciously or unconsciously designed to incarcerate more minorities is a question that may be debated. In essence though, what we have seen are policy choices that have not only failed to reduce the scale of the problem but have seriously eroded the life prospects of the very targets of those policies.

It should come as no surprise to find that arrest policies beginning in the 1980s have disproportionately affected African Americans and other minorities. Between 1986 and 1991, the number of whites held in state prisons on drug charges grew to 30,000 from 16,000, while the number of blacks increased to 80,000 from 65,000 (Hatchett, 1995). Due to increased aggressiveness of police forces in certain neighborhoods, African Americans are being arrested and taken to prison at unprecedented rates. Some say that soon an inner city African American male under 35 years of age who has not been arrested will be a "fluke" (Hatchett, 1995). As the numbers of arrests grow, so do the proportion of African Americans incarcerated for drug use and possession (see Table 5).

Compounding the higher arrest rates for drug offenses have been changes in sentencing policies for drugs that have disproportionately affected blacks. The advent of a renewed generation of mandatory sentence statutes for drugs, now in place in all states and the federal system, has led to dramatic increases in the number of incarcerated drug offenders. According to Mauer and Huling (1995) minimum sentencing statutes have led to a 510% increase in the number of incarcerated drug offenders between 1983 and 1993 (see Table 5). One out of 4 inmates now serving time or awaiting trial are doing so for a drug offense. The cumulative impact of arrest and sentencing policies on African Americans can be seen in Figure 2. Looking at minorities overall, it

TABLE 5. Drug Offenders in Prison and Jail–1983 and 1993

	Total # Inmates		% Drug Offenders		# Drug Offenders	
	1983	1993	1983	1993	1983	1993
Jail	223,552	459,804	9.3%	23.0%	20,790	105,755
Federal Prison	31,926	89,586	27.6%	60.8%	8,812	54,468
State Prison	405,322	859,295	7.0%	22.5%	28,373	193,341
Total	**660,800**	**1,408,685**	**8.8%**	**25.1%**	**57,975**	**353,564**

FIGURE 2. African Americans and Drug Possession

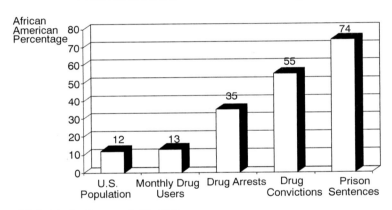

Criminal Justice Response to Drug Use.
Note: Data are for 1992 or 1993 depending on the most recent available figures.

was found by Mauer and Huling that African Americans and Hispanics represented almost 90% of all sentences to state prisons for drug offenses in 1992 (see Table 3). In the federal system, the impact of sentencing policies is already being felt, with the average time served by drug offenders increasing 50%, from 22 months in 1986, to 33 months by 1992.

The most explosive discussion today revolves around the disparity in sentencing between crack cocaine and powder cocaine, which represents racism in the criminal justice system (see Table 4). Persons convicted of crack possession receive a mandatory prison term of 5 years by possessing only one-hundredth of the quantity of cocaine as those charged with powder cocaine possession. In 1995, fourteen states had statutes that distinguished between crack and powder cocaine in sentencing. The U.S. Sentencing Commission found that African Americans accounted for 84.5% of federal crack possession convictions in 1993, while comprising 38% of those who report using crack in the past year. The Sentencing Commission has also calculated that a person convicted of trafficking in 5 grams of crack with a maximum retail value of $750 will receive the same sentence as an offender charged with selling 500 grams of powder cocaine retailing for $50,000. Professor Michael Tonry (1995) summed up the impact of prevailing drug policies with the following statement:

> All that is left is politics. The war on drugs and the set of harsh crime control policies in which it was enmeshed were undertaken to achieve political, not policy, objectives. It is the adoption for political purposes of policies with foreseeable disparate impacts, the use of disadvantaged black Americans as means to achieving politicians' electoral ends, that must be in the end justified. It cannot. (p. 39)

In discussing sentencing for crack vs. powdered cocaine, some young black inmates interviewed are appalled at the difference in sentencing, others burst into tears due to the unfairness of a system that brags about being fair.

TENSION AND RAGE IN U.S. PRISON SYSTEMS

The growth of the African American prisoner population began in the 1960s and 1970s and added a racial element to already high tensions in the prison systems (Johnson, 1987). This was a time when "black rage" (Grier & Cobbs, 1980) had surfaced in social movements in the free world, first in muted form in the civil rights movement, later in more virulent form in the black power movement (Carmichael & Hamilton, 1967). During this time, many of the African American prisoners drew inspiration from their angriest brethren on the streets, some of whom were subsequently incarcerated for standard felonies but who assumed the status of self-proclaimed political prisoners. At the same time, the failure of correctional programs took on an almost conspiratorial tone; the larger system was rigged against the down-and-outs and so was the correctional system (Dorin & Johnson, 1978). As a result, prisoner militancy and black power became synonymous at the outset of what has come to be known as the "prison movement." Violence between militant black prisoners and the largely white prison authorities became increasingly commonplace, and violence against fellow inmates became more open and bold.

But, it has been observed that militant prisoners were often not the dedicated and selfless revolutionaries they made themselves out to be (Irwin,

1980; Carroll, 1982). More often than not, their commitment, like that of gang members and lone predators, was to survive in a hostile environment rather than try to effect radical social change (Dorin & Johnson, 1978).

As order yielded to disorder, violence and fear fed upon one another, producing a climate of terror in many prisons throughout the nation. Increasingly, correctional officers in the trenches refrained from enforcing the rules in order to avoid conflict (Carroll, 1982). Officers with seniority (and presumably the competence to mediate those conflicts properly) elected administrative assignments or retreated to the towers on the prison walls far from the dangers of the cellblocks and the prison yard (Sheehan, 1978; Cressey, 1982). Informal accommodations between staff and inmates broke down, undermining the various "opportunity systems" that had given stability to the convict culture of the prison. With little reason to conform to staff directives or even authorities like me (a warden), violence became the order of the day and the preferred mode of adjustment among convicts.

Today, state and federal prisons remain arenas of tension and rage, too often serving as proving grounds for aspiring tough guys (and women), gang members and wannabes, infused by design with an "us versus them" atmosphere. In the most populous jurisdictions, those charged with the monumental task of simultaneously protecting public safety, themselves, and constantly growing numbers of inmates must deal on a daily basis with sporadic outbursts of violence on the part of individuals and organized gangs. Meanwhile, inmates who are unwilling or unable to cope with the stresses and strains of prison-often those who are the targets of others' violence and intimidation– are finding their own way out through escape and increasingly, suicide.

This information most of which represents my professional and personal insights, does not paint a pretty picture, and rising populations coupled with current political and societal attitudes toward the treatment of convicts offer little hope for a more peaceful future. All in all the abolishment of good time and parole opportunities, along with legislative mandates such as "three strikes" sentencing, threaten to create widespread frustration and hopelessness among inmates. Thus, predictably inmate management will become more difficult and the propensity for violence among inmates, who have abandoned dreams of a civilized life on the outside, will continue to escalate.

THE USE OF PRISON SLAVE LABOR

The increase in the prison population and subsequent cost to the state has compelled some to believe that alternative prison management methods should be employed. One proposal for addressing this problem is the privatization of prisons. In this arrangement, what has been presented to prison officials by high paid lobbyists is that the private sector can operate parts of the prison system more effectively, efficiently and cheaply than can state systems (See & Khashan, 2001). Further, by using existing prison labor the federal government's fulfillment of meaningful work for prisoners will be accomplished. The provisions of this plan call for actually hiring inmates to work for private companies contracted to run the prison and corporations seeking cheap labor. Part of the wages earned from this work will be paid to the prison as 'Room and Board,' part sent to the inmate's family, and part sent to the victim. In this way the prisoner funds his or her own imprisonment and makes restitution, and the private contracting company becomes rich with the help of the state and endorsement from the government (U.S. Department of Justice, 1990). See and Khashan (2001) argue that employing the privatization system is a way of building a Prison Industrial Complex, and is a means of exploiting prisoners who are sentenced to serve time for their misdeeds. Davidson (1997) had this to say about the privatization phenomenon:

> . . . feeding the correctional-industrial complex is a series of laws, policies and practices in the criminal justice system that make young black people in particular fodder for the swelling network. Criminal behavior, combined with a system biased against the poor and Black, provides the industry with a steady stream of human cargo. The war on drugs sweeps thousands of young people off the streets and into crowded prisons . . . [thus a potent, ready-made workforce is available to those who own the private prison system]. (pp. 36-48)

This new prison system is congruent with the observation made several decades past by Hall (1935) who offers an all-encompassing view regarding the purpose of the government. He affirms that in a capitalist system conditions that maximize profit are frequently achieved through legislation and the creation and implementation of certain regulations. Thus, powerful economic interests influence specific laws, including those that would grant permission for big business and corporations to maximize profit by using prison labor.

Similarly, some Marxist theorists have moved one step further in their analysis of a capitalist economic system. For example, Braverman (1964) contends that the capitalist state is an essential vehicle for inducing cheap labor in order to maximize profit for big business. And Braverman (1964), and Offee (1973) assert that in a capitalist society the state is obliged to provide a cheap labor force by enacting laws helpful to capitalism. Furthermore, they argue that in the political economy, the state operates directly in the interest of capitalists and the infrastructure consciously expands the work force with a huge available working-class population. From these perspectives, the belief is strong that the function of the capitalist state is to look after the vested interest of big business and corporations at the expense of the powerless, including blacks and minorities placed behind prison bars. Correspondingly, this means that with reference to the criminal justice system, the state must impose harsher punishments to keep a fresh labor force coming into the prison industrial complex as laborers, as it takes a considerable workforce to control all prison operations from building the prison cells, to supplying food and medicine, to staffing the guard positions, to selling hair products (See & Shashan, 2001). For some in our society this arrangement is hailed as a brilliant move, but to most social scientists the use of human beings as slave laborers is an American tragedy. But Black prisoners are not only used as slave labor but also for political purposes.

PRISONERS USED FOR POLITICAL PURPOSES

Unfortunately, the variable of discrimination in the criminal justice system has shamefully reached upward into the decision-making apparatus of this nation, and black prisoners are used as campaign fodder. A case in point is the 1988 Presidential campaign when George Bush used the Willie Robert Horton Jr. case to embarrass his opponent, Michael Dukakis. According to Anderson (1995) this case was a turning point in the incarceration of black males for violent offenses. The Massachusetts correctional system had permitted a prison furlough to Horton, a black male murderer. Horton committed several violent crimes in Maryland while on furlough. During one he burglarized the home of Clifford Barnes, a computer specialist, assaulted him and allegedly raped Angela Miller, Barnes's girlfriend. It would be hard to find a better case for portraying a politician as "soft on crime and solicitous toward criminals." The Bush camp was able to use this incident to raise questions regarding the managerial competence or foolhardiness of Dukakis. Violent crime then, became a major public issue for the nation.

But there was also the racial aspect. Willie Horton was black and his Maryland victims were white. That racial nexus roused emotions, and Dukakis was branded with using the furlough system to permit a black man to rape a white woman. What was not told by the news media is that this was not the first occasion Willie Horton had used the furlough system, as he had been granted nine previous furloughs without incident. Even more telling was that Dukakis did not institute the prison furlough program it was started under Francis Sargent, a Republican Governor. What this incident points up is that a politician running for the highest office in the land was not beyond vilifying a black prisoner to win the presidential election. Bush's raising of primal fears about black criminals was responsible for substantially reduced prison furlough programs across the country, and was a setback to the entire criminal justice system, particularly regarding the disenfranchisement of Blacks where 1 in 7 (or 14%) are denied a right to vote (C. Collands, Internet).

Yet, the vehicle that could help humanize the criminal justice system has failed miserably its role as "the third estate," and the beacon of objectivity.

NEWS MEDIA

Most Americans get their news from television. Thus, a major contributing factor in the increase of African Americans entering the criminal justice system is the volume of crime and violence committed by blacks displayed in the visual media. Coverage of crime on the three major network television news shows tripled from 571 stories in 1991 to 1,632 stories in 1993–despite the fact that crime declined slightly over that period. In 1993, crime was the leading story on the major networks surpassing economic and healthcare news. Unfortunately, most of the negative coverage was directed toward young African Americans.

In their publication, *Young Black Americans and the Criminal Justice System*, Mauer and Huling (1995) emphasize the part the media has played in the incarceration rates of African Americans. In recent years, a succession of media images and racially divisive political campaigns has created public images of a violent young African American. One need only to turn on the evening news to witness that day's evidence of young black men engaging in murder and mayhem. To what extent is such an image justified? An examination of crime rates and criminal justice populations shows that the issue is more complex than it might appear on the evening news. What most people do not know is that the typical African American male in the criminal justice system is not a violent offender as usually portrayed by the media. Combining the four components of the criminal justice system–prison, jail, probation, and parole–about three-fourths of all offenders under supervision have been convicted of a non-violent offense. However, media interest in portraying violent and sensational crimes clearly contributes to the lack of understanding of this issue and has perpetuated the myth that African Americans commit more violent offenses.

Thus the image on the evening news, while indicative of some disturbing trends is highly misleading in its overall impact. In recent years, we have seen the far-reaching impact that media images have played on public policy. For example, in its comprehensive report on crack cocaine, the United States Sentencing Commission (1995) described how the adoption of harsh federal sentencing policies for crack followed upon the intense media attention devoted to the death of basketball star Len Bias in 1986 from cocaine intoxication. While it was widely reported at the time that Bias had probably died of "free-basing" cocaine, it was not until a year later that Bias's drug supplier revealed that Bias and other players had snorted powder cocaine on the night of his death. Not only has the media exploited black men imprisoned for minor drug offenses, but also they have targeted blacks to negatively impact the political process.

CONCLUSIONS

It is clear from this article that there is much work to be done and many seemingly insurmountable hurdles to encounter in America's Criminal Justice System. The author suggests the following measures to consider, at a minimum, when processing the information included in the article. First, the entire criminal justice system needs to be revisited. In the process, special emphasis must be given to racism, discrimination and sexism. Second, within the criminal justice system, the sentencing process needs to be more egalitarian–all groups must be treated equally and the punishment absolutely must fit the crime. Nowhere is this problem more evident than in the instance of drugs and sentencing, particularly in the case of crack cocaine vs. powder.

Third, it is important to consider the role of the American politician in the process of revamping the criminal justice system. It is imperative that politicians refrain from using the prison system as a vote-getting device at the expense of prisoners (specifically black prisoners). Fourth, the issue of privatization of the prison system is fraught with controversy and should be given time and attention. The issue is whether or not this mode is the way we want our prisons to be run.

And finally, the media needs to be challenged and their "feet held to the fire" when they present half-truths and partial facts. The consequences of fast action reporting, before well thought out and researched documentation of facts are ascertained is a disservice to those who are affected. Without a doubt the media has been responsible for the termination of rehabilitation for prisoners, and consistently, bias is shown in terms of prisoners.

It is not the intent of the author to provide a wholly bleak picture of the criminal justice system now to have the answers to the many challenges presented in this writing. In fact, even with a quarter century of experience all the answers are not known. The information provided herein is set forth for more thought, discussion and primarily education on the issues plaguing our criminal justice system today. Also, it serves as raw data for generating hypotheses for research efforts that should be tested in order to gain deeper knowledge of the criminal justice system.

REFERENCES

Altin, G. (2000). Interview with Georgia Altin, a native of Greece, and MSW, University of Georgia. March, 2000.

Anderson, D. C. (1995). *Crime and the politics of hysteria: How the Willie Horton story changed American justice.* New York: Times Books.

Becker, H. (1963). *Outsiders: Studies in the sociology of deviance.* New York: Free Press.

Braverman, H. (1964). *Labor and monopoly capital: The degradation of work in the twentieth century.* New York: Monthly Review Press.

Brown, H. R. (1997). Violence. *The new international Webster's pocket quotation dictionary* (pp. 295-296). Slovenia: Trident Press International.

Carmichael, S., & Hamilton, C. (1967). *Black Power.* New York: Random House.

Carroll, L. (1982). Race, ethnicity, and the social order of the prison. In R. Johnson & H. Toch (eds.). *The pain of imprisonment* (pp. 181-203). Beverly Hills: Sage.

Clark, R. (1970). *Crime in America: Observations on its nature, causes, prevention, and control.* New York: Simon and Schuster.

Cole, G. F. (1992). *The American system of criminal justice.* Pacific Grove, CA: Brooks/Cole.

Collands, C. Internet

Colvin, M. (1982). The 1980 New Mexico prison riot. *Social Problems, 29*(5), 449-468.

Compton, B. R. (1999). *Social work processes* (6th ed.). Pacific Grove, CA: Brooks/Cole.

Cressey, D. R. (1982). Foreword. In F. Cullen & K. E. Gilbert (Eds.). *Reaffirming rehabilitation.* Cincinnati: Anderson.

Currie, E. (1985). *Confronting crime: An American challenge.* New York: Pantheon Books.

Davidson, J. (1997). Cashing in on black prisoners. *Emerge, Oct.,* 36-48.

Donziger, S. R. (1996). *The real war on crime: The report of the national criminal Justice commission.* New York: HarperCollins.

Dorin, D. D., & Johnson, R. (1978). Violence and survival in prison: The case of George Jackson. In J. Inciardi & A. Potheger (Eds.). *Violent Crime: Historical and contemporary issues* (pp. 125-142). Beverly Hills: Sage.

Douglas, W. O. (1997). Violence. *The new international Webster's pocket quotation dictionary* (pp. 295-296). Slovenia: Trident Press International.

Federal Bureau of Investigation (1996). *Crime in the United States 1996* [Uniform Crime Reporting Program statistics]. Washington, DC: U.S. Department of Justice.

Fleck, G. (1981). Racial discrimination in criminal sentencing: A critical evaluation of the evidence with additional evidence on the death penalty. *American Sociological Review 46,* 783-805.

Forer, L. G. (1994). *The rage to punish: The unintended consequences of mandatory sentencing.* New York: W. W. Norton & Co.

Frazier, M. B. (1995). *From behind the wall: Commentary on crime, punishment, race, and the underclass by a prison inmate.* New York: Paragon House.

Friedman, L. M. (1993). *Crime and punishment in American history.* New York: Basic Books.

Gordon, D. R. (1994). *The return of the dangerous classes, drug prohibition and policy politics*. New York: W. W. Norton and Company.

Grier, W. H., & Cobbs, P. M. (1980). *Black Rage*. New York: Basic Books.

Hall, J. (1935). *Theft, law and society*. Indianapolis: Bobbs-Merrill.

Hatchett, D. (1995). Crackin' down on crack and crime. *Crisis, 102* (7), 18-20.

Henderson, J. H. (1994). *Crime of the criminal justice system*. Cincinnati: Anderson Publishing.

Horne, M. (1996). Race and the criminal justice system. *Crisis, 103* (1), 10.

Hudson, C. G. (2000). At the edge of chaos: A new paradigm for social work. *Journal of Social Work Education, 36* (2).

Irwin, J. (1980). *Prisons in turmoil*. Boston: Little Brown.

Johnson, R. (1987). *Hard time: Understanding and reforming the prison*. Belmont, CA: Wadsworth, Inc.

King, M. L., Jr. (1997). Violence. *The new international Webster's pocket quotation dictionary* (pp. 295-296). Slovenia: Trident Press International.

Lemert, E. (1967). The juvenile court quest and realities. In President's Commission on Law Enforcement and Administration of Justice. Task force report: *Juvenile delinquency and youth crime* (pp. 91-106). Washington, DC: U.S. Government Printing Office.

Mann, C. R. (1993). *Unequal justice: A question of color*. Bloomington: Indiana University Press.

Marable, M. (1984). *Race, reform and rebellion*. Mississippi: University Press of Mississippi.

Mauer, M., & Huling, T. (1995). *Young black Americans and the criminal justice system: Five years later*. The Sentencing Project.

May, R. (1972). *Power or innocence: A search for the sources of violence*. New York: W. W. Norton.

McCall, G., & Simmons, J. L. (1966). *Identities and interaction*. New York: Free Press.

Merton, R. K. (1968). *Social theory and social structure* (4th ed.). New York: Free Press.

National Institute of Justice (1990). *Recovering correctional costs through offender fees*. Washington DC: U.S. Department of Justice.

Niehoff, D. (1999). *The biology of violence*. New York: Free Press.

Offee, C. (1973). Political authority and class structures: An analysis of late capitalistic societies. *International Journal of Social Sciences 2, Spring*.

Overby, A. (1971). Discrimination against minority groups. In L. Radzinowicz & M. Wolfgang (Eds.). *Crime and justice, volume II: The criminal in the arms of the law* (pp. 569-581). New York: Basic Books.

Platt, A. (1977). *The child savers: The invention of delinquency* (2nd ed.). Chicago: University of Chicago Press.

Reiman, J. (1995). *The rich get richer and the poor get prison: Ideology, class, and criminal justice* (p. 1). Boston: Allyn and Bacon.

Rubington, E., & Weinberg, M. S. (1968). *Deviance: The interactionist perspective*. New York: Macmillan.

Schur, E. (1973). *Radical non-intervention: Rethinking the delinquency problem*. Englewood Cliffs, NJ: Prentice-Hall.

See, L. A., & Khashan. (2001). Violence in the suites: The corporate paradigm. *Violence as Seen Through the Prism of Color.*

See, L. A. (1998). *Human behavior in the social environment from an African American perspective.* New York: The Haworth Press, Inc.

Selke, W. L. (1993). *Prisons in crisis.* Bloomington: Indiana University Press.

Sheehan, S. (1978). *A prison and a prisoner.* Boston: Houghton Mifflin.

Shelly, L. (1981). *Crime and modernization* (p. 76). Carbondale: Southern Illinois University Press.

Shireman, C. H., & Reamer, F. (1986). *Rehabilitating juvenile justice.* New York: Columbia University Press.

Sutherland, E. H., & Cressey, D. R. (1970). *Principles of Criminology.* Philadelphia: J. B. Lippincott.

Tannenbaum, F. (1951). *Crime and community* (2nd ed.). New York: Columbia University Press.

Tonry, M. (1995). *Malign neglect: Race, crime, and punishment in America.* New York: Oxford University Press.

United States Department of Justice, Bureau of Justice Statistics (1999). *Prisoners in 1998.* Washington, DC: author.

United States Sentencing Commission (1995). *Cocaine and Federal Sentencing Policy* (pp. 129-134). Washington DC: author.

Valentine, V. (1998). Youth crime, adult time. *Emerge, 10* (1), 48-52.

Vold, G. B., Bernard, T. J., & Snipes, J. B. (1998). *Theoretical Criminology* (4th ed.). New York: Oxford University Press.

Webb, W. J. (1990). *Psychotrauma: The human injustice crisis* (pp. 52-53). Lima, Ohio: Fairway Press.

Wellman, D. T. (1977). *Portraits of white racism.* New York: Cambridge University Press.

Wilson, A. N. (1990). *Black on black violence.* New York: African World InfoSystems.

Violence Against African American Women in Prisons and Jails: Who's Minding the Shop?

Alicia R. Isaac

Lettie L. Lockhart

Larry Williams

SUMMARY. The United States prison population is bulging and in recent years, the percentage of African American women being incarcer-

Alicia R. Isaac, DPA, currently teaches at Clayton College and State University in Atlanta, Georgia. She recieved her Doctor of Public Administration and MSW degrees from the University of Georgia. She is the President of the A.R. Isaac Group, a consulting firm specializing in policy analysis, program design, implementation and evaluation. Her first book, *The African American Students' Guide to Surviving Graduate School*, published by Sage Publishing Company, is widely used by graduate students. Her second book related to the human potential of surviving traumatic life events is scheduled for completion in summer, 2001.

Lettie L. Lockhart, PhD, is Professor of Social Work at the University of Georgia in Athens. She received her PhD from Florida State University and teaches research, methods, and women's studies. Dr. Lockhart is a member of the prestigious Commission on Social Work Education, and has served on several editorial boards in the field of social work. Her research interest is domestic violence and she has written widely in that area.

Larry Williams, MSW, Director of the Salvation Army (Atlanta, Georgia) is a doctoral student in the School of Social Work at Clark-Atlanta University. He holds a BA degree in social work from Hunter College (NY), and an MSW from the University of Georgia. His areas of interest include criminal justice, power and oppression of minority populations, and clinical practice. He has broad experience working in prison systems, and with minority and oppressed groups.

[Haworth co-indexing entry note]: "Violence Against African American Women in Prisons and Jails: Who's Minding the Shop?" Isaac, Alicia R., Lettie L. Lockhart, and Larry Williams. Co-published simultaneously in *Journal of Human Behavior in the Social Environment* (The Haworth Social Work Practice Press, an imprint of The Haworth Press, Inc.) Vol. 4, Nos. 2/3, 2001, pp. 129-153; and: *Violence as Seen Through a Prism of Color* (ed: Letha A. (Lee) See) The Haworth Social Work Practice Press, an imprint of The Haworth Press, Inc., 2001, pp. 129-153. Single or multiple copies of this article are available for a fee from The Haworth Document Delivery Service [1-800-342-9678, 9:00 a.m. - 5:00 p.m. (EST). E-mail address: getinfo@haworthpressinc.com].

129

ated far outnumber any other group. As the Black women in jails and prisons grow, so do the whispers about sexual abuse and labor abuse inside these institutions. This article discusses the nature of violence directed against incarcerated Black women and why it is important to direct national attention to this problem. It argues that though the violence may be individually directed, it is institutionally founded. Strategies are proposed for humanizing local jails and federal and state prisons. *[Article copies available for a fee from The Haworth Document Delivery Service: 1-800-342-9678. E-mail address: <getinfo@haworthpressinc.com> Website: <http://www.HaworthPress.com> © 2001 by The Haworth Press, Inc. All rights reserved.]*

KEYWORDS. Prison violence, sexual abuse, Prison Industrial Complex, incarceration, prisons, jails

Today more than ever before, violence in America's prison systems is attracting widespread attention among criminologists and social science researchers. Racism, injustice, oppression, strained relations between prison authorities women and criminals, and the lack of communication between authorities and prisoners are some of the most salient themes posing serious concern to social scientists. For thousands of Americans, "three strikes and you're out," has been the common response by the criminal justice system to crime in America. Routing non-violent women criminals into crowded and punitive correctional institutions has become the panacea for America's frustration with crime. Yet, research confirms that prisons and jails have become little more than breeding grounds for the same type of violent behavior that is endemic to American society.

Most Americans view prison violence primarily in terms of highly publicized male uprisings, such as the riots staged in California, New Mexico State penitentiary and in New York's Attica prison. However, violence in prison institutions is no longer directed solely against the prison system but is directed toward the prisoner him or herself, prison authorities, and other inmates (Martin & Zimmerman, 1990). "In-house" violence in America's prisons for women is a continuous problem but is seldom reported in the media. Besides the female inmate's sentence, the physical and psychological violence that these women experience at the hands of correctional staff, and other inmates, is so severe that it amounts to double jeopardy. For example, in 1990, nearly 100 inmates (men and women) in United States prison were murdered, and more than 10,000 were victims of assaults severe enough to require medical attention (Martin & Zimmerman, 1990). In addition, if one were to include the number of inmates who were murdered and severely assaulted in the nation's local jails, (which are operated and administered by local governments) these figures would show a dramatic increase (Perlins, Stephan & Beck, 1995).

Although inadequate, much of the literature on prison violence has focused primarily on the characteristics of male rather than female inmates. The past several decades, however, have seen a surge in the numbers and proportion of incarcerated women (mostly Black) in the United States and without a doubt this situation is troubling. The available data reveals that the rate of imprisoned Black females is growing at a faster rate than the rate for men (Mumola & Beck, 1997). For example, between 1985 and 1995, the number of incarcerated men doubled, from 691,800 to 1,437,600; while the number of incarcerated women (disproportionately Black) tripled, from 40,500 to 113,100 (Morash, Bynum & Koons, 1998; Bureau of Justice Statistics, 1997). The question then is: What is causing the increase in black women prisoners? (see Figures 1, 1.1, and 1.2).

While there is no consensus about the causes for the increase in female incarceration, it is nevertheless a fact that once imprisoned, these women experience egregious abuses, sexual exploitation and physical and psychological violence within prison walls. (Human Rights Watch 1998). These abuses go unreported for two salient reasons. First, there exists a sinister wall of secrecy that pervades prison life. Secondly, those who bravely smuggle their stories of horror to the news media face the risks of parole denial and stronger disciplinary actions against them. Therefore, most women in their efforts to survive conform to unscrupulous prison practices. Those who fail to conform experience retaliation more punitive and severe than those who acquiesce (Collins, 1997).

The purpose of this article is to examine violence against African American women in America's prison systems from a structural perspective. This focus will examine the mistreatment of these women on two fronts: (1) sexual

FIGURE 1

Variables Accounting for Disproportionate Black Female Incarceration

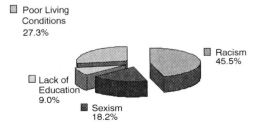

Source: Figure constructed from data based on Collin's research and U.S. Department of Justice Survey data. Values assigned by Collins.

FIGURE 1.1. Females by Race and Sex in the Prison System

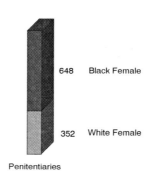

648   Black Female

352   White Female

Penitentiaries

Source: Prepared from Nichole Hahn Rafter, data: *Partial Justice: Instate Prisons, 1800-1935*, p. 146.

FIGURE 1.2. Adult Women Inmate Population by Race and Ethnicity, 1983, 1988

Yr–1985   Yr–1988

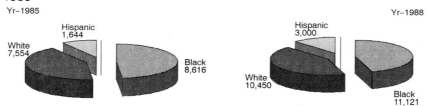

Source: *Vital Statistics in Corrections*, 1985 (p. 41). 1988 (p. 42). Numbers reflect a 20 percent increase in the female prison population since 1988.

abuses and (2) abuses in the prison workplace. In examining the sexual exploitation suffered by African American women in America's prison, one can draw a parallel similar to the inhumane treatment they suffered as slaves (Franklin, 1947). The only difference being, in contemporary America, Black guards are also the perpetrators. In this article, the fundamental focus is on how the system facilitates the mistreatment of Black women in the penal system. The term, 'mistreatment' will be discussed with the following questions in mind: (1) how does privatization of prisons, as a structural phenomenon, affect incarcerated black women? (2) Is the Black women's labor used to generate revenues for the states and to extend the profit margin of giant corporations? If so, how? These questions are raised to stimulate conceptual thinking that will, hopefully, generate hypotheses for future testing. In the meantime, suggestions are presented on how to humanize prison systems to a level that will allow all women to repay their debts to society without undue victimization.

VIOLENCE AND ABUSE
OF FEMALE PRISONERS DEFINED

To bring us closer to an understanding of the abuse of black women in the penal system, it is necessary to have a clear definition of abuse. Prison abuse is defined as any forceful or intimidating behavior (e.g., pressure, threats, and/or other actions and communications) that is perpetrated by one or more correctional employee and/or inmate (Federal Bureau of Prisons, 1995). Prison violence, for the purpose of this article, is defined as pushing shoving, maiming, forceful rape, murder, stabbing, etc.

THEORETICAL FRAMEWORKS

In order to provide structure, coherence and bounds to the treatment of women in jails and prisons, a search was made for an overreaching theoretical framework. Two primary paradigms have emerged as the most highly regarded: the structural-institutional approach and the individual characteristics of prisoners. Both models were developed from research on men's penal institutions. Consequently, neither takes into account, in a direct meaningful way, the cultural complexities associated with the incarceration of African American women or for that matter, women in general. In fact, Collins (1997, p. 24) states that the ever-increasing number of African American women entering the criminal justice system and the total disregard, of the need to address their specific issues, is an example of social neglect and abuse. This stems from the structure of a system that devalues women.

The structural-institutional theory posits that the organizational structure and working methods of a prison institution produces an atmosphere that encourages violent behavior (Schneider, 1996, p. 5; Johnson, 1986). The individual characteristics model further contends that violence in prisons may be due to specific characteristics of the inmates' personalities, including personal histories of violence (Sylvester et al., 1977, p. 78). In both instances, inmates assume an adaptive role determined by their social and ethnic culture, their street-smarts, their previous contact with the police or prison system, and their psychological selves (Palermo, Palermo, & Simpson, 1996, p. 182). These roles, which often lead to victimization, can be either aggressive or passive.

STRUCTURAL–INSTITUTIONAL MODEL

The structural–institutional approach focuses on how the inequitable distribution of power, culture of degradation, imposed isolation, and other social conditions created by the prison environment combines to create conditions of violence. The violence perpetrated against Black women, and women in general, is systemic and operates on a number of different structural levels ranging from indirect assault by legislators to direct attack by prison staff and administrators. First, penal institutions wield a significant discretionary and inequitable power over inmates because of (1) their legislative authority and (2) the lack of public concern for the well-being of prisoners. Based on the structural institutional premise, institutions perpetuate crimes of violence against African American women in prisons because the power differential at the highest levels of decision making condones it. A second facet of the model is that the availability of unbridled power allows prison staff and administrators to create a culture of degradation, which contributes to the violence. A negative social climate in which persons are purposefully degraded, belittled, dehumanized, and morally and socially destroyed is a contributor to violence (Schneider, 1994; Feltes, 1990; and Hurrelman, 1990). This environment is created through a series of acts designed to evoke shame and cause a woman to so severely dislike and loathe herself that she cannot imagine anyone else would see value in her as a person.

Socially imposed isolation is the third pivotal link in the structural–institutional framework. In this model, prisoners and prisons are designed to be isolated from the citizenry. Just as the public is isolated physically from prisons, it is also isolated from the severe injustices being carried on inside these facilities. Without social support, (orchestrated by the prison system) incarcerated women have few avenues for increasing their self-esteem, reframing negative experiences, and strengthening coping mechanisms. Lastly, other social conditions such as overcrowding, layout of prisons, and the prison–industrial complex contribute to the power available to agents of structural-institutional violence.

INDIVIDUAL–CHARACTERISTICS MODEL

The second framework, the individual–characteristics model, follows the structural model in current popularity. It contends that certain personality characteristics of inmates, either aggressive or passive, make them prime targets for prison violence. For example, aggressive prisoners require the use of more force from guards and other inmates. This force is exerted not only to enforce the rules but also to affect the feelings of self-worth of the prisoner.

On the other hand, passive prisoners exhibit what Seligman (1975) refers to as "learned helplessness." Seligman's theory proposes that a person learns through continuing experiences that no matter what their behavior, they are unable to avert negative consequence. Thus, they believe certain consequences will occur despite any purposeful action they may take. In the individual characteristic model, individuals believe that it is prudent to remain mute rather than attempt purposeful action. Thus, the individual will simply just submit to pressure.

Though this theoretical framework has some merit, its primary shortcoming lies in the heightened importance of the prisoner's behavior in the violence process. When comparing the two theories, neither can stand alone in explaining prison violence. A more comprehensive paradigm must be developed that encompasses both structural and interpersonal characteristics in a culturally sensitive light. Although lacking in some respects, the aforementioned theoretical formulations serve some purpose toward helping us, as we will later see, to understand how Black women respond to sexual abuse in prison settings.

DEMOGRAPHICS OF FEMALE INMATES NUMBER AND PROPORTION OF FEMALE INCARCERATION IN U.S. JAILS AND PRISONS

First however, we must look at the general demographic profile of female inmates, and later at the data on incarcerated Black women. According to the U.S. Census, population estimates for July 1, 1998 indicated that there were 230,861,000 females and males who were 10 years of age or older in the United States. Females accounted for 51.6% (n = 119,010,000) of this population (Greenfeld & Snell, 1999). Because the United States has the incredulous notoriety of incarcerating the largest known number of prisoners in the world, (Human Rights Watch, 1996), it is not surprising that many of these females over the age of 10 are now incarcerated in local jails and in federal and state prisons. A special report of *Women Offenders* published by the Bureau of Justice Statistics (1999) reported that in 1998, women offenders accounted for about 16% (942,448) of the total (5,890,300) correctional population (this number includes parolees). But between 1990 and 1998, the per capita number of women on probation climbed 40%; the jail rate grew 60%; the imprisonment rate increased 88%; and the parole rate was up 80%. Additionally, between 1990 and 1998, the number of women confined in state and federal prisons grew by an annual average of 8.5%, while the overall nation's prison populations increased an average of 6.7% (Greenfeld & Snell, 1999). According to Harlow (1996), women also accounted for an increasing percentage of inmates in local jails. In 1983, 7.1% (n = 15,900) were females; and in 1996, 10.2% (n = 52,600). What this data suggests is that women, in increasing numbers are rapidly filling jails and prisons and will in due course equal the number of men who are imprisoned.

CHARACTERISTICS OF WOMEN HOUSED
IN STATE AND FEDERAL PRISONS AND JAILS

As presented in Table 1, there is a comparison of arrest data based on the offense committed. Clearly women (of all colors) were more likely to be incarcerated for crimes such as larceny, forgery, embezzlement, and prostitution. In 1995, an increasing percentage of women were sentenced to state and federal prisons for non-violent drug-related offenses. In 1995, all offenses for women increased in percentage with the exception of offenses for murder and non-negligent manslaughter, weapon violation (e.g., carrying, possessing), prostitution, commercialized vice, and sexual offenses. However, even the percentages of women sentenced for these offenses slightly decreased over two decades (Bureau of Justice Statistics, 1999).

The demographic characteristics of women who were arrested, confined to state and federal prisons and granted probation are presented in Table 2. Women housed in our nation's jails and state and federal prisons are mostly poor minorities with children under the age of 18. The median age of these women range between 31-36 and most are between the ages of 25 and 34 years old. Thirty-seven percent have never been married and are single parents with one to three children (62%). Most came from a single parent home, and 50% have other family members (mostly Black men) who are incarcerated. Thirty-six percent have been the victims of sexual and/or physical abuse prior to their sentencing. Women in federal prisons tend to use more drugs and used them more frequently than those in state prisons and local jails (Bureau of Justice Statistics, 1999).

DRUG USE OF WOMEN PRISONERS

As presented in Table 1, 72% of the most serious offenses committed by women are drug related (e.g., this includes embezzlement and stealing to supply the habit (Bureau of Justice Statistics, 1999; U.S. Department of Justice, 1998; McShane & Williams, 1996). The rapid increase in female prisoners therefore can be partially attributed to the nation's war on drugs, a structural initiative that was launched in the 1980s and led to stiffer sentencing for drug offenses (Johnson, 2000; Bush-Baskette, 1998). Reacting to the Amnesty International's report, *Not Part of My Sentence*, Bernice Powell

TABLE 1. Percentage Distribution of Female Arrests by Offense Over Two Decades for Women in State and Federal Prisons

Type of Offenses	%–Based on 1975 population of 179 million	%–Based on 1995 population of 196 million
Murder and non-negligent manslaughter	15.6	9.5
Forcible rape	1.0	1.2
Robbery	7.0	9.3
Aggravated assault	13.1	17.7
Burglary	5.4	11.1
Larceny–Theft	31.2	33.3
Motor vehicle theft	7.0	13.1
Arson	11.3	15.7
Forgery and counterfeiting	28.9	35.9
Fraud	34.2	41.0
Embezzlement	31.1	43.6
Stolen property	10.7	14.2
Vandalism	8.0	13.6
Weapons: Carrying, possessing, etc.	8.0	7.9
Prostitution and commercialized vice	74.3	1.1
Sex offenses	7.7	8.0
Drug abuse violations	13.8	16.7
Gambling	8.8	15.2
Offenses against family and children	11.7	0.2
DUI	8.1	14.6
Liquor law violations	14.3	18.9
Disorderly conduct	17.6	21.7
Vagrancy	10.5	19.4
Curfew and loitering law violations	20.3	29.6
Runaways	56.9	57.4

Source: Bureau of Justice Statistics, *Sourcebook of Criminal Justice Statistics,* 1996, p. 380. Bureau of Justice Statistics, *Sourcebook of Criminal Justice Statistics,* 1977, p. 486.

Jackson (1999), Executive Director for the Commission for Racial Justice, United Church of Christ, stated that the rapid rise of women incarcerated is attributable to some of the draconian drug laws of the past. The report indicated that the war on drugs has become a war on women. For example, women in our criminal justice system are placed at a distinct disadvantage by "gender-neutral" federal sentencing guidelines, which do not allow the court to consider the impact of imprisonment on single mothers. Further, it does not consider the minor role that many women play in drug possession and trafficking as a result of abusive relationships. The problem of drugs, it seems, is a factor that is causing an increase in women prisoners.

WOMEN OFFENDERS BY RACE,
WITH SPECIAL ATTENTION TO AFRICAN AMERICANS

Kirk and Okazawa-Rey (1995) reported that from 1989 to 1994, young African-American women experienced the greatest increase in incarceration than any other demographic group (Mauer & Huling, 1995, p. 20). Although the U.S. Department of Justice reports that white women committed more murder and

TABLE 2. Characteristics of Adult Women on Probation, in Jail, and in Prison, December 1998.

Characteristics of Adult Women Prisons	Local Probation	State Jails	Federal Prisons	
Race/Hispanic Origin				
White	62%	36%	33%	29%
Black	27	44	48	35
Hispanic	10	15	15	32
Other	1	5	4	4
Age				
24 or younger	20%	21%	12%	9%
25-34	39	46	43	35
35-44	30	27	34	32
45-54	10	5	9	18
55 or older	1	1	2	6
Median Age	32 yrs	31 yrs	33 yrs	36 yrs
Marital Status				
Married	26%	15%	17%	29%
Widowed	2	4	6	6
Separated	10	13	10	21
Divorced	20	20	20	10
Never Married	42	48	47	34
Education				
8th grade or less	5%	12%	7%	8%
Some high school	35	33	37	19
High school graduate/GED	39	39	39	44
Some college or more	21	16	17	29
Women with Children				
With minor children				
(under 18 years of age)	72%	70%	65%	59%

Source: Bureau of Justice Statistics (December, 1999) *Special Report on Women Offenders*, U.S. Department of Justice, (1998) *Special Report on Women in Criminal Justice System–A Twenty Year Update.*

homicide (see Figures 2 and 3) nationally during this period, Black women in state and federal prisons grew 278%, while the number of African-American men grew only 186%. In 1998, over 64% of the women in local jails, 67% in state prisons, and 71% in federal prisons were minorities (Mauer and Huling, 1995, p. 20). Notwithstanding the fact that estimates from the U.S. Census Bureau for July 1, 1998 indicated that African-American comprised only 12.2% of the population nationally, they represented over 52% of the jailed and imprisoned population in this country (Bureau of Justice Statistics, 1999), and are the largest minority group represented in our federal prisons (Human Rights Watch, 1996). As shown in Figure 4, African American females are sentenced to prison at a rate that outpaces other ethnic groups (117 per 100,000 residents), with estimates doubling in 1998 to a projected estimated rate of 212 sentenced prisoners per 100,000 residents. For white women, the numbers are far less significant; they were sentenced prisoners in 1990 at a rate of about 31 per 100,000 residents and with a projected rate of 57 per 100,000 in 1998. For example, in Florida, Black females constitute 55.6% of the incarcerated female population in 1983, 58.3% in 1993, and 59.3% in 1994 (Florida Department of Corrections, 1993/1994).

Again, Mann (1984, p. 197) found that drug violations were the primary reasons for the upward spiral of incarceration for Black women (see Figure 2). Among deadly crimes, (see Figure 3) the second most frequent incarceration offense committed by Black women was for murder, and the third was larceny. These patterns have not drastically changed over the past 15 years.

FIGURE 2. Crimes Commited by Female Inmates in Federal Prisons, by Race, 1992

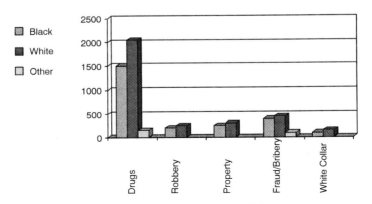

Source: U.S. Department of Justice, *Sourcebook* 1993, Table 6.85, p. 636.

FIGURE 3. Deadly Crimes Committed by Female Inmates of State Prisons by Race

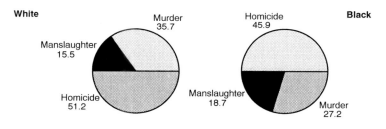

Source: U.S. Department of Justice, Sourcebook, 1990, p. 620.

FIGURE 4. Federal Female Inmates by Race, Ethnicity, 1960-96

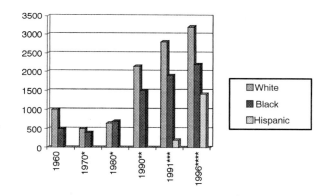

*Inclusive minorities.
** U.S. Department of Justice, Sourcebook 1990.
*** U.S. Federal Bureau of Prisons, October 1991.
**** U.S. Federal Bureau of Prisons, January 1996.

Source: U.S. Federal Bureau of Prisons, Annual Statistical Report, Table 1A.

The current "war on drugs" initiated by the Reagan administration and continued by the Bush and Clinton administrations, has been a structural policy which has affected poor African-American and Latino communities; despite the fact that whites make up the majority of drug users and traffickers. African-American women comprise over half of the female prison population. Therefore, it could be surmised that poor African-American women and other poor women of color have been the main target of the "drug czar's" initiatives on the "war on drugs" (Kirk & Okazawa-Rey, 1998; Bureau of Justice Statistics, 1999; Bush-Baskette, 1998). Though Blacks are more highly represented in prison ranks, Greenfeld and Snell (1999), reported in one study which was congruent with Mann (1984) research that over half of female violent offenders were described by their victims as White in comparison to over a third described as black. Clearly, Black and White offenders accounted for virtually equal proportions of women committing robbery and aggravated assault, but simple assault female offenders were more likely to be described as white (Greenfeld and Snell, 1999).

Foley and Rasche (1979) found that women of color received more punitive treatment in the criminal justice system than White women. In their longitudinal study of one of Missouri's state institutions over a 16-year period, Foley and Rasche found that African-American women received on average longer sentences (55.1 months) than White women who were sentenced to 52.2 months. They further stated that White women who were imprisoned for murder served one-third less time than African-American women for the same offense. This supports the Kirk and Okazawa-Rey (1998) thesis that some women may receive harsher sentences and treatment for some crimes. Additionally, women who do not fit the traditional stereotypes (passive and gentle), may receive more punitive sentences and may serve longer sentences than women who fit the stereotypes. Lewis (1981) concluded from her analyses of San Francisco jail data and Glick and Neto's national data, that racism seems to affect Black women more than Black men (see Figure 1). She further stated that Black women are treated more harshly than their White counterparts by police officers, judges, and correctional guards (Mann, 1989; Jackson, 1999).

These data pose questions about how female offenders are treated in prisons and jails run and administered by male criminal justice officials who uphold the structural policies of this nation. Also, based on the American history of racism and sexism, are African-American female offenders and other females of color treated any differently than their White counterparts? These are issues, as we will see, that deserve attention.

SEXUAL ABUSE IN JAILS AND PRISONS: IS THIS THEIR PUNISHMENT?

As stated, in most prisons, employees have total authority over female prisoners. As a result these women often cannot attend their basic intimate needs in a secure atmosphere free from intrusion. In the alleged name of performing their jobs, male employees can engage in a number of abusive behaviors. According to a two-and-a-half year investigation of the sexual abuse of female prisoners at the hands of male employees at eleven state prisons located in Georgia, California, Illinois, New York, Michigan, and the

District of Columbia, "being a woman prisoner in U.S. state prisons can be a terrifying experience" (Human Rights Watch, 1996, p. 1).

An understanding of the full extent, as well as the nature, of sexual abuse of female offenders in local jails and in state and federal prison by male employees cannot be determined. This is due partly to the failure of jails and prisons to keep accurate records of sexual assaults and other abuses of women in penal facilities and partly to the women's reluctance to report these abuses. (Kim, 1999). In federal prisons, and in 41 states and the District of Columbia, there are laws criminalizing sexual abuse of prisoners. District of Columbia Congresswoman, Eleanor Holmes-Norton, asserts that without comprehensive data, "it remains unclear the extent to which these laws are routinely enforced and policies and procedures followed." Thus, Representative Norton, a non-voting delegate to the House of Representatives, requested that the Government Accounting Office (GAO) study the extent of sexual abuse of female prisoners (Kim, 1999).

According to an Associated Press article by Kim (1999) between 1995 and 1998, the GAO studied female inmates from three of the largest prison jurisdictions (i.e., Texas, California, and the Federal Bureau of Prisons). These prisons were selected because they house more than one third of the nation's 80,000 female offenders. Findings of the investigation indicated that 506 female inmates from California, Texas, and federal prisons reported sexual abuse by correctional staff. Only 92 (18%) of the reports resulted in a resignation, termination, or disciplinary action. The District of Columbia had 111 allegations of sexual abuses from December 1995 to June 1998, where 12% resulted in disciplinary actions or resignations (Kim, 1999).

In Michigan, male correctional employees are employed at all women's prisons. For example, at Crane prison, approximately 80 percent of the staff is male and open dormitories are divided into cubicles. The officers' desks are next to the bathroom and the bathroom doors must be left open at all times. Also, male correctional employees are allowed to conduct body shake-down, where as previously stated, officials run their hands freely over the women's bodies–their breasts, genitalia, legs, and thighs (Kurshan, 1998).

The use of strip searches, a common practice in law enforcement facilities and correctional institutions, is often a degrading and a harmful means of obtaining contraband. This practice is designed to send a message that severe consequences exist for lawbreakers. Although all facilities employ female officers who have responsibility for strip searches, countless stories have been told of female officers overstepping their boundaries by conducting searches in front of male officers, and male officers attempting to retrieve contraband from a woman's outer vaginal area before the "alleged" contraband could be placed far inside a woman's body (*New York Times*, December 1996).

As the Humans Right Watch (1996) reported in *All Too Familiar: Sexual Abuse of Women in United States Prisons*, often female prisoners find it difficult to stop unlawful conduct by male correctional employees or have the perpetrator brought to justice. The Human Rights Watch Report present the case of Robin Lucas, who was housed in a men's facility and who filed a lawsuit against U.S. authorities in 1996, stating that she was raped, sodomized, and made a sex slave by guards who "sold" access to her cell to male inmates in a federal prison in California. Lucas' case was filed along with two other fellow female prisoners and was settled out of court for $500,000 and an agreement by the U.S. Bureau of Prisons to institute major prison reforms.

The above has not been the only case where suits were filed against federal and state prisons for violating the constitutional rights of female prisoners. In 1994, a federal judge ruled that the D.C. Department of Corrections had violated the constitutional rights of 13 female prisoners after they filed a class action suit accusing guards of fondling and raping them along with other instances of sexual and physical misconduct. In a *Boston Globe* (1999) editorial, it was reported that the Human Rights Watch Report presented an incident at a state-run Massachusetts facility (e.g., MCI-Framingham) where 112 female prisoners and pre-trial detainees were roused from bed and strip-searched by masked guards conducting a training exercise. The Massachusetts Department of Correction settled the lawsuit regarding this case in 1998.

The Human Rights Watch Report (1996) further indicated that even when a prisoner succeeded in pursuing a complaint of sexual misconduct, internal investigatory procedures are often fraught with conflicts of interest and a bias against prisoner testimony. At times, officer's accused of sexual misconduct were assigned to investigate themselves. Given the closed nature of the prison environment, and the reluctance of officers to testify against their peers, such evidence is often very hard to obtain. Thus, complaints of sexual misconduct can be extremely difficult to substantiate. Frequently, prison administrators fail to deal appropriately with cases that are presented to them because the allegations do meet prosecutional standards. An employee who may not have been found to commit a crime, but who may nonetheless have violated prison rules, can thus escape punishment altogether (Human Rights Watch, 1996).

In some states and the District of Columbia, a first offense of this sort is classified as a felony. In others, it is classified merely as a misdemeanor. But no matter how the offense is classified, state laws are rarely enforced, and when they are, they often carry light penalties. The failure of many states to uphold their own laws regarding custodial sexual misconduct reflects their reluctance to prosecute such crimes. This is largely due to an ingrained belief, except in the most egregious cases, that the prisoner is responsible for the sexual abuse. In this sense, state officials still widely view criminal sexual misconduct as a victimless crime (Human Rights Watch, 1996).

RETALIATION

Incarcerated Black women who report mistreatment clearly feel they are punished for reporting sexual abuse by guards. This punishment is frequently referred to as retaliation. Retaliation is defined as any act by a corrections officer, corrections employee, or administrative official in the penal system, which is directed towards the inmate in order to punish him/her for having reported an abuse(s) (Amnesty International, 1998). Virtually every prisoner interviewed, who had lodged a complaint of sexual misconduct, faced retaliation by the accused officer, his colleagues, or other prisoners. In some cases, they also faced punishment by correctional officials (Amnesty International, 1998). These punishments generally took the form of write-ups for sexual misconduct, the loss of "earned good time" accrued towards early parole, or prolonged periods of administrative segregation. In other cases, officials did not overtly discipline prisoners but made use of administrative segregation, ostensibly a protective mechanism, designed to punish inmates. Thus, prisoners who had committed no disciplinary infraction were still subjected to the same treatment as prisoners serving disciplinary sentences.

The belief among women prisoners that retaliation is a reality, is supported by the testimonies of other inmates, prison guards, and prisoner' rights advocates. Reports are to the effect that participation in rehabilitative programs such as work, school, visitation privileges, and physical and mental health are denied as a form of retaliation. As described in a 1998 report by Amnesty International, most women prisoners are afraid to report sexual abuses, because they feel the consequences may be more devastating than the abuse.

CASE STUDY

Jane Doe 2 entered the corrections system in 1995. At the time of her incarceration, she spoke very little English. After she had been in the prison for several months, she was approached by a guard who asked her to give him oral sex. She did not want to agree, but because she did not feel comfortable talking with any of the guards or administrators, she went along with the guard's request. The sexual abuse continued over a two-year period until the guard transferred to another facility. As she became more comfortable in the system and her English improved, she decided to seek outside counsel and approached a lawyer about what she could do to stop the abuse. However, once she realized that it would be impossible to file a complaint without her identity being revealed, she decided not to take any action. (Amnesty International, 1998)

This story demonstrated the chilling effect that retaliation has on female prisoners. In some cases, women choose to live with the sexual abuse rather than risk being targeted for retaliation. Others, who were brave enough to report the abuse, ultimately expressed regret for coming forward. Regardless, it is commonly believed that if one chooses to file a complaint against a guard for sexual harassment, she may suffer unrelenting retaliation. This may include loss of credit for good behavior that could adversely affect the inmate at her parole hearing.

The question arises: why do other corrections' officers refuse to speak out against the sexual abuse and retaliation? Under oath, Kennedy-Carpenter, a Corrections Officer, talked about the fear corrections officers have about speaking out against the abusive guards:

> They're afraid of their supervisor setting them up and getting them fired. They're afraid of some of the dirty officers doing things to them; setting them up, running them off the expressway, all the things they've been doing. A lot of them know what's right and what's wrong, but they don't have the guts to put up with it on a daily basis. The harassment they are going to have. . . . You are going to have to guarantee them jobs within other state systems here; transfer them to another department . . . because there's no way they're going to be able to function here afterwards. You can't put them in another prison. There is not an officer here that doesn't know people at twenty other prisons. And word gets out. Before that person ever hits the front gate, word will get to that prison that he was a snitch. There's just no way you're going to be able to protect these officers.

> Given that a corrections officer within the system despairs at the possibility of protecting a fellow officer from retaliation if he or she speaks out about the abuse or retaliation, it is clear that prisoners are even less able to protect themselves. No attempt is made to keep the names of prisoners who file grievances against officers confidential. (Amnesty International, 1998)

The invisibility of custodial sexual misconduct, and hence its repudiation, are further fueled by the failure of many states and the District of Columbia to establish credible internal grievance and investigatory procedures that do not expose complainants to retaliation or punishment. In virtually every prison investigated by Amnesty International, grievance procedures required that the prisoner informally confront the implicated officer before she can file a formal grievance. In many cases the targeted officer of a complaint had supervisory contact with the complainant. Both procedures exposed complainants to retaliation or punishment and routinely deterred them from filing sexual misconduct complaints (Amnesty International, 1998).

Coupled with feelings of shame for having being imprisoned, and the problem of trying to survive in a hostile prison atmosphere, some women suffer long periods of deep depression.

SEXUAL ABUSE OF AFRICAN AMERICAN WOMEN

Some forms of sexual abuses to which female prisoners are routinely subjected to by male correctional employees include: (1) vaginal, anal, and oral rape of women; (2) watching women fight each other, (3) watching them shower and dress, (4) selling women for sex to other guards and male inmates, and (5) groping and or touching female prisoners' breasts, buttocks, and vaginal areas during strip searches and pat-downs. In 1996, the Human Rights Watch Report found that in the course of committing such gross misconduct, male officers not only used actual or threatened physical force but have also used their discretionary authority to provide or deny goods and privileges to female prisoners. Because prisoners are completely dependent on officers for their most basic necessities, the offer or (by implication) threat to withhold privileges, or goods, is a very powerful inducement.

No one group of women prisoners appears to suffer violent sexual misconduct more than African Americans. Among this group, those who are in prison for the first time, lesbians, the young and the mentally ill are particularly vulnerable to demands for sexual relations. In some instances, women have been impregnated as a result of sexual misconduct, and some of these prisoners experienced additional abuses in the form of inappropriate segregation, denial of adequate health care, and/or pressure to seek an abortion (Kirk & Okazawa-Rey, 1998; Bush-Baskette, 1998).

African American women in correctional institutions find themselves in extreme emotional conflict because of their intense desire to fight against prison abuses. Traditionally, these women have been providers, and protectors for themselves, their children, and their elders. Thus, willingly acquiescing to their captors' sexual abuses is contrary to their nature. Hence, once a Black woman in a correctional institution takes a stand, she becomes branded as someone to demoralize–someone to be "put in her place" in a very abusive and public way. Because the African American woman will not back down easily, the struggle continues until the system with its many resources, and lack of accountability, overpowers her. Once the woman has been "broken" she becomes easy prey for continuous abuse from multiple correctional staff and other inmates.

The bulging prison population in Federal and State prisons is disproportionately African American (51%) and Hispanic 11%. Of the entire population of incarcerated women in federal, state and local jails, 71%, 67% and 64% respectively are women; most of whom are African American and Hispanics (Human Rights Watch, 1999). Thoughtful analysis of the demographic characteristics of incarcerated African American women identifies the tremendous risk and propensity for sexual abuse solely due to their numbers. First, African American women are likely to be incarcerated for longer periods of time because of the nature of offenses committed. Second, African American women represent the largest population group that may serve as a threat. Third, because African American women are more likely to have a "debilitating" substance use/abuse problem with crack cocaine as the reported drug of choice, they are easy prey for "black market violence" in these facilities. Lastly, because the general public has limited interest in the effective operation of correctional facilities, it is mostly unaware about injustices occurring behind prison walls. The public appears to have even less interest if the primary target group service is Black or minority. There is evidence that prisons mirror the same racial injustices as seen in the larger society. According to Smiley (1996) a power gap exists between Black people and those in power who make major decisions in this country. Thus Black women prisoners are affected by the sharpening of conflict on the outside and the increasing national oppression visited upon Black people in general. Further, there exists an ethical/moral feeling that if prisoners, who are feared and disliked by other women, are victimized by each other, guards would then be free of charges of sexual harassment. Thus, in some sense, the prevailing attitude would be: "it serves them (the prisoners) right" (Schneider, 1996, p. 10). These consequences are believed to "go with the territory of doing the crime and the time" and after all, "jail is supposed to be harsh and punitive." The collaboration of these identified risk factors for violence against incarcerated African American women creates a volatile social justice problem that is only expected to worsen because of emerging trends in Black juvenile female crime.

Violence in correctional institutions, therefore, is an even more devastating problem to African American females who represent 50% of all women incarcerated in this country, and who are treated more harshly than other imprisoned (Daily, 1989; Foley & Rasche, 1979; Sari, 1986; Hake and Shields, 1992; Mann, 1996, p. 126). Yet, Black women suffer other atrocities aside from the sexual abuse experienced at the hands of male prison officials–they perform slave labor.

PRISON LABOR ABUSE

Steadily emerging as an important issue, in violence against incarcerated women, mostly Black, is prison labor abuse. This abuse is defined as cruel and unusual involuntary servitude within prison confines beyond the specified punishment for the crime committed. In 1984, Congress created the Prison Industry Enhancement Program to allow federal and state prisons to sell inmate-made products on the open market. Additionally, the program allowed private companies to contract with prisons for inmate labor (Cozic, 1997, p. 95). This provided the impetus for inmates to work long, grueling hours in prison factory settings with intense heat, unsafe machinery, and health hazards. Further, inmates are often paid wages ranging from $.25-$.40 per hour. If inmates refuse to work, they serve longer sentences, lose privileges, and risk solitary confinement (Erlich in Cozic, 1997, p. 103). The violence imposed on African American women is formulated at the highest levels of decision-making and is a disgrace to any civilized society.

Clearly, the treatment of many women in U.S. prisons, mostly Black, is an abuse of human rights. It is one more indication that the U.S. stands on shaky moral ground when it calls into account other nations of the world for their human rights abuses. In recent months, the U.S. Government has been justifiably critical of the practice of some foreign governments, such as China, for using the prison population as a source of forced, underpaid laborers. What is not so widely known and understood is that similar practices, namely the Prison Industrial Complex, occur in the U.S. under conditions that amount to prohibited forced labor and the use of prison labor as punishment. At a prison facility in Texas, for instance, current employers of prisoners include among other laborers a circuit board assembler, an eyeglass manufacturer, and a maker of valves and fittings. Many of these companies have closed their factories outside the prisons, and now rent factory space in the prisons. Practices such as these violate the Universal Declaration of Human Rights, the International Covenant on Civil and Political Rights, and the Standard Minimum Rules for the Treatment of Prisoners. Many U.S. government practices fit the United Nations definition of genocide when it comes to the treatment of the poor and people of color.

Privatization of prisons in the United States has fueled the fires of the Prison Industrial Complex. Prisons are a growth industry and many new corporate players are taking advantage of a new trend to contract for private prison services (See & Khashan, 2001). The new Prison-Industrial Complex is establishing a network of political contacts and local constituencies–wardens, prison guard unions, subcontractors and suppliers, and local government officials–that benefit from increased incarceration (See & Khashan, 2001). Just as the country now struggles to rid itself of unnecessary military bases and weapons systems, in years ahead, the Prison-Industrial Complex may lobby to maintain unnecessary prisons or promote laws that help fill them (Erlich in Cozic, 1997, p. 108). Though no empirical data exists that clearly links the Prison-Industrial Complex to heightened arrest and the incarceration rates for Black women, Erlich may be alluding to the whispers being heard across the country. What is known is that because African American women constitute the largest percentage of those incarcerated in prisons, and because prisons more intensely mirror the racism and oppression found in the larger society, African American women are more likely to be adversely affected by the Prison-Industrial Complex.

In many areas of the country, mostly in inner cities, young people feel that the police are an occupation army and inner cities are militarized zones. They feel that the courts are used to funnel young Blacks and Latinos into prisons where their labor potential is valuable. Once incarcerated, inmates are forced to work long hours in "sweatshop" conditions, including unprotected exposure to hazardous chemicals and materials and unsafe machines. The work is hard and abusive and the jobs teach very few skills that will benefit offenders once outside of the prison. Critics such as Erlich (in Cozic, 1997) purport that the mistreatment in the form of prison labor is also a way to maintain social control in heavily populated facilities. If prisoners refuse to work, they are moved to disciplinary housing and lose canteen privileges. Most importantly, they lose "earned good time" credit that reduces their sentences (p. 103).

The issue of prison labor abuse is hotly debated. Many do not feel that putting prisoners to work is detrimental. Former Delaware Governor, Pete Du Pont, argues that increasing the use of inmate labor would benefit prisoners, prisons, and society (Du Pont in Cozic, 1997, p. 96). Du Pont also goes on to say that allowing prisoners to work will make the streets safer for the rest of us (p. 101). Across the country, a million prisoners are serving time in jail. Each month, 40,000 are released under mandatory supervision, on parole or at the conclusion of their sentences. Critics of the prison work programs assert streets would be safer and the crime rate would be lower if these newly returned members of society had a skill, a job, and the beginning of a future. Unfortunately, others disagree that few, if any, of these benefits will actually be realized.

SOLUTIONS FOR HUMANIZING PRISONS AND JAILS

One of the greatest obstacles to the eradication of custodial sexual misconduct against women in general, and Black women in particular, is lack of attention to their plight at both state and national levels. In the Georgia and District of Columbia correctional systems, for example, it took class action suits in 1992 and 1994, respectively, to expose the problem of sexual misconduct inside the confines of the correctional system. Only after a class action suit was filed against both states, did the departments of corrections admit that the problem of custodial sexual misconduct exists in their facilities for women. It is likely that the same course of action will need to be taken, before prison labor abuses are eradicated.

Any culturally sensitive remedy for change, must lean heavily on the beliefs that the milieu of custodial violence is primarily institutional. The remedy must begin at the societal level and descend to the institutional and individual levels. The framework must also include a philosophical premise that incarcerated offenders are offered certain protections by the constitutional and administrative laws that govern this country. Further, African American women should be equally protected by those same tenets of the Constitution. Just because African American women make up the largest population of incarcerated women, it does not give society the right to turn a "deaf ear" to prison violence.

Thorough and long-lasted eradication of custodial violence must occur as a result of a multi-tiered process. First, there must be a change in public moral thinking and a shift from archaic ideas that inmates deserve whatever happens to them in prison facilities. Second, policies and procedures must reflect a systemic desire to identify and punish those who break the law by engaging in the custodial mistreatment of incarcerated women. The effort to eradicate this abuse must seek violators on all levels from the lowest classification of prison staff to the boardroom of corporate giants. The privatization of prisons and the prison-industrial complex must be studied and closely scrutinized for their merit in allowing offenders to pay their debt to society. Third, prison structures and environments must be changed to embrace a more culturally sensitive program. The following steps must be taken: (1) enhance physical designs of buildings and services that increase safety and decrease violence risk factors; (2) employ more female administrators and staff with extensive training; (3) create a climate of zero tolerance for abuses against women; (4) establish accessible systems for women to report and receive assistance in stopping the abuse; (5) provide counseling and other necessary services to alleviate the trauma of abuse; and (6) ensure the safety of correctional staff who seek to report egregious abuses against inmates. The safety of women in custodial care and the priority for change must be seen on every step of the judicial process including federal, state and local levels (Human Rights Watch, 1998).

Clearly, there is much work yet to be done to address this still "invisible" problem. Little hard data exists about custodial violence against African American women. The questions and implications raised in this article, along with others, provide an important starting place for future research.

REFERENCES

Amnesty International (1999) United States of America. Violation of Human Rights of Women in Custody. New York: Amnesty International.

Amnesty International (1999) United States of America. *"Breaking the Chain"*: *The Human Rights of Women in Prison*. New York: Amnesty International.

Beverly, C. (1998). Black on Black Crime: Compensation for idiomatic purposeless-ness. In See (Ed.) *Human behavior in the social environment from the African American perspective*. New York: The Haworth Press, Inc.

Bureau of Justice Statistics (Aug. 15, 1999). The nation's prison population grew by 60,000 inmates. (News Release). Washington, D.C.: U.S. Department of Justice.

Bureau of Justice Statistics (Dec. 5, 1999). About 2.1 million violent female offenders (News Release). Washington, D.C.: U.S. Department of Justice.

Bureau of Justice Statistics (1999). Women Offenders: Summary Findings. *Criminal Offenders Statistics*. Washington, D.C.: U.S. Department of Justice.

Bureau of Justice Statistics (1998). *Sourcebook of Criminal Justice Statistics*, 1997. Washington, D.C.: U.S. Department of Justice.

Bureau of Justice Statistics(1997). *Sourcebook of Criminal Justice Statistics*, 1996. Washington, D.C.: U.S. Department of Justice.

Bureau of Justice Statistics (1977). *Sourcebook of Criminal Justice Statistics*, 1996. Washington, D.C.: U.S. Department of Justice.

Bush-Baskette, S. R. (1988). The War on Drugs As a War Against Women. In *Crime, Control and Women*: *Feminist Implications of Criminal Justice Policy*. (pp. 113-124) by Susan L. Miller. Thousand Oaks, CA: Sage Publications.

Collins, C. (1997). *The Imprisonment of African American Women*. Jefferson, NC: McFarland & Co.

Cozic, C. (1997). *America's Prisons*. San Diego: Greenhaven Press.

DuPont, P. (1997). Inmate Labor is Beneficial. In *America's Prisons*. (pp. 96-101) by Charles Cozic. San Diego, CA: Greenhaven Press.

Erlich, R. (1997). Inmate Labor May Not Be Beneficial. In *America's Prison*. (pp. 102-110) by Charles Cozic. San Diego, CA: Greenhaven Press.

Feltes, T. (1990). Gewalt in der schule. In H.D. Schwind, J. Bauman et al. (Eds.) Ursachen, praevention und Kontrolle von Gewalt. Berlin: Duncker & Humblot.

Fletcher, B., Dixon-Shaver, L., Moon, D. (1993). *Women Prisoners*: *A Forgotten Population*. Wesport, CT: Praeger.

Florida Department of Corrections (1994/1995). *Florida Department of Corrections Annual Report: Corrections as a Business*. Tallahassee, FL: State of Florida.

Foley, L. and Rasche, C. (1979). The affects of race on sentencing, actual time served and final disposition of female offenders. In *Theory and Research in Criminal Justice*, edited by J. Conley. Cincinnati: Anderson.

Franklin, J.H. (1947). From Slavery to Freedom. New York: Knopf.

Greenfeld, L. & Snell, T. (1999). Women Offenders. Bureau of Justice Statistics Special Report. Washington, D.C.:U.S. Department of Justice.

Harlow, C. (1998). *Profile of Jail Inmates*. 1996. Bureau of Justice Statistics Special Report. Washington, D.C.: U.S. Department of Justice.

Harlow, C. (1994). *Comparing Federal and State Prison Inmates*. 1991. Bureau of Justice Statistics Special Report. Washington, D.C.: U.S. Department of Justice.

Haney, C., Banks, C., & Zimbardo, P.G. (1973). Interpersonal dynamics in a simulated prison. *International Journal of Criminology and Penology*, 1, 69-67.

Human Rights Watch Project. (Winter 1997). All too familiar: Sexual abuse of women in U.S. state prisons. *Women's International Network News*, 23, (1), 43.

Human Rights Watch Telephone Interview: Jane Doe, former corrections officer at Scott Correctional Facility. Ann Arbor, MI. March 27, 1998.

Human Rights Watch (1998). *Nowhere to Hide: Retaliation Against Women in Michigan State Prisons*. New York: Human Rights Watch.

Hurrelman, K. (1990). Gewalt in der schule. In H.D. Schwind, J. Bauman et al. (Eds.). Ursachen, Praevention und Kontrolle von Gewalt. Berlin: Duncker & Humblot.

Jackson, B. (1999). Not a Part of Their Sentence. *Civil Rights Journal*. Cleveland, OH: Commission for Racial Justice, United Church of Christ.

Kirk, G. & Okazawa-Rey, M. (1998). *Women's Lives: Multicultural Perspectives*. Mountain View, CA: Mayfield Publishing.

Kurshan, N. (1998). Behind the walls. In *Women's Lives: Multicultural Perspectives*. (pp. 343-354). Edited by Kirk and Okazawa-Rey. Mountain View, CA: Mayfield Publishing.

Mann, C.R. (1995). Women of Color and the Criminal Justice System. In the *Criminal Justice System and Women*. Edited by Price and Sokaloff. New York: McGraw-Hill.

Mann, C.R. (1993). *Unequal justice: A Question of Color*. Bloomington: Indiana University Press.

Mann, C.R. (1989). Minority and Female: A Criminal Justice Double Bind. *Social Justice*. 16(4),95.

Mann, C.R. (1984). *Female Crime and Delinquency*. Birmingham: University of Alabama Press.

Martin, R. & Zimmerman, S. (1990). "A Typology of the Causes of Prison Riots and an Analytical Extension to the 1986 Virginia Riot." *Justice Quarterly* 7: 711-37.

Mauer, M. & Huling, T. (1995). *Young Black American and the Criminal Justice System Five Years Later*. Washington, D.C.: The Sentencing Project.

McShane, M. & Williams, F. (1996). *Encyclopedia of America Prisons*. London: Garland.

Morash, M., Bynum, T., & Koons. (1998). *Women Offenders: Programming Needs and Promising Approaches*. National Justice Institute of Justice Research in Brief. Washington, DC: U.S. Department of Justice.

Mumola, C. and Beck, A. (1997). *Prisoners in 1996*. Bureau of Justice Statistics. Washington, D.C.

Palermo, G., Palermo, M., & Simpson, D. (1996). Death by inmate: Multiple murder in a maximum security prison. *International Journal of Offender Therapy and Comparative Criminology*, 40,(3), 181-191.

Platt, A. (1994). Politics of law and order. *Social Justice*, 21, 3(57), fall, 3-13.

Pollock-Byrne, J. (1990). *Women, Prison and Crime*. Pacific Grove, CA:Brooks/Cole.

Schiele, J. (1998). Cultural alignment, African American male youths, and violent crime. In See (Ed.). *Human Behavior in the social environment from the African American perspective*. New York: The Haworth Press, Inc.

Schneider, H. (1996). Violence in the institution. *International Journal of Offender Therapy and Comparative Criminology*, 40,(1), 5-18.

See, L. (1998). Human behavior theory and the African American experience. In See (Ed.). *Human behavior in the social environment from the African American perspective*. New York: The Haworth Press, Inc.

See, L & Khashan, IV (2001). Violence in the suites. In L. See (ed.) *Violence as Seen Through a Prism of Color*. New York, The Haworth Press, Inc.

Seligman, M.E.P. (1975). *Helplessness: On depression, development, and death*. San Francisco, CA: Freeman.

Shoham, S., Rahan, B., Rubin, R. (1987). Family parameters of violent prisoners.

Smiley, T. (1996) *Hard Left*. New York: Anchor Books.

Race Backwards:
Genes, Violence, Race
and Genocide

Gerald Horne

SUMMARY. This article discusses recent highly criticized National violence initiatives and behavioral interventions. These interventions include drug therapy and psychosurgery aimed at preventing later adult violence. The article provides an overview of the roots of eugenic violence. It charges that science is being misused to justify racism at the highest levels of government. A case is made that by failing to factor in socio-economic causes of violence black and brown youth, and despised and persecuted minorities are targets for experimentation. Strategies for preventing black genocide are offered. *[Article copies available for a fee from The Haworth Document Delivery Service: 1-800-342-9678. E-mail address: <getinfo@haworthpressinc.com> Website: <http://www.HaworthPress. com> © 2001 by The Haworth Press, Inc. All rights reserved.]*

KEYWORDS. Genes, violence, race, genocide

INTRODUCTION

Within the past decade, the psychiatric literature is abundant with studies reporting the effectiveness of phenothiazine, and other drug treatments in

Gerald Horne, PhD, JD, is Professor of history and communications at the University of North Carolina at Chapel Hill. Dr. Horne received his PhD from Columbia University, and his law degree from the University of California at Berkeley. He has authored over 100 articles, and published approximately 15 books. Currently he is completing a research project in Hong Kong, China.

[Haworth co-indexing entry note]: "Race Backwards: Genes, Violence, Race and Genocide." Horne, Gerald. Co-published simultaneously in *Journal of Human Behavior in the Social Environment* (The Haworth Social Work Practice Press, an imprint of The Haworth Press, Inc.) Vol. 4, Nos. 2/3, 2001, pp. 155-166; and: *Violence as Seen Through a Prism of Color* (ed: Letha A. (Lee) See) The Haworth Social Work Practice Press, an imprint of The Haworth Press, Inc., 2001, pp. 155-166. Single or multiple copies of this article are available for a fee from The Haworth Document Delivery Service [1-800-342-9678, 9:00 a.m. - 5:00 p.m. (EST). E-mail address: getinfo@haworthpressinc.com].

altering the behavior of mentally ill patients. Seemingly, however, these studies are inching closer to performing experimentation on human beings who are deemed socially aggressive, and who may not be welcome in our social system. This may not have occurred to Dr. Frederick Goodwin but quick reaction to some of his controversial reactions no doubt brought this realization sharply home to him. For when he took the podium to address the National Health Advisory Council on February 11, 1992, Dr. Goodwin, then head of the Alcohol, Drug Abuse and Mental Health Administration (ADAMHA), did not know he was about to ignite a major crisis. By the time he finished his remarks, he was embroiled in a raging controversy that has raised profound questions about efforts to deal with escalating problems in urban areas. Goodwin told his audience:

> If you look, for example, at male monkeys, especially in the wild, roughly half of them survive to adulthood. The other half die by vio-lence. That is the natural way of it for males, to knock each other off and, in fact, there are some interesting evolutionary implications of that because the same hyper aggressive monkeys who kill each other are also hypersexual, so they copulate more and therefore they reproduce more to offset the fact that half of them are dying. Now, one could say that if some of the loss of social structure in this society, and particular-ly within the high impact inner city areas, has removed some of the civilizing evolutionary things that we have built up and that maybe it isn't just the careless use of the word when people call certain areas of certain cities jungles, that we may have gone back to what might be more natural, without all of the social controls that we have imposed upon ourselves as a civilization over thousands of years in our own evolution. . . . (Leary, 1992)

By associating African-Americans with monkeys and "hyper sexuality," Goodwin tapped into a wellspring of racist sentiment. He also provoked anti-racist anger. Rep. John Conyers (D-Mich.), a leading member of the Congressional Black Caucus (CBC), objected strenuously to Goodwin's re-marks and helped draft a letter signed by all 26 CBC members. It raised the issue of whether Dr. Goodwin had the necessary sensitivity and approach to continue heading a major government agency. Conyers asserted that:

> Goodwin's dangerous and simplistic explanation for the violence in our cities evokes a type of social Darwinism that has long been discredited and continues to function as a smoke screen for the separate and dis-criminatory treatment of African-Americans. It ignores a complex set of root causes of drug use and violence in our society. (Conyers, 1992)

The Congressional Black Caucus was joined in its denunciation by Senator Edward Kennedy (D-Mass.) and Congressman John Dingell (D-Mich.), as well as the 114,000 member American Psychological Association and the 137,000 member National Association of Social Workers (Editorial, 21 March 1992; Leary, 1992). Administration and most of the media reactions were more supportive of Goodwin. The *Wall Street Journal* invoked the specter of the "speech-police" and rushed to Goodwin's defense (Editorial, 9 March 1992). Although Health and Human Services Secretary Dr. Louis Sullivan criticized the remarks, he in effect rewarded Goodwin by appointing him head of the similarly influential National Institute of Mental Health–a post not requiring Senate approval or presidential appointment (Leary, 1992).

THE NATIONAL VIOLENCE INITIATIVE

And if the "monkey" remarks were not bad enough, Goodwin, during his notorious February 11 speech, casually revealed plans for a new National Violence Initiative. This proposal was slated to become the number one funding priority for the National Institute of Mental Health by 1994–the agency Goodwin would soon head. The Department of Health and Human Services (HHS) has since declined to clarify the current status of the National Violence Initiative except to deny that it includes genetic research. Due to the widespread criticism that continued to mount, the General Accounting Office, then, began looking into the entire research portfolio.

The National Violence Initiative came as a surprise to many in Congress, Rep. Conyers was upset not only with the proposal but with the lack of public disclosure surrounding it. Health and Human Services, he charged, had not been able to "supply us with the paper work on this initiative and the two African-American members of the Mental Health Advisory Panel were unfamiliar with the program" (Conyers, 1992). Under the Initiative, researchers will use alleged genetic and biochemical markers to identify potentially violent minority children as young as five for biological and behavioral interventions–including drug therapy and possibly psychosurgery–purportedly aimed at preventing later adult violence. The Initiative specifically rejects any examination of social, economic, or political questions, such as racism, poverty, or unemployment. Instead, this biomedical approach focuses heavily on the alleged role of the brain neurotransmitter, serotonin, in violence. Not coincidentally, this approach is favored by many in the medical industry. As Dr. Peter Breggin, the leading analyst in the field, has observed:

> This [approach] corresponds with the current financial interests of the pharmaceutical industry, since several drugs affecting serotonin, neurotransmission have been submitted for approval to the Food and Drug

Administration. . . . The controversial antidepressant, Prozac, is the first of these serotonergic drugs, and it has become the largest moneymaker in the pharmaceutical industry. (Breggin, 1992).

Against this backdrop, NIH provided a hefty $100,000 grant for a conference entitled "Genetic Factors in Crime: Findings, Uses and Implications." It was to be sponsored by the Institute for Philosophy and Public Policy at the University of Maryland and slated for October 1992. The promotional brochure promised that:

> Genetic research holds out the prospect of identifying individuals who may be predisposed to certain kinds of criminal conduct, of isolating environmental features which trigger those predispositions, and of treating some predispositions with drugs and unintrusive therapies. (Anderson, 1992). . . . Genetic research also gains impetus from the apparent failure of environmental approaches to crime–deterrence, diversion and rehabilitation. (Bielski, 1992)

With this last statement, the conference planners appeared to write off an entire generation, and focus exclusively on various genetic and medical solutions.

The ensuing protest caused NIH to freeze conference funding–temporarily. The objections were led by enraged African-Americans concerned that, in these dangerous times, such a project could easily be transformed into directed genocide. Their concern was not assuaged when it was revealed that Reagan appointee Marianne Mele Hall proclaimed that black and brown people are culturally or even genetically inferior. She said, in essence, that "they have been conditioned by 10,000 years of selective breeding for personal combat and the anti-work ethic of jungle freedoms, and are therefore unfit for civic life." Great Society programs just "spoiled" them, she argued, encouraging a sense of entitlement that led to laziness, drug use, and crime, particularly crime against whites (Di Leonardo, 1992).

Despite the fear that such a conference would encourage racism and broaden the path for potentially genocidal efforts, the NIH revealed that it was considering unfreezing the funds so that the conference could go forward in 1993 (Wheeler, 1992).

THE DISEASE MODEL

As previously stated, the last time an initiative such as genetic research was proposed, a firestorm of protest erupted. The context, not unlike today, stemmed from rising unemployment and poverty in the euphemistically termed "inner cities." Then Neurosurgeon William Sweet testified in 1968 before the New York state legislature that those participating in urban uprisings were suffering from brain disease (psychomotor epilepsy); i.e., blacks who rebelled against their plight could be "cured" by carving their brains or drugging them (Bird, 1968).

That same year "successful" psychosurgery was performed on California prisoners (Aarons, 1968; Breggin, 1975) and other "undesirables" (Fields, 1972). Dr. Jewell Osterholm and his associate, Dr. David Matthews, confessed to performing psychosurgery, or cingulotomies, on drug addicts, alcoholics, and "neurotics." According to Dr. Peter Breggin, "a cingulotomy is nothing more than the newest version of lobotomy. It can turn a person into a zombie. It makes the patient docile, subdued and easy to manage" (Mason, 1973). This latter description was precisely what certain U.S. elites desired for often-rebellious blacks in prison described as belligerent trouble makers, or "smart niggers."

Perhaps Sweet and his colleagues, Dr. Frank Ervin and Dr. Vernon Mark, were inspired by these programs. In any case, they went directly to Congress for funding and in 1971, the NIMH awarded them a $500,000 contract, with the Justice Department kicking in a supplemental grant. Their mission was to research the causes of violence, with particular attention to possible genetic factors and to investigate treatments, including psychosurgery and amygdalotomy (Breggin, 1975). Although public pressure eventually caused them to lose their funding, the effort to disguise racism and "black genocide" as objective research and the search for a medical "cure" for socioeconomic problems did not die.

In 1972, the state of Michigan moved forward with funding for research into controlling violence through psychosurgery and chemical castration. Fortunately this project, too, was aborted in the face of public protest. In light of similar approaches today, the words of the neurologist in charge of this 1972 project, Ernest Rodin, remain relevant. Children of "limited intelligence" tend to become violent, he suggested, when treated as "equals," and were better brought up in an "authoritarian life style." Much violence could be avoided by castrating "dumb young males. . . . It is also well known," he went on, "that human eunuchs, although at times quite scheming entrepreneurs, are not given to physical violence" (Breggin, 1975; Rodin, 1973).

The next year, the popular African-American monthly, *Ebony* reported a disturbing story about Dr. 0. J. Andy, a neurosurgeon at the University of Mississippi Medical Center, who had been performing psychosurgery, or thalamotomies. Dr. Andy revealed that the kind of brain damage that could necessitate such radical surgery might be manifested by participation in the Watts Uprising. Such people, he diagnosed, "could have abnormal pathologic brains." In addition to inducing docility, side effects to such surgery could include loss of memory, dreams and daydreams, intellectual emptiness, lack of awareness, lack of creativity, and loss of the ability to get angry. The desired result was enforced passivity for black and other communities perceived as dissident (Mason, 1973).

Fortunately, the scientific community did not rest supine in the face of this atrocity. Dr. Seymour Pollack, among others, challenged sharply the idea that participating in a civil insurrection was a sign of mental disorder (Pollack, 1967). A remarkably diverse coalition sprang up in Congress to stymie the original violence initiative that had begun 20 years earlier.

ROOTS OF THE EUGENIC SOLUTION

The historical roots of viewing rebellion against intolerable conditions as symptoms of disease go back more than a century. In the early years of the 19th century, Samuel Cartwright, a physician, argued that particular forms of mental illness caused by nerve disorders, were prevalent among slaves. Drapetomania, for example, could be diagnosed by a single symptom: the uncontrollable urge to escape from slavery. The symptoms exhibited by slaves who "suffered" from *dysathesia* aethiopica were more complex and included destroying plantation property, disobedience, talking back, fighting with their masters, or refusing to work. Despite the aura of expertise and the Latin terms, Dr. Cartwright and his 19th and 20th century counterparts were not practicing neutral science. Rather, they were providing convenient explanations that served to justify and rationalize the systemic exploitation practiced by their paymasters (Tavris, 1992).

In addition to blaming disease, some scientists (black and white) have concocted a genetic model to explain their own presumed superiority and justify exploitation and repression of their "inferiors." Such structured, organized disinformation has been part of social science since the "Age of Enlightenment." At that time, Sir Francis Galton, a cousin of Charles Darwin, coined the term eugenics for his study of how humans inherit physical and behavioral traits (Coleman, 1992).

Proponents of genetically-based inferiority hold that a whole race is biologically, irredeemably inferior. The endemic nature of this racism tells less about the individuals who promote it than about the society that fosters their rise to positions of power. Remarks like Goodwin's, comparing blacks with monkeys, are not isolated. In the wake of the 1965 Watts uprising, ultra-right Los Angeles Police Chief William Parker anticipated Goodwin's analysis by comparing African-Americans to "monkeys in a zoo" (*Time*, 1965). The L.A. police who beat Rodney King echoed the slur when they used the term "gorillas in the mist."

The genetic model has endured not because it has any scientific basis, but because it is useful. Around the turn of the century, eugenics took the ethnically-diverse U.S. by storm. It provided a "scientific" justification for stigmatizing African-Americans, Asians, and Eastern and Southern European immigrants and forcing them to work for less. Theories of genetically determined inferiority also legitimated calls for forced sterilization. Theodore Roosevelt was not alone in calling for this radical solution to social problems (Dyer, 1980). In 1907, Indiana passed the first law allowing involuntary sterilization of "confirmed criminals, idiots, imbeciles and rapists." A 1937 survey found that compulsory sterilization of so-called habitual criminals was supported strongly by "progressive" intellectuals and policymakers who were keen on applying social science to society. In 1939, the prominent Harvard anthropologist, E.A. Hooten, advocated "ruthless elimination of inferior types" and "biological housecleaning." By 1940, 30 states had sterilization laws, often for such vaguely defined crimes as "moral degeneracy"; 22 states continue to have such laws on the books (Finkelstein, 1992).

The legal basis for sterilization in the U.S. had been established by a 1927 Supreme Court decision: "[It] is far better for all the world," proclaimed Justice Oliver Wendell Holmes on the constitutionality of sterilization, "if instead of waiting to execute degenerate offspring for crime . . . , society can prevent those who are manifestly unfit from continuing their kind" (Buck v. Bell, 1927). Thus, chillingly, the U.S. preceded the Nazis down this genocidal path. It was not until 1933, that Germany approved the Nazi Eugenics Sterilization Law. It was, noted New York University Professor Norman Finkelstein, "the first fateful step toward the final solution" (Finkelstein, 1992).

The misuse of social science to justify racism had deep roots in Europe. French research in 1857 "demonstrated" that criminality was hereditary. In 1874, Richard Dugdale published a study of an Irish family he called Jukes in which he purported to trace their hereditary tendency toward crime. In Italy in 1876, in his study, *L'Uomo Delinuene*, Cesare Lombroso asserted that criminals were the products of heredity and could be recognized by features such as small restless eyes (thieves) or bright eyes and cracked voices (sex criminals). Sadly, he did not leave us with a reliable method by which a robber baron could be recognized.

Quaint and vicious as that 19th century research now appears, it differs little from the intellectual offspring it has spawned in the last years of the 20th century. Contemporary "scientists" have simply become more sophisticated in delineating alleged "markers" that predict who will become a "criminal." In the 1970s, for example, the XYY chromosomal configuration was said to be associated with crime and violence (Coleman, 1992). And as the 1992 *Violence Initiative* and the proposed Maryland conference demonstrate, the misbegotten search continues. Like Dracula, "scientific racism" continues to rise from the dead to stalk black America, in particular.

DÉJÀ VU ALL OVER AGAIN

Not only science and government, but the media have been complicit in perpetuating the mythological link between genes and crime. Shortly before Goodwin's remarks to the advisory council, *The New York Times* gave front-page coverage to a modern Jukes study. "More than half of all juvenile delinquents imprisoned in state institutions and more than a third of adult criminals in local jails and state prisons have immediate family members who have also been incarcerated, according to figures compiled by the Justice Department" (Butterfield, 1992). Backing up the article were predictable quotes from Harvard Professor Richard Herrnstein, coauthor with Charles Murry of *The Bell Curve*. His position was not unusual since he had been attacked in the past for taking stands on genes and crime perceived widely as racist. "These are stunning statistics," he said, accepting the unproven innuendo of genetic causality.

Some of the studies to determine "markers" for crime are indeed stunning. In Nebraska, seven genetic marker systems were analyzed from liquid blood and dried bloodstain specimens and submitted from various law enforcement agencies throughout the state to the Nebraska State Patrol Crime Laboratory. The reported results indicated that criminal facial and body types correlated with crime statistics ("Distribution," 1990). Thus, it could be concluded easily that darker peoples may be committing more crime, not necessarily because of socioeconomic conditions, but because of genetic predisposition. And if bad genes are the cause, the cure is certainly not education, jobs, equality of opportunity, decent health care, and an end to racism. Rather, the solution is that people of color must reproduce less, be pharmacologically or surgically "repaired," or incarcerated.

THE MEDIA AND THE MYTH OF NEUTRAL SCIENCE

Given the present climate, exploring the "nature" side of the *nature-nurture* controversy relating to crime and race is, in principle, objectionable. In the context of a declining capitalist economy suffused with racism, such research could be transmuted easily into a bludgeon wielded especially against people of color. Research is never "neutral." Who asks the questions, what questions are asked and what ones ignored, who pays for the research which interprets the results, are all subjective decisions outside the realm of "pure science?" The bias is built in.

It is not only the kind of research that is problematic, but how the elite media choose to report it that promotes and perpetuates those biases. *The New York Times*, as noted, placed on the front page a pedestrian–at best–study suggesting genetic links between race and crime. In contrast, in 1988, Prof. Delbert Elliott, of the University of Colorado-Boulder, published the results of his 10-year study demonstrating that black youth from poor sections of cities are only slightly more likely to commit crimes than are white youths from affluent neighborhoods. He factored in that the latter are more likely to have connections allowing them to escape punishment. Prof. Elliott was correct in his euphoric assertion that, "These findings have really challenged the old concepts about crime." Perhaps that is why the study received little attention (Rensberger, 1988).

TARGET:
BLACK AND BROWN YOUTH

Science, which seeks explanations for crime and violence without carefully factoring in socioeconomic conditions, is of special concern to those who see black youth as a targeted and endangered population. Inevitably, as the U.S. continues its foreign-born population input, the country will increasingly face organized challenges such as the Black Panthers and inchoate uprisings such as the one that shook Los Angeles in spring 1992. Inevitably, the government will respond. Even without a formal violence initiative, other, similarly odious initiatives have already been implemented to control young urban blacks. Despite Jesse Jackson's admonition that it is more expensive to send a youth to jail than to Yale, and to the state pen than to Penn State, incarceration has become the government's option of choice. In Baltimore, for example, on any given day in 1991, 56 percent of the city's African-American men ages 18-35 were in jail or in prison, on probation or parole, awaiting trial or sentencing, or being sought on warrants for their arrest. That year, of nearly 13,000 individuals arrested on drug charges in Baltimore, more than 11,000 were African-Americans. An African-American youth was 100 times more likely to be charged with the sale of drugs in Baltimore than a Euro-American youth (Hobbling and Generation, 1992).

California, the most populous state, reflects the national picture. The state's prison population has more than quadrupled from 22,500 inmates at the beginning of the 1900s, to over 100,000 eleven years later. In the decade ending in 1991, California had imprisoned seven times more people than during the 30 years between 1950 and 1980. There are 40,000 more inmates in California than in all of Great Britain or Germany. A disproportionate percentage of California's inmates are African-American and Latino (Zimring & Hawkins, 1992). In short, rather than attacking the roots of crime by addressing socioeconomic questions, the authorities have chosen to lock up a generation of young blacks and throw away the key.

Mass imprisonment is supplemented by another disquieting example of institutionalizing those who cannot be controlled. *Southern Exposure* documented the disproportionate number of blacks involuntarily committed to state-run mental hospitals in the southern U.S. In 1987, nearly 37 percent of those committed against their will were black. Consistently diagnosed with more severe mental illnesses than whites, they have been subjected to heavier doses of drugs and longer hospital stays as well as (in a number of southern states), indefinite commitment without judicial review. The pattern of over-institutionalizing and over-medicating blacks, the article suggests, may not be confined to the South (Ramm, 1989).

Nor–despite the fact that the greatest weight of overt repression falls on young minority males–do women escape society's "remedies." In late 1990, an editorial in the *Philadelphia Inquirer* suggested the ghastly scenario that the 5-year contraceptive, Norplant, be implanted in black women so that what was seen as their excessive number of babies would not swell the welfare rolls. Although the editors were sufficiently squeamish to acknowledge, "All right, the subject makes us uncomfortable, too," they did not jettison the macabre idea (Editorial, 1990).

PREVENTING GENOCIDE

The U.S. faces stiffer challenges abroad not only from the so-called Third World but also from erstwhile allies in Western Europe and Japan. Simultaneously, restive minorities at home have made clear–through the fires of spring in L.A.–that they will not be recumbent in the face of massive unemployment, increased homelessness, and draconian cuts in education. Norplant, ethnic weapons, psychosurgery and the *Violence Initiative* are sophisticated stratagems designed to deal with these festering problems. As has happened often in the past, fundamental socio-economic questions are redefined as biomedical problems, and these in turn are redefined as stemming from defective and possibly sub-human individuals. Hence, Goodwin's references to urban youth as "monkeys."

It is not enough for the targets to be viewed as less than human. Children as young as five years old–some of the most defenseless members of this society–are singled out for intervention. And, it is not enough for the targets to be young, they must also come from the ranks of despised and persecuted minorities. It will only be enough when minorities offer no more resistance and simply do as they are told.

Sadly, these kinds of initiatives have not disappeared. Only recently it was reported that several psychiatric experiments were being conducted on more than 100 New York City Black and Latino boys using the now banned diet drug fenfluramine. This took place at the New York State Psychiatric Institute, which is affiliated with Columbia University and Queens College of the

City University of New York. The boys were given this drug to test a theory that violent criminal behavior may be predicted by levels of certain brain chemicals (Hilts, 1998).

It appears that certain U.S. "scientists" have been taking their cues from apartheid South Africa. There the Truth and Reconciliation Commission has reported that the previous regime sought to develop "race-specific biochemical weapons targeting blacks" and other vaccines designed to make Africans infertile. There were plans to distribute infected T-shirts in the black townships to spread disease and infertility (Cockburn, 1998).

Lest some in the U.S. consider that this could never happen here, note that U.S. military researchers of biochemical warfare in the 1950s conducted race-specific experimentation. In 1980 the U.S. Army admitted that Norfolk Naval Supply Center was contaminated with infectious bacteria in 1951 to test the Navy's vulnerability to biological warfare attack. The Army disclosed that one of the bacteria types was chosen because blacks were known to be more susceptible to it than whites (Cockburn, 1998).

In short, when racism meets science a combustible brew is created. Science is not "neutral" and all scientific initiatives in a society that is not free of white supremacy must be viewed with this in mind.

REFERENCES

Aarons, L.F. (1972, February 25). Brain surgery is tested on three California convicts. *Washington Post*.

Anderson, Christopher. (1992, July 10). NIH, under fire. *Nature*.

Bielski, V. (1992, July 15). Hunting the crime gene. *San Francisco Weekly*.

Bird, D. (1968, August 14). More stress urged on cause of civil disorders. *The New York Times*.

Breggin, P., (1992). The violence initiative–A racist biomedical program for social control. *The Rights Tenet, Center for the Study of Psychiatry*. Also see (1972), Psycho-surgery for political purposes. *Duquesne Law Review* (13) 1, 841-862.

Buck v. Bell. (1927). 274 US 207.

Butterfield, F. (1992, January 31). Study finds a link to criminality. *The New York Times*.

Cockburn, A. (1998, June 21). South Africa's dirty secrets have echoes. *Los Angeles Times*.

Coleman, D. (1992, September 15). New storm brews on whether crime has roots in genes. *The New York Times*.

Conyers, J. (1992, April 1). Letter to the editor. *Wall Street Journal*.

Di Leonardo, Micaela. (1992, September 22). White lies: Rape, race and the myth of the black underclass. *Village Voice*.

Distribution of genetic markers in a Nebraska population. (1990, September). *Journal of Forensic Violence*, 35 (5),1207-1210.

Dyer, T. (1980). *Theodore Roosevelt and the idea of race*. Baton Rouge: Louisiana State University Press.

Editorial. (1990, December 12). Norplant and poverty. *Philadelphia Inquirer.*

Editorial. (1992, March 9). The speech police. *Wall Street Journal.*

Editorial. (1992, March 21). The Fred Goodwin case. *Washington Post.*

Fields, Larry. (1972, March 13). Addict who died had brain surgery to fight habit. *Philadelphia Daily News.*

Finkelstein, Norman. (1992, September 19). Letter to the editor. *The New York Times.*

Hallinan, C. (1989, April 6). Using CBW at home and abroad.

Harris, R. and Paxman, J. (1982). *A Higher Form of Killing: The Secret Story of Chemical and Biological Warfare.* New York: Hill and Wang, 266.

Hobbling Generation: Young African-American Males in the Criminal Justice System of America's Cities. (1992). Baltimore, Maryland; Alexandria, Virginia.

Hilts, P.J. (1998, April 15). Experiments on children are reviewed. *New York Times.*

Lawler, J. (1978). *IQ, Heritability and Racism.* New York: International.

Leary, W. (1992, March 8). Struggle continues over remarks by mental health official. *The New York Times.*

Mason, B.J. (1973, February). Brain surgery to control behavior: Controversial options are coming back as violence curbs. *Ebony.*

Piller, C. and Tamamoto, K. (1988). *Gene Wars: Military Control over the New Genetic Technologies.* New York: Beech Tree Books, 24, 100.

Pollack, S. (1967, November 13). Letter. *Journal of the American Medical Association.* (1965, August 27). Races. *Time.*

Ramm, D. (1989). Over committed. *Southern Exposure*, 14-17.

Rensberger, B. (1988, August 15). Study discounts race, class as studies in youth crime. *Washington Post.*

Rodin, E. (1973, July 10). A neurological appraisal of some episodic behavioral disturbances with special emphasis on aggressive outbursts. Exhibit 3 for American Orthopsychiatric Association, Kaimowitz v. Department of Mental Health, Civil No. 73-19, 434-AW. Michigan: Circuit Court, Wayne County.

Tavris, C. (1992). *The Mismeasure of Woman.* New York: Simon and Schuster, 176-177.

Wheeler, D.L. (1992, September 30). Genetic-in-crime meeting may get funds from NIH. *Chronicle of Higher Education.*

Zimring, F. and Hawkins, G. (1992). Prison population and criminal justice policy in California. *California Policy Seminar.* 4 (8), 1-7.

SECTION III:
VIOLENCE
IN EDUCATIONAL INSTITUTIONS

Violence in Predominantly White Institutions of Higher Education: Tenure and Victim Blaming

Laura J. Lee
Curtis A. Leonard

SUMMARY. This chapter examines the patterns of violence associated with the tenure process for the African American professor in tradition-

Laura J. Lee, DSW, is Associate Professor of Social Work at Fordham University, New York. She holds three degrees with a DSW from the University of Pennsylvania. Her scholarly interests include social work practice and education, diversity, school social work, and children and families. She is the author of articles on school social work, substance abuse, staff development, and African American professionals.

Curtis A. Leonard, PhD, is Professor and Dean of the School of Social Administration, Temple University, Philadelphia. He earned his PhD from the University of Pennsylvania, and has broad experience as an administrator. His scholarly interests include social work practice, administration, and social policy. He has written in the areas of diversity, administration, and organizational behavior. His current interest is on tenure and promotional issues in university systems.

The terms "African American" and "black" are used interchangeably in this chapter.

[Haworth co-indexing entry note]: "Violence in Predominantly White Institutions of Higher Education: Tenure and Victim Blaming." Lee, Laura J., and Curtis A. Leonard. Co-published simultaneously in *Journal of Human Behavior in the Social Environment* (The Haworth Social Work Practice Press, an imprint of The Haworth Press, Inc.) Vol. 4, Nos. 2/3, 2001, pp. 167-186; and: *Violence as Seen Through a Prism of Color* (ed: Letha A. (Lee) See) The Haworth Social Work Practice Press, an imprint of The Haworth Press, Inc., 2001, pp. 167-186. Single or multiple copies of this article are available for a fee from The Haworth Document Delivery Service [1-800-342-9678, 9:00 a.m. - 5:00 p.m. (EST). E-mail address: getinfo@ haworthpressinc. com].

ally white higher education institutions. In this article, violence is examined in the context of its psychological and demeaning effects. The following dimensions are reviewed: recruitment of African American faculty; the review process for tenure; the politics of tenure; socialization and orientation of faculty; junior faculty as victims and tenure denial. Intervention strategies for addressing the problems of violence are recommended. *[Article copies available for a fee from The Haworth Document Delivery Service: 1-800-342-9678. E-mail address: <getinfo@ haworthpressinc.com> Website: <http://www.HaworthPress. com> © 2001 by The Haworth Press, Inc. All rights reserved.]*

KEYWORDS. Violence, African American, white institutions, recruitment, socialization, tenure, authority, oppression, victim blaming

INTRODUCTION

African Americans scholars at predominantly white institutions of higher education are a group at risk. This endangerment is related in part to the systemic and structural violence perpetrated within universities, colleges, schools and academic departments. In spite of several decades of aggressive recruitment by white universities and colleges, the proportion of black faculty members remains miniscule (Mickelson and Oliver, 1990). Recent studies suggest that this dire situation may be more critical than had been suspected. Recruitment efforts and current faculty numbers appear stagnant. The actual overall numbers of African American faculty have gradually declined in the last two decades for all states (Myers & Wilkins, 1995). For example, in 1993 only 4.6 percent of the nation's faculty were African American. And nearly half of that number were employed at historically black colleges and universities (Phillips, 1993). But by 1995, the National Research Council reported that African Americans received only 3% of the PhD's degrees awarded in the United States (Taylor, 1998). The result has been that fewer blacks were available to enter academe as professors.

This endangerment may be accounted for in two ways. First, African Americans who were recruited during the late 1970s and early 1980s are now tenured and are nearing retirement. Moreover, new black tenure-track appointments will not replace retiring Black faculty (Wilson, 1987). Not surprising, this point has fueled debate on whether black candidates are in short supply or if this is a chronic condition of exclusion that maintains privilege of those persons already in the systems. The literature reveals there is support for both positions. Secondly, as important as those issues are, they fail to address the functional role of the tenure system as a methodical, highly structured process that has contributed to the thinning of African American faculty ranks. The tenure system then, in spite of its venerable place in higher education, is symptomatic of continued structural racism and violence in predominantly white universities of higher education. (Mickelson & Oliver, 1990).

The purpose of this chapter is to examine patterns of structural violence associated with tenure review. Specifically, this paper addresses: (1) politics, power and oppression; (2) the recruitment of African American faculty; (3) socialization of new faculty; (4) the tenure review system; (5) tenure denial and (6) recommended strategies for survival. To be sure, other minorities and women, in addition to African Americans, have undergone devastating experiences owing to the abusive nature of the tenure process. However, the focus addresses violence that is committed against African American faculty. The tenure process is viewed as a primary factor in the declining presence of African American scholars on white campuses. Scant attention has been given to African American faculty involved in tenure review and the aftermath of denial of tenure. (Farmer, 1993). Thus our focus offers a beginning basis for research and knowledge building. As such, the chapter is written from an African American perspective that draws upon the forty plus combined years of academic experience of the authors in predominantly white institutions.

WHAT IS ACADEMIC VIOLENCE?

Contemporary studies and discussions on the nature of violence have generally conceded that there is no single "act" that constitutes a definition of violence. Rather, violence is now understood as reflecting a continuum of behaviors from the most dramatic of using a handgun to eye rolling (Straus, Gelles, & Steinmetz, 1980). Moreover, within that continuum such actions as ridiculing, threatening, intimidation, and gossiping are all considered violent behavior. Although violence within academe seems unthinkable at first glance, it is the manner in which that violence is employed that holds significance (Farmer, 1993). In that regard, the tenure process, which is heavily dependent upon evaluating the qualifications of others, often becomes the conduit for the emergence of violent behaviors.

Academic violence, then, is defined as any combination of personal behaviors and systemic practices that are demeaning to African Americans in predominantly white universities and colleges as a result of the misuse of power and influence. Predominantly white institutions refer to universities and colleges where the majority of students and faculty are white (Mickelson and Oliver, 1990). With respect to blaming the victim and victimization ideology, Ryan (1978) refers to these notions as a pattern through which committed acts are justified and made palatable. Thus, the term victimization aids in understanding African American faculty's relationship to the tenure review process.

According to one published source, academic violence not only occurs in the 3,200 institutions of higher learning, but it is also well concealed (American Governing Boards of Universities and Colleges, 1985). What has been learned about violence in American universities and colleges is that it is no aberration. Its' existence is inherently perilous to the psychological well-being of African Americans (Moore, 1988). Academic violence, unlike physical violence which is reported in news articles, is basically psychological (Farmer, 1993). It is notably obvious by the seemingly innocuous statement proffered by a colleague about one's publications. It may be encountered when opinions offered by black faculty are condescendingly ignored and when ideas are received in a hostile or patronizing manner (Farmer, 1993). At a structural level, academic violence becomes even more evident when African American faculty are seldom elected to university Senates or selected as departmental chairpersons (Goldenberg, 1998). In short, African American faculty are rendered "invisible," and as a result of feeling isolated may elect to leave the university (Ellison, 1964; Gregory 1993). In brief, academic violence is a threat to one's career, can thwart ambitions, and impair scholarly intent (Blum, 1988; Shils, 1982; Moore, 1988). As a precursor to such outcomes, academic violence in its predominant mode may be found in the tenure review process.

THEORETICAL FRAMEWORK:
POLITICS, POWER AND OPPRESSION

Most, if not all organizations, seek a structure that will enable them to meet their specified goals or objectives (Child, 1972). The degree to which such goals are met becomes then a basis for determining their effectiveness (Lawrence and Lorsch, 1967). Highly bureaucratic organizations tend to rely upon tightly contained structures where authority is situated at the top and policy initiatives are carried out by subordinates lower in the organization (Weber, 1946). At the same time many other organizations, while maintaining their formality, are structured as "flat," or "loosely coupled," i.e., authority and power are diffuse and less dependent upon formal rules and position (Weick, 1976; March & Olson, 1976). Universities and colleges with their various departmental alignments conform to the latter depiction of loosely coupled systems (Weick, 1976). These systems are characterized as having ambiguous goal centers, rules are often vague, and they contain multiple levels of authority (Hasenfeld, 1983).

Within universities and colleges deans hold broad formal authority over the college and their departments. The essential work of the college is carried out within departments through their various committee structures. It is within such contrived environments that opportunity for political contest and the exercise of power emerges through faculty committees. More significantly, however, it is through the university's structural arrangements of the university that academic violence is permitted. Politics in universities, as with many other organizations, is the concern for the acquisition and distribution of scarce resources (Gummer, 1990). In academe, resources are an accessible supply of expert or technological capital that can be called upon as needed and can be exchanged for profitable support and goal attainment.

The acquisition and control over faculty as a resource by departments is often based on an "exchange theory" perspective (Asley and Sachdeva, 1984). Blau (1970) indicated that exchange theory is the basis for understanding an individual's relationship to an organization. The exchange of resources is characterized by reciprocity. Faculty provides service to the university in exchange for future tenure. That such resources may in fact be scarce is both obvious and motivational. An appreciation of the department's limited resources makes the need to conserve or barter them all the more critical. This urgency is often the impetus for the exercise of power and influence. Power emerges "when one person controls resources that another wants, cannot get elsewhere, and cannot do without" (Gummer, 1990). On the other hand, power and authority are not the same. Power is the ability to gain compliance through influence, force or coercion. Authority, however, is positional power without the intimation of force (Hall, 1982; Hasenfeld, 1983).

It is generally agreed that deans have authority within their respective colleges. This authority is given legitimacy by the dean's position (Barnard, 1938; Hasenfeld, 1983). At the same time departmental chairs and chairpersons of departmental committees also hold authority. They exercise their influence in the areas of faculty selection, nominations, retention and tenure review proceedings. In spite of the above differential authority bases, deans continue to wield substantial influence over tenure decisions. That influence can extend to the make-up of committees, appointment of the chair, and the manner in which the dean advocates for a candidate. Obviously not all deans have a style that preempts the role of faculty in tenure decisions, although the dean's judgement very often can seal a candidate's fate.

Related in part to the multiple and diffused centers of authority residing in departments, the misuse of authority can have oppressive overtones. Oppression is based on power and control which delimits the range of choices available to individuals. According to Goldenberg (1998), the concept of oppression may be understood as having four major components: (a) containment which seeks to limit physical and psychological movement; (b) expendability which infers the possibility that individuals can be replaced involuntarily; (c) compartmentalization that refers to the variety of ways individuals are prevented from developing integrative work styles; and (d) personal culpability which assigns and interprets deficits, failures and shortcomings as a predisposed force within the individual. Taken as a whole, these four oppressive components along with the misuse of power and authority represent the core of violence in academe.

This overview on the nature of politics and power provides merely one of several existing perspectives for understanding the organizational and interpersonal dynamics within academic departments. Fueled in part by a combination of differential power centers and ubiquitous structure, deans, academic department heads, and their committees exercise enormous discretion in their decision of making career options. This influence is particularly pronounced in the recruitment phase for African American candidates and in the later tenure review process. It is within this context that the emergence and perpetration of violence on the career aspirations of African American scholars will be examined.

THE RECRUITMENT OF AFRICAN AMERICAN FACULTY

A common perception is that affirmative action efforts have aided African American faculty in securing academic positions. The results are mixed. For example, in a study of 500 white and 500 minority faculty, blacks were far more likely to support affirmative action than whites. Not surprisingly, untenured African American faculty were somewhat more supportive of affirmative action than tenured African American faculty (Niemann & Dovidio, 1998). Still, a different study revealed that affirmative action policies were of limited effectiveness in producing changes in African American hiring, promotion and tenure practices in the 1990s. That study noted that affirmative action policies needed to be measured in terms of actual numbers of African Americans hired, promoted and tenured rather than by inputs or planned strategies and guidelines (Smith, 1993).

More relevant to the discussion is that African American professors enter academe with the same aspirations as their white colleagues do. They want to teach and prepare students for critical and analytical thinking. These faculty members are interested in research, advancing knowledge in their fields, and have a desire to be a part of the academic community (Newman, 1999). Clearly, a black intellectual presence on America's campuses has boded well for higher education in general and for our larger society in particular. African American faculty have enormously contributed to the reputations of their universities and colleges (Mickelson, and Oliver, 1990). In so doing they have dispelled long-standing myths concerning their intellectual ability (Wilson, 1987). Nonetheless, troublesome issues persist for African American faculty in determining what constitutes "real" access as they confront the continual and violent aspects of the "glass ceiling" (Jones, 1986).

African Americans, as with their white counterparts who are new to the academy, have little substantive knowledge of the modern university (Newman, 1999). As new faculty they rightfully should believe that their appointments have been based on the careful review of their credentials and in the fulfillment of other criteria as established by hiring committees. Yet, far too often African American faculty assume that their intellect, heavy teaching schedules, and leadership in committee work is all that is required for tenure (Newman, 1999). Of course not all newly appointed faculty (whether white or black) will necessarily warrant tenure. Nonetheless, that decision should be based on clearly defined procedures that include, but not limited to, the traditional criteria of scholarship, teaching, and service (Alger, 1999).

For new faculty the political context of the modern university is woefully under appreciated. Given the current complexities facing universities as reflected through their diversity, multiple constituencies, limited resources, and mixed consensus on goals, they are continuously engaged in "phantom" resource practices (Gummer, 1990). Even politically astute deans often become enmeshed in these exchange rituals with central administration. In those instances available resources in the form of new hires become the bargaining chips for central administration's need to control operating costs as against the educational needs of academic units.

Those administrative rituals are nothing more than transparent efforts for instilling accountability within academic units. The "unintended consequences" of such practices, however, is that deans, department heads, and committees seek alternative remedies for securing resources (Merton, 1940). In periods of fiscal austerity the use of black adjunct faculty rather than tenure line appointments is viewed as achieving both diversity needs and flexibility in operating costs. Yet, black adjunct faculty rarely moves into tenure track positions. The use of TA's (teaching assistants) is another strategy to counterbalance limited faculty lines. At other times encouraging an early tenure decision (e.g., a three-year review rather than the typical six years) could mean an administrative coup in meeting long-range departmental needs.

Each of these administrative strategies, regardless of intent, serves as a deterrent to recruiting and retaining tenure-track African American faculty. A commitment to equity in higher education is determined by the number of minority faculty which are present (Wilson, 1987). The above decisions are typically caused by an imbalance between resource allocations and existing need. But they also reflect the priorities of both the dean and central administration. New African American hires become the victims in this academic drama by those who control access to positions and resources.

THE SOCIALIZATION OF NEW FACULTY

Many new faculty members are far removed and little concerned with the above administrative scenarios. A great deal of time and energy is devoted to getting "settled," and acclimated to the demands of their new role. African American faculty may enter academe not anticipating or prepared for the socialization process required of tenure track appointees. White (1998) found that those who survive the rigors of graduate school in spite of socialization deficiencies would be handicapped entering faculty ranks. Inadequate socialization stems from many sources. The faculty person may not have had the experience of meaningful mentoring relationships during undergraduate and graduate school. Or the faculty person may not have considered the psychological cost to being the sole minority faculty. In other instances, there is a lack of attention to the nuances of verbal and non-verbal communication patterns between mainstream and black neophyte faculty members.

The inability of junior faculty to understand (let alone contend with) the psychodrama within departments can significantly effect their own retention. That situation can create expectancy levels of "cognitive dissonance" for faculty who hold idealized expectancies of the academy (Festinger, 1957). Of the many areas associated with becoming socialized into the academy's culture, none is as important for African Americans as an awareness of organizational stakeholders (Luthans, 1989). This cognitive "mapping" of key actors within the department (which includes psycho-social-political orientations) is a first step in the deconstruction and demystification of professorial realities. Uzell (1983) has suggested that both formal and informal relationships can embody exploitative and racist practices. These relational patterns may range from how teaching loads are assigned to which department committees are "recommended" and who shares lunch with the new appointee.

Clarity on the part of new African American faculty of the "who" and the "what" within their departments is premised on gaining a more precise understanding of how colleagues align themselves and the issues and conditions which support those alignments (Uzzell, 1983). To be sure, positive and long-standing departmental friendships can and do occur. They are the expected outcomes resulting from sustained academic and scholarly interests. Bonds between colleagues are important sources of support during times of stress. However, violent behavior can abruptly occur which can be perplexing, hurting, and shocking for those who misread a "friendship." New faculty orientation often does not include discussions on the contextual framework within which the tenure system operates. Four primary contextual dimensions of this process are tokenism, and unwritten performance expectations, productivity and communications.

TOKENISM

As discussed earlier African American faculty constitute a small percentage of all faculty numbers in white institutions of higher education (Phillips, 1993). Those who do exist are located more differentially within the academic hierarchy than are their white counterparts. The result of this positioning provides African American faculty with high visibility (thus improving the institution's public image) but with little autonomy or influence (power remains concentrated with white faculty). Under such conditions people of color, as with their scholarship, are "given a place but not importance" (Farmer, 1993, p. 202).

In the absence of a critical mass, token African Americans are expected to serve in a variety of roles and capacities that far exceeds the expectations for whites. Steinhorn and Diggs-Brown (1998) refer to this phenomenon as "managed tokenism." Assignments are given formally and informally but they are always made or suggested by key stakeholders. On the other hand, competing faculty stakeholders offer alternative suggestions as to when to say "no" to an assignment that carries limited status and rewards. These double messages can create dilemmas for the non-tenured professor, since they are often without the advantage of other blacks to crosscheck "paranoia" or their own reality. Small numbers of black faculty means there is no critical mass which will have an impact; there are limited network support opportunities, and fewer occasions to effect the vision of higher education and the isolation which surrounds the African American professor (Tack & Patitou, 1992). Unfortunately, it is precisely under these conditions that violence can be expertly executed.

INSTITUTIONAL EXPECTATIONS

New faculty are bombarded with voluminous information about the university upon his/her arrival. This is often supplemented by additional sources of information emanating from the college and department on mission, types of students, along with teaching and advising schedules. Yet, an important source of information is the "informal group" process or "grapevine" which provides an "introduction to the culture" of the department (Luthans, 1989). An understanding and assessment of this information is a first step in the acculturation process of African American faculty.

Formal expectations for junior faculty are scholarship, exemplary teaching and community service. The definition and weighting of those expectations varies among disciplines, departments and institutions. Maintaining good standing on the tenure track means meeting expectations, completing assignments and exhibiting decorum. The process is characterized by ambiguity. When one of the authors questioned a colleague about a blatantly inequitable treatment of another faculty member the response was: "Don't you understand? We have flexible ethics here." Equally important is the discovery of existing departmental standards of performance. Performance standards are often subsumed within the written procedures for tenure and promotion and serve as directional guides for faculty responsibilities. However, in many instances, those standards only surface during periods of review. This "rationing" of information results in a control on the availability of essential information (Lipsky, 1980).

Structural violence occurs in academia when there is absence of open discussions about standards of performance. African American faculty are at risk to the vagaries of unethical practices during the formal review stage. A lack of consensus on performance standards creates a reliance on informal data sources. While those sources may have a basis in fact, they often are the result of fragmented information, hearsay, rumor or plain gossip (Luthans, 1989). The six year tenure review period allows for opinions to be formed based on "institutional fit," and the ability to "play the game" (Robinson, 1996). One nationally prominent social work professor noted a critical standard as "is this a person with whom I want to have lunch?" Another social work educator reported that the size of her earrings and her expensive clothing were perceived as a nuisance! (See, 1999).

Unless the appointed black professor is an academic "superstar" he/she is under constant scrutiny. To be the only minority professor merely compounds the issue. Vargus (1980) notes if the professor has been brought in to appease other minorities, and to increase minority presence, or represent the black community perspective, the professor will likely fail at those expectations. Black constituents and black colleagues will question the validity of the Black professor's credentials. In a faculty search interview one applicant had the experience of having the only black professor on the interview team conspicuously turn his chair to gaze out the window throughout the interview. The candidate was not hired.

COMMUNICATION DISCREPANCIES
AND SCHOLARSHIP

Communication is the fourth socialization issue not covered in junior faculty orientation. Differential messages can create cognitive dissonance for the unsuspecting professor. African American faculty bring a sense of commitment to the principle of academic freedom and hold a sense of expectations of participating in a community of scholars. These expectations are often given a rude awakening as the professor meets head on the verbal and non-verbal communications between colleagues (Bowser et al., 1993). In a meeting on curriculum one of the authors made a suggestion bearing on the topic. The room immediately became silent. After a moment discussion resumed without acknowledging the suggestion. Later in the meeting a senior, white, male professor made the identical suggestion. His comment was met with much nodding of heads in agreement and to the excellence of his proposal. These intentional "silencing" mechanisms in addition to being an affront also conveys a sense that minority faculty ideas are not worth listening to much less using (Farmer, 1993).

According to Blum (1988) black faculty may run into roadblocks associated with minority experiences as they engage in scholarly research. Often publishing companies shy away from material that may be in conflict with the institution's notion of scholarly writing. In some institutions, qualitative research is frowned upon and number crunching is the only acceptable measure of scholarship. Collaboration and working with colleagues is valued behavior. On the other hand single authored publications have a higher valence in some departments than co-authored publications (McKay, 1998). This situation is compounded when teaching schedules, advising, liaison work and other extraneous assignments are forced upon junior faculty. Obviously, the need to engage in community service only exacerbates the black professional's sense of frustration and reinforces the violence against them.

THE TENURE REVIEW SYSTEM: AN "UNHOLY" QUEST?

The tenure system at colleges and universities represents one of the most distinctive features of higher education in the United States. Moreover, tenure and its seemingly inviolate nature have been predicated on the assurance of academic freedom to the mission of teaching and research (Statement of Principles on Academic Freedom and Tenure, 1940). Aside from critics of the tenure system few would disagree with that perspective. Tenure is specifically designed for full time faculty of a college or university who meet the criteria for teaching, scholarship, and service as established by collegial committees. The granting of tenure is for all practical purposes a contractual guarantee of lifetime employment between the university and members of the faculty. And while tenure may be revoked and lead to dismissal, such instances are few, and center on either financial exigency faced by universities or due to "incompetence, grave misconduct, and neglect of duty" (Anderson, 1992; Temple University, Faculty Guide, 1993). For many critics of tenure, those factors, along with others, are enough to suggest abolishment of the system.

The process of tenure at most universities and colleges follow fairly similar protocol (Statement of Principles, 1940). First, tenure is the consideration of three major categories: teaching, scholarship, and service. Second, within those broad parameters academic disciplines through their departments (e.g., sociology, psychology, social work, political science, etc.) determine the criteria that best exemplifies outstanding performance in the three areas (Anderson, 1992). As expected different disciplines have alternative methods for evaluating the above categories. It is, however, those three categories, which guide committee deliberations; they also provide the necessary ingredient of consistency between and among different disciplines. And finally, the process of tenure is decidedly collegial. The process begins as peer-review at the departmental and collegiate levels, and subsequently involves the dean and other central administrative review bodies.

The review for tenure is by design a rigorous process. As a prerequisite to fulfilling the mandate for excellence in teaching and research, departments engage in the evaluation of the skills, competence, and knowledge base of faculty seeking permanent positions. To do otherwise is to compromise the basic tenets that support excellence in higher education. It is that view which the tenure system purports to uphold. Typically, tenure review is initiated through elected faculty committees and guided by written procedures. The procedures vary from one department and discipline to the next. Overall, they tend to specify the format by which credentials are to be presented, the role of outside reviewers, the role of the chair, and the manner in which eligible candidates are to be received and notified. Additionally, it is expected that each discipline and department will have delineated what constitutes excellence in teaching, scholarship and service. For example, teaching evaluations may be based on observations of teaching from peer-review teams, yearly evaluations from the department chair, student evaluations of teaching, and innovations in course development. These methods for evaluating performance are used to develop more precise criteria for each category in the tenure review process. As such, criteria used by departmental review committees are established for the department as a whole rather than for specific candidates. It goes without saying, then, that departments are obliged to develop standards of performance and the means by which those standards are to be met (Alger, 1990).

As described earlier, the format of review for excellence in teaching, scholarship, and service has almost become a universal pattern for most colleges and universities (See AAUP 1940 Statement of Principles). Where variations in this format exist they are usually found in the degree of weighting given to one or more of the three categories. That is, greater significance may be given to scholarship and teaching than service, or some variation thereof. The differences in approaches to tenure review, are likely to be dictated by the discipline and the long-term structural needs of the university, than to disagreements with individual categories.

THE POLITICS OF TENURE

The above delineation of the tenure review process brings us to the more central and significant features of the system and how it may be subverted. To the extent that all candidates have been identified and informed of the review procedures, one could assume that the process, although difficult and time consuming, should proceed with a minimum of difficulty. Often that is the case. Yet, in far too many instances, where the candidate is African American the review process is a pretext for the emergence of prejudice sentiments and personal animus based on race (Bowser, 1993). In rare instances race and gender are actually minor factors in the review, and become the backdrop to long-held conflict between one or more faculty members.

Hypothetically, professor **A** finds an opportunity to obstruct professor **B**'s support for candidate **C**. This is a result of professor **B**'s previous lack of support for professor's **A** pet project. When both of these two senior professors are perceived as having influence, mediating the conflict may be difficult. Moreover, given the nature of the "power" holders' perception of influence, the chair may also encounter constraints in redirecting this imbroglio. Candidates in the above hypothetical case are clearly compromised and may have limited recourse.

For African American candidates the situation may become even more stressful. When affirmative action is viewed within the context of scarce resources and diminished opportunities African American faculty may perceive themselves at a disadvantage (Jayaratne et al., 1992). Although excellence in teaching, scholarship and service are the parameters for tenure review, race does enter the deliberations. At this level long-standing racial biases may subtly surface. The difficulty for "persons of color" and members of the review committee resides in the committee deliberations. That is, rarely if ever, are open discussions held on the subject of racial identity. This is obvious since the candidate's race is likely already known. In addition, discussions about race are a blatant violation of principles of fairness and the purpose of the review process. The exception may be found in hiring committees who seek to increase diversity in their teaching ranks by recruiting and hiring minority faculty and women. But even those efforts come perilously close to violating Title VII of the Civil Rights Act of 1964, and as amended in 1972, which bars employers from using diversity as a basis for employment decisions based on race, color, religion or national origin (Title VII, Equal Employment Opportunity Act, 1974).

Tenure review committees are more likely to discuss the candidate in terms of his/her pedagogy and research portfolio. Since the deliberations are not "racial" and presumably focused on substantive issues, individual committee members have the opportunity to discuss the candidate in subtly coded ways that reinforce their personal racial biases. A discussion and subsequent concern about a specific publication and its lack of "quality" and impact often can achieve this purpose. A similar method may be used to evaluate a journal in which a publication appears, and by inference, suggest that the article would not meet the publication standards of so-called "top-tier" journals. The dilemma is that these questions are not likely to be construed as "racist," and therefore, are equally applicable to white candidates. But how is one to judge the motivation behind the questions? Do the statements and queries offer a legitimate basis for concern? How should committee members react and evaluate such ambiguous comments? At what point did the discussion shift? Obviously, these are difficult and serious issues and do not lend themselves to simplistic answers, but can result in imposing violence against African American applicants.

Surrounding all of the potential ways in which minority candidates' applications for tenure may be negatively impacted is the principle of confidentiality. Confidentiality is basic to the tenure system as a means of ensuring fairness. Ironically, however, that same principle may tend to preserve reliance on subjectivity rather than on more valid sources of information. The degree to which confidentiality plays a harmful role is related to the chair's ability to exercise leadership in controlling the proceedings. That leadership, if executed properly, can delimit unwarranted "fishing expeditions" that have at their root racially motivated biases.

TENURE DENIAL:
VICTIM BLAMING AS RITUAL

A review yielding a negative vote or decision means tenure is denied. The "rationale" used to deny tenure is always formal and most often criteria based. In part, this rationale is in response to the potential of litigation on tenure applications. For each criterion on which the candidate fell short a "blame the victim" perspective is applied (Ryan, 1981). The formal notice of tenure denial often specifies the reasons for denial. See (1998) notes that at white universities black faculty have been denied tenure with the explanation that their work was not sufficiently quantitative and thus not rigorous. Victim blaming is almost always cloaked in perfunctory acts of concern and kindness. Committee members may express disappointment about the decision, question its fairness and even attempt to console the candidate (Honolulu Advertiser, 1999).

A faculty member's academic performance is very personal and represents that person's core reason for being. Scholarship, teaching and service all reflect the person's essence; this is embodied in their values, priorities, skills, and aspirations. Webb (1991) observes that "losing a job is not just the termination of an income that is so injurious and damaging, but one's reputation and status in the community is also affected. These adverse reactions set off a chain reaction that compounds the violence and pain and is more than some people can bear."

A fairly common psychological reaction to the denial of tenure is depression that may manifest itself in sadness, sleep deprivation, and weight loss. The person feels alone, desolate and battered. The sense of grieving is due to the assault on the self and its length may vary from person to person (Kübler-Ross, 1969). In addition to depression and other emotional responses trauma may also be experienced. Termination is indeed a traumatic act. A negative decision causes trauma simply because it was not anticipated. As a result of the trauma the emotional ordeal is magnified and may set into motion the "flight" or "fight" syndrome. In either case, the faculty person remains consumed with his/her violent ordeal.

Denial of tenure involuntarily launches the professor into an unwanted period of transition (Golan, 1981). This may mean contesting the decision through available grievance procedures, seeking employment at other universities or withdrawing from higher education altogether. If the rejected faculty member chooses to remain in academe, the tasks become finding a new position and resolution of the stigma attached to denial of tenure. Word of the African American faculty's tenure denial quickly travels. The message of "we do not want X university's rejects" has the effect of further stigmatizing and adding to the professor's distress (Goffman, 1963). The typical aftermath of the terminal year is for the university to recruit another African American professor and the process of assault begins anew.

STRATEGIES FOR SURVIVAL AND RENEWAL

The process of surviving systemic violence, while difficult, is surmountable. The following strategies may be useful in this effort. Exposure is a sure method of eliminating violence. Discussions of the African American's plight must occur in open forums, published articles, through the sharing of experiences and See (1999) suggests use of newsletters and conferences. Dickens and Dickens (1982) offer clear suggestions on how to create opportunities for success and survival at white institutions (see Figure 1). Development of a mentor relationship is a critical rung on the career ladder for black faculty in white institutions (Kalbfleisch & Davies, 1991; Strozier-Newell, 1994; Conley, 1998).

CONCLUSIONS

Entering the 21st century African American faculty at white universities and colleges have fallen well below the numbers reported in 1970 (Wilson,

1987). The earlier gains made have been eroded by new interpretations of affirmative action through court rulings, the reemergence nationally of more contentious race relations, and the lack of courage on the part of university administrations in sustaining a black intellectual presence on the nation's campuses. Equally important is the limited number of African Americans in the PhD pipeline that has traditionally served as the catalyst for black faculty.

While those factors have contributed greatly to the plight of African American faculty, the systemic and violent practices emanating from within white institutions of higher education is deemed a major structural factor in the thinning of black faculty ranks. As in the larger society race does matter in academe. Recruitment practices of deans and hiring committees, in spite of

FIGURE 1. Individual Strategies for Academic Success and Achievement

INTERNAL
- Having an effective style of one's persona
- Understanding one's responsibilities
- Managing anger as a constructive tool
- Resisting power when logic and explanation fail
- Regularly performing/documenting self-evaluation
- Developing action plan to achieve goals
- Maintaining positive self-identity

EXTERNAL
- Management of racial attitudes
- Effective working relationship with superiors and colleagues
- Identifying and cultivating resources
- Understanding non-verbal communications to break into informal networks
- Selectively choosing your battles
- Managing conflict

ENVIRONMENTAL
- Strategic management of superiors and colleagues
- Effective negotiation skills
- Passing and receiving personnel information through the grapevine
- Empowering oneself through position, expertise, influence and/or charisma
- Maintaining one's power
- Improving one's skills
- Sharing one's skills with faculty and other African Americans

Source: Dickens, F. & Dickens, J. (1982) *The Black Manager.* New York: AMACON. pp. 221-287

rhetorical intents of seeking diversity, continue to rely on strategies that are self-fulfilling and archaic. African American candidates who are hired often are tokens within their departments. Unfortunately, through a combination of isolation, heavy workloads, and suspect committee work, African American faculty find themselves enmeshed in a culture that withholds emotional and professional supports. Of course, the race factor is a hardship for white and African American professors alike. Many African American faculty leave rather than endure the emotional trauma assigned to college teaching. For those who stay, and believe that they have a fair opportunity, the tenure review system must be based on equity. The tenured African American professor in the white university has been able to use internal and external resources in support of the tenure goal even though each such survivor can show battle scars and tell war stories.

The denial of tenure for African American faculty becomes the final assault on their dignity. It is both a violent betrayal of academic expectations and the dream that now must be deferred. The tenure system is flawed not by its intents, but rather by a culture of arrogance and internecine pettiness that perpetuates conformity. For many African American junior faculty this psychodrama has become a pathological "no-win" affair. In far too many instances the old dictum of "last hired and first fired" has become "first hired and now first fired."

The systemic violence perpetuated on African American faculty at white campuses is no longer hidden. Indeed, this edited volume represents a clear signal and concrete example that the second "civil rights" revolution is under way. There is renewed resolve that "business" will not be conducted "as usual." Continued efforts must be given to exposing and eliminating abusive practices, even as African American faculty refines their negotiating skills within white institutions of higher education. That first step has already been taken.

REFERENCES

Alger, Jonathan (1990) How to recruit and promote minority faculty: Start by playing fair. AAUP Hoe Page. *Diversity and Affirmative Action in Higher Education.* Washington, DC. American Association of University Professors.

American Association of University Professors. 1940 Statement of principles on academic freedom and tenure with interpretative comments. Washington, DC.

Anderson, M. (1992). *Imposters in the Temple.* New York: Simon & Schuster. *(1986).* *Association of Governing Boards of Universities and Colleges.* p. 3

Asley, W.G., & Sachdeva, P.S. (1984). Structural sources of interorganizational power: A theoretical synthesis. *Academy of Management Review.* (1): pp.104-113.

Barnard, Chester. (1938). *The function of the executive.* Harvard U. Press.

Blau, P. (1970). Exchange Theory. In O. Grusky & G. Miller (Eds.). The Sociology of Organizations: Basic Studies. New York: The Free Press. pp. 127-148.

Blum, Debra (1988). Black woman scholar at Emory University loses three year battle to overturn tenure denial but vows to fight on. *Chronicle of Higher Education.* June 22. pp. A15-17.

Bowser, Benjamin, Auletta, Gale, & Jones, Terry (1993). *Confronting Diversity Issues on Campus.* Newbury, CA: Sage Publications.

Chids, James (1972) Organizational structure, environment and performance: The role of strategic choices. *Sociology.* (6): 2-22.

Conley, Frances (1998). *Walking Out on The Boys.* New York: Farrar, Straus & Giroux.

Dickens, F. & Dickens, J. (1982) *The Black Manager.* New York: AMACON.

Ellison, Ralph (1964). *The Invisible Man.* New York: New Amsterdam Library.

Equal Employment Opportunity Act, Title VII (1974 Amended).

Farmer, Ruth (1993). Place but not importance: The race for inclusion in academe. In J. Jams & R. Farmer (Eds.) *Spirit, Space & Survival: African American Women in (White) Academe.* New York: Routledge.

Festinger, Leon (1957). *A Theory of Cognitive Dissonance.* Stanford: Stanford U. Press.

Goffman, Erving (1963). *Stigma: Notes on a Spoiled Identity. New York: Simon & Schuster.*

Golan, Naomi (1981). *Passing Through Transitions.* New York: Free Press

Goldenberg, I. (1996). *Oppression and Social Intervention.* Chicago: Nelson-Hall.

Gordon, Mike (1999). Tenure denial shatters scholarly calm in Manoa. *The Honolulu Advertiser.* Honolulu, HI: June 17. p. 1.

Gregory, Shelia (1995). *Black Women in The Academy.* New York: University Press of America, Inc.

Gummer, Burton (1990). *The Politics of Social Administration.* Englewood Cliffs, NJ: Prentice-Hall.

Hall, Robert (1982). *Organizations: Structure and Process.* Englewood Cliffs, NJ: Prentice-Hall.

Hasenfeld, Yeheskel (1983). *Human Service Organizations.* Englewood Cliffs, NJ: Prentice-Hall.

Jayaratne, Srinka et al. (1992). African American practitioners perceptions of their supervisor's emotional support, social undermining and criticism. *Administration in Social Work.* 16(2): 27-43.

Jones, Edward (1986) Black managers: The dream deferred. *Harvard Business Review.* (64): 84-93.

Kalbfleisch, Pamela & Davies, Andrea (1991) Minorities and mentoring: Managing multicultural institutions. *Communication Education.* 4(3) July: 266-271.

Kübler-Ross, Elizabeth (1969) *On Death and Dying.* New York: Macmillan.

Lawrence, P.R. & Lorch, J.W. (1967) *Organization and Environment.* Boston: Harvard Business School, Division of Research.

Lipsky, Michael (1984) The rationing of services in street level bureaucracies. In F. Fisher & C. Sirianni (Eds.) *Organizations and Bureaucracy.* Philadelphia: Temple U. Press.

Luthans, Fred (1989) *Organization Behavior.* New York: McGraw Hill Book Co.

March, James & Olson, John (1976) *Ambiguity and Choice in Organizations.* Bergen, Norway: Universitestsforlaget.

McKay, Nellie (1998) What does genuine respect for African American literature mean? *The Chronicle of Higher Education.* July 17.

Merton, Robert K. (1940) Bureaucratic structure and personality. *Social Forces.* (18): 560-568.

Mickelson, Roslyn & Oliver, Martin (1990) Making the short list: Black candidates and the faculty recruitment process.

Moore, W. (1987-1988) Black faculty in white colleges: A dream deferred. *Educational Record.* Fall/ winter. pp. 117-121.

Newman, Kathy (1999) Nice work if you can keep it: Confessions of a junior professor. *Academe.* 85(3): May/June. Washington, DC: American Association of University Professors.

Niemann, Yolanda & Dovidio, John (1998) Tenure, race/ethnicity and attitude toward affirmative action. *Sociological Perspectives.* 41(4).

Phillips, Mary C. (1993) Tenure trap. Black Issues in Higher Education. 10(27): 42-44.

Robinson, Adriane (1996) Perceived factors that influence achievement of tenure for African American faculty at Virginia Polytechnic Institute and State University and Old Dominion University. Dissertation. Virginia Polytechnic Institute and State University.

Ryan, William (1976) *Blaming the Victim.* New York: Vintage Books.

Scott, Janny (1998) Discord turns academe's hot team cold. *The New York Times.* November 21.

See, Letha A. (Lee) (1998) Human behavior theory and the African American experience. *Journal of Human Behavior in the Social Environment.* 1(2/3).

_____ (Ed.) (2001) Violence as Seen Through a Prism of Color. *Journal of Human Behavior in the Social Environment.* 4(2/3)(4): Fall/Winter.

Shils, Edward. (1982) *The Academic Elite.* Chicago: U of Chicago Press.

Smith, E. & Jordan, M. (1993) Faculty stress and retention of junior Black faculty in U.S. universities. *Research in Higher Education.* 34(2): 229-242.

Steinhorn, Leonard & Diggs-Brown, Barbara. (1998) *By the Color of Our Skin: The Illusion of Integration and the Reality of Race.* New York: Dutton Press.

Straus, M., Gelles, R., Steinmetz, S.K. (1980) Behind closed doors: Violence in the American family. In L.A. See (Ed.) *Human Behavior in the Social Environment from an African American Perspective.* Binghamton, NY: The Haworth Press, Inc. p. 111.

Strozier-Newell, Linda (1994) Perceptions of African American male and Caucasian male senior level administrators in higher education concerning cultural characteristics, motivational factors and barriers associated with their leadership roles. Dissertation. University of Southern California.

Tack, M., Patitou, C. (1992) *Faculty Job Satisfaction: Women and Minorities in Peril.* Eric Digest. Washington, DC: Eric Clearinghouse on Higher Education.

Temple University Faculty Guide (1993).

Uzzell, Odell (1983) Black decision-makers: An exploratory study in role perceptions and role performance. *Journal of Black Studies.* 14(1): 83-98.

Vargus, Ione (1980) The Black administrator. In F. Perlmutter (Ed.) *Leadership in Social Administration*. Philadelphia: Temple U Press. 216-229.

Webb, Willie J. (1990) *Psychotrauma: The Human Injustice Crisis*. Ohio: Fairway Press.

Weber, Max (1946) *From Max Weber: Essays in Sociology*. (Eds.) H. Gerth &C.W. Mills. New York: Oxford Press.

Weick, Karen (1976) Educational organizations as loosely coupled systems. *Administrative Science Quarterly*. (21): 1-19.

White, Joseph S. (1998) Perceptions of the tenure process by Black faculty at Tennessee Board of Regents universities. Dissertation. University of Memphis.

Wilson, Reginald (1987) Recruitment and retention of minority faculty and staff. *American Association of Higher Education Bulletin*. (13) February. pp. 2-5.

Fighting Violence
in and Around Schools:
A Challenge for School Social Workers

Robert O. Washington
Freddie L. Avant

SUMMARY. Violence in and around schools in America is a common occurrence. Cliques, bullies and gangs that taunt "straight children" are attracting millions of followers who feel caught in a maze with no escape route. This article presents a model that may assist administrators and social workers to deal with violence in America's schools. *[Article copies available for a fee from The Haworth Document Delivery Service:*

Robert O. Washington, PhD, who was recently deceased following submission of this article, was President of the Social Policy Research Group, a New Orleans-based public policy organization that specializes in research, social planning and human service delivery systems. He was also Professor of Urban Planning Analysis in the College of Urban and Public Affairs at the University of New Orleans. Dr. Washington was Vice Chancellor for the Graduate Studies and Research and Dean of the Graduate School at the University of New Orleans. He was Dean of the Graduate School of Social Work, University of Illinois at Urbana-Champaign, and was Dean of the College of Social Work at the Ohio State University. He had written hundreds of articles and was one of social work's most renowned scholars.

Freddie L. Avant, BS, MSW, is Associate Professor and BSW Program Director, Stephen F. Austin State University, Nacogdoches, Texas. He is enrolled in the Jackson State PhD program. Professor Avant has extensive experience working with youth in schools, community based programs, and residential facilities in the field of mental health, mental retardation, and criminal justice. His primary research interest is rural social work practice, school social work, diversity, and social work education.

[Haworth co-indexing entry note]: "Fighting Violence in and Around Schools: A Challenge for School Social Workers." Washington, Robert O., and Freddie l. Avant. Co-published simultaneously in *Journal of Human Behavior in the Social Environment* (The Haworth Social Work Practice Press, an imprint of The Haworth Press, Inc.) Vol. 4, Nos. 2/3, 2001, pp. 187-208; and: *Violence as Seen Through a Prism of Color* (ed: Letha A. (Lee) See) The Haworth Social Work Practice Press, an imprint of The Haworth Press, Inc., 2001, pp. 187-208. Single or multiple copies of this article are available for a fee from The Haworth Document Delivery Service [1-800-342-9678, 9:00 a.m. - 5:00 p.m. (EST). E-mail address: getinfo@haworthpressinc.com].

1-800-342-9678. E-mail address: <getinfo@haworthpressinc.com> Website: <http://www.HaworthPress.com> © 2001 by The Haworth Press, Inc. All rights reserved.]

KEYWORDS. Violence, schools, school violence, ecological perspective, youth violence

INTRODUCTION

Violence in the classroom and on the schoolyard has become an unsettling state of affairs and a national menace. Unless America can keep children and youth safe from bullies, gangs and other forms of school-based violence, it cannot expect schools to achieve the performance that society demands. The recent massacre at Columbine High School in Littleton, Colorado, calls attention to the senseless violence and social problems children and youth live with in their homes, schools, and communities. The incidents of violence from Pearl, Mississippi to Jonesboro, Arkansas to Springfield, Oregon demonstrate the severity of the epidemic of gun violence among school age children. This condition undoubtedly compounds the problem of maintaining schools as safe havens for learning. However, schools are responding to the challenge of creating and maintaining a safe environment in numerous ways, ranging from increased school security to conflict-resolution classes. Criminal justice experts, behavioral psychologists, educators and social scientists have begun to pool their intellectual resources and research to fight violence in schools. Their findings show that schools with the greatest amount of success seem to be those that adopt a comprehensive program designed to prevent as well as punish criminals.

This article examines some of these results and the sociological dimensions of violence in today's society and their connections with violence in schools. It examines factors associated with an increased risk of violent behavior among school age youth that social workers are uniquely trained to treat. A basic assumption underlying the paper is that in order to change violent behavior children manifest at schools, professionals must change the environmental circumstances that influence and contribute to that behavior (Minahan, 1982; Germain, 1991; Gitterman, 1996). In other words, this paper takes an ecological perspective in examining violence in schools and subsumes that to mitigate violence in schools requires improving the quality of person-environment exchanges. This is a challenge that social workers understand, but the problem extends far beyond the domain of schools and social workers in schools. It requires the attention of the whole community.

The paper also incorporates a descriptive analysis of two school systems, one urban and one rural, in order to compare how these districts as prototypes cope with the various dimensions of violence and how each mobilizes resources to address them. It concludes with some comments regarding public policy implications and suggests leadership roles social workers can play as public advocates against violence.

AN ECOLOGICAL PERSPECTIVE

Behavioral scientists contend that violence is a cultural artifact of society and is deeply woven into the fabric of our day-to-day activities. Americans purchase toys for children that accentuate violence. They make movies that extol violence as a means of settling disputes, and write history books that celebrate frontier days when it was considered chivalrous to defend one's honor through violence. Children watch an average of 4,000 hours of television programming before they are six years old; and they watch Saturday morning programs that contain on the average, 25 acts of violence every 60 minutes. The average American child at the time of graduation from high school has spent more time watching TV–15,000 hours–than in school–11,000 hours. By age 18, the average child has witnessed approximately 250,000 acts of violence on TV and/or in films. There is no wonder then that research shows that violent behavior is linked to television viewing (*TV Guide*, August 1992).

Other social and behavioral science data show that a complex interaction or combination of predisposing factors contribute to an increased risk of violent behavior in school-age children (AACAP, 1997). These risk factors include previous aggressive or violent behavior, being the victim of physical abuse and/or sexual abuse, exposure to violence in the home and/or community, genetic (family heredity) factors, exposure to violence in media (TV, movies, etc.), use of drugs and/or alcohol, presence of firearms in home, combination of stressful family socioeconomic factors (poverty, severe deprivation, marital breakup, single parenting, unemployment, loss of support from extended family), brain damage from head injury. Other data also show that children associated with any of these factors and who manifest intense anger, frequent loss of temper or blow-ups, extreme instability and impulsiveness or frustration in routine, day-to-day activities are even more likely to be candidates for exhibiting violent behavior. What these data suggest is that children who are at risk of violent behavior must be protected from weapons of violence. This imposes a major responsibility upon the family and the home.

American's Romance with Guns

Americans have had a long-standing romance with guns. The Second Amendment of the U.S. Constitution declared, "a well regulated militia, being necessary to the security of a free State, the right of the people to keep and bear arms, shall not be infringed." This statement has served for many as mantra for the possession of arms. "Right to Carry" gun laws have increased from eight states in 1985 to 31 in 1998. A recent *Time* magazine story noted that there are almost as many firearms in the United States as there are people (estimates range from 132 million to 270 million). Millions in the U.S. believe passionately that their liberty and safety are bound up with the availability and right to carry guns. The consequence is that gun murders in the U.S. are far more common than they are in any other Western industrial nation. ". . . Guns are still very much with us, murderous little fixtures of the cultural landscape. We live with them as we live with computers or household appliances, but with more difficult circumstances–some of them paid in blood. Among the industrial nations, this cultural predicament is ours alone" (Lacayo, July 6, 1998, p. 34). Other facts seem to support this point of view. For example, from the Civil War to the present, 567,000 Americans have died in combat; but since 1920 alone, firearms have killed over one million American civilians (Pacific Center, 1994). Handgun Control, a lobbying organization in Washington, D.C., offers the following astonishing fact: "In 1996 handguns were used to murder two people in New Zealand, 15 in Japan, 30 in Great Britain, 106 in Canada, 213 in Germany and 9,390 in the United States" (Herbert, 1999). To offer another perspective, in a 1993 speech before the Congress of the United States, the Surgeon General, M. Joycelyn Elders noted that every year, over 23,000 U.S. citizens die by violent acts, an average of 65 people a day. Another 600 persons each day suffer injuries related to violence. In 1987, America spent an estimated $19.9 billion on long-term medical and mental health treatment, emergency response, productivity losses, and administration of health insurance and disability payments for injuries from violent assaults (Elder, 1993). It is not unrealistic to assume that the romanticism with guns displayed by adults may be imitated by children and youth at an early age.

VIOLENCE AMONG YOUTH

Perhaps the most devastating trend in our society is the increasing number of youth who are both perpetrators and victims of violence. According to the Office of Juvenile Justice and Delinquency Prevention (OJJDP), in 1994 almost 2.6 million youth ages 12 to 17 were victims of crime–simple and aggravated assaults, rape, and robbery (Bureau of Justice Statistics, "National Crime Victimization Survey," 1994). In the same year, an estimated 3.1 million children were reported to public welfare agencies for abuse or neglect. More than 1 million of those children were substantiated as victims. FBI data show that in 1997, about 900 murder victims were below the age of

13 and 2,100 persons under the age of 18 were murdered. This level, however, was 27% below that of the peak year of 1993, when 2,900 youth were murdered. However, this decline only returned the level to that of 1989. The number of youth murdered in the United States in 1997 was still over 300 more than in a typical year in the 1980s (Juvenile Justice Bulletin, December 1998). The OJJDP declared in 1995 that youth gun violence in our country had reached epidemic proportions. Teenagers 15-19 committed suicide in 1991; a rate of 11 per 100,000 youths in that age group. Between 1979-1991 at the rate of suicide among this group increased 31%. Firearms were used in 6 out of 10 suicides. FBI estimates show that in 1997, 68% of all murder victims were killed with firearms. Fifty-six percent of youth murdered during this period were slain with firearms. Eighteen percent of murdered youth under age 13 were killed with firearms and 84% of thirteen year olds or older were killed with firearms. No other age group had a higher incidence of murder by firearms.

James A. Fox (1998) noted that recent reports of a declining rate of violent crime in cities across the country would seem to be at odds with the growing problem of youth violence. The overall drop in crime hides the grim truth that there are actually two crime trends in America–one for the young, one for the mature–which are moving in opposite directions. He noted that from 1990-94, for example, the overall rate of murder in America changed very slightly, declining a total of four percent. For this same time period, the rate of killing at the hands of young adults, ages 18-24 rose barely two percent; however, the rate of murder committed by teenagers, ages 14-17 jumped a tragic 22 percent.

The recent surge in youth crime actually occurred while the population of teenagers was on the decline. As a consequence of the "baby boomerang" (the offspring of the baby boomers), there are now 39 million children in this country who are under the age of ten, more young children than we have had for decades. Millions of them live in poverty. Most do not have fulltime parental supervision at home guiding their development and supervising their behavior. In a short period of time, these children will reach their high-risk years. As a result we are likely to face a future wave of youth violence that will be even worse than that of the past ten years.

Many studies show that youth carrying firearms do so out of fear and protection. *A Washington Post*–ABC News poll of 500 public and private high school teenagers and 522 parents in April 1999 showed that 40% of the youth surveyed said they had fear about potentially violent classmates. In other studies, youth expressed fear about violence in their homes. The following case illustrates one circumstance under which some youth get involved in violence.

Darryl is a sixteen-year-old boy convicted of manslaughter in the fatal shooting of his mother's boyfriend. Court records and testimony show that Darryl had suffered years of beatings, neglect and verbal abuse at the hands of the boyfriend. Testimony also revealed that Darryl had asked the juvenile court to remove him from the home three days before he fatally shot the boyfriend; and the child protective worker claimed she didn't do anything because "her hands were tied." When challenged in court as to why she did not intervene after the child told her he was being abused, the worker replied, "He didn't have any visible bruises. I was afraid that if it were investigated, the case would have been closed. There would have been no documentation and it could have gotten worse for him."

Court testimony showed that Darryl admitted shooting the boyfriend in the chest with a .22 caliber rifle as the man strode through the door of the house, but said it was the escalation of abuse and a beating a few hours earlier that precipitated the incident at that time. It seems that both the court and the social service system missed the clue in this case.

VIOLENCE IN AND AROUND SCHOOLS

The incidence of crime and violence in society and its spillover in schools have generated public concern about how safe schools are as places of learning. According to the Centers for Disease Control and Prevention, at least 2.5 million U.S. teens carry guns, knives, razors, and clubs; and some undoubtedly bring these weapons to schools. For example, Lockwood (1997), in his study of violence among middle schools and high school students, found that the number of incidents at school among both boys and girls was about the same. He noted, however, that while boys tended to fight mainly with other boys, girls were involved in almost as many fights with boys as with other girls. Moreover, girls were the offenders in all incidents in which knives were used. Most of these knife incidents began in school.

Inspired by then-President George Bush and the nation's governors during an "Education Summit" in 1989, the 1991 National Education Goals Panel Report, *Building a Nation of Learners*, declared that one of its goals was that by the year 2000 "all schools in America will be free of drugs and violence and the unauthorized presence of firearms and alcohol, and offer a disciplined environment that is conducive to learning." In response to this goal, the Congress passed the Safe and Drug Free Schools and Communities Act of 1994, which provides the support for drug and violence prevention programs. As part of this legislation, the National Center for Education Statistics (NCES) is required to collect data to determine the "frequency, seriousness, and incidence of violence in elementary and secondary schools." A report jointly issued by the U.S. Department of Education and the U.S. Department of Justice concludes, "While this fear is understandable, it is not based on fact." The report, the First Annual report on School Safety (1998) points to research that shows students in school today are not significantly more likely to be victimized than in previous years. A smaller percentage of students bring weapons to school today than earlier this decade. Yet, certain conditions exist that make students more vulnerable to crime, according to the report. Students in the upper grades are more likely to be victims of or witness crimes, and more serious crimes, in school than younger students. More crime occurs in larger schools than in smaller ones. The presence of gangs and drugs also increases the chance of crime occurring at school–and gang activity has increased "sharply" notes the report.

The NCES study, conducted in the spring of 1997, found that in 1996-97, 10 percent of all public schools reported at least one serious violent crime to the police or a law enforcement representative. Serious violent crimes included murder, rape or other types of sexual battery, suicide, physical attacks or fights with a weapon, or robbery. Another 47 percent of the public schools reported a less serious violent or nonviolent crime. These included physical attacks or fights without a weapon, theft/larceny, and vandalism. Elementary schools were much less likely than either middle or high schools to report any type of crime in 1996-97. They were much more likely to report vandalism (31 percent) than any of the other crimes (19 percent or less). At the middle and high school levels, physical attacks or fights without a weapon were generally the most commonly reported crimes in 1996-97 (9 and 8 per 1,000 students). Theft or larceny was more common at the high school than the middle school level (6 versus 4 per 1,000 students).

According to the National Education Goals Panel Weekly (April 28, 1999) the State of Vermont is a top-performing state on two Goal 7 indicators: student victimization and physical fights. In 1997, Vermont was one of the top 10 states, with only 7% of public high school students reporting that they were threatened or injured with a weapon on school property during the past 12 months. In that same year, Vermont was one of the top nine states on a related indicator, with only 13% of public high school students reporting that they were in a physical fight on school property at least once during the past 12 months.

Small schools in communities where people know each other help. Vermont earned top scores in the area of safe schools, claims Bill Reedy, legal counsel for the state Department of Education. He also lauds the state's "Building Effective Supports for Teaching," or BEST, program for keeping the peace at schools. Now in its fifth year, BEST is "designed to help schools develop effective strategies and interventions to anticipate, prevent, and respond to the challenging behaviors of students." BEST began in response to complaints by principals that between 5% and 8% of the student population was so disruptive they "interrupted the flow of instruction," explains Richard Boltax, coordinator of BEST.

South Dakota is a top-performing state in three Goal 7 indicators examined by the NEGP Weekly. Only 5% of South Dakota public high school students reported in 1997 that they were threatened or injured with a weapon on school property during the past 12 months, the best record of any state in the nation. Only eleven percent of public high school students reported during that year that they were in a physical fight on school property, earning South Dakota the best record of any state on this indicator as well. South Dakota ties with its neighbor, North Dakota, as the highest-performing state in the area of teacher victimization. Only 8% of its public school teachers reported that they were threatened or physically attacked by a student from their school during the past 12 months. Other states in which school violence has been reduced in the last few years include Nevada, Connecticut, Hawaii, Iowa, Kentucky, Montana, New York and Wyoming.

Violent Deaths at Schools

Seventy-six students were murdered or committed suicide at schools during the combined 1992-93 and 1993-94 school years. Non-student violent deaths also occurred at schools. For example, during this period there were 105 violent deaths at schools of which 29 involved non-students (NCES, 1998).

Most murders and suicides among young people occurred while they were away from school. In the combined 1992 and 1993 calendar years, 7,357 young people ages 5 through 19 were murdered, and 4,366 committed suicide. Students in urban schools had a higher level of risk of violent death at school than their peers in suburban or rural schools. The estimated rate of school-associated violent death for students in urban schools was nine times greater than the rate for students in rural schools and two times greater than for students in suburban schools during the combined 1992-93 and 1993-94 school years. During the 1995 school term, more than 6,000 students were expelled from schools for carrying guns and other weapons (OJJPP, 1995). Vice President Gore, in reporting these data to the nation, noted "our schools must be places where kids aren't bullied, where guns and other weapons do not get through the door, where teachers aren't threatened, and where drugs are not used, sold or distributed." The period of 1997-99 saw an escalation in violent deaths in U.S. schools. For example, of the 2,100 killings of youth in 1997, thirty-four occurred at schools (NCES, 1998). Wire reports show that in 1998 there were nine persons killed by youths, two of whom were teachers and thirty-four persons were wounded. In 1999 there were 24 violent deaths on school grounds. These included the aforementioned 15 fatalities from the massacre at Columbine High School and three suicides. The scenes of the carnage in the Colorado killings, which included the two suspected killers, who were students at the high school, will perhaps become the most devastating school massacre for the next half-century. This crime was perpetrated by members of a hate group, "the Trench Coat Mafia," that secretly stashed weapons and explosive devices, including three bombs, a semi-automatic rifle and pistol and two shotguns in the school.

Copycat Behavior

Following the unanticipated tragedy of the April 20, 1999, Columbine massacre was a series of copycat activities, which occurred within the next ten days. Following is a list:

- A 13-year-old boy from Bakersfield, California, was arrested in class on a tip from classmates with a loaded .40 caliber semi-automatic hand gun and a hit list of thirty names, with the notation that "they deserved to die."
- In Enid, Oklahoma, a school employee found a pipe bomb in a restroom of a high school on April 29th. Classes were canceled for the 1,400 students and state troopers disabled the device.
- A middle school in Petaluma, north of San Francisco, was evacuated after five devices that looked like pipe bombs were found in the backpacks of two students. The devices were detonated but contained no explosive material.
- In Taber, Alberta, Canada, a 14-year-old boy was charged with first-degree murder and attempted murder in a shooting at a Canadian high school on April 28th that left one student dead and another seriously wounded.
- In Tavares, Florida, a 10th grader playing hooky on April 29th was arrested for making bomb threats that led to the evacuation of 27,000 students from 39 schools in central Florida.
- A threat found on the Internet led school officials in Sylvania, Ohio, to close two high schools for the day so the buildings could be searched. An 18-year-old student was charged with threatening that Sylvania would be the target of a rampage worse than the shootings in Colorado. The student later told detectives the computer message was a prank.
- A day after the bomb threats at seven Detroit schools, the police chief promised to prosecute those involved in such incidents.

These incidents illustrate how susceptible youth are to trends and fads and how quickly they imitate events and activities that they think may bring them popularity or notoriety.

Gangs and Bullies

Most studies show that while gang-related activities are still prominent on school campuses, there has been a decrease in gang-related killings stemming from disputes between individual students or groups of students. In 1992-93, the earliest school year for which figures are available, there were 18 deaths due to disputes between students and 13 gang-related slayings. During the 1998-99 school year, there have been three deaths related to disputes and one gang-related death. The Colorado deaths were called hate-crime killings because witnesses said the shooters targeted groups, specifically athletes and blacks. Many students claim that shootings on campus are a result of a combination of things–including being the victim of school bullies. While bullies play a role in the behavior of school shooters (the Pearl, Mississippi case) seldom is the shooting directed at bullies. The case of the teenager, Luke Woodham, and the slayings of his mother, his girlfriend with whom he had just broken up and her friend, and the wounding of seven students at Pearl High School, Mississippi–". . . I started shooting anybody I could find"–is an example of how and why bullied students associate with gangs.

Luke was a student who suffered from obesity and felt that his mother" . . . always never loved me" and believed that "nobody cared about me." Luke joined a gang known as the Kroth, which participated in satanic rites and assisted him in plotting the high school murders. He explained, "My whole life, . . . I just felt outcast, alone. Finally, I found some people who wanted to be my friends. I was just trying to find hope in a hopeless world, man." At his trial, Luke admitted that students picked on him". . . it just made me really mad. It just really hurts. I didn't feel like I really had any friends. Nobody I could trust. So I kept everything inside of me. I didn't care about the world."

This case is a glaring example of why schools must control gang activities and protect vulnerable children from bullies on school grounds. Social workers' understanding of the person-in-environmental concept can play an important role in nipping gang and bully activities in the bud .

We turn now and examine how two school systems, one urban and one rural, attempt to create non-violent schools.

THE ORLEANS PARISH SCHOOL DISTRICT

The New Orleans Public School District serves a community of 496,000 citizens, of which a breakdown in population includes 62% blacks, 35%

whites and 3%, others. Thirty-eight percent of the persons living in the parish have an income below the poverty level, with 28% of the households headed by females. The school system houses 81,000 students on 126 campuses with a faculty of 4,935 (1997-98). Average attendance during the 1997-98 term (the period for which we were able to get the latest data) was 90.33%. Total dropout reported to the State Board of Elementary and Secondary School Education for this period was 3,761 which is roughly 4.5%. There were 10,225 out-of-school suspensions and 709 out-of-school expulsions. The school system is financed by a parish mileage rate of 165.0, which nets an annual school budget of $591,942,000.

The New Orleans school district adopted a zero-tolerance policy in 1996–a policy, which suspends and arrests students who fight on school property, and it charges them with a misdemeanor crime. In 1995-96, there were 93 weapons incidents on campuses and 6,408 student injuries; however, it is not clear how many of these injuries resulted from acts of violence.

CONDITIONS MANDATED BY THE STATE

The New Orleans school board violence prevention and mitigation program is governed principally by mandates from the State Superintendent of Education and a 35-member statewide School Safety Task Force composed of students, teachers, principals, supervisors, superintendents, school board members, parents, law enforcement representatives, corrections officials, district attorneys, and municipal officials which was established in response to the 1997-98 New Orleans school board.

In early 1998, the "Safe Schools" Task Force issued a report, which set forth eleven action steps to guide safe schools programs in the state. Each school must:

- Design and adopt a code of conduct with explicit attention to violent behavior
- Design or adopt a zero tolerance policy for violent behavior
- Conduct a critical review of discipline statutes, regulations, rules, policies, and procedures
- Develop a security plan
- Install specific security measures
- Develop a climate of trust among students with adults
- Develop student leadership to create safe and violence-free campuses
- Develop high quality staff training programs on safe school topics
- Increase priority for guidance and counseling services to students
- Develop early and quick intervention for troubled students
- Improve community support for safe schools

Following is a brief description of programs and activities adopted by the New Orleans public schools to respond to these mandates.

Project Respect

This program began in 1995 and has two primary goals: (1) to create a climate in schools that enables all students to be treated with respect and (2) to create ways for students to share their concerns without retribution or intimidation. The program maintains zero tolerance of students who mistreat or bully other students because of ethnicity, gender, race, etc. It also provides a mechanism for students to report troubling situations and threats of violence. Since the initiation of the program, zero tolerance policies have increased suspensions and expulsions and in a recent survey, 84% of the students surveyed said that they felt safer in their respective school campuses because of Project Respect.

Project Respect includes such activities as Peer Assistance Conferences where students learn the skills of self-awareness, communication, and conflict resolution. Conflict resolution strategies include programs in anger management, peer leadership, and mediation.

Code of Conduct

Each school site is expected to develop a code of conduct developed through a participatory process involving students, educators, community members, and parents. The code must give explicit attention to violent behavior and each student's responsibility toward safety and deterrence of violence. All 126 campuses have adopted codes of conduct, which were printed and distributed to students.

Zero Tolerance Policy

All New Orleans schools maintain a zero tolerance policy for violent behavior. The policy is developed with extensive public participation and sets the tone for the respective schools and governs policies and procedures for student conflicts, code of conduct, and school regulations, which are posted and consistently enforced. Depending upon the school, these rules and regulations may govern dress codes, and contraband items, display of gang colors or bandannas, beepers, portable phones and radios.

According to the National Center for Education Statistics (1998) more than 75% of the schools in its study had zero tolerance policies on violence, use of tobacco, alcohol, drugs and weapons other than firearms. Most students who violate these standards are suspended or expelled. The New Orleans zero tolerance policy is similar to the national norm. Most studies show, however, that with respect to suspension and expulsions zero tolerance policies that offer suspended and expelled students alternative education during their period away from regular school are more effective. Although zero tolerance programs have proved to be effective, they are financially burdensome in some rural school districts. For example, in rural communities outside of New Orleans, zero tolerance policies have placed additional pressures on juvenile justice systems that are already so over burdened that they only have resources to focus on punishment rather than rehabilitation.

Metal Detectors and Searches

Zero tolerance policies in some New Orleans schools permit metal detectors or searches at their respective schools as part of its security and anti-violence procedures. Because of the limitations imposed upon search and seizures by the fourth amendment, all schools are advised to adhere to the guidelines developed by the National Association of Attorneys General on search and seizure.

Security Measures

Schools in the district use a variety of measures to secure their schools. For example, all schools in the district require visitors to sign in before traveling through the building. All schools have a closed campus policy that prohibits most students from leaving campus during school hours. Most high schools in the district conduct drug sweeps. In addition to the security measures described above, all of the schools have police or other law enforcement representatives stationed in the schools.

"Teen Life Counts"

In 1998, the New Orleans school system along with surrounding school systems participated in a program run by the Jewish Family Service called "Teen Life Counts" which provided counseling to teens concerning suicide and depression and to serve as an adult support system. During this two-year period, 6,500 teenagers participated in this program.

School Social Work Services

In addition to the service mentioned, a staff of 87 district-side school social workers operate the following programs and services:

- Crisis prevention
- Crisis trauma response teams

- Manage death and grief groups
- Manage behavior modification groups
- Parent focus groups
- Alternative placement programs

In collaboration with the Department of Family Services, the social work program participated in the following:

- Prevention, Education Advocates (PEA)
- Peer mediation
- Remove, Recover and Referral programs ("Triple R")
- Teen court

NACOGDOCHES INDEPENDENT SCHOOL DISTRICT

Nacogdoches Independent School District (NISD), located in Nacogdoches, Texas is a rural school district that serves a community of 30,000 citizens. The population breakdown includes 16% Africans Americans, 75% Caucasian, 7% Hispanics and 1% others. Twenty-five percent of the persons living in the county and 31% of the city's population have incomes below the poverty level. NISD is the largest school district in Nacogdoches County and has a population of 59,250. According to the 1996-97 NISD District Snapshot, the district serves 6,281 students on eight campuses with a faculty of 412 (TEA, 1997a). The ethnic breakdown of students consists of 48% Caucasian, 32% African American, 19% Hispanic, and Other (1%) (TEA,1997a). Fifty-five percent of the students are considered economically disadvantaged, 13% receive special education services, 6% participated in the gifted and talented program, and 10% participated in the bilingual English as a Second Language (ESL) education program (1997a). The ethnic breakdown for faculty includes 84% Caucasian, 12% African American, and 4% Hispanic (TEA, 1997a).

According to Texas Education Agency Report (1998) there were 200,000 assaults against students and 18,000 assaults against teachers in the last four academic years throughout the state. In addition, there were more than 31,000 weapons confiscated in schools across Texas. In 1995 there were 3.6 million students on 6,343 campuses in 1,046 school districts statewide attending public schools in Texas. According to the Texas Independent School District Crime Report (1995), in 1993-94 about 3% of the 1,456 districts were considered urban (major urban and other central city districts), while 66% of all Texas students are enrolled in rural school districts. These data indicated the significance and importance of developing violence prevention programs in rural school districts in Texas. Moreover, considering the recent increase in violent and homicidal incidents in school systems across the nation, it is very apparent that many are occurring in rural communities. Consequently, rural as well as urban school districts must place emphasis on prevention to create a safe learning environment for their students.

Conditions Mandated by the State

According to the Texas Independent School District Crime Report (April 1995), the overall crime rates in Texas are decreasing, but violent crime rates among juveniles are on the increase. A recent Policy Research Report (TEA, 1994) highlights major themes emerging from state-level efforts to address the problems of juvenile crime and crime in the schools, including the exchange of information among schools, law enforcement, and juvenile probation agencies, and the need for accurate record keeping and reporting of misconduct at school, particularly criminal misconduct. These factors contributed to the state-level initiative Senate Resolution 879 which was passed during the 73rd session of the Texas legislature. This resolution directed the Texas Department of Public Safety (DPS) and Texas Education Agency (TEA) to conduct a study of crime on public school campuses, and to collaborate in developing a statewide crime reporting system for schools. This information is helpful to school districts in evaluating, developing and implementing prevention programs to eradicate violence.

Following is a brief description of programs and activities adopted by the Nacogdoches Independent School District to respond to violence prevention.

The Nacogdoches Independent School District
(NISD) Police Department

The NISD Police Department is an independent, fully functioning law enforcement agency, receiving its authority from the Texas Education Code. Nacogdoches ISD police officers have full authority to provide protection any place in the school district, which is comprised of approximately 262.5 square miles. The NISD Police Department works closely with the Nacogdoches Police Department on cases occurring within their overlapping jurisdiction.

NISD's first attempt at addressing school violence occurred in the Fall of 1993. Prior to this, the school had been experiencing an increase in violence throughout the district. The final incident that influenced the district to take action occurred when a 14 year old student fired a .220 caliber pistol on the junior high campus as a threat to another student. According to the Nacogdoches Daily Morning News, the local newspaper, following this incident school administrators recommended to the school board that a school district police department be established as a proactive measure to prevent student violence on campus. The NISD Police Department was officially initiated on November 1, 1993 with the hiring of one police officer. Within five years the department has expanded to include one Chief of Police, two police officers, one security guard, and a dispatcher/secretary (NISD Report 1998). According to a department report (1993), it was formed with three objectives:

- To be an enforcement agency
- To be a preventive measure and to deter violence on campuses
- To educate students about laws and school policy, to teach them about the consequences of not obeying laws and to teach students about the dangers of drug and alcohol abuse.

Today the Police Department's philosophy is very similar to its founding objectives and covers two major areas:

Intervention. The NISD police officers are assigned to individual campuses and spend their days interacting with students and faculty. Officers are available to meet with students or faculty on an individual or group basis to help resolve issues concerning criminal matters or situations that may result in a criminal offense. By building rapport with the students, officers often find out about offenses before they take place and are therefore able to intervene quickly.

Education. The NISD police officers engage in classroom instruction by speaking on a variety of law enforcement topics that are geared towards the different grade levels. Officers also make presentations to faculty, parents, and community groups on various topics. One of the officers is assigned to teach safety-related issues to the elementary and intermediate campuses.

Types of Offenses Identified in District

Tables 1, 2, and 3 illustrate the nature and extent of violence in NISD during the period of 1995 through 1998. These data are separated into three major categories: crimes against person, crimes against property, and common crimes.

In 1997-98 NISD found the majority of its problems were confined to the senior high school campus. This was consistent with findings from data across the state. The most common offenses were disorderly conduct (28%), simple assault (18%), disruption (15%) and theft (12%). There was a 50% decrease in thefts, 38% decrease in disorderly conduct and a 68% decrease in simple assaults since 1995.

TABLE 1. Crimes Against Persons

Criminal Offenses	95/96	96/97	97/98
Assault (Simple)	34	13	23
Assault (Aggravated)	2	3	0
Disorderly Conduct	53	34	20
Robbery	0	1	0
Deadly Conduct	0	0	0
Retaliation	3	6	2
Terroristic Threat	1	2	3

TABLE 2. Crimes Against Property

Criminal Offenses	95/96	96/97	97/98
Theft (Misdemeanor)	24	15	12
Theft (Felony)	0	1	0
Criminal Mischief (Misdemeanor)	5	3	2
Criminal Mischief (Felony)	1	0	0

TABLE 3. NISD Common Offenses Three Year Report, 95-98

Offense	Number Reported
Disorderly Conduct	107
Simple Assault	70
Disruption (Public School/Transportation)	57
Theft (Misdemeanor)	51
Narcotics/Drug Cases (Misdemeanor)	17
Criminal Trespass	13
Retaliation	11

INTERVENTION PROGRAMS

Zero Tolerance Policy

NISD implemented zero-tolerance policies in 1995 to deal with the increase in campus violence. This policy requires that if you throw a punch, you will be suspended. This approach is very effective in decreasing the number of violent incidents on the campuses.

Crime Stoppers Focusing on Teen Violence

The NISD Police Department was instrumental in starting the Teen Crime Stoppers program, which has aided in the enforcement and intervention of crime related problems (*NISD Police Report* 1999). It works collaboratively with NISD and serves as the eyes and ears throughout the school district. According to the Nacogdoches Police Department, the organization enhances the awareness of teen violence by focusing on the Crime of the Week in this area, and it encourages anonymous reporting by participants and provides information on gang activity and other crimes committed by young people.

Dragon Dads

NISD is very much aware of the importance of family involvement. Special attention has been given to the inclusion of fathers in the educational environment. Because of the increase in violence at the Junior High School, specifically during the last six weeks of school, a volunteer program was implemented to encourage the father's presence on campus. Dragon Dads, which was named for the NISD mascot, started in 1993. Dads of students attending the Junior High School patrol the campus. Dragon Dads' primary goal is to provide a parental presence on the Junior High campus during the peak hours of unstructured activities like the beginning of school, lunch times and dismissal times, and strive for positive contacts with all students while building rapport, establishing trust, and adding to the overall educational environment.

Accelerated Learning Center

Some students have a difficult time learning in the regular academic environment for a variety of reasons. Typically, these students become two or three grade levels behind, drop out of school or their attendance is so sporadic it is virtually impossible for them to graduate. Many times their frustration predisposes them to violence. The Accelerated Learning Center (ALC) was developed and implemented in an attempt to address the needs of students who fall in this category. ALC is an educational environment where students receive self-paced instruction. Students are required to meet credit requirements in all subjects taught. The curriculum, however, is designed to allow flexibility in terms of timeliness for completion of grade level units. This flexibility also allows the student who has failed due to poor attendance and lack of performance to demonstrate mastery of learning objectives and moves ahead more rapidly to regain an academic standing in an appropriate grade level. Another advantage of this flexibility is that it enables the slow learner to acquire skills at his/her own pace without the stigma of retention (ALC Manual).

Social Workers in the School Systems

Nacogdoches Independent School District hired its first social worker six years ago to work with the school's teen pregnancy program. Later, three more social workers were added to work with the growing number of Hispanic students to address their needs and concerns. The job description calls for the NISD social worker to work with other personnel and students in the identification and alleviation of any barriers that interfere with students' learning. School social workers are in a unique position to help students, parents, and communities more effectively prevent or reduce violent incidents and to minimize further damage after a crisis has occurred (NASW 1999). School social workers practice principles support a comprehensive school plan that focuses on prevention, with ongoing activities at the elementary, middle, and high school levels. They also place emphasis on strategies that deal with the dual threat of drugs and violence, peer mediation, curricula geared toward violence prevention, dress codes, pupil and staff ID cards, alternative schools, and alternative disciplinary actions.

CONCLUSION

This paper set out to provide an overview of the ubiquity of violence in American society and its consequential impact on schools. What our findings show is that all sectors of the community must be committed to making schools safe. Schools that have ties to families, human service agencies, community police, faith-based organizations and the community at large–creating what some experts call social capital–are more likely to develop safe schools. Social workers play a primary role in creating social control and developing links and partnerships with other stakeholders in the community.

Historically, schools have been the first line of defense against societal acts, which violate societal norms and values. They teach children how to become socially competent and they socialize children to society's values. School officials, particularly social workers in schools see evidence that clearly point to the social and economic deprivations so many youngsters live with. The argument proposed here is that social workers, because they are uniquely trained to understand and mitigate the ill effect of those conditions that breed poverty, ignorance and violence, must therefore provide stronger leadership in advocating the elimination of these conditions. They can begin by taking a stronger, affirmative position on the proposition that bearing children is not a sine quo non for raising them. Raising children in poverty is in and of itself violence. Society must rescue children early from home and environmental conditions that condemn them to violence.

Recent acts of violence in schools demonstrate that violence and economic deprivation are not the only culprits contributing to violence. Although most social scientists argue that our knowledge is inadequate in isolating causes and cures of violence, what is indisputable is that Ritalin and Prozac offer little long-term hope. What is called for is more professional attention and more competent parenting supported at the highest levels of government. Children's problems start early and thus early childhood intervention programs and services must be devised to aid children before they reach schools. Social workers are uniquely trained to help schools and communities understand that violence is contextual. Violent and aggressive behavior as an expression of emotion may have many antecedent factors–factors that exist with the school, the home, and the larger social environment. In fact, for those children who are at risk of participating in aggression and violence, certain environments or situations can serve as the trigger of these activities. Some children may act out if stress becomes too great, if they lack positive coping skills, and if they have learned to react with aggression (U.S. Dept of Education, August 1998).

What the authors argue further is that violence in children must be controlled before they begin school. Nationally recognized programs such as "Parents as Teachers" and "First Step to Success" have demonstrated that early intervention can reduce anti-social behavior.

Study findings from the comparison of the Orleans Parish school district with the Nacogdoches Independent School District were consistent with what is generally known about rural and urban school districts. Both rural and urban districts have a common set of intervention programs that include zero tolerance policies, formation of prevention and response teams, codes of conduct, dispute resolution strategies, monitoring school campuses during school hours, building safety audits, opportunities for students to express concerns, to name a few. The NPSD has more and a greater variety of programs that address violence prevention than Nacogdoches. This is in part because urban school programs serve more children and have a significantly larger budget for dealing with violence prevention. Rural programs such as Nacogdoches have limited funds for education and devote most of them to instruction.

Establishing school district police forces to handle non-instructional problems is a growing trend in both rural and urban school districts. According to the National School Safety Center in California, many school districts have developed their own independent police force. Organized police forces on campus presents its own set of problems. In schools where the police force creates a fortress or suppressive atmosphere, it may impair the learning environment.

In the final analysis, social work intervention in schools can be reduced to a home-school-community liaison paradigm. While this is an important function, social workers in schools cannot be all things to all people in controlling violence in schools. Theirs is a partnership that requires resources and collaborative efforts of the total community. There is room, however, for social workers to enhance their leadership in this partnership. The profession must exert more influence in the public policy arena. For example, the national leadership can join forces with local chapters to advocate expanding the corps of social workers in school. Local chapters can join school social workers in improving social capital in the community.

REFERENCES

Allen-gagen, B., Sickmund, M., and Snyder, H.N. (1994). *Juveniles and Violence: Juvenile Offending and Victimization*. Fact Sheet #19. Washington, D.C.: Office of Juvenile Prevention, U.S. Department of Justice.

American Academy of Child and Adolescent Psychiatry (1996). "Facts for Families: Understanding Violent Behavior in Children and Adolescents." Fact No. 55 *<http://www.aacup.org/factsfam/behavior.htm>*.

Elders, M. Joycelyn, M.D. Surgeon General, U.S. Public Health Service, Statement before the U.S. House of Representatives Committee on Energy and Commence, Subcommittee on Telecommunications and Finance, Wednesday, September 15, 1993.

Fox, James A. (1998) *Trends in Juvenile Violence: A Report to the U.S. Attorney General on Current and Future Rates of Juvenile Offenders*.

Germain, Carol B. (1990, 1991) "An Ecological Perspective on Social Work in Schools," in R. Constable et al. (Eds) *School Social Work Practice and Research Perspectives*, 2nd edition, Chicago: Lyceum.

Gitterman A. (1996) "Life Model theory and Social Work Treatment," in F.J. Turner (Ed.), *Social Work Treatment*, 4th edition. New York: Free Press.

Gould Publication of Texas Inc. (1998). Texas criminal law and motor vehicle handbook. Longwood, FL: Author.

Herbert, Bob (1999) "Are We a Land Addicted to Violence," *The New York Times*.

Kaufman, Phillip; Chen, Xianglei et al. (1998). *Indicators of School Crime and Safety, 1998*. Washington, D.C.: Bureau of Justice Statistics, U.S. Department of Justice.

Lacayo, Richard. "Still Under the Gun" *Time*, July 6, 1998.

Lockwood, Daniel (1997). Violence among middle school and high school students. Washington, D.C.: U.S. Dept of Justice, Office of Justice Programs, National Institute of Justice.

Minahan, Ann (1982) *Encyclopedia of Social Work*. Washington, D.C., NASW.

Nacogdoches Independent School District. (1998). Accelerated learning center standards [Brochure]. Nacogdoches, TX: Author.

Nacogdoches Independent School District. (1998). Dragon dads [Brochure]. Nacogdoches, TX: Author.

Nacogdoches Independent School District. (June, 1998). Nacogdoches Independent School District crime report (Three Year Summary). Nacogdoches, TX: Author.

National Association of Social Workers. (1999). National Association of Social Workers Position Paper: Reauthorization of the Elementary and Secondary Education Act. Washington, D.C.: Author

National Association of Social Workers/Arkansas. (1998) School Social Workers November/December. Chapters 10, 7.

National Center for Educational Statistics (1998) "Violence and Discipline Problems in the U.S. Public Schools: 1996-97"

Office of Juvenile Justice and Delinquency Prevention (1995). "Reducing Gun Violence: A Summary of Programs and Initiatives.

Pacific Center for Violence Prevention. (1994). *Preventing Youth Violence: Reducing Access to Firearms* (Policy paper funded by The California Wellness Foundation). San Francisco, CA: Pacific Center for Violence Prevention.

Texas Education Agency (1997). Texas Independent School District Crime Report (April 1995). Austin, TX: Author.

Texas Education Agency (1997). *Texas Independent School District Crime Report.*

Texas Education Agency. (1997a). District snapshot. [on-line]. Available: <*www.tea. state.tx.us./cgi/broker?_service=hogg&_program=melinda.snap97ds*>.

T.V. Guide, August 22, 1993, p. 9.

U.S. Department of Education (1998). *Early Warning, Timely Response: A Guide to Safe Schools.*

SECTION IV:
VIOLENCE IN RELATIONSHIPS

The Structural Components of Violence in Black Male-Female Relationships

Delores P. Aldridge
Willa Hemmons

SUMMARY. An Afrocentric perspective provides a point of departure for the understanding of black male-female violence. American society

Delores P. Aldridge, PhD, is Grace Towns Hamilton Professor of Sociology at Emory University, and Associate Director of the Women's Health Service Research, School of Medicine. Dr. Aldridge was founding director of the first BA degree granting Black Studies program in the South. She has more than 150 publications including six books in the fields of sociology, social work, and African American Studies. Two of her books, *Focusing: Black Male-Female Relationships* and *Black Male-Female Relationships: A Resource Book of Selected Materials* address the thorny problem of black male-female relationships.

Willa Hemmons, PhD, JD, received her Doctorate in Sociology from Case-Western Reserve University and her law degree (JD) from the University of Illinois. She is currently employed in Cleveland State University's Department of Social Work. Her book, *Black Women in the New World Order*, published by Prager Press (1996), foretold the elimination of the welfare state as it has been known for 60 years. She is completing a new book, which looks at the manner in which the legal system deals with African American men and women who are engaged in domestic violence issues.

[Haworth co-indexing entry note]: "The Structural Components of Violence in Black Male-Female Relationships." Aldridge, Delores P., and Willa Hemmons. Co-published simultaneously in *Journal of Human Behavior in the Social Environment* (The Haworth Social Work Practice Press, an imprint of The Haworth Press, Inc.) Vol. 4, No. 4, 2001, pp. 209-226; and: *Violence as Seen Through a Prism of Color* (ed: Letha A. (Lee) See) The Haworth Social Work Practice Press, an imprint of The Haworth Press, Inc., 2001, pp. 209-226. Single or multiple copies of this article are available for a fee from The Haworth Document Delivery Service [1-800-342-9678, 9:00 a.m. - 5:00 p.m. (EST). E-mail address: getinfo@haworthpressinc.com].

209

is defined by and derived from core or dominant values, which have differentially impacted its diverse populations. The Lens Model presented in this discourse focuses on these values as being counterproductive for black male-female relationships. Capitalism, racism, sexism and the Judeo-Christian ethic comprise the four-prong institutional or structural value components of the Lens Model. This dynamic framework is instructive as it helps social scientists view domestic violence in black adult relationships from a different perspective. The Lens Model has a connection to the "scientific method" which purports detachment, objectivity, and impartiality. *[Article copies available for a fee from The Haworth Document Delivery Service: 1-800-342-9678. E-mail address: <getinfo@haworthpressinc.com> Website: <http://www.HaworthPress.com> © 2001 by The Haworth Press, Inc. All rights reserved.]*

KEYWORDS. Lens model, violence, black male-female relationships, Afrocentric, capitalism, racism, sexism Judeo-Christian

While the literature coupling African Americans (blacks) to a discussion of violence is prolific, the scholarship analyzing the dynamics of this relationship is scant (Aldridge, 1984, 1989, 1991; Rodgers-Rose, 1985). Even more tenuous is a ubiquitous reluctance on the part of social scientists to effect a discourse on both topics–violence and black male-female relationships in the context of their societal background (Aldridge, 1991). An analysis of this crucial relationship is essential to forming an accurate and comprehensive understanding of how, why, and when, the purported interpersonal relationships between blacks of opposite gender explode or erode into violence. More tenuous still, is for the analysis of the relationship between black men and women to take place within a well formulated conceptual or theoretical framework. Indeed, it has been convenient for conventional European-centered wisdom to have discussions surrounding violence between black men and women devoid of a framework that includes institutional or structural factors. Such a non-contextual discourse lends itself to a "blaming the victim" (Ryan, 1965). In this perspective the female who is often the "victim" bears the burden of being at fault for her vulnerable situation. The fact that her circumstances, far from being situational are more the result of structural factors in the society are camouflaged by focusing primarily on Eurocentric, interpersonal "Who shot Jane?" or "dumping ground" approaches.

Karenga's (1982) observations of black male-female relationships are most instructive. He points out that these interactions are no more problem ridden than those of other groups, and that life itself, is characterized by conflicts and problem-solving. Further, he asserts that, while many black male-female relationships are sufficiently healthy, enough are in trouble or non-existent to require that they undergo a sustained critical examination. Karenga cautions however, that criticism of black male-female relationships must always be accompanied by an in-depth review of the structure of our social system, complete with all of the variables that shape and mold individuals and ultimately their relationships.

The purpose of this paper is to focus primarily on structural factors that influence violence in black male-female relations. In this writing the Lens Model as a conceptual framework for analyzing these relations will be presented. Specifically, the paper will (1) look at the structural components that impinge upon black male-female relationships (2) present the Lens Model and discuss its usefulness as a theoretical construct (3) against the backdrop of the Lens model suggestions are made on ways of improving the relations between black males and females who must occupy the same space and live in harmony in our society.

DEFINITION OF TERMS

Any discourse on black male-female relationships must ultimately begin with a definition of terms. For some, conjuring up memories of past atrocities involved in these relationships is not a useful undertaking–mainly because this is a calamitous, or at worse, hurtful process. However, an examination of past behavior can be cleansing and assist one to move on with ones life.

Obviously the definition of black males and females require no explanation however "relationships" and "violence" are more troublesome concepts and require specific, definitive, and candid appraisal. In this writing "relationships" transcends beyond courtship, dating, and even marriage, and moves into a threshold of connectedness, where there is no subordination but unity of purpose effected between two individuals.

Violence is defined in many ways. However, in the criminological literature it is more often defined in terms of physical force or as a threat or use of physical force–all of which may stem from antecedent acts and consequences to attain a given end (Steinmetz & Straus, 1974). In this paper however, the force of strained relationships, aggression, cruelty, and destructive acts may be directly traceable to the structure of the American society, which has severely oppressed each partner in black relationships. Although there are still ambiguities in the literature, the true definitions of "relationships" and "violence" seem to lie just below the surface of a paradigm, which will later be described as the "Lens Model."

In examining the societal structure that often impinge on black male and female relationships it can be seen that American society is defined by and derived from core or dominant values which have differentially impacted diverse sub cultural groups. The Lens perspective presented in this discourse focuses on these values as being counter-productive for an understanding of black male-female relationships. In the structure of this society, capitalism, racism, sexism, and the Judeo-Christian ethic comprise the four-pronged institutional or structural value components that focus on an understanding of these relationships (see Figure 1). The numbers in Figure 1 represent blurred vision of focusing on relationships. Twenty-twenty (20/20) vision represents optimum focusing on any given object or subject. As the vision moves away from 20/20, the focusing loses varying degrees of sharpness. By focusing on capitalism racism, sexism and Judeo-christianism, analysis can sharpen or assess differing degrees of impact on male-female relationships among African Americans and for that matter on any group in the American society.

FIGURE 1. The Lens Model for Focusing on Black Male-Female Relationships

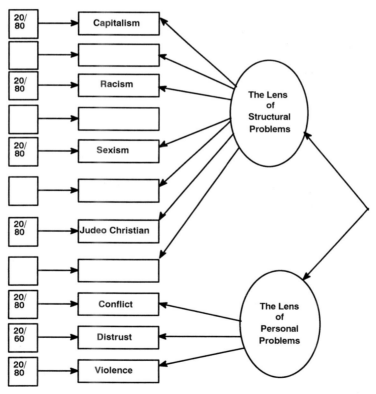

Note: This Figure was designed by Dr. Delores P. Aldridge for the book, *Violence as Seen Through a Prism of Color*. The Haworth Press , Inc., New York, NY

Capitalism, which drives our economic system, may be defined as a socio-economic system in which private ownership is the primary means of satisfying human needs. One salient characteristic of capitalism is a strong and continuous pursuit of profit (Weber, 1950; Tawney, 1952; Marable, 1980). In capitalism the private ownership of goods and services tend to shape the view of human relationships. For example, the conceptual conversion of human beings into organisms to be owned, or an attitude in which people may subconsciously be viewed as objects for purchase and resale.

Concomitantly, racism may be defined as a system of denial and deformation of a people's history and humanity based primarily on the specious concept of race and hierarchies of races. Racism in America was born out of European feelings of racial superiority and is bred within the moral contradiction between Christian concepts and economic beliefs (see for example Max Weber, *The Protestant Ethic and the Spirit of Capitalism*, 1950; Richard Tawney, *Religion and the Rise of Capitalism*, 1952). Slavery, on the other hand, represented an attempt at dehumanization of both the proponents as well as those who were enslaved. Slavery with its extension of private ownership and profit fragmented and almost destroyed the realm of all human relationships in this country. In the contemporary world new colonialism links capitalism and racism. Moreover, this linkage may result in any effort to effect an even-handed approach. In this context it is important to understand that capitalism and racism extended their influence from the interpersonal system to the world system of human organization.

Sexism is the political oriented "ism" that results in using gender or sex as an ascriptive and primary determinant in the establishment, maintenance, explanation, and justification of relationships and exchanges. As a system, sexism is composed of assumptions and acts, theories and practices that imply and impose unequal, oppressive and exploitative relationships based upon gender. When capitalism and racism are reviewed for their effects upon human relationships–especially between black men and women it seems that sexism converts those who are dominated into an assortment of subordinate feminine stereotypes. Thus, they are sitting targets to be "used."

The Judeo-Christian tradition is a religiously weighted system, which has its roots in Judaism and Christianity and draws heavily upon the cultural and social experiences of Jews, whites, and males. This tradition encourages identification with males as leaders and heroes. But more importantly, it emphasizes the leader-hero tradition as being one with elite males and their socio-economic experiences. Thus, any man who does not comply with such an ideal falls short within the value construct of American society. It is clear therefore, that a racist, sexist, capitalist, and Judeo-Christian macro systems form the basic structural value framework for analyzing black male-female relationships from an African centered or Afrocentric perspective (Aldridge, 1989).

AN AFRICAN CENTERED
OR AFROCENTRIC PERSPECTIVE

In the journey toward the development of the "Lens Model" one needs to define all theoretical tenets that led to the development of this new framework. Thus, at this juncture the specific characteristics of the Afrocentric paradigm must be delineated. Nobles (1972, 1980), Ak'bar (1984), Baldwin (1985) and Asante (1988) are among contemporary scholars who have identified an Afrocentric approach to philosophy and human behavior and contributed to the development of what has come to be known as the Afrocentric paradigm. Daly, Jennings, Beckett and Leashore (1995), describe the Afrocentric approach as proposing that in Africa "cultural humanity is viewed as a collective rather than as individuals and that this collective view is expressed as shared concern and responsibility for the well being of others (Ak'bar, 1984; Houston, 1990; Schiele, 1990).

The Afrocentric paradigm acknowledges feeling and emotions as well as rational and logical ways of thinking equally. Friendship, compassion, sharing, honesty, courage and self control are among the other virtues of this perspective. It follows therefore, that the need for an African centered perspective in studying issues involving an African people is particularly salient when the dynamics of black male-female violence is so deeply mired in the function of the U.S. criminal justice system that is specifically designed to separate these two groups.

Ostensively, since blacks in the United States are an identified "out group," the function of the criminal justice system for black people whether alleged perpetrator or victim, has essentially been oppressive. Hence, it is postulated that the structural components of U.S. social institutions, including the criminal justice system prohibits the improvement of black male-female relationships. The resulting effects are expressed as violence, misuse, mistrust, and exploitation. Furthermore, given the fact that both black men and women are an oppressed people, the harsh ramifications of societal policies and practices work a severe hardship upon the black community in general, and negate the notion of communism or "I am, because we are."

We turn now to a discussion of the "Lens Model"–which is the centerpiece of this paper.

THE LENS MODEL:
A CONCEPTUAL FRAME FOR ANALYZING
BLACK MALE-FEMALE RELATIONSHIPS

A considerable number of writings have been published by African American and other scholars in which they painstakingly addressed the breakdown in black male-female relationships from an Afrocentric perspective. These writings have been thought-provoking, intellectually challenging, and polemics have emerged over whether the relationships have been unequal, exploitative, oppressive, and irresponsible. The writings although brilliant have produced no specific conceptual framework to help explain various aspects of the relationship phenomenon. The "Lens Model," an unadorned framework seeks to close that gap in the literature. It has multifaceted or eclectic attributes, which makes it a paradigm with considerable usefulness. This model was developed by first asking this question, what is a model? The literature is consistent neither in nominal definitions of what a model "is," nor in usage of the term. For example, Rubenstein and Haberstroh's (1960) discussing of organizational theory argue that a model gives "intuitive understanding" of the thing modeled; a model comes first, and contributes to theory-building. Miller (1956) reserves the term model for a formal identity between a conceptual system and an empirical one. According to Levi-Strauss (1953), social structure is to be regarded as a model. The Lens Model then, is a biological perspective that is crafted or "taylor-made" for usage in the social sciences. It selects the eyes as organs that can be employed to show that Black males and females must see the same objects through the same pair of lens.

According to the Webster Dictionary, a lens is a piece of glass, or other transparent object with two curved surfaces, or one plane and one curved surface. When brought together, the lens spread rays of light which is remarkably intensified. Using this definition we see that historically, black men and women have experienced considerable difficulty attempting to come together or spread rays of light that will not "frost over," become cloudy, murky, or "out of focus." However, the societal structure has prevented them from shining bright as a couple by using every device at their disposal to keep the two groups divided to include amicable relations that would normally be exchanged with each other. The Lens Model addresses that deficiency.

OPERATIONALIZING THE LENS MODEL

A description of the Lens paradigm sets the stage for operationalizing this framework against a backdrop of black male-female relationships. Accordingly, the following postulates are set forth for this framework: (1) Black males and females have different experiences in a racist society and these are grossly different than those of white Americans. Accordingly, their relations must be viewed through the lens of a societal structure, which has denied and deformed Black history and humanity based on the specious concept of race and hierarchies of race. (2) Sexual and gender oppression is as much an issue for African American males as it is for females. Thus racism and sexism are interactive and inseparable as both are oppressed in similar yet different ways. Indeed, an analysis of sexism and the experiences of black men is needed which is different from the requirements of white men. The solving of this problem will cause the societal Lens to retract, and for vision to become clear. (3) Demographics is a primary determinant of developing relationships between African American males and females. There is a significant shortage of available desirable, educated black men for black women to choose as mates. This shortage poses significant problems and prohibits the converging of the lens. (4) Capitalism and racism have generated situational inequities and sustained oppression which define the lives of people of African descent. These twin banes prohibit the Lens of society from becoming equal. (5) God-Christianism rooted in the social and cultural experiences of Jews, and white men provide images and models that encourage identification with white men as leaders/heroes. Thus, acting superior to black men and women causes the lens of the latter groups to misfocus, as they mistake the superficial for "the real thing." As can be seen therefore, the Lens Model analysis is a simple and comprehensive construct that enables practitioners to organize information in terms of relevance for change. It highlights areas of uncertainty, determines the feasibility of change and evaluates alternative interventions. At the heart of this paradigm is the conception that one's view of a situation is a dynamic force, and it is more powerful if black men and women will join efforts and work as a team rather than as separate entities. The case study of Mr. X will exemplify the point made so far in this writing.

THE CASE OF MR. X

Mr. X is a 26 year old African American male and father of Doris X, age 6. He was accused of threatening his former wife, age 26 and her boyfriend when he came to pick up Doris for her regular weekly visit with him. As a dialysis patient Mr. X had never entered the home of his former wife and generally parked in the driveway and signaled by honking his car horn that he was waiting for Doris. The child's mother had always been ambivalent about the court-ordered visitation rights, so on this day she had not prepared Doris for the visit with her father. After waiting in the car for an hour, Mr. X blew his horn continuously. Mrs. X's boyfriend came to the door and ordered him to cease the intimidation. Mr. X cursed at his former wife's boyfriend. At that point Mrs. X came to the door and he cursed at her also. Mrs. X called the police who arrested Mr. X for disturbing the peace. His bond was set at $30,000. Upon being contacted and apprized of the case a private attorney interviewed the arresting officers, the investigating detectives, bondspersons, judges, bailiffs and court clerks. Her objective was to obtain a release order for Mr. X to receive his dialysis treatment in order to prevent his lapsing into a coma. He was temporarily released with the understanding that he could not leave the city. This restriction made it impossible for Mr. X to travel to the college campus located 6 miles outside the city limit, where he had been awarded a scholarship to pursue a baccalaureate degree. The judge hearing the case had established a reputation as one who was "death on domestic violence." In fact, witness-victim advocates and court watchers who frequented his courtroom, as well as other judges in the municipality, remarked that he would not retract one inch from the "letter of the law." Mr. X's court appearance was not uneventful. During one session Mrs. X's boyfriend became unruly, had to be restrained, and was escorted from the court hearing. On another occasion the boy friend attempted to physically assail Mr. X, the dialysis defendant. Finally, the case was dismissed. So, a case, which had begun in April 1999, had dragged on until mid-September. By then it was too late for Mr. X to properly enroll in college, so he lost his scholarship. He had not been able to comply with the conditions of his scholarship, which included making a campus visit, meeting with his advisor, and completing the final documents for enrollment. Additionally, with his arrest and court trial Mr. X could no longer write on this financial packet that he had no arrest record. Thus, with this case a young African man's potential for improving his life was sabotaged by a black female that was caught in the crossfire–between a former husband, and a current lover.

If the Lens Model were applied to this case from a purely Eurocentric view to Black male-female violence one would most likely overlook the nuances of how the law was applied in this case. Such an approach would perhaps ignore how the economic, health and educational forces affected, in this instance the legal stages of the purported violence in black male-female relationships. Moreover, it is clear that there is need to consider the dynamics of black male-female violence from a Lens perspective–which means this case would be "viewed" through Afrocentric lens which take into consideration all the variables associated with this family conflict.

Many authors have written eloquently on the importance of black male-female relationships (Aldridge, 1989; Gordon, 1987; Hare & Hare, 1989; hooks, 1990, 1992; Karenga, 1982; Rodgers-Rose and Rodgers, 1985). In sum, the perspective of these scholars is that if people have been oppressed, fragmented, dehumanized and demeaned by external forces, ultimately they will begin to oppress, fragment dehumanize each other (Fanon, 1967). Aldridge, (1991) Rodgers-Rose and Rodgers (1985) point out that black male-female relationships from the inception of their formation have been influenced by their societal environment. Karenga (1982) posits:

> Any criticism of black male-female relationships is at the same time and in equal measure a criticism of U. S. society which has shaped them to fit and function "properly" in it. For social conditions create both social consciousness and social conduct and failure to recognize this

can lead one to see racial defects where social ones are more real and relevant. (1982, p. 291)

Results such as the case described above have led to the conclusion that, alternatives other than incrimination in situations involving domestic disputes should be pursued (Davis, 1998). This might be particularly true where the evidence is equivocal in as much as there is no apparent physical or mental injury and the situation has not been continuous. As Aldridge (1989 p. 291) further indicates in her discourse:

Analyses of the major defects in black male female relationships clearly reveal their social rather than genetic or purely personal basis. Thus, to understand the negatives of the relationship we must understand the negative characteristics of society which have shaped them.

ECONOMIC DISPARITY EXPERIENCED BY AFRICAN AMERICANS

In the case narrated above, the violence stemming from faulty black male-female relationships can be viewed from the Lens Model. This means that Mr. X's case could be viewed through lens that take into consideration the structural value systems of capitalism and racism which often operate synchronistically with each other (Glasglow, 1981; Mills, 1959; Marable, 1980). For example, the economic disadvantages faced by black men and women were exacerbated during the last half of the twentieth century. According to the U.S. Bureau of Census, the median family income of a family with a white male head of household was approximately $39,000 while a black female headed household results in a loss of almost $7,000 a year in annual income or $32,000. In general, families headed by blacks have incomes, which are sixty percent of those of whites (see Table 1). Thus, if the income disadvantages suffered by black family members is not frustrating, the prospects for economic improvement is serious. Despite, relatively low unemployment rates in the 1990s black people still were twice as likely to be unemployed than whites. Further, their poverty rates around the country averaged three times that of their white counterparts. Continuing this economic backdrop of black interpersonal dynamics, African Americans are still very conclusively shut out of the higher managerial levels of corporate operations not to speak of ownership (Blackwell, 1991, p. 303). Even if they mind their " P's" and "Q's" they still will be unable to move beyond token levels of middle management responsibility.

The economic situation is exacerbated likewise by two major political trends in the U. S. that plagued the post Reagan-Bush era (Blackwell, 1991,

TABLE 1. Comparison of Summary Measures of Income by Selected Characteristics: 1989, 1997, and 1998

Characteristics	1998 Median Income			Median Income in 1997 (in 1998 dollars)		Median Income in 1989 (in 1996 dollars)		Percent Change in Real Income 1997 to 1998		Percent Change in Real Income 1989-1996	
	Number (1,000)	Value (dollars)	90-percent confidence interval(+/−) (dollars)	Value (dollars)	90-percent confidence interval(+/−) (dollars)	Value (dollars)	90-percent confidence interval(+/−) (dollars)	Percent change	90-percent confidence interval(+/−)	Percent change	90-percent confidence interval(−/−)
HOUSEHOLDS											
All households	103,874	38,885	378	37,581	286	37,884	344	*3.5	0.6	*2.6	0.8
Type of Household											
Family Households	71,535	47,469	410	46,053	394	45,343	413	*3.1	0.6	*4.7	0.8
Married-couple families	54,770	54,276	530	52,486	388	50,702	458	*3.4	0.6	*7.0	0.9
Female householder, no husband present	12,789	24,393	655	23,399	657	22,662	603	*4.2	2.0	*7.6	2.5
Male householder no wife present	3,976	39,414	1,633	37,205	1,201	39,717	1,607	*5.9	2.8	−0.8	3.5
Non-family households	32,339	23,441	467	22,043	347	22,568	363	*6.3	1.3	*3.9	1.6
Female householder	17,971	18,615	462	17,887	428	18,143	474	*4.1	1.8	2.6	2.2
Male householder	14,368	30,414	559	28,022	770	29,489	660	*8.5	1.8	*3.1	1.8
Race and Hispanic Origin of Householder											
All races[1]	103,874	38,885	378	37,581	286	37,884	344	*3.5	0.6	*2.6	0.8
White	87,212	40,912	336	39,579	413	39,852	320	*3.4	0.7	*2.7	0.7
Non-Hispanic White	78,577	42,439	401	41,209	354	40,792	331	*3.0	0.6	*4.0	0.8
Black	12,579	25,351	653	25,440	720	23,950	789	−0.3	1.9	*5.8	2.7
Asian and Pacific Islander	3,306	46,637	2,135	45,954	2,102	47,337	2,007	1.5	3.2	−1.5	3.7
Hispanic Origin[2]	9,060	28,330	896	27,043	792	28,631	882	*4.8	1.8	−1.1	2.7

TABLE 1 (continued)

Characteristics	1998 Median Income — Number (1,000)	1998 Median Income — Value (dollars)	1998 Median Income — 90-percent confidence interval(+/−) (dollars)	Median Income in 1997 (in 1998 dollars) — Value (dollars)	Median Income in 1997 (in 1998 dollars) — 90-percent confidence interval(+/−) (dollars)	Median Income in 1989 (in 1996 dollars) — Value (dollars)	Median Income in 1989 (in 1996 dollars) — 90-percent confidence interval(+/−) (dollars)	Percent Change in Real Income 1997-1998 — Percent change	Percent Change in Real Income 1997-1998 — 90-percent confidence interval(+/−)	Percent Change in Real Income 1989-1996 — Percent change	Percent Change in Real Income 1989-1996 — 90-percent confidence interval(−/−)
Age of Householder											
15 to 24 years	5,770	23,564	730	22,935	822	24,401	755	2.7	2.4	−3.4	2.6
25 to 34 years	18,819	40,069	696	38,769	755	39,041	603	*3.4	1.3	*2.6	1.5
35 to 44 years	23,968	48,451	730	47,081	637	49,310	675	*2.9	1.0	−1.7	1.2
45 to 54 years	20,158	54,148	877	52,683	727	54,575	893	*2.8	1.1	−0.8	1.4
55 to 64 years	13,571	43,167	989	42,000	783	40,569	878	*2.8	1.5	*6.4	2.0
65 years and over	21,589	21,729	395	21,064	406	20,719	381	*3.1	1.3	*4.9	1.0
Nativity of the Householder											
Native born	92,853	39,677	390	38,229	381	(NA)	(NA)	*3.8	0.7	(X)	(X)
Foreign born	11,021	32,963	1,230	31,806	802	(NA)	(NA)	3.6	2.3	(X)	(X)
Naturalized citizen	4,877	41,028	1,808	(NA)	(NA)	(NA)	(NA)	(X)	(X)	(X)	(X)
Not a citizen	6,143	28,278	1,199	27,379	971	(NA)	(NA)	3.3	2.8	(X)	(X)
Region											
Northeast	19,877	40,634	772	39,535	877	42,780	709	*2.8	1.5	*−5.0	1.5
Midwest	24,489	40,609	600	38,913	747	37,685	642	*4.4	1.3	*7.8	1.5
South	36,959	35,797	500	34,880	580	33,933	471	*2.6	1.1	*5.5	1.0
West	22,549	40,983	681	39,772	910	40,705	696	*3.0	1.4	0.7	1.4
Residence											
Inside metropolitan areas	83,441	40,983	352	39,994	448	40,776	346	*2.5	0.7	0.5	0.7
Inside central cities	32,144	33,151	638	32,039	456	(NA)	(NA)	*3.5	1.5	(X)	(X)
Outside central cities	51,297	46,402	512	45,364	568	(NA)	(NA)	*2.3	0.8	(X)	(X)
Outside metropolitan areas	20,433	32,022	630	30,525	690	29,393	636	*4.9	1.5	*8.9	1.9

EARNINGS OF FULL-TIME YEAR-ROUND WORKERS										
Male	56,951	35,345	219	34,199	535	35,727	242	*3.4	0.9	*−1.1	0.6
Female	38,785	25,862	194	25,362	259	24,614	270	*2.0	0.7	*5.1	0.9
PER CAPITA INCOME										
All races[1]	271,743	20,120	199	19,541	202	18,280	132	*3.0	0.7	*10.1	0.8
White	223,294	21,394	237	20,743	239	19,385	147	*3.1	0.8	*10.4	0.8
Non-Hispanic White	193,074	22,952	268	22,246	271	(NA)	(NA)	*3.2	0.9	(X)	(X)
Black	35,070	12,957	322	12,543	346	11,406	253	*3.3	1.9	*13.6	2.1
Asian and Pacific Islander	10,897	18,709	1,094	18,510	1,128	(NA)	(NA)	1.1	4.4	(X)	(X)
Hispanic origin[2]	31,689	11,434	410	10,941	393	10,770	294	*4.5	2.3	*6.2	2.7

*Statistically significant change at the 90-percent confidence level.
¹Revised to reflect the population distribution reported in the 1990 census.

[1]Data for American Indians, Eskimos, and Aleuts are not shown separately. Data for this population group are not tabulated from the CPS because of its small size.
[2]Hispanics may be of any race.

Source: U.S. Census Bureau, Current Population Survey, March 1990, 1998, and 1999.

p. 483); One was the rampant explosion of criminal legislation that resulted in the incarceration of almost two million people, over half of whom are non-white origin, and the creation of essentially, a police state with a policy of zero tolerance for any black "deviance." The second was the passage of federal and state "Personal Responsibility" laws obliterating 'welfare' [as we know it], (42 U.S.C. Sec. 601-678). However, no matter how inadequately implemented, eradicating any "safety-net" for millions of children–many of whom are non-white is brutal.

Hence, capitalism is the Lens through which any meaningful discussion of black male-female violence must take into consideration. Black male-female relations do not take place in isolation. They are formed maintained and /or destroyed in a structural societal setting which is not geared toward the well-being of black men, black women, and their children.

Oliver (1994) suggests that the incidence of domestic violence is probably higher among blacks than among whites. Theoretically, he agrees with other African American scholars who contend that the major reason for difference is due to racism. The internal devaluation of their self-worth as individuals precipitates much black violence, against other blacks, and toward whites. Since many blacks have little power to effect change, overwhelming obstacles and hopelessness produce high levels of frustration. Poussaint, (1972, p. 72) states that . . . "frustrated men may beat their wives in order to feel manly, and these violent acts are an outlet for a desperate struggle against feelings of inferiority." Oliver (1994), observes that beatings and arguments precipitated by a husband seem to occur particularly when there is a discrepancy between the demands on him as a provider and his ability to meet those demands. Consequently, his response is an attempt to regain status and respect for his role as head of the family.

Aldridge (1991) has employed her Lens Model to underscore how the structural/value systems of capitalism, racism, sexism and Judeo-Christianism impose strains upon black male-female relationships. However, additional insights may be revealing. Karenga (1982, p. 292) contends that with blacks strains can be expressed "as a transformation of the relationship into what can be described as 'connections.'" He posits that the four basic relationships in the U.S., and by extension between black males and females are: (1) the cash connection (2) the flesh connection (3) the force connection and (4) the dependency connection. But the economic motif in the U. S. transforms everyone into a commodity including the black female who according to this perspective can be bought and paid for because everyone has a price. In short, the "cash" connection causes black men and women to lose sight of each other as human beings and treat each other as market items. What Karenga (1982), is suggesting is that the connection allows both parties to exploit each other without remorse and treat each other in a heartless manner thus contributing to their mutual dehumanization without assessing their predicament through 20/20 vision.

TOWARD NEW MODALITIES
IN BLACK MALE-FEMALE RELATIONSHIPS

New modalities in black male-female relationships demands that the quality relations between the two groups must grow out of a conscious struggle for change. A quality relationship is a stable association defined by its positive sharing and mutual investment in the emotional and psychological well-being of each other. African American women have the responsibility to select mates/partners who affirm their strengths, capabilities, and potentials. The complementary nature of the support provided by each member of the relationship sustains a resilience and a positive assertion of love, respect, and trust. It is thus incumbent upon the black male and female to find solutions to shield their relationship from violence. This means developing means to offset the interpersonal and institutional components imposed by the structure of the society. Hill-Collins (1991, p. 188) is among those who subscribe to the Lens Model by concluding that:

> . . . we need a holistic analysis of how race, gender, and class oppression frame the gender ideology internalized by both African women and men. By deconstructing violence as a seemingly inevitable outcome of racism and sexism, other alternatives become possible. (p. 188)

In the *Psychology of Blacks: An Afro-American Perspective,* White (1984, p. 73) captures the essence of the matter in the following description:

> The ideal male-female relationship within extended family networks and in the black community at large would be characterized by the Afro-American values of interdependence, cooperation, and mutual respect, without a fixed classification of household, economic and social responsibilities based on sex. Male-female relationships that are built on a bond of sharing, nurturance, tenderness and appreciation have the strong psychological foundation necessary to cope with the social and economic stresses that usually confront black couples living in a country dominated by Euro-Americans impact on male-female relationships.

In the future more research is needed to examine status devaluation as a racial group and how such status is expressed in violent behavior and what mediating factors control violence in some relationships while fostering it in others. Further, a crucial area of needed research is an analysis of employment trends and male-female violence. Does this violence increase as the rate of unemployment increases? What relationship exists, if any, between the type of status of occupations and the incidence of male-female violence? Finally, exploration of the relationship of strong religious orientation to violence would be a useful lens through which to examine the structural value system in the African American community.

CONCLUSION

The dynamic Lens Model allows social scientists to focus upon and approach an understanding of the complexity of the relations between black males and females. In the U. S. society, the integrity of being both black men and black women is constantly under assault. They both have sought refuge in the sanctity of their relationship with each other not recognizing that the long arm of the "master" has found its way into their bedroom. It will only take an intensive program of self awareness and working together to gain some control of the political, economic, educational, health and communication institutions that help structure and determine the nature and quality of their relationship and to improve it. If the violence against the integrity of their personhood is taken away or diminished, likewise so will the violence which permeates their most intimate relationship be eliminated.

REFERENCES

Ak'bar, Naim. (1984). Afrocentric social services of human liberation. *Journal of Black Studies*, 14, 395-413.

Aldridge, Delores P. (1989). *Black male-female relationships: A resource book of selected materials* (Ed.). Dubuque, Iowa: Kendall/Hunt Publishing Company.

_____. (1991). *Focusing: Black male-female relationships*. Chicago: Third World Press.

_____. (1984). Toward a theoretical perspective for understanding black male-female relationships. *The Western Journal of Black Studies*, 8, 184-191.

Allen, Walter R. (1981). "Moms, dads and boys: Race and sex differences in the socialization of male children. In Lawrence E. Gary (Ed.) *Black men*. Beverly Hills, Calif.: Sage Publications, pp. 99-114.

Asante, Molefi. (1987). *The afrocentric idea*. Philadelphia: Temple University Press.

_____. *Afrocentricity*. Trenton, NJ: Africa World.

Blackwell, James E. (1991). *The black community: Diversity and unity*. Third Edition. New York: Harper Collins Publishers,

Daly, Alfrieda, Jeanette Jennings, Joyce O. Beckett, and Bogart R. Leashore (1995). Effective coping strategies of African Americans, *Social Work*, 40, 240-248.

Davis, Richard I. (1998). *Domestic violence*. Westport, CT: Praeger Publishers.

Fanon, Franz (1967). *The wretched of the earth*. New York: Grove.

Gelles, Richard J. (1993). Family violence, In *Introduction to Social Problems*, C. Calhoun and G. Ritzer (Eds.), pp. 553-571.

Glasglow, Douglas (1981). *The black underclass: Poverty, unemployment, and entrapment of ghetto youth*. San Francisco, CA: Jossey-Bass Publishers.

Gordon, Vivian V. (1987). *Black women, feminism, and black liberation: Which way?* Chicago: Third World Press.

Hemmons, Willa. (1996). *Black women in the new world order: Social justice and the African American female*. Westport, CT.: Praeger Publishers.

Hill-Collins, Patricia. (1991). *Black feminist thought: Knowledge, consciousness, and the politics of empowerment*. New York: Routledge.

hooks, bell. (1990). *Ain't I a Woman: Black Women and Feminism*. Boston: South End Press.

Houston, L. N. (1990). *Psychological principles and the black experience*. New York: University Press of America.

Karenga, Maulana. (1982). *Introduction to black studies*. Los Angeles: The University of Sankore Press.

Levi-Strauss, Claude. (1953). Social structure, In A. L. Kroeber (Ed.), *Anthropology today*. Chicago: The University of Chicago Press, pp. 524-553.

Marable, Manning (1980). *How capitalism underdeveloped black America: Problems in race, political economy and society*. Boston: South End Press.

Miller, James G. *Toward a general theory for the behavioral sciences, in the state of the social sciences*. Leonard D. White (ed). Chicago: The University of Chicago Press, pp. 29-65.

Mills, C. Wright (1959). *The power elite*. New York: Oxford.

Nobles, Wade W. (1980). African American family life: An instrument of culture. In H. P. McAdoo (ed.), *Black families* (pp. 77-86). Beverly Hills, CA: Sage Publications.

Oliver, William (1994). *The violent social world of African American men*. New York: Lexington.

Poussaint, Alvin (1972). *Why Blacks Kill Blacks*. New York: Emerson Hall.

Rodgers-Rose, LaFrancis and James T. Rodgers (1985). *Strategies for resolving conflict in black male and female relationships*. Plainfield, NJ: Traces Institute Publications.

Rubenstein, Albert H. and Chadwick J. Haberstroh (eds.) (1960). *Some theories of organization*. Homewood, Il: The Dorsey Press and Richard D. Irwin, Inc. Also see, Morgan, G. (Ed.).

Ryan, William. (1965). Savage Discovery: The Moynihan Report. *Nation*, November 22.

Schiele, Jerome H. (1990). Organizational theory from an Afrocentric perspective. *Journal of Black Studies*, 21, 145-161.

Social Security Act. 42 US.C. Secs. 401 et al. (As Amended 1996).

Steinmetz, Suzanne K. & Straus, Murray A. (1974). *Violence in the family*. New York: Dodd, Mead.

Tawney, Richard. (1952). *Religion and the rise of capitalism*. New York: Harcourt, Brace and Co., Inc.

U.S. Bureau of the Census. *Current population survey, March 1990, 1998, and 1999*.

Weber, Max. (1950). The protestant ethic and the spirit of capitalism, translated by Talcott Parsons. New York: Charles Scribner's Sons.

White, Joseph L. *The psychology of blacks: An Afro-American perspective*. Englewood Cliffs, NJ: Prentice-Hall, 1984.

Young, Carlene. (1989). Psychodynamics of coping and surviving of the African American female in a changing world, *Journal of Black Studies*.

_____. (1986). Afro-American family: Contemporary Issues and implications for social policy. *In On being black: An in-group analysis* (ed.) David Pilgrim. Wyndham Hall Press.

Is Domestic Violence
a Gender Issue,
or a Human Issue?

R. L. McNeely
Philip W. Cook
José B. Torres

R. L. McNeely, PhD, JD, is Professor of Social Welfare at the University of Wisconsin-Milwaukee and he is a practicing attorney. He received his PhD from Brandeis University, and was a Fellow of the American Council on Education. Dr. McNeely has published two edited books and more than sixty articles in social science and educational journals. He testified before Congress as an expert on the issue of domestic violence and has served as domestic violence consultant for the U.S. Army.

Philip W. Cook, BS (Professional Journalist) is an author and journalist and a former broadcast journalist who has won awards for his reporting from the Associated Press, and from the Professional Journalism Society. His books, *Abused Men: The Hidden Side of Domestic Violence*, has won widespread acclaim from, among professional news outlets, the West Coast Review of Books, the London University Medical Center, and from "Dear Abby" (Abigail Van Buren). He has produced broadcast media documentaries, and educational materials for the print media. His work focusing upon selected human rights issues includes domestic violence.

José B. Torres, PhD, is Associate Professor at the School of Social Welfare, University of Wisconsin-Milwaukee. Additionally, he is an Associate Scientist with the Center for Addictions and Behavioral Health Research Center at the University of Wisconsin-Milwaukee. He teaches courses that focus on direct social work and social work with multi-cultural populations. He is a certified marriage and family therapist, and an approved supervisor for trainees of the American Association and Family Therapy.

[Haworth co-indexing entry note]: "Is Domestic Violence a Gender Issue, or a Human Issue?" McNeely, R. L., Philip W. Cook, and José B. Torres. Co-published simultaneously in *Journal of Human Behavior in the Social Environment* (The Haworth Social Work Practice Press, an imprint of The Haworth Press, Inc.) Vol. 4, No. 4, 2001, pp. 227-251; and: *Violence as Seen Through a Prism of Color* (ed: Letha A. (Lee) See) The Haworth Social Work Practice Press, an imprint of The Haworth Press, Inc., 2001, pp. 227-251. Single or multiple copies of this article are available for a fee from The Haworth Document Delivery Service [1-800-342-9678, 9:00 a.m. - 5:00 p.m. (EST). E-mail address: getinfo@haworthpressinc.com].

227

SUMMARY. Domestic violence, like all violence, is a human issue. It is not merely a gender issue. Classifying spousal and partner violence as a women's issue, rather than a human issue, is erroneous. In domestic relations, women are as inclined as men to engage in physically abusive acts. Yet most reports appearing in the popular press, and in scholarly journals, have framed the issue as essentially a masculine form of assaultive behavior, thereby imbedding into the national consciousness a false and inaccurate view of the problem. This article presents the results of selected empirical studies that contradict the popular view of domestic violence, briefly focuses on the phenomenon as it relates to race, offers several elucidating case accounts, and suggests that the popular view of domestic violence not only contributes to men's increasing legal and social defenselessness, it also leads to social policies that obstruct efforts to address the problem of domestic violence successfully. *[Article copies available for a fee from The Haworth Document Delivery Service: 1-800-342-9678. E-mail address: <getinfo@haworthpressinc. com> Website: <http://www.HaworthPress.com> © 2001 by The Haworth Press, Inc. All rights reserved.]*

KEYWORDS. Domestic violence, spousal abuse, abused men, gender abuse, human issue

INTRODUCTION

The question of whether domestic violence is a human issue remains nearly as vibrant and compelling today as when it was posed, first, more than ten years ago (cf. McNeely and Robinson-Simpson, 1987). When that question was asked and then answered in the affirmative by McNeely and Robinson-Simpson, in an article published by the National Association of Social Workers, the reaction of incredulous readers was, mildly stated, shock, disbelief, and anger (cf. Saunders, 1988; McNeely & Robinson-Simpson, 1988).[1] Among other reactions, the chancellor of author McNeely's university was sent a letter from a women's group threatening to do everything in its power to terminate McNeely's federal funding, and co-author Robinson-Simpson, then a female assistant professor, was characterized as a woman, duped, and under the domination of male professor, McNeely, despite the fact that Robinson-Simpson had uncovered some of the most compelling scientific evidence undergirding the position that women are no less violent than men (Cook, 1997). But the reaction to McNeely and Robinson-Simpson has by no means been unique.[2] Among other things, in efforts to stop researchers from presenting evidence to professional and other audiences of the proclivity of women to engage, as do men, in the production of domestic violence, false reports of sexual harassment and wife abuse have been asserted, and bombing threats have been made, as have threats against the safety of the researcher's children (cf. Cook, 1997, pp. 112-116).

But why should presentation of scientific proof provoke such reaction? Readers contemplating this question need look no further than to the historically documented fates of those who had the audacious guile to question conventional wisdom, such as Socrates, Copernicus, and Galileo. Indeed, and returning to the present day, those who insist either on denying or repudiating countless, empirically sound studies, showing women to be no less violent than men, are very much like those who once vehemently insisted that the earth is flat, and then proceeded to brand the purveyors of new knowledge as heretics. But it is not just that the idea of women's complicity in interpersonal violence[3] challenges old ideas, and challenges what many regard as common sense, it generates fear among those with vested interests in the perpetuation of federal and other funding that is based on the notion that spousal violence is a male-perpetrated phenomenon (cf. George, 1998, p. 4; Hoff-Sommers, 1995). Too, it is perceived by some feminist advocates as undercutting power derived from the presentation of women *only* as culpable victims, a power that leads uninformed and well-meaning sponsors to fund women's services (not people's services), and to enact legislation, such as the $1.6 billion 1994 *Violence Against Women Act*, and legal doctrines, such as the "battered woman's defense," that empowers women, not people (cf. Rittenmeyer, 1981). Consequently, the notion that women are no less violent than men *is* threatening to those wishing to empower one gender at the expense of the other gender (cf: Straus, 1991), particularly given the fact that there are virtually no data demonstrating that federally-funded feminist approaches to resolving domestic violence are effective (cf. Satel, 1997).

None of this denies the fact that many women are victimized, brutally, at the hands of vicious males. Indeed, prior to working with Robinson-Simpson, and after asking the same questions ("Who are these men?" and "Why do these men do it?") as did Erin Pizzey, whose seminal (1974) work launched the era in which woman battering became classified as a severe social problem, McNeely was publishing articles encouraging the development of domestic abuse shelters exclusively for women (cf. McNeely & Jones, 1980). What happened in the interim? What happened in the interim is that a review of astonishing scientific and other evidence compelled the asking of a new question: "Is domestic violence a human issue, rather than a gender issue?" (cf. McNeely & Mann, 1990; Fiebert, 1998). Traveling an analogous road, this article's co-author, Philip Cook, who recently published the seminal (1997) work, *Abused Men: The Hidden Side of Domestic Violence*, found his previously conventional views on domestic relations to be equally challenged when in performing work for a charitable organization he found an astonishing number of male questionnaire respondents who checked "yes" to the question of whether they had ever been a victim of physical attack by a domestic partner. This led him to a more rigorous study of the phenomenon that ultimately resulted in the publication of his controversial volume on abused men. But neither the road traveled by McNeely, nor the road traveled by Cook, are unique: It is clear from presentations made at professional conferences and elsewhere that nearly every scholar conducting domestic violence studies has found data obtained by survey research to be astonishing. Simply put, it is initially astonishing, even to domestic relations professionals, that the robust belief of men being the more-or-less exclusive perpetrators of interpersonal violence is false.

But those who subscribe to the view of women's more-or-less equal propensity to initiate, engage, and perpetuate interpersonal violence, base their view, principally, on a particular type of data. More, subscribers to the view that women are no less likely than men to engage in interpersonal violence regard the data upon which their view rests as being superior to other forms of evidence. The evidence being referred to here is data generated by survey research methods. Survey data, where people selected by known sampling techniques comprise sample frames that are representative of the general population, yield a different view of interpersonal violence than research based on interviewing known victims of domestic violence. Known victims of domestic violence, most often, are women who are, or have been, housed in domestic abuse shelters. Indeed, some images of the problem are formed by sample frames composed exclusively of women. It seems to us that a sine qua non with respect to research methods is that *if* one wishes to generate a full view of a social problem, one must utilize research methods that represent the entire population. Obviously, sample frames that include only known victims who currently or formerly have been housed in domestic violence shelters (who invariably are women), or sample frames that include only women, will not be representative of the domestic violence phenomenon with respect to male victims (McNeely & Robinson-Simpson, 1987; Stets & Straus, 1990, p. 151).

So what have been the findings of research utilizing samples representative of the population, or at least those utilizing samples not limited exclusively to women? A selected chronology of this research, which is intended to be illustrative, not exhaustive, follows. Before proceeding to those investigations, however, a caveat is in order. Readers must appreciate that the results of social science investigations are rarely completely consistent. This is due to a variety of factors, including, for example, the fact that different researchers use different sampling techniques that can cause findings to vary in unknown ways, various protocols used by researchers also can cause research findings to vary in unknown ways, the relationship of respondents to those who collect the data can vary, affecting findings, and concepts such as "violence" can be defined differently by different researchers, causing research findings to vary (cf. Straus, 1990a). Consequently, the findings generated by survey and other forms of research can, and do, vary.[4]

If one appreciates this fact about the domestic violence literature, and if one limits one's analysis to methodologically sound domestic violence studies involving samples not constructed exclusively of known female victims of abuse, it is difficult to argue that women are less likely than men to engage in interpersonal violence. Indeed, to date, every empirical study surveying both men and women has found that women comprise a significant percentage of domestic violence perpetrators. As noted by Satel (1997, p. 9), an analysis of the domestic violence literature reveals that about 25 to 30 percent of violence among married and cohabiting couples is initiated solely by women, about 25 five percent is initiated solely by men, and the remainder is mutually initiated (Straus, 1980; Straus et al., 1980; cf. Nisonoff & Bitman, 1979, p. 138).

Purpose

The purpose of this article is to demonstrate that domestic violence, like all violence, is a human issue, and not merely a women's issue. To achieve this purpose, illustrative survey research investigations, conducted over three decades, are reviewed, and elucidating anecdotal evidence also is presented.

THE INVESTIGATIONS

1970s

In the same year as Pizzey's previously cited seminal volume was published, Murray Straus, commenting in the foreword of a 1974 volume on family violence, noted that selective attention had characterized prior research on family violence, "because husband-wife violence has been a taboo topic" (Gelles, 1974, pp. 13,15). The publication, in 1974, of Gelles's *The Violent Home* constituted a step of substantial research importance because the study, unlike prior investigations utilizing divorce-prone individuals or subjects who were known abusers, involved a comparison group of individuals presumed to be more representative of "normal" families. Pointing out that at the time of the study family violence was assumed to be a rare event, Gelles noted that the possibility of drawing a random sample was ruled out because of common agreement that too many subjects would have to be interviewed to generate a sufficient number of abusers (Gelles, 1974, p. 33). Admittedly, because the comparison group consisted mainly of neighbors of subjects classified by police, or a social service agency, as abusive, no claim could be made that the neighbor group was truly representative. Nonetheless, the neighbor families provided the best data then available on family violence occurring among families with no known history of domestic violence. Among other findings, Gelles's study determined that 26 percent of all families participating in the study engaged in domestic violence regularly, that whereas 2.5 percent of neighbor wives had been victimized between two and five times during the course of marriage, 12.5 percent of husbands had been so victimized. Five percent of both husbands and wives had been victimized as much as once every two months, and 7.5 percent of wives compared to 2.5 percent of the husbands were victimized at least once per month, in some cases, daily. As stated by Gelles: "Although the wives were less violent than their husbands, they were far from passive" (1974, p. 52).

Suzanne Steinmetz, who was later victimized by bombing threats and threats against her children's safety, published the results of two family violence studies, in 1977. One was a small exploratory study involving self reports generated by students at a large urban university (1977a), and the second involved 57 families residing in New Castle County, Delaware (1977b). In the first study, students enrolled in two sections of a university course were requested to fill out questionnaires designed to assess the modes of conflict resolution employed by family members. Each participating student also was requested to obtain two additional questionnaires to be filled out by individuals 18-30 years of age who were not affiliated with the university. Among other findings, Steinmetz determined that 95 percent of all husbands and wives employed verbal aggression against each other (arguing a lot, yelling, screaming and insulting each other, sulking, stomping out of the room), and that 30 percent employed physical aggression (throwing and smashing things; threatening to hit or throw something at a spouse; did throw something at a spouse; pushed, grabbed or shoved; hit or tried to hit the other; hit or tried to hit the other person with something).

Perhaps because no claims could be made as to the sample's representatives, Steinmetz secured a public-opinion polling company to select subjects for a second study. Subjects who were members of intact families with at least two children between the ages of three and eighteen were selected randomly until quotas proportionately representative of the population were filled. Findings indicated that 93 percent of the families used verbal aggression, and 60 percent had used physical aggression at least once to resolve marital conflicts. Thirty-nine (39%) percent of husbands versus 37 percent of wives had thrown things. Thirty-one (31%) percent of husbands compared to Twenty-two (22%) percent of wives had pushed, shoved, or grabbed. Twenty (20%) percent of both husbands and wives had struck their spouses with their hands, and 10 percent of both husbands and wives had hit spouses with a hard object. Steinmetz observed that there were few differences between husbands and wives in the type and frequency of physical aggression, that wives were sometimes the aggressors, husbands were the aggressors in other cases, and that many families experienced reciprocal aggression. Steinmetz also noted that women were as likely as men to select and initiate physical violence to resolve marital conflicts, and that men and women were equal in their intentions when using physical violence. Having reviewed homicide data, Steinmetz noted further that when differences in physical strength were neutralized by weapons use, about as many men as women were victims of homicide. [Additionally, compelling evidence refutes the notion that female killers are helpless angels avenging former abuse: About eighty percent of murderesses have been found to have prior arrest records (Mann, 1996)].

Murray Straus, in 1977, presented findings (during a conference held at Stanford University) from the first study of domestic violence in the U.S. involving a large and nationally representative sample. Subsequently, the findings were published in a journal article appearing later that year (Straus, 1977-78), in books Straus published with George Hotaling (1980), and with Richard Gelles and Suzanne Steinmetz (1980). The study involved a national probability sample of 2,143 married and unmarried couples, examined in 1975, whose demographic profile closely matched the nation as a whole in regard to age, race, and socioeconomic status. Straus used an ascending continuum (The Conflict Tactics Scale) of violent acts including the following: (1) Throwing things at spouse; (2) pushing, shoving or grabbing; (3) slapping; (4) kicking, biting, or hitting with the fist; (5) hit or tried to hit with something; (6) beat up; (7) threatened with a knife or a gun; and (8) used a knife or a gun. Items 1-4 were regarded as an overall "Violence Index" whereas items 4-8 were considered to constitute a "Severe Violence Index."

So what did Straus find? Findings indicated that, in a given year, men perpetrate an average (median) of 2.5 "assaults" per year (items 1-8), but women perpetrate an average of 3.0 "assaults per year (items 1-8). When means rather than medians were used to assess central tendencies, men engaged in an average of 8.8 assaults per year, but women were found to engage in 10.1 assaults per year. Women also engaged more often than men in serious transgressions (items 4-8). Whereas males perpetrated a yearly average (median) of 2.4 acts of severe violence, women committed an average (median) of 3.0 acts of severe violence against male intimates. The mean severe violence rate for men was 8.0 acts per year, but women committed 8.9 acts of severe violence. But men beat up women more often (1.7 times per year) than females beat up men (1.4 times per year). But when all severely violent acts (items 4-8) were examined, violent females were found to transgress against males more often than males transgressed against females, and numerically more males (2.1 million) are victimized by females than females are victimized by males (1.8 million).

These findings were, and are, stunning to casual observers of the domestic violence phenomenon. This is because people have difficulty with the notion of women inflicting injuries on men because men, on average, are larger, stronger, and more adept at fighting. But the average man's size and strength are neutralized by guns and knives, boiling water, fireplace pokers, bricks, and baseball bats. Many fail to realize that domestic assaults do not involve pugilistic fair play, or to consider that attacks occur when males are asleep, or incapacitated by alcohol, age, or infirmities (McNeely & Mann, 1990). Perhaps more surprising is that young husbands are not spared victimization. Military men in their fighting prime are not uncommonly stabbed or shot in unprovoked episodes of violence (Ansberry, 1988).

1980s

In 1985, Straus and Gelles presented the findings of a study (at the annual conference of the American Society of Criminology) that sought to replicate the Straus survey reported above. Subsequently, the presented paper was published (Straus & Gelles, 1986). Although the original sample frame consisted of 2,143 families, 3,250 families were involved in the second survey. Both samples were representative of the nation, and a primary purpose of the study was to compare domestic violence rates for 1975 versus 1985. Again, the Conflict Tactics Scale was utilized to assess violence.

Findings revealed that the incidence of violence against females decreased between 1975 and 1985.[5] About 12.1 percent of all women had experienced at least one instance of violence in 1975, whereas 11.3 percent reported being victimized in 1985. Severe violence against women also decreased, from 3.8 percent having been assaulted in 1975, to only 3.0 percent having been assaulted in 1985. As noted by Straus and Gelles, this meant that approximately 432,000 fewer females were beaten than would have been the case if the 1975 rate had prevailed (Straus & Gelles, 1986, p. 470). However, although a slightly smaller percentage (4.4%) of men were victimized by overall violence in 1985 by severe violence compared to 1975 (4.6%), a higher proportion of men were victimized in 1985 (12.1%) versus 1975 (11.6%). Additionally, while the incidence of males using objects to strike females decreased from 2.2 percent in 1975 to 1.7 percent in 1985, no change was reported for women, with 3.0 percent using objects to strike males in both 1975 and 1985. Contemplating their findings, Straus and Gelles reported:

> Violence by wives has not been an object of public concern . . . no funds have been invested in ameliorating (violence against males) because it has not been defined as a problem . . . Our 1985 finding of little change in the rate of assaults by women on their male partners is consistent with the absence of ameliorative programs. (1986, p. 472)

But antagonists assailed the conclusions of Straus and Gelles, asserting that their research was faulty because their instrument, the Conflict Tactics Scale, critics argued, failed to take into account the context of violence. Simply put, the critics had argued that the scale failed to assess whether women's violence was in response to male aggression, and failed to assess if abused women were injured more seriously than male abuse victims. Responding to these criticisms, Straus thereafter compared rates generated in his surveys to self-reported rates of female-to-male assaults reported exclusively by women. What did Straus find? He found no significant differences in the rates reported by the general surveys, and the self-reported rates disclosed by the women (Straus, 1993, p. 69; cf. Straus, 1997, pp. 217-218; Straus, 1990b). What differences were found were not substantive with women, again, perpetrating more violence: Violence by men occurred in 23 percent of the cases while violence by women occurred in 28 percent of the cases, and women reported that they struck the first blow in 52.7 percent of the cases although, when the severest forms of violence were examined, women were more likely than men to require medical care, to take time off from work, and to be bedridden, but the differences in comparison to men were not particularly strong or large (Stets & Straus, 1990, pp. 154-158). This latter finding, of women being more likely to need medical care, contrasts with findings reported by Maureen McLeod for a study group in which 77 percent of the male victims were African American. Analysis of her data led McLeod to state: "Clearly, violence against men is much more destructive than violence against women . . . Male victims are injured more often and more seriously than are female victims" (McLeod, 1984). Given the fact that Straus's study group did not have such a disproportionate number of African-American males, it is possible that African-American males, when acts of severe violence are perpetrated against them, tend to be more severely brutalized than male European-Americans. Indeed, whereas European-American women receive "slap the cad" instructions from mothers, lower-class African-American women typically receive specific instructions in the use of hot water, hot cooking oil, etc., for scaldings.

1990s

Just as had been the case in the U.S., most British studies of domestic violence initially focused exclusively on battered women (Smith, 1989), or on community samples of women (Andrews & Brown, 1988). To correct this, Carrado et al. (1996), decided to conduct a study with a nationally representative sample of both male and female heterosexual respondents in 1994. Their sample frame was comprised of 1,978 adults residing in the United Kingdom who, to enhance confidentiality, completed questionnaires in their homes instead of being interviewed on a face-to-face basis in their homes. Anticipating that criticism of their study might focus on the oft-repeated arguments that survey research (1) does not identify whether female aggression is in response to male aggression, (2) does not identify if female aggression is in response to anticipated male aggression, (3) does not identify if female aggression is in response to prior male aggression, and (4) does not differentiate expressive female violence, versus instrumental male violence, Carrado et al. designed their instrument to ascribe reason and context to reports of victimization.

Findings revealed that about 10 percent of the men admitted committing an act of physical aggression, whereas 11 percent of women indicated committing these acts. Although men were more likely to push or grab intimates, women were more likely to slap their intimates, but women also were more likely to punch, kick, throw objects, and to strike their intimates with a sharp object. The study also found that with respect to multiple transgressions, about one-third of assaulted women experienced three or more types of assaults, whereas about one-fourth of men experienced three or more types of assaults. Women who were married or cohabiting reported less overall victimization than single women, but relationship status had little effect in mitigating the victimization of men, and men, compared to women, suffered a higher overall incidence of victimization, and a higher incidence of more severe forms of violence. The latter finding, that of men suffering more victimization, was consistent with prior smaller scale United Kingdom studies showing females to commit more severe violence than their male partners (cf. Archer & Ray, 1989; Russell & Hulson, 1992). Finally, as has been the case with studies performed in other countries (cf. Sommer, 1994), data obtained by Carrado et al. did not corroborate the erroneous notion indicated above that female violence is only in response to male violence. The study also failed to find substantive contrasts in the reasons given for violence, with prevalent reasons given by both men and women for inflicting violence including a number of motives, such as to (1) get a partner to do something the perpetrator wanted, as (2) a response to something said or threatened, to (3) stop a partner from doing something, or (4) as the means by which a perpetrator "got through" to a partner.

But the U.S. and Great Britain are not the only countries in which survey research involving national samples has trumpeted similar findings. Presenting his Canadian findings in a German journal, Eugen Lupri reported that approximately 2.5 percent of Canadian men and 6.2 percent of Canadian women admitted to having beaten up their partners, that women reported more acts of violence than did men, that 18 percent of the men compared to 23 percent of the women reported directing physical aggression against their mates, and that 10 percent of the men, but 13 percent of the women, had perpetrated acts of severe violence (Lupri, 1990).

It comes as a shocking surprise that military men, who are in their fighting primes, also are victimized by female-perpetrated domestic violence. In a study commissioned by the U.S. Army that was conducted by Behavioral Research Associates, data obtained from a final sample that included 33,762 randomly selected married active duty respondents stationed at 38 installations, located in all fifty states, revealed the following: More than nineteen (19.3%) percent of married males reported having been victimized by moderate wife-to-husband violence, and 6.6 percent reported having been victimized by severe violence. This contrasts with 18.5 percent of married females who reported being victimized by moderate level husband-to-wife violence, with 9.7 percent indicating having been victimized by severe violence. Interestingly, when males were asked to report their own aggression against their spouses, 17.6 percent indicated having perpetrated moderate violence, and 5.2 percent indicated perpetrating severe violence. When females were asked to report their aggression against spouses, 24.6 percent indicated having engaged in moderate-level assaults against husbands, and 6.5 percent indicated having engaged in severe violence (Heyman et al., 1996).[6]

Another question has to do with the extent to which verbal and symbolic aggression directed against partners is gender related. Straus and Sweet (1992) turned their attention to this issue by examining verbal/symbolic aggression among a nationally representative sample of 5,232 American couples (the study had 6,002 respondents; some respondents were not involved in coupled relationships). Pointing out that the literature provides little in the way of findings on the questions as to whether one gender is more verbally aggressive than the other, Straus and Sweet utilized telephone surveys to interview respondents during the summer of 1985. Categories of verbal/symbolic aggression included: insulting, swearing at, sulking, refusing to talk, stomping out of the room or yard, saying things to spite a partner, threatening to strike a partner, threatening to throw something at a partner, and actually throwing, hitting, kicking, or smashing something. Findings revealed that 74 percent of the men, and 75 percent of the women, engaged in verbal/symbolic aggression. Consequently, similar to physical aggression, there is no significant difference between man-to-woman and woman-to-man aggression.

African American Males

A common misconception is that African American males are more violent in their treatment of women than European American males. Even Straus and his co-investigators, whose survey is the most comprehensive and methodologically sound of all domestic violence investigations, have contributed to this misconception. Reporting in 1980 that wife abuse was 400 percent higher among African American couples than among European American couples (Straus, Gelles, & Steinmetz, 1980), the researchers failed to take into account that social class differences between the races, rather than race itself, might explain discrepant rates. But in a premier study that was specifically designed to take social class into account, Lockhart (1985; 1991) found virtually no differences between the races. Although a higher percentage of African American women reported at least one victimization event, the median rate of violent episodes experienced by middle-class European American women was somewhat higher than that experienced by middle-class African American women. Subsequent research has shown the salience of other factors, such as a residential area's percentage of female-headed families, level of population density, and residential mobility (cf. Hampton et al., 1998, pp. 15-19).

ANECDOTAL EVIDENCE

Many readers of scientific research find it difficult to digest what they regard as abstract numbers and statistical analyses needing, instead, concrete examples in order to place the nature of a problem, such as domestic violence, into perspective. Although anecdotal evidence in the form of violent female-to-male episodes are replete in the media, such events often are regarded as being rare. One stunning example of anecdotal evidence appeared when an emergency room physician wrote to *Time* magazine to report his objection to the claim, reported in a previous issue of the magazine, that because women are smaller than men, they are not as likely to inflict serious injury. Injuries this physician had treated included ax assaults, scaldings, smashing with fireplace pokers and bricks, and many gunshot wounds. As noted by the physician:

> [I]n my experience as an emergency room physician, I treated more men than women for [domestic violence] injuries, perhaps because a woman is more likely to use a weapon (Letter to the Editor, *Time.* January 11, 1988, p. 12).[7]

Although this sort of abbreviated evidence is replete in the popular press (usually presented to evoke humor), it is presented only episodically, and only in disparate fashion. But numerous substantive case accounts presented systematically are now available for the first time in a single source. That source is Philip Cook's volume, *Abused Men: The Hidden Side of Domestic Violence.* Selected briefs from some of the case accounts appearing in that volume follow.

Selected Case Accounts

The briefs presented herein profile cases of domestic violence, including accounts of verbal/symbolic as well as actual physical aggression, ranging from those that were very minor to those that were quite serious. Readers should be aware that few published accounts of abused men appear in the literature. The sum total of published accounts amounts only to about 90 referenced cases. Although a study of a large number of cases (N = 150) has been performed by clinical psychologist, Carole Hammond-Saslow (1997), her work remains an unpublished doctoral dissertation. Additionally, although Erin Pizzey (1982) has detailed accounts of male victimization, these accounts have been presented only from the viewpoints of female perpetrators.

Incidents reported below regarded as being minor involved slapping, pushing, grabbing, shoving and/or throwing things, while serious incidents involved hitting, kicking, biting, threatening to use a weapon and/or actual use of a weapon. Male victims, in many respects, appeared to be similar to female victims. A significant number of male victims, for example, believed that their spouses used violence or threats of violence to control their behavior. One male victim, Steve J., expressing frustration with his marriage, stated the following:

> She made all the decisions, about everything. She would decide how and where to spend money, what discipline there would be for the children, when we could make love, just everything. After awhile, I began to view my own opinions as wrong . . . She would constantly contradict me, especially in front of the children . . . I would make a decision, say about not having any TV because homework wasn't done, that kind of thing, and she would find out about it, and then overturn it, saying they could have TV. This happened constantly, and it became another area where I just gave up trying.[8]

Males interviewed by Cook for his volume, *Abused Men*, also expressed difficulty in leaving their abusive situations. Patricia Overberg, Director of the Valley Oasis Crisis Center in Sacramento California, one of the rare shelters that admits men, contends that men have a more difficult time not only admitting they are victims and seeking help, but they also have a more difficult time leaving the abusive relationship: "Because if you leave, you are abdicating your responsibility, and you are less than a man" (Cook, 1997, p. 60). Mark K., who was frequently kicked, hit, scratched, and had things thrown at him, says this sense of responsibility was the primary reason he didn't leave his marriage sooner. Asked the question, *"Did you feel responsible, as a man, for the family?"* Mark replied:

Yes, definitely. Just like when she quit working. I said to heck with it, stay home, take care of the baby–I'll just work overtime; and that's what I did.

Noted twenty years ago by Steinmetz (1977-78, p. 506), and more recently by Cook (1997), male abuse victims tend to find that leaving an abusive situation is especially difficult. Many of those interviewed by Cook expressed the belief that it was their responsibility to provide for their children, and in many cases they acted as protector or buffer between their spouses and children, sometimes becoming the targets of physical aggression that otherwise would have been directed to their children. Many of the interviewed men also believed strongly that no matter what their partner did to them, the judicial system would be against them. Thus, not only would they fail to gain custody of their children, if they left the marital relationship, visitation also would be blocked by their spouses as a continuation of controlling and abusive behavior, with husbands having little or no recourse under the law. Tom W.'s wife, for example, had thrown knives at him, resulting in a cut on one occasion, and she also was verbally and emotionally abusive. He explained the aftermath when he lost physical custody, and visitation thereafter was controlled by his former spouse, as follows:

She is still very controlling. She enjoys the power she has. I've been denied visitation many, many times. She had moved, and I would get there, and I couldn't see the children because they had done something, or not done something, that she wanted them to do. I'd try calling the police, but there's nothing they would do, because it's a civil domestic situation, and I was told I would have to go back to family court. Well, that still meant I would lose my weekend visitation, and going back to court meant an expense, and lawyers, and I just couldn't afford it.

Abused males often are victimized when they step in to protect their children from being abused (Steinmetz, 1977-78). However, males also expressed to Cook what Cook regarded as masculine reasons for staying in a relationship, and not hitting back, after being physically assaulted by wives. Jeff W. explains:

It's almost like it was ingrained in me, from the time I was a little kid. You don't hit girls, you just don't. I would hold her arms, I guess pretty tightly in the heat of the moment. She did get some finger mark bruises on her arms once, but what was I supposed to do, just let her keep hitting me? Still, I couldn't hit back.

Abused males also are more restrained than women in revealing their victimization (cf. Szinovacz, 1983) partly for fear of being ridiculed. Many of the men interviewed had never even told close family members about the abuse. Tim S. a twenty-five year old college student, never told anyone, until he was interviewed: "Because they would assume that I had done something to her, or that I deserved it."

While both abused women and men often feel shame over revealing instances of marital violence, men, unlike women, fear being characterized as a "wimp," or worse. Sacramento California's Valley Oasis Crisis Center shelter director, Patricia Overberg, explains how the lack of empathy for male victims was expressed in one case:

> I worked with a man who was an ironworker. Now an ironworker is the epitome of macho. This guy was big, and his wife was tall, but thin, probably no more than a hundred pounds. She kept putting him in the hospital. She kept beating him up with a baseball bat. Every time he came out of the hospital, they [his co-workers] were laughing him off the girders. They had no sympathy or empathy for him.

A significant number of the interviewed men said they would not have called a crisis line even if they had known that one was available for men. However, a nearly equal number said they would have called, if there had been some place to call, as Tom W. explained:

> It seems as though I had no one to really turn to. To say, you know, "How can I cope with this?" I felt as though I was out in a boat in the ocean all by myself. I saw so many opportunities for help for women in my situation. I don't deny them that opportunity, because I think there have been quite a few situations . . . But the other side is, I felt I had been an abused husband, and an abused parent, with really nowhere to turn.

Bewilderment and betrayal are the most common feeling of bruised men finding themselves in the above situation. Each interviewed man expressed this in one form or another. Many said it outright: "What was I supposed to do?" Their isolation was extreme. Shame and fear of ridicule helped keep their problems hidden[9] while societal views of proper masculine behavior and a lack of resources insured that the most hidden form of domestic violence would remain hidden. One of the interviewed men said: "I wonder how many homeless men on the streets there are who were in my situation . . . I had resources, there are those who don't." Some of the men claimed to no longer trust women, others had difficulty adjusting to a new relationship, while others had little difficulty putting their abused past behind them. The longest lasting negative effects seemed present with those who were fathers. It did not seem to matter whether the fathers had physical custody of their children. Readers may wish to contemplate one implication flowing from these remarks: Although the indicators reported above are sparse, the psychological harm visited upon men victimized by wife-to-husband violence tend to contradict those who subscribe to the view that abused men do not suffer psychologically. Indeed, when the issue of psychological harm was examined, empirically, findings revealed no significant gender differences in psychosomatic illness, or stress, although abused women were more likely than men to be depressed (Stets & Straus, 1990).

DISCUSSION–DIFFERENTIAL RATES

As noted previously, not all research, not even all survey research, shows such equivalent rates of violence for the sexes. Despite the fact that more than one hundred family conflict studies have shown approximately equal rates of violence in domestic relations (Straus, forthcoming), one type of survey tends repeatedly to show lower rates for women. The type of study being referred to is what might be characterized as "crime surveys" (such as the National Crime Victimization Survey/National Crime Survey discussed previously in footnote 4). Also, "crime studies" (such as those using official police call data or Uniform Crime Report data) show lower rates for females (but women are more likely than men to initiate official intervention, and men are less likely to obtain official intervention, even when it is sought). Straus, on this issue, was confronted by a *U.S.A. Today* reporter to explain why family conflict studies, which show equal gender rates of involvement in domestic violence, appear to be contradicted by crime surveys, such as the 1997 National Violence Against Women in America (NVAW) Survey (see: Tjaden & Thoennes, 1997), which showed men to be three times as likely as women to commit domestic abuse. Even if one were to accept the findings of the NVAW survey, which examined victimization, rather than victimization *and* perpetration, it would mean that 835,000 men are victimized each year. Straus responded to the reporter's inquiries with the following paraphrased explanation:

> Crime surveys are presented to respondents as studies of crime, whereas family conflict surveys are presented to respondents as studies of family problems. Although most people would regard being kicked by a spouse as horrendous, few would think of having been kicked by a spouse as a crime. Thus, respondents, who are likely to regard, e.g., the victimization event of kicking a spouse as a "family argument," would be unlikely to report the kicking instance as a "crime" to crime-survey interviewers (Straus, in press).

Straus noted further that family conflict studies report injury rates of about three (3%) percent, whereas crime studies report injury rates ranging, recently, from fifty-two (52%) percent to seventy-six (76%) percent. Straus (in press) also commented that:

> The implausibly high injury rates from the (crime surveys) are prob-ably the result of the crime threat to safety focus of those studies, i.e., partner assaults tend to not be reported unless there is something, such as injury, that moves them from the category of a "family fight" to a "crime" or a threat to safety.

Straus reported other reasons for discrepant rates in crime survey/study data versus family conflict studies (see: Straus, in press), and still other reasons for discrepant rates between family conflict studies and studies in-volving clinical populations (cf. Stets & Straus, 1990), in which he and Jan Stets implicitly reprimanded writers such as Daniel Saunders (cf. Saunders, 1988). Among the uninformed conclusions drawn and presented by Saund-ers, whose views of domestic violence had been based virtually exclusively on clinical samples, was the erroneous assertion that women rarely or never initiate assaults (Saunders, 1986). The danger of basing views of a societal-wide phenomenon exclusively on the far "tail" of a distribution curve, such as on a subpopulation of women who sought clinical services at a battered women's shelter, were discussed, herein, previously (cf. McNeely & Robin-son-Simpson, 1987; 1988).

Meanwhile, data obtained from nationally representative surveys de-signed specifically to assess domestic violence rates within the general public continues to accumulate. Most recently, British researchers, Catriona Mirrlees-Black and Carole Byron, who surveyed respondents comprising a nationally representative sample of the British population, found, as re-ported in banner headlines by London's *The Guardian*: "Both Sexes Equal-ly Likely to Suffer Domestic Violence" (4.2% of both sexes reported being assaulted). Announced by the newspaper on January 22, 1999, one day after this British governmental study (Mirrlees-Black and Byron, 1999) was released to the public, some readers were overwhelmed. One of those read-ers was Erin Pizzey, whose startling 1974 seminal book, *Scream Quietly or the Neighbors Will Hear*, had founded the movement by which wife abuse ultimately became defined as a social problem. Pizzey, in fact, also estab-lished the world's first shelter for battered women, the Chiswick Women's Refuge. Writing to Phil Cook, Pizzey, who, after penning *Scream Quietly or the Neighbors Will Hear*, had traveled a road similar to that of McNeely and Cook, commented to Cook:

> This morning, I opened *The Guardian* and saw the headlines . . . This should be a great day in our lives. So many of us have been fighting for so long but . . . I wonder how the feminists in this country will react . . . If

the whole thing will be swept under the carpet . . . If this will affect other countries? Who will answer for all the years of fathers losing their families and in some cases, their lives, because of huge lies? Can you pass this on to as many people as possible? (Personal correspondence to Phil Cook, Jan. 22, 1999)

These comments may surprise many, but not those who know of Pizzey's plight after she published her 1982 volume, *Prone to Violence*. In this book, Pizzey, having interviewed women housed within Chiswick Women's Refuge, presented her findings that sixty-two (62%) percent had participated in a mutually violent relationship. Thereafter, Pizzey was excommunicated from feminist ranks, her publisher was threatened with having his windows smashed, Pizzey was picketed, she was required, officially, to have a police escort for her book tour in England, and someone shot at her in her home in the United States (Thomas, 1993, pp. 185-191). Commenting about her new status, Pizzey remarked:

Time and again I've dealt with men who are physically attacked by women. In fact, the ophthalmologist I used to go to in Santa Fe [New Mexico] said that one of the major injuries he saw was men who had [pieces of] bottles and glasses in their eyes . . . I suppose that at the end of five years in America . . . I just came to the conclusion that not only did I have hardly any American women friends, but they were the most aggressive and dangerous women I'd ever met in the world . . . terrifying. (Cook, 1997, p. 121)

CONCLUSION

Although there is compelling evidence showing the complicity of individual attributes in the interpersonal production of domestic violence, particularly where anti-social personality disorders and alcoholism are combined (cf. Bland & Orn, 1986), the influence of social-structural factors is an exceedingly complicitous precipitant of violence (cf. Straus, 1994). Such mezzo and macro-level factors are far ranging, including, for example: (1) highly *stressful environments*, including those associated with alienating working environments (McNeely, 1979), and including those associated with certain military bases, where domestic violence is more pronounced than on lesser-stress military bases (Cook, 1997, p. 5); (2) features inherent in the structure of nuclear family households, such as the fact that conflicts must be settled by the two antagonists (husbands and wives) themselves, rather than via tension-reducing mechanisms such as democratic majority-group consensus, and also because of traditional gender-related roles assigned by societal norms, such as male authoritarianism and dominance (Straus & Hotaling, 1980); and, as some writers have noted, (3) because interpersonal violence is but a natural reaction to inegalitarian structures (racism, sexism, class inequalities) in society that inhibit personal growth (Gil, 1986; 1984). Moreover, given the magnitude of the problem, it is unlikely that psychotherapeutic approaches can successfully address it, or even that psychological disturbance is the root of family violence in most instances. As noted by Gil (1996, p. 77):

> The futility of violence prevention efforts by government, professional organizations, and social advocacy movements should not be surprising, since the aim of these efforts has been primarily to control, punish, and modify the behavior of individuals involved in violence, rather than to discern and eliminate its root causes in the fabric of societies.

Indeed, in the view of psychiatrist and previously cited author, Sally Satel, as stated in a conversation occurring on February 15, 1999, with the instant article's senior author: "I am writing a book on public health and want to mention in it that feminist-run batterer treatment should be considered malpractice."

Solutions that involve gender inclusion practices within the provider community can be achieved fairly easily. Staff of some shelter and crisis-line services have been trained to properly differentiate between perpetrators and abusers of both genders, and to recognize predominantly mutual combat situations. Funding is not affected. What seems to be lacking is a coordinated educational effort that supports workers in victim assistance, law enforcement, and those in the legal and social service systems who desire more information about an underserved victim population in order to aid their efforts to serve this population.

One-sided governmental policies that fund women-only resources, based on the assumption that women rarely, or never, engage as perpetrators in domestic violence, is key to the problem. Given this, we agree with Stets and Straus who have argued that primary prevention efforts to curb domestic violence, rather than concentrating on male violence, should pay as much attention as possible to assaults by women on their partners (1990, p. 165). On the other hand, we disagree with Straus, who has urged that priority be given to women victims because they are more likely to sustain serious injuries, and because of greater financial and emotional injury (Straus, in press). In our view, priority needs to be assigned to the victims of domestic violence, regardless of gender, particularly given the fact that men can be victimized brutally (McLeod, 1984; Cook, 1997), suffer serious financial hardship (Steinmetz, 1977-78, p. 506), and evidence no robust differences in their need to see physicians, take time off from work, or become bedridden, following victimization (Stets & Straus, 1990, p. 158) We would agree, however, that a disproportionate share of governmental resources should be targeted to women because, among people who are victimized by severe violence, proportionately more women than men suffer very serious injuries. Yet, in our view, to give less priority to the victimization experiences of men, compared to women, would be discriminatory (Young, 1999). After all, domestic violence is a human problem.

NOTES

1. See also the numerous letters to the editor, as published in *Social Work* 33(2) 1988, that assailed authors McNeely and Robinson-Simpson. Indeed, the journal's editor, in the same issue of the journal, noted that the journal had been challenged for publishing the McNeely and Robinson-Simpson article. Perhaps in deferential response to the hundreds of letters sent in opposition to the article, the journal failed to publish even one letter supporting McNeely's and Robinson-Simpson's article, although many supportive letters were received.

2. Indeed, Murray Straus, who was accused falsely of wife abuse and of harassing female students after publishing articles showing women to be as likely as men to commit domestic abuse, has compared his plight, at the hands of feminists, to that of Salman Rushdie, who was condemned to death by Islamic fundamentalists for what they regarded as Rushdie's heretical views on the Islamic religion (Straus, in press).

3. "Interpersonal violence," as used in this paper, refers only to spousal/partner violence. It does not include other forms of violence, such as violence against elders, dating violence, or parent-child violence. Readers may be surprised to learn that women, historically, have been the primary perpetrators of infanticide (Steinmetz, 1977b, p. 89), that women are 62 percent more likely than males to abuse children, that male children are more than twice as likely as female children to suffer physical injury (Steinmetz, 1980), that typical infanticide victims are male children (Mitchel, 1987), and that women are twice as likely as men to assault an elderly spouse (Satel, 1997). They may be surprised also to learn that women are not less likely than men to engage in violence during dating, or in other forms of non-stranger violence, such as in non-marital cohabitation, etc. (cf. Fiebert and Tucci, 1998; Fiebert and Gonzalez, 1997; Lane and Gwartney-Gibbs, 1985; Szinovacz, 1983; Laner and Thompson, 1982).

4. Research findings generated by the National Crime Survey (NCS) as originally designed provide a good illustration of how varying research protocols and varying definitions of "violence" may significantly affect domestic violence findings. The NCS also is a good illustration because it demonstrates that some studies utilizing survey research methods have resulted in the finding that women are *less* likely than men to engage in domestic violence. The NCS is a longitudinal study funded by the Department of Justice that was begun in 1973 and conducted by the Bureau of the Census (cf. McNeely, 1983, p. 138). Data obtained by the NCS have shown women to be victimized by domestic violence at a rate of about 3.9 per 1,000, while men were victimized at a much lower rate of .3 per 1,000. However, seeking to estimate all types of victimizations, the NCS differs from studies reported in the section of this article titled *The Investigations* because it was

not specifically designed initially to answer questions on domestic abuse. Spouse abuse was defined by NCS researchers as: "Assault without theft in which the offender was the victim's spouse or ex-spouse" (Gaguin, 1977-78, p. 635). Consequently, data obtained from respondents reporting domestic victimization involving co-habitant couples or those involving theft were excluded. Additionally, no special interviewing protocols sensitive to the peculiar problems involved in obtaining domestic violence data were incorporated into the study. This is especially important because, without such protocols, men are particularly less likely to report domestic abuse victimizations than are women (cf. Szinovacz, 1983, p. 641). Indeed, NCS researchers have stated their conviction that male victimization is much higher in the general population than that reported by NCS data (McNeely & Robinson-Simpson, 1987: see footnote 9) and, perhaps, this was part of the reason it was later redesigned to include some specific domestic violence questions, and renamed as the National Crime Victimization Survey (NCVS). Consequently, the NCS should underscore for readers how different research protocols can significantly affect a study's findings, and that even if survey research methods are used, such findings may be at odds with the weight of findings obtained by other survey research studies employing methods that are designed specifically to examine domestic violence. Studies reported in the *Investigations* section were designed from their inception specifically to examine domestic violence. For a recent critique and analysis of why crime studies (national crime surveys, police calls, etc.) underestimate male victimization, see: Straus, (in press).

5. Despite the decline in violence against females, authors such as Satel argue that a one-sided treatment approach focusing only on men ultimately exposes women to more danger (Satel, 1997, p. 10).

6. Contrary to recent reports in the print and broadcast media that domestic violence rates are much higher in the Army than in the civilian population, Heyman and Neidig (in press) have shown that once age and race are controlled, husband-to-wife violence is only slightly higher in the military than in the U.S. civilian population.

7. Domestic assault patients in hospital emergency rooms have been surveyed by confidential self-administered questionnaires. When one such survey was performed in Detroit, Michigan, researchers Goldberg and Tomlanovich failed to find any statistically significant differences between the number of male and female victims (1984). In another survey of hospital room patients, conducted in Pennsylvania, fully thirty percent of the battered women questioned were identified positively as batterers (McLeer & Anwar, 1989).

8. Married couples in which the female is dominant frequently result in situations where the male partner loses libido or becomes impotent (cf. Crowe & Ridley, 1990).

9. But, increasingly, male victimization is becoming more and more visible. For example, Ernst et al. (1997), after examining patients in an "inner-city" emergency department, concluded: "Recognition of the global nature of violence may be more realistic than assuming that only women are victims." In this survey, 20% of the men and 19% of the women reported physical violence in their current domestic relations. It should be noted that data reported by emergency room studies that have been crime-focused have shown more female than male victimization (cf. Rand, 1997).

REFERENCES

Andrews, B. and G. W. Brown. (1988). Marital violence in the community: A biographical approach. *British Journal of Psychiatry*, 153, 305-312.

Ansberry, C. (1988). "Calling sexes equal in domestic violence article stirs clash among rights groups," *The Wall Street Journal*, May 5, 27.

Archer, J., and N. Ray (1989). Dating violence in the United Kingdom: A preliminary study. *Aggressive Behavior*, 15, 337-343.

Bland, R. & Orn, H. (1986). Family violence and psychiatric disorder. *Canadian Journal of Psychiatry*, 31, 129-137.

Carrado, M., George, M. J., Loxam, E., Jones, L., & Templar, D. (1996). Aggression in British heterosexual relationships: A descriptive analysis. *Aggressive Behavior*, 22, 401-415.

Cook, P. W. (1997). *Abused Men: The Hidden Side of Domestic Violence*. Westport, CT: Praeger.

Crowe, M. & Ridgely, J. (1990). *Therapy with couples: A behavioral systems approach to marital and sexual problems*. Oxford, England: Blackwell Scientific.

Ernst, A. A., Nick, T. G., Weiss, S. J., Houry, D., & Mills, T. (1997). Domestic violence in an inner-city Emergency Department. *Annals of Emergency Medicine*, 30, 190-197.

Fiebert, M. S. (1998). References examining assaults by women on their spouses/partners. *Sexuality and Culture*, 1, 273-286.

Fiebert, M. S. & Tucci, L. M. (1998). Sexual coercion: Men victimized by women. *The Journal of Men's Studies*, 6, 127-133.

Fiebert, M. S. & Gonzalez D. M. (1997). College women who initiate assaults on their male partners and the reasons offered for such behavior. *Psychological Reports*, 80, 583-590.

Gaguin, D. (1977-78). Spouse abuse: Data from the National Crime Survey. *Victimology*, 2, 632-643.

Gelles, R. J. (1974). *The violent home: A study of physical aggression between husbands* and wives. Beverly Hills, CA: Sage.

George, M. J. (1998). *Beyond all help*? London: DeWar Research (Tel: 01344 621167).

Gil, D. (1984). Reversing dynamics of violence by transforming work. *Journal of International and Comparative Social Welfare*, 1, 1-15.

Gil, D. (1986). Sociocultural aspects of domestic violence. In M. Lystad (Ed.) *Violence in the home* (pp: 124-149. New York: NY: Brunner/Mazel.

Gil, D. ((1996). Preventing family violence in a structurally violent society: *Mission impossible*. *American Journal of Orthopsychiatry*, 66, 77-84.

Goldberg, W. & Tomlanovich, M. (1984). Domestic violence victims in the emergency department. *Journal of the American Medical Association*, 251, June 22-29, 3259-3264.

Hammond-Saslow, C. (1997). *Domestic Abuse and Levels of Depression Self-Esteem and Assertiveness*. Unpublished doctoral dissertation, U.S. International University (San Diego).

Hampton, R., Carrillo, R. & Kim, J. (1998). Violence in communities of color. In R. Carrillo & Tello, J. (Eds.), *Family Violence and Men of Color* (pp. 1-30). New York: Springer.

Heyman, R. & Neidig, P. (in press). A comparison of spousal aggression prevalence rates in U.S. Army and civilian representative samples. *Journal of Consulting and Clinical Psychology.*

Heyman, R., Schaffer, R., Gimbel, C., & Kerner-Hoeg, S. (1996). *A comparison of the prevalence of Army and civilian spouse violence: Final report.* U.S. Army Community and Family Support Center.

Hoff-Sommers, C. (1995). *Who stole feminism: How women have betrayed women.* New York: Simon and Schuster.

Lane, K. & Gwartney-Gibbs, P. (1985). Violence in the context of dating and sex. *Journal of Family Issues* 6, 45-59.

Laner, M. & Thompson, J. (1982). Abuse and aggression in courting couples. *Deviant behavior: An Interdisciplinary Journal*, 3, 229-244.

Lockhart, L. (1985). Methodological issues in comparative racial analyses: The case of wife abuse. *Social Work Research and Abstracts*, 21, 35-41.

Lockhart, L. (1991). Spousal violence: A cross-racial perspective. In R. L. Hampton (Ed.). *Black Family Violence: Current Research and Theory* (pp. 85-101). Lexington, MA: Lexington Books.

Lupri, E. (1990). Harmonie und aggression: Uber die dialektick ehlicher gewalt. *Kolner Zeitschrift fur Soziologie und Sozialphycholgie*, 42, 479-501.

Mann, C. R. (1996). *When women kill.* Albany, NY: Suny Press.

McLeer, S. V. & Anwar, R. (1989). A study of battered women presenting in an emergency department. *American Journal of Public Health*, 79, January, 65-66.

McLeod, M. (1984). Women against men: An examination of domestic violence based on an analysis of official data and national victimization data. *Justice Quarterly*, 1, 171-193.

McNeely, R. L. (1979). Sources of alienation at work and household violence within middle-class families: A theoretical perspective. *Social Development Issues*, 3, 12-34.

McNeely, R. L. & Jones, J. M. (1980). Refuge from violence: Establishing shelter services for battered women. *Administration in Social Work*, 4, 71-82.

McNeely, R. L. (1983). Race, sex, and victimization of the elderly. In R. L. McNeely and J. N. Colen (Eds.), *Aging in Minority Groups* (137-152). Beverly Hills, CA: Sage.

McNeely, R. L. & Robinson-Simpson, G. (1987). The truth about domestic violence: A falsely framed issue. *Social Work*, 32, 485-490.

McNeely, R. L. & Robinson-Simpson, G. (1988). The truth about domestic violence revisited: A reply to Saunders. *Social Work*, 33, 184-188.

McNeely, R. L., & Mann, C. R. (1990). Domestic violence is a human issue. *Journal of Interpersonal Relations*, 5, 129-132.

Mirrlees-Black, C. & Byron, C. (1991). *Domestic violence: Findings from a new British crime survey self-completion questionnaire* (pp. 1-126). Home Office Research Study 191, London: HMSO,

Mitchel, L. (1987). *Child abuse and neglect fatalities: A review of the problem and strategies for reform.* Working Paper 838. Monograph of the National Center on Child Abuse Prevention Research, National Committee for the Prevention of Child Abuse, Chicago, Illinois.

Nisonoff, L. & Bitman, I. (1979). Spouse abuse: Incidence and relationship to selected demographic variables. *Victimology*, 4, 131-140.

Pizzey, E. (1974). *Scream quietly or the neighbors will hear.* Middlesex, England: Penguin Books.

Pizzey, E. (1982). *Prone to violence.* Middlesex, England: Hamlyn.

Rand, M. R. (1997). *Violence-related injuries treated in hospital emergency departments.* Washington, DC: U. S. Department of Justice, Bureau of Justice Statistics, August, (Report NCJ-156921).

Rittenmeyer, S. D. (1981). Of battered wives, self-defense and double standards of justice. *Journal of Criminal Justice,* 9, 389-395.

Russell, R. J. H., & Hulson, B. (1992). Physical and psychological abuse of heterosexual partners. *Personality and Individual Differences,* 34, 457-473.

Saunders, D. G. (1986). When battered women use violence: Husband-abuse or self-defense? *Violence and Victims* 1, 47-60.

Saunders, D. G. (1988). Other truths' about domestic violence: A reply to McNeely and Robinson-Simpson. *Social Work,* 33, 179-183.

Satel, S. L. (1997). It's always his fault. *The Women's Quarterly,* Summer, 12, 4-10.

Smith, L. F. J. (1989). *Domestic violence: An overview of the literature.* (Monograph), Home Office Research Study No. 107. London: HMSO.

Sommer, R. (1994). *Male and female perpetrated partner abuse: Testing a diathesis-stress model.* Unpublished doctoral dissertation. Winnipeg, Canada: University of Manitoba.

Steinmetz, S. K. (1997a). The use of force for resolving family conflict: The training ground for abuse. *The Family Coordinator,* 26, 19-26.

Steinmetz, S. K. (1977b). *The Cycle of Violence: Assertive, Aggressive, and Abusive Family Interaction.* New York: Praeger.

Steinmetz, S. K. (1980). The battered husband syndrome. *Victimology,* 2, 499-509.

Steinmetz, S. K. (1980). Women and violence: Victims and perpetrators. *American Journal of Psychotherapy,* 34, 334-350.

Szinovacz, M. (1983). Using couple data as a methodological tool: The case of marital violence. *Journal of Marriage and the Family,* 45, 633-644.

Stets, J. E. & Straus, M. A. (1990). Gender differences in reporting marital violence and its medical and psychological consequences. In M. A. Straus & R. J. Gelles (Eds.), *Physical violence in American families: Risk factors and adaptations to violence in 8,145 families* (pp. 151-165). New Brunswick, NJ: Transaction.

Straus, M. A. (1977-78). Wife-beating. How common and why? *Victimology,* 2, 443-458.

Straus, M. A. (1980). Victims and aggressors in marital violence. *American Behavioral Scientist,* 23, 681-704.

Straus, M. A. (1990a). The Conflicts Tactics Scale and its critics: An evaluation and new data on validity and reliability. In M. A. Straus & R. J. Gelles (Eds.), *Physical Violence in American Families: Risk Factors and Adaptations to Violence in 8,145 Families* (pp. 49-74). New Brunswick, NJ: Transaction.

Straus, M. A. (1990b). Injury and frequency of assault and the 'representative sample fallacy' in measuring wife beating and child abuse. In M. A. Straus & R. J. Gelles (Eds.), *Physical Violence in American Families: Risk Factors and Adaptations to Violence in 8,145 Families* (pp. 75-92). New Brunswick, NJ: Transaction.

Straus, M. A. (1991). New theory and old canards about family violence research. *Social Problems*, 38, 180-197.

Straus, M. A. (1993). Physical assaults by wives: A major social problem. In R. J. Gelles & D. R. Loseke (Eds.), *Current Controversies on Family Violence* (pp. 67-87). Newbury Park, CA: Sage.

Straus, M. A.(1994). State-to-state differences in social inequality and social bonds in relation to assaults on wives in the United States. *Journal of Comparative Family Studies*, 25, 7-24.

Straus, M. A. (1997). Physical assaults by women partners: A major social problem. In M. R. Walsh (Ed.), *Women, men and gender: Ongoing debates* (pp. 210-221). New Haven, CT: Yale University Press.

Straus, M. A. (In press). The controversy over domestic violence by women: A methodological, theoretical, and sociology of science analysis. In X. B. Arriaga & S. Oskamp (Eds.), *Violence in Intimate Relationships*. Thousand Oaks, CA: Sage.

Straus, M. A. & Hotaling, G. (1980). (Eds.). *The social causes of husband-wife violence*. Minneapolis, MN: University of Minnesota Press.

Straus, M. A., Gelles, R. & Steinmetz, S. (1980). *Behind closed doors: Violence in the American family*, New York, NY: Anchor Press/Doubleday.

Straus, M. & Gelles, R. (1986). Societal change and change in family violence from 1975 to 1985 as revealed by two national surveys. *Journal of Marriage and the Family*, 48, 465-479.

Straus, M. & Sweet, S. (1992). Verbal/symbolic aggression in couples: Incidence rates and relationships to personal characteristics. *Journal of Marriage and the Family*, 54, 346-357.

Thomas, D. (1993). *Not guilty: The case in defense of men*. New York: William Morrow and Co.

Tjaden, P. G. & Thoennes, N. (1997). *The Prevalence and Consequences of Intimate Partner Violence: Findings from the National Violence Against Women Survey.*" Paper presented at the 49th Annual Meeting of the American Society of Criminology, San Diego, CA.

Tjaden, P. G. & Thoennes, N. (1998). *Prevalence, incidence, and consequences of violence against women: Findings from the National Violence Against Women Survey* (Research in Brief), (pp. 1-16). Washington, DC: National Institute of Justice Centers for Disease Control and Prevention.

Young, C. (1999). *Ceasefire! Why women and men must join forces to achieve true equality.* New York: The Free Press.

PART V:
CHILDREN AND VIOLENCE

When White Boys Kill:
An Afrocentric Analysis

Jerome H. Schiele
Ron Stewart

SUMMARY. The image of male youth homicide is primarily associated with young black males. However, recent school shootings in which multiple innocent victims were murdered indicate that young white males may be at serious risk of a much more tragic homicidal phenome-

Jerome H. Schiele, DSW, is Associate Professor, School of Social Work at Clark-Atlanta, University, Atlanta, Georgia. He received his doctorate degree from Howard University, Washington, DC. His scholarly work focuses on Afrocentric social theory and social work practice, cultural oppression, and race and gender stratification among social work faculty. Dr. Schiele's new book, *Human Services and the Afrocentric Paradigm* has recently been released, and is being well received in the social work community.

Ron Stewart, PhD, is Associate Professor in the Department of Sociology at Suny-Buffalo State College. He received his PhD from Howard University, after obtaining two master's degrees from Ohio State University. Dr. Stewart teaches courses in Race Relations, African American Studies, Research, and Sociological Theory. He is an expert on the African American male and much of his writing has centered on problems involving this population.

[Haworth co-indexing entry note]: "When White Boys Kill: An Afrocentric Analysis." Schiele, Jerome H., and Ron Stewart. Co-published simultaneously in *Journal of Human Behavior in the Social Environment* (The Haworth Social Work Practice Press, an imprint of The Haworth Press, Inc.) Vol. 4, No. 4, 2001, pp. 253-273; and: *Violence as Seen Through a Prism of Color* (ed: Letha A. (Lee) See) The Haworth Social Work Practice Press, an imprint of The Haworth Press, Inc., 2001, pp. 253-273. Single or multiple copies of this article are available for a fee from The Haworth Document Delivery Service [1-800-342-9678, 9:00 a.m. - 5:00 p.m. (EST). E-mail address: getinfo@haworthpressinc.com].

253

non known as *multicide*. This paper offers a conceptual framework to explain multicide and violence generally among young white males by employing an Afrocentric analysis. This analysis assumes that multicide among young white males can be explained by the convergence of three structural-cultural factors, which are (1) the concept of manhood that places considerable emphasis on physical aggression; (2) the phenomenon of spiritual alienation; and (3) the anxiety and stress associated with concerns over maintaining white male privilege. The paper also presents recommendations that describe how the effects of these three factors could be prevented and mediated, and it offers suggestions for future research that applies an Afrocentric framework to investigate young, white male violence. *[Article copies available for a fee from The Haworth Document Delivery Service: 1-800-342-9678. E-mail address: <getinfo@haworthpressinc.com> Website: <http://www.HaworthPress.com> © 2001 by The Haworth Press, Inc. All rights reserved.]*

KEYWORDS. White males, violence, Afrocentric analysis, multicide

INTRODUCTION

Perhaps one of the most tragic indicators of the overemphasis on physical aggression in American society is that of kids killing kids. While homicide arrests for persons under 18 have declined precipitously since 1993 (United States Department of Justice, 1999), recent school shootings in Santee, California; Littleton, Colorado; Conyers, Georgia; Stamps, Arkansas; and Pearl, Mississippi have compelled the American public to once again confront its violent cultural proclivities. What has been particularly somber about these school shootings is that they were multiple victim homicides, that is, situations in which more than one innocent person was murdered. The number of these types of homicides, which some now, along with recent mass workplace shootings, refer to as *multicide* (see Anonymous, 1998; Holmes & Holmes, 1992), rose from just one in school year 1994-95 to five in 1997-98 (United States Department of Education and Justice, 1999). The 1999 shooting at Columbine High School in Littleton, Colorado has been the most devastating: 13 were left dead, and the two perpetrators also took their lives. A striking observation of these multicides is they have occurred in predominantly white middle class communities and the perpetrators have been young white males.

The image of young white male homicide perpetrators challenges the much heralded nightly news image of the young black male homicide offender. Recent national data, however, reveal that while the proportion of black male homicide offenders between 14-24 has declined since 1993, the proportion of white male homicide offenders of the same age group has slightly increased (Fox & Zawitz, 1999). The proportion of young black male homicide offenders decreased from 33% of the total homicide offenders in 1993 to 26% of the total in 1998. Comparatively, young white male homicide offenders, as a proportion of the homicide offender total, slightly increased from 16% in 1993 to 19% in 1998. Although this increase was modest, it should be juxtaposed against the simultaneous decline in the overall population of young white males, which implies that a lesser number of young white males increasingly represent a higher percentage of homicide offenders (Fox & Zawitz, 1999). Moreover, the phenomenon of multicide is most likely to be committed by white males (Anonymous, 1998; Holmes & Holmes, 1992).

The above data, and recent school shootings, suggest that there may be a critical need to devote greater attention to violence among young white males. Though studies have attempted to explain young white male violence, many have attempted to do so by comparing young white males to young black males (see, for example, Cao, Adams, & Jensen, 1997; Harris, 1992; Kingery, Biafora, & Zimmerman, 1996; Paschall, Ennett, & Flewelling, 1996). However, little attention has been dedicated to explicating violence among young white males specifically.

This paper suggests that violence among young white males, especially of the multicide form, may be a function of the confluence of three structural-cultural factors: (1) the concept of manhood, prevalent in American culture, that places considerable emphasis on physical aggression; (2) the phenomenon of spiritual alienation; and (3) the anxiety and stress associated with concerns over maintaining white male privilege. While Oliver (Forthcoming) defines structural-cultural as the dynamic interplay between macro societal pressures and dysfunctional cultural adaptations, the term structural-cultural in this paper is conceptualized as the way in which specific cultural values in American society have been institutionalized to shape and justify America's social structure (i.e., the manner in which social roles, statutes, privileges, and positions are organized) structural-cultural. The acknowledgment of factors in explaining multicide in young white males is assumed in this paper to affirm an Afrocentric paradigm. After articulating some core themes of the paradigm, an examination of how the themes underscore the potential role of these structural-cultural factors in comprehending multicide among young white males is presented. Last, specific community interventions that might prevent multicide in young white males, as well as areas for future research, are provided.

THE AFROCENTRIC PARADIGM
AS A STRUCTURAL-CULTURAL CRITIQUE

Since the mid 1970s, an increasing cadre of African American social scientists and community activists has raised the critical question of whether

European American models of society and human behavior were sufficient in not only explicating the behavior and solving the problems of African Americans, but also at identifying shortcomings of the American cultural landscape (see, for example, Akbar 1979, 1984, 1994; Ani, 1994; Asante, 1988, 1990; Baldwin, 1985; Baldwin & Hopkins, 1990; Boykin & Toms, 1985; Carter, 1997; Cook & Kono, 1977; Dove, 1995, 1996; Harvey & Rauch, 1997; Hilliard, 1989; Kambon, 1992; Karenga, 1993, 1996; Khatib, Akbar, McGee, & Nobles, 1979; Myers, 1993; Nobles, 1980; Robinson & Howard-Hamilton, 1994; Schiele, 2000; Shujaa, 1994; Stewart, 1995). Referring to themselves as Afrocentrists, these writers have suggested that the shared cultural values, experiences, and visions of people of African ancestry can and should be codified into a formal social science paradigm that can and should be employed to explain and resolve social problems. Afrocentrists believe that the cultural legacy of traditional African societies, especially those of West Africa, continue to inform and influence the cultural ethos of contemporary people of African descent. They further contend that this ethos also has been shaped by people of African descent's experiences with racial oppression. Thus, the combined factors of the survival of the African cultural legacy and experiences with racial oppression underlie the philosophical underpinnings of the Afrocentric, or what some refer to as the African-centered, paradigm.

Afrocentrists avouch that the dual factors of *Eurocentric domination* and the *Eurocentric worldview* are the primary sources of the social problems prevalent in American society. Eurocentric domination can be defined as the ubiquitous control people of European descent exercise over influencing the contour and character of American political, economic, educational, religious, and knowledge validation institutions. The Eurocentric worldview can be defined as a distinct set of philosophical assumptions, which emanate from the diverse traditions and future visions of people of European descent, that provide explications of and prescriptions for human behavior and human civilizations.

Afrocentrists avouch that together, Eurocentric domination and the Eurocentric worldview have engendered a structural-cultural milieu that confines the positive potentiality of all people (Akbar, 1984; Karenga, 1996; Myers, 1993; Schiele, 2000). Eurocentric domination limits positive potentiality because it fosters extreme political and economic inequities and peculiar psychological distortions about human self-worth, mainly along the color line (Ani, 1994; Atwell, & Azibo, 1991; Kambon, 1992; Schiele, 2000). The primary societal implication for the political and economic inequities is that material resources and valuable social positions are distributed to validate and favor people of European ancestry over people of color, particularly African Americans (Asante, 1988; Asante & Abarry, 1996; Everett, Chipungu, & Leashore, 1991; Henderson, 1995). The peculiar psychological distortions of Eurocentric domination are attributed to cultural oppression (Akbar, 1984; Dove, 1996; Kambon, 1992). Young (1990) conceives cultural oppression as "the universalization of a dominant group's experience and culture and its establishment as the norm" (p. 59). The imposition of the dominant group's culture is attained by their control of major societal institutions and resources, and it creates the psychological illusion that the cultures of less powerful groups are marginal, invalid, or nonexistent (Ani, 1994; Schiele, 1998; Young, 1990). As a method of vilifying the humanity of one group to the celebration of another's, cultural oppression nurtures a false sense of group inferiority in the culturally oppressed and a false sense of group superiority among the culturally dominant (Ani, 1994; Atwell & Azibo, 1991; Baldwin, 1985; DuBois, 1961; Fanon, 1961; Welsing, 1991). From an Afrocentric perspective, this disparity in human self-worth is socially detrimental because it supports psychological misrepresentations that manifest in immense intergroup (and intragroup for the oppressed) animosity, envy, suspicion, and discomfort (Akbar, 1996; Ani, 1994; Fanon, 1961; Welsing, 1991).

The Eurocentric worldview also restricts the positive potentiality of people. Two core values–individualism and materialism–upon which the worldview stands not only have implications for reinforcing unsettling intergroup and intragroup relations, but also more personal ramifications for the individual's capacity to function optimally (Myers, 1993; Nobles, 1984; Rowe & Grills, 1993). For example, the value of individualism can generate an uncompromising insularity that downplays the importance of others in shaping whom and what the individual becomes, in short, denying the values of collective success and collective failure (Gyekye, 1987; Myers, 1993; Schiele, 2000). Because of its disavowal and marginality of collective success and failure, this insularity also can influence an over concern for aggressive competition, an insatiable desire to exploit the weaknesses of others to demonstrate prowess and power (Ani, 1994; Kambon, 1992; Myers, 1993). The value of materialism can be psychologically deleterious in two ways: (1) it supports the notion that material items mean more than the quality of interpersonal relations and that material possessions are the cornerstones of human self-worth (Akbar, 1984; Myers, 1993; Wilson, 1992); and (2) it encourages the belief that reality is determined primarily by sensory perception and that unseen, nonmaterial phenomena are less credible or nonexistent (Asante, 1990; Horton, 1993; Kambon, 1992). Additionally, if life is restricted to a material reality, the spiritual essence, assumed to pervade and to conjoin all life, is underestimated or denied (Asante, 1990; Ameen, 1990; Paris, 1995). Due to its values and their potential to encourage human alienation and conflict, some suggest that the Eurocentric worldview is particularly suited to buttress and sustain political and economic oppression in the United States (Ani, 1994; Baldwin, 1985; Nobles, 1984; Schiele, 1996).

The structural-cultural critique of American society offered by the Afro-centric paradigm supports the earlier contention that multicide among young white males may be a result of three structural-cultural factors: (1) an aggressive concept of manhood; (2) spiritual alienation; and (3) anxiety and stress around concerns over persevering white male privilege. Next, the Afrocentric critique is applied to explain how it underscores each of the three structural-cultural factors.

AFROCENTRIC CRITIQUE
AND MALE AGGRESSION

The factor of male aggression is highlighted by the Afrocentric critique of the Eurocentric world views emphasis on individualism. It is the competitive feature of individualism that can generate a veneration for aggression. Although all who are exposed to and who internalize the Eurocentric worldview are at risk of behaving aggressively, if only subtly, men are placed in greater jeopardy than are women (Baldwin, 1991; Ghee, 1990; Oliver, 1989; Schiele, 1998). This can be explained by two factors: (1) the role of provider in traditional European American culture is almost exclusively ascribed to men, despite recent changes in female work participation rates (Abramovitz, 1996; Jimenez, 1999); and (2) the expectation in traditional European American culture that males display emotional toughness, which can effectuate fascinations over physical prowess and fearless violence (Akbar, 1991; Baldwin, 1991; Garbarino, 1999; Oliver, 1989; Schiele, 1998).

Walker (1995) proposes that white males are notably prone to the allure of and tolerance for violence in the United States. He suggests that the origins of this preoccupation can be found in the nation's origins: "It is a nation formed in revolution against the British by tax-hating, angry white men with guns"(Walker, 1995, p. 28). Walker further observes that this inception laid the foundation for many later acts of aggression by gun toting white males ". . . that always ended in success" (p. 28). Examples of these historical successes are the annihilation of First Nation (Native American) people, the racial terrorism of all white male groups such as the Ku Klux Klan, and major white intraracial conflicts such as the American Civil War and World Wars I and II. With the aid of the mass media, educational institutions, and lore, these historical triumphs have become ingrained in the American ethos and consciousness. While all who are exposed to this cultural hallmark are at risk of engaging in and justifying violence, especially gun violence, the primary historical actors in America have been white males, who were often young (Walker, 1995; Zinn, 1999).

From a historical framework, young white males may be more susceptible than others to the belief in the effective use of guns in advancing a political cause and resolving social and interpersonal conflicts. Possible evidence for this assumption may be revealed by national data indicating that more whites own guns than blacks and that more males own guns than females (Cook & Ludwig, 1997), which suggest that white males are more likely to own guns than other race/gender groups. In addition, since U.S. history of gun violence often included mass murder (i.e., multicide), the attraction it poses to vulnerable, young white males may be substantial.

AFROCENTRIC CRITIQUE
AND SPIRITUAL ALIENATION

Spiritual alienation, the second structural-cultural factor, also derives from an Afrocentric critique and may be important in explaining multicide among young white males. The notion of spiritual alienation emanates from the two central values of the Eurocentric worldview examined earlier, particularly the value of materialism. Spiritual alienation can be defined as " . . . the disconnection of nonmaterial and morally affirming values from concepts of human self-worth and from the character of social relationships" (Schiele, 1996, p. 289). It represents an extreme materialist worldview in which humans become objectified. This objectification is possible because the spiritual essence that binds humans to each other and to nature is underestimated and repudiated (Ani, 1994; Cohen, 1996). This sense of interrelatedness and interdependence, some say, is necessary to promote moral consciousness, mutual respect, and peaceful communities (Etzioni, 1993; Ward, 1995).

Because of its denial of the sacredness of human life and the spiritual nexus that underlies it, spiritual alienation contributes to a *cutthroat morality* that encourages a hostile social environment (Ward, 1995). In this callous social milieu, the exclusive interests, needs, feelings, and desires of an individual or group can foster indifference toward other individuals and groups. This condition is not only a function of the individual's or group's disregard for *alien others*, but also from an underlying belief, regnant in Eurocentric societies, that human beings are innately evil, aggressive, and selfish (Ani, 1994; Schiele, 2000). This belief can produce pessimism and cynicism about the intent and actions of others, and xenophobia (Ani, 1994; Schiele, 2000). It has been suggested that xenophobia was a central motivation in the historical massacres perpetuated by white males against groups such as First Nation people and African Americans in the United States (T'Shaka, 1995; Zinn, 1999). Today, xenophobia is believed to be demonstrated in the growth of white supremacist groups and Internet sites, diatribes on affirmative action, and protests against the rising immigration of people of color that are mostly spearheaded and supported by white males (Ferber, 1998; Dobratz & Shanks-Meile, 1997).

Another aspect of spiritual alienation that might affect young white male multicide is the feeling of disempowerment, of being dispossessed. This might appear illogical if one considers the political and economic power and privilege white males have held historically in the United States. However, a critical Afrocentric assumption undergirding spiritual alienation as an explanatory factor is that humans cannot elicit their full positive potentiality if they do not acknowledge and tap into the power inherent in spiritual interconnectedness (Myers, 1993; Phillips, 1990; Schiele, 2000). When humans recognize and draw upon this interconnectedness, they are in a better position to expand their sense of self, to recognize that life has greater meaning beyond the confines of material possessions and the material realm, to integrate the knowledge and wisdom of others who may be different, and to gain inspiration from the simple, yet complex, beauty of life itself. If depression is associated with feelings of disempowerment, which is assumed here to be related to a lack of spiritual interconnectedness, and if depression is a precursor to the most devastating self-destructive act, suicide, then suicide may be an indicator of one's lack of spiritual interconnectedness. This point about the potential role of spiritual interconnectedness in suicides may be especially relevant to white males in that national data reveal they commit suicides at a greater rate than any other race/gender group in the United States (Hoyert, Kochanek, & Murphy, 1999).

AFROCENTRIC CRITIQUE
AND WHITE MALE PRIVILEGE

The potential lower likelihood of spiritual interconnectedness among white males may suggest that one factor involved in young white male multicide is the concern over continuing white male political and economic privilege. The significance of this concern stems from the Afrocentric focus on Eurocentric domination, that is, the continuation of political and economic power among European Americans, particularly European American males. While the factor of white male privilege may appear to be the less relevant structural-cultural factor since young white males–especially teens–have not fully entered the workforce, it nonetheless may be indirectly pertinent to this population. Although young white males may not participate fully in the workforce, and thus may not be as directly affected by recent workplace changes in American society, their socialization as white males may compel them to consider these transformations as they approach adulthood. Furthermore, their conscious observations of the lives of adult white males–those they know and do not know–may sensitize them to the anxiety and stress experienced by these men as they attempt to negotiate alterations in the demographic, political, and economic character of America that increasingly are perceived as discriminatory against white males (Gillian, 1999; Lynch, 1997).

From an Afrocentric viewpoint, the anxiety and stress over maintaining white male privilege, which is assumed to play a pivotal, yet indirect, role in young white male multicide, is a result of three relatively recent phenomena: (1) the globalization of the economy, (2) changes in and projections of the demographic picture of the U.S. population, and (3) the ascendancy of the political and legal power of people of color and women.

The Global Economy

The globalization of the American economy has caused manifold layoffs, considerable company downsizing, and the frequent relocation of American companies to other nations (Blau, 1999; Karger & Stoesz, 1998; Rifkin, 1995; Wilson, 1996). These trends have been fueled by the increasing mechanization of labor, the desire among American companies to locate new pools of low wage labor and regulatory free business environs, the enactment of free trade policies such as the North American Free Trade Agreement (NAFTA), the declining power of nation states, and the avarice among corporations to accumulate and appropriate a greater amount of capital (Blau, 1999; Rifkin, 1995; Karger & Stoesz, 1998; Wilson, 1996).

Although these trends have been devastating for many American workers and their families, blue-collar white males and their families may have been particularly caught off guard (Pfeil, 1997; Rifkin, 1995). This may be attributed to not only the economic stability these men enjoyed for so long, but also to the elimination of psychological power or what DuBois (1935) referred to as the *psychological wage*. The psychological wage, DuBois contended, was a feeling of privilege and power extended to all white males because of their racial and gender status. The psychological wage ensured that white men from all socioeconomic groupings would be treated better than others, and would be afforded a stronger sense of psychological security. What the recent changes from globalization have generated is an emotional disconnection between blue-collar white males and their employers (Pfeil, 1997). These males no longer have the psychological security that companies will protect them and their families and guarantee perpetual employment. Pfeil (1997) contends the fundamental source of blue collar white men's bewilderment is their " . . . bafflement, grief, and rage at the breakdown and/or removal of a profoundly undemocratic patriarchal and neofeudal hierarchy into which they once believed they fit organically, with their own zones of autonomy and . . . privilege, no matter how small" (p. 30). Young white males who read and hear about these psychoemotional changes and who may experience them vicariously through their fathers or other white male relatives and friends may become disillusioned about their future and their ability to benefit economically from being white and male.

Demographic Changes

Demographic projections indicate that by 2050, the United States likely will be comprised mostly of nonwhite people (United States Bureau of the Census, 1998). This social change has ocurred in California where over 50% of its residents are now nonwhite (United States Bureau of the Census, 2001). This population shift in California and the rest of the country usually is ascribed to the massive immigration of Hispanic and Asian Americans since 1980, and to disparities in fertility rates between white and nonwhite people (United States Bureau of the Census, 1998).

This demographic change, while perhaps trivial to some, has caused others to express passionate concerns about the biological and cultural survival of the white race in the United States (Lane, 1995; Thornton, 1995; Unz, 1999). The critical question is how can whites, especially white males, sustain political, economic, and cultural dominance if their numbers are dwindling? With their cultural and biological survival at stake, European American adults generally, and European American men specifically, may be desperate for solutions to quell the seemingly irreversible demographic tide, and this consternation also may be discerned by and inculcated to many young white males.

Enhanced Power Among People of Color and Women

The final potential source of anxiety and stress associated with sustaining white male privilege is the ascension in the political and legal power of people of color and women, especially as revealed in the growth in Affirmative Action programs. Ever since President Nixon's *Philadelphia Plan* in 1969, which set quotas and time tables for the hiring of construction workers of color (Quadagno, 1994), people of color and women have successfully won major legal victories that have created meaningful opportunities in education and the workplace (Jansson, 1997; Quadagno, 1994). People of color, primarily African Americans, and women are now found in positions that just a generation ago little, if any, were in. Moreover, the labor force participation of women increased dramatically between 1950, when the participation rate for women was 33.9%, and 1998, when the participation rate was 59.8% (Fullerton, 1999).

For many white males, these employment and workplace trends suggest a form of reverse racism and an anti-white male agenda (Gillian, 1999; Lynch, 1997). The allegations of reverse racism and anti-white maleness can be illustrated in the following views and actions of white men: (1) white males overwhelmingly oppose employment preferences for both African Americans and women (National Opinion Research Center, 1996); (2) white males are highly likely to sue for reverse discrimination in the workplace (Gillian,

1999; Lynch, 1997); (3) they constitute the majority of the membership in white advocacy and racial hate groups in the United States (Dobratz & Shanks-Meile, 1997); and (4) white males are more likely than any other group to commit hate crimes that are motivated by racial hostility (United States Department of Justice, 1999).

If modeling–both personal and societal–is a significant component of socialization, then these adult, white male role models may be projecting messages of hate, anxiety, and intergroup intolerance to younger white males. More fundamentally, these messages may cultivate an entrenched, yet unobtrusive, depression in vulnerable young white males, who may perceive its cure, or at least its alleviation, as lashing out at innocent victims conveniently located in their immediate community surroundings. Perhaps it is this depression, germinating from the structural-cultural themes of Eurocentric domination and the Eurocentric worldview, that is the final straw that pressures distraught white boys to commit the unforgettable calamity of multicide.

AFROCENTRIC RECOMMENDATIONS
TO END THE VIOLENCE

Enhancing Spirituality

Since the Afrocentric paradigm assumes that the spiritual or nonmaterial component of human beings is just as important as the material, one way of reducing the violence committed by young white males is to eliminate their condition of spiritual alienation. In the main, American society encourages a high degree of individualism. Conceivably, this rabid individualism removes one from a spiritual core, leaving the material as paramount. Americans in general, and young white males in particular, should recapture their spiritual grounding. Spiritual and moral development ought to be at the forefront of social policies aimed at alleviating violence committed by young white males. Young men today live in a world where morality seems irrelevant (Garbarino, 1999). There has to be a concerted effort to bring back or reinvigorate moral standards of living. This effort has to entail collaboration and cooperation on the part of parents, schools, churches, and community leaders. A *moral minimum* (Karenga, 1993) should be established, setting into place an ethos that should be adhered to by youth growing up today. Mutual respect and tolerance of others should be an unyielding cornerstone of this ethos.

Garbarino (1999) outlines a novel set of steps that if implemented can enhance the spirituality of young males. First, these males need experiences that put an emphasis on empathy, feeling as others feel. The callousness of recent school shootings clearly demonstrates an absence of empathetic understanding. Empathy is important because it can assist boys in connecting abstract principles of morality with real-life situations and feelings. Second, spiritual connectedness should entail a reduction in the exposure to socially demeaning images. Parents and community members could be integral components of this process if they collaborate in protecting boys from degrading and dehumanizing images. Limiting the access and exposure to violent movies, video games, and comic books could reduce the development of a calculating, cold-blooded, and uncaring disposition. Third, encouraging boys to participate in non-punitive religious experiences also could contribute to spiritual development. Churches should move away from coercive traditional methods of captivating potential parishioners. The days of making a person feel as if he or she is a "sinner" if minor violations of church doctrine occur should end. Moreover, this step may have the effect of increasing the religious participation of a spiritually marginalized segment of the population.

Relatedly, at the family, community, and societal levels, there is a need to provide greater integration of religious concepts and dialogue. Particular attention should be given to integrating religious content in public schools. In December of 1999, the United States Department of Education Secretary, Richard Riley, sent guidelines for teaching religion content to public school principles throughout the country (Riley, 1999). The guidelines are aimed at dispelling the myth that religious content cannot be infused in school curricula and offer specific recommendations on how to explore religious content in the classroom without violating first amendment rights (see First Amendment Center, 1999). The guidelines are not only concerned with providing a cognitive understanding of diverse religious beliefs but also with the relationship between religious content and character education that focuses on enhancing the moral life and consciousness of students. An Afrocentric analysis would strongly encourage schools to incorporate these guidelines in their curricula so as to increase the exposure of students to deeper values of community and civic responsibility and mutual tolerance and respect.

Grappling with Male Aggression

In any discussion of masculinity or manhood in Eurocentric societies, invariably the notion of aggressiveness, particularly physical aggression, finds its way into the discourse. Other Eurocentric conceptions of manhood include the view that men are competitive, dominant and unemotional (Franklin, 1984, 1988). Young white males who believe and internalize these conceptions of manhood are more likely to use violence than those that do not (Garbarino, 1999). Thus, it becomes imperative to transform what young males believe exemplifies manhood. The Afrocentric paradigm does this by departing substantially from placing considerable emphasis on physical aggression.

Akbar (1991) delineates several characteristics in terms of a definition of manhood. No where in his definition does one find physical aggression. Using a group of renown models of African American manhood (i.e., Martin Luther King, Jr., Elijah Muhammad, Paul Roberson, Cheikh Anta Diop), Akbar (1991) offers an image of manhood that embodies the qualities of (1) excellence; (2) courage; (3) defiance; (4) economic solvency; (5) uncompromising integrity; and (6) scholarship. Echoing Akbar's conception of manhood, Madhubuti (1990) conceives of manhood as exemplifying quiet strength, scholarship, resource sharing, justice, truth and honesty, sensitivity, commitment, spirituality, and vision. A conception of manhood placing primacy upon these values can enable young white males to de-emphasize physical aggression and violence and place more emphasis upon prosocial behaviors.

Recommendations that may usher in these conceptions of manhood include the following:

1. *Encouraging participation in character building programs such as the Boy Scouts of America or the Big Brother Program*;
2. *Improvements in mentoring programs especially those where older successful males mentor young white males who have a demonstrated propensity to become violent*;
3. *Involvement of media outlets and representatives to help change the definitions of manhood.* As alluded to above, the media, particularly movies and video games, may be particularly culpable in fostering violence among white male youths. Evidence for this assertion has been documented by Price, Merrill, & Clause (1992) who, in their content analysis of prime-time programming of major television networks, found that white males were portrayed as gun users in more than 75% of the scenes observed. Since it is assumed the media foster violence, they should play a central role in eradicating violence committed by white boys. Media campaigns entailing the development of public service and awareness announcements concerned with positive, prosocial attributes of manhood may lead to a cessation of the violence committed by white boys. This effort also should require involvement from many human service professionals such as teachers, school administrators, social workers, child development experts, juvenile justice officials, and clergy;
4. *Development of manhood training programs during early adolescence.* One should not presume that young white males are being adequately socialized to elicit their vast positive potentiality. More deliberate strategies of socialization that expose young white males to more socially affirming and humanistic conceptions of manhood might be needed. In the African American community, these deliberate strategies are referred to as *Manhood Training or Rites of Passage Programs* (see Harvey & Rauch, 1997; Jeff, 1994; Stewart, 1995). For young white males, these programs may help to reinforce those characteristics Akbar (1991) and Madhubuti (1990) believe are exemplars of manhood.

The Challenge of White Male Privilege

To address the last structural-cultural factor that may engender violence among young white males, the importance of the Afrocentric assumption that human identity is a collective identity should be upheld (see Akbar, 1984; Mbiti, 1970; Nobles, 1980; Schiele, 1996). Positing the violence committed by white boys is associated with the anxiety and stress associated with the perceived loss or abatement in white male privilege may illustrate how vulnerable white boys do not perceive human identity as a collective identity. White male privilege may unconsciously induce young white males to develop an ethos of insularity and entitlement. This privilege may encourage a separate and distinct identity wherein white men may believe they deserve most, if not all, of society's resources. If they perceive a decrease in what they believe to be rightfully theirs, they may be at risk of becoming violent (Walker, 1995; Ferber, 1998). In a critical examination of Western thought and European American culture, Myers' (1993) views could be construed to suggest how it is possible that white boys may have developed the erroneous perception of their privileged status in American society:

> Starting with the basic ontological assumption that the nature of reality is principally material, we are set up for a world view in which the resources necessary for survival exist in only a finite and limited amount (e.g., the pie is only so big). The process of life is such that to survive we must compete (*aggress*) [italics added] for the limited resources. Highest value is placed on their acquisition. If we accept the materialist perspective, even our worth as human beings becomes fragile and diminished: our worth is equal to what we own, how we look, and what kind of car, house, education we have, and so on. Because of its nature this system does not work even for the dominant group, and it will most certainly not work for the racially and sexually oppressed. That basic sense of worth, peace, and security all human beings so desperately need cannot be achieved through material, external criteria. What happens is that we get only some of what we want, and we want more; we get more, and we want more and more, and so on. We are left feeling insecure, anxious, depressed, and looking outside ourselves for something else to make everything better. (Myers 1993, p. 10)

Referring to the limited resources mentioned by Myers, white males who believe their piece of the pie is constantly shrinking may resort to violence to compensate for their feelings of material loss. Fostering a collective identity among young white males might compel them to share the pie rather than hoard it for themselves.

To reduce the anxiety and stress associated with maintaining white male privilege among white male youths, the following recommendations are offered: (1) Developing and implementing programs that stress the importance of diversity; (2) The use of programs that teach tolerance such as the ones used by The Southern Poverty Law Center; (3) Designing social activities that break down the social distance between young white males and others; and (4) Highlighting alternative indicators of success that accentuate nonmaterial aspects of achievement (e.g., one's success in interpersonal relationships and in demonstrating compassion for others).

ADDITIONAL IDEAS

Whereas the aforementioned recommendations relate to the three structural-cultural factors that are thought to contribute to the violence committed by white boys, the following are some general, school-based recommendations that could help preclude and reduce multicide:

- Targeted prevention, intervention and remedial programs aim at youth who commit serious violent crimes; those who commit less serious offenses, and the growing population of at-risk youth (Biden, 1998).
- Development and enforcement of school safety drills and zero-tolerance gun control legislation including gun-free school zones (Lamberg, 1998; Page and Hammermeister, 1997; American Academy of Child and Adolescent Psychiatry, 1999).
- Teacher training in preventing youth violence (Wood et al., 1996).
- Curriculum development with emphasis upon diversity.
- Responsible media coverage of acts of school violence (Dority, 1999).
- Development of effective school-based hate prevention programs.
- Development of curricula that encourage feelings of empowerment and positive self-worth.
- Development of effective response plans to school violence (Dwyer et al., 1998).

SUGGESTIONS FOR FUTURE RESEARCH

Although an Afrocentric analysis may be helpful in explaining why young white males commit multicide, more research employing the Afrocentric paradigm needs to be conducted in the area of youth violence. Some possible research questions might include: (1) Would specific quantitative measures of male aggression, spiritual alienation, and anxiety over maintaining white male privilege help to discriminate young white males prone to multicide from those who are not? (2) For what reasons are white male youths more likely to engage in multicide than youths from other racial and ethnic groups? (3) Will an increase in gun control and gun safety laws significantly reduce violence among white boys? (4) Are young white males exposed to diverse cultural and ethnic backgrounds early in life less likely to be violent than those white males not exposed to such diversity? (5) What additional structural-cultural factors, other than the three examined here, could explain white boys who kill? and (6) How effective are violence prevention programs that rely on Afrocentric principles? Future research of this kind could augment the applicability of the Afrocentric paradigm in explaining and diminishing multicide among young white males.

CONCLUSION

This paper has applied the Afrocentric paradigm to explain and provide recommendations to prevent multicide in young white males. A physically aggressive concept of manhood, spiritual alienation, and anxiety and stress associated with white male privilege were offered as three structural-cultural factors pivotal in understanding and obviating multicide among young white males. These factors were further assumed to emerge from Eurocentric domination and the Eurocentric worldview, which were presented as concepts essential to an Afrocentric critique of American society.

While some may suggest the application of the Afrocentric paradigm to interpret and prevent violence among young white males is politically inappropriate, the Afrocentric paradigm can and should be employed to address all social problems stemming from Eurocentric domination and the ubiquity of the Eurocentric worldview. The Afrocentric critique, though reflecting the cultural traditions of people of African descent and their intergenerational experiences with racial oppression, should focus just as much on the adverse effects that Eurocentric domination and the Eurocentric worldview have had on the psychosocial functioning of European Americans as it should on the deleterious consequences they have had on people of African descent. Although many young white males, like European Americans generally, have benefited politically and economically from Eurocentric domination and the pervasiveness of the Eurocentric worldview, they have suffered socially, psychologically, and spiritually, and this has acutely compromised their humanity. Perhaps an Afrocentric analysis can be most useful in helping vulnerable young white males to recapture and repair their humanity that has been undercut by a cultural model that diminishes human potential for maximum peace, love, and mutual cooperation and respect.

REFERENCES

Abramovitz, M. (1996). *Regulating the lives of women.* Boston: South End Press.

Akbar, N. (1979). African roots of black personality. In W.D. Smith, H. Kathleen, M.H. Burlew, & W.M. Whitney (Ed.), *Reflections on black psychology,* (pp. 79-87). Washington, DC: University Press of America.

Akbar, N. (1984). Afrocentric social sciences for human liberation. *Journal of Black Studies,* 14(4), 395-414.

Akbar, N. (1991). *Visions for black men.* Nashville, TN: Winston-Derek Publishers, Inc.

Akbar, N. (1994). *Light from ancient Africa.* Tallahassee, FL: Mind Productions.

Akbar, N. (1996). *Breaking the chains of psychological slavery.* Tallahassee, Fl: Mind Productions & Associates.

Ameen, R.U.N. (1990). *Metu neter, Vol.1.* Bronx, NY: Khamit Corporation.

American Academy of Child and Adolescent Psychiatry. (1999). Violent behavior in children and youth: Preventive intervention from a psychiatric perspective. *Journal of the American Academy of Child and Adolescent Psychiatry.* 38(3), 235-245.

Ani, M. (1994). *Yurugu: An African-centered critique of European cultural thought and behavior.* Trenton, NJ: Africa World Press.

Anonymous, (1998). A profile of multicide. *Occupational Hazards,* 60(8), 28-30.

Asante, M.K. (1988). *Afrocentricity.* Trenton, NJ: Africa World Press, Inc.

Asante, M.K. (1990). *Kemet, afrocentricity, and knowledge.* Trenton, NJ: African World Press.

Asante, M.K. & Abarry, A.S. (1996) (Ed.). *African intellectual heritage: A book of sources.* Philadelphia: Temple University Press.

Atwell, I. & Azibo, D. (1991). Diagnosing personality disorder in Africans (Blacks) using the Azibo nosology: Two case studies. *Journal of Black Psychology,* 17(2), 1-22.

Baldwin, J. (1985). Psychological aspects of European cosmology in American society. *The Western Journal of Black Studies,* 9(4), 216-223.

Baldwin, J. (1991, October). *An Afrocentric perspective on health and social behavior of African American males.* Presented at the National Conference on Health and Social Behavior of African American Males, Institute for Urban Affairs & Research, Washington, DC.

Baldwin, J. and Hopkins, R. (1990). African-American and European-American cultural differences as assessed by the worldviews paradigm: An empirical analysis. *The Western Journal of Black Studies,* 14(1), 38-52.

Biden, J. (1998). Attacking Youth Violence. *Criminal Justice Ethics.* 17(1), 2-5.

Blau, J. (1999). *Illusions of prosperity: America's working families in an age of economic insecurity.* New York: Oxford University Press.

Boykin, W. and Toms, F. (1985). Black child socialization: A conceptual framework, in H.P. McAdoo (ed.) *Black children.* Beverly Hills: Sage Publications.

Cao, L.Q., Adams, A., & Jensen, V.J. (1997), A test of the black subculture of violence thesis: A research note. *Criminology,* 35(2), 367-379.

Carter, C.S. (1997). Using African-centered principles in family-preservation services. *Families in Society,* 78(5), 531-538.

Cohen, G. (1996). Toward a spirituality based on justice and ecology. *Social Policy,* 26(3), 6-18.

Cook, N. & Kono, S. (1977). Black psychology: The third great tradition. *The Journal of Black Psychology*, 3(2), 18-20.

Cook, P.J. & Ludwig, J. (1997). *Guns in America*: *National survey on private ownership and use of firearms*. Washington, DC: U.S. Department of Justice, National Institute of Justice.

Dobratz, B. & Shanks-Meile, S. (1997). *"White power, white pride!" The white separatists movement in the United States*. New York: Simon & Schuster.

Dority, B. (1999). The Columbine tragedy: Countering the hysteria. *The Humanist*, 59(4), 7-12.

Dove, N. (1995). An African-centered critique of Marx's logic. *The Western Journal of Black Studies*, 19(4), 260-271.

Dove, N. (1996). Understanding education for cultural affirmation. In E.K. Addae (Ed.), *To heal a people: African scholars defining a new reality*, (269-298). Columbia, MD: Kujichagulia Press.

DuBois, W.E.B. (1935). *Black reconstruction in America-1860-1880*. New York: Russell & Russell.

DuBois, W.E.B. (1961). *The souls of black folk*. New York: Fawcett World Library.

Dwyer, K., Osher, D., & Warger, C. (1998). *Early warning, timely response: A guide to safe schools*. Washington, DC: Department of Education.

Etzioni, A. (1993). *The spirit of community*. New York: Pantheon.

Everett, J., Chipungu, S., & Leashore, B. (1991, Ed.). *Child Welfare: An Afrocentric perspective*. New Brunswick, NJ: Rutgers University Press.

Fanon, F. (1961). *Black skin, white masks*. New York: Grove Press.

Ferber, A.L. (1998). *White man falling*: *Gender, race, and white supremacy*. New York: Rowman & Littlefield.

First Amendment Center (1999). *A teacher's guide to religion in the public schools*. Nashville, TN: First Amendment Center.

Fox, J.A. & Zawitz, M.W. (1999). *Homicide trends in the United States*. Washington, DC: U.S. Department of Justice, Bureau of Labor Statistics.

Franklin, C. (1984). *The changing definition of masculinity*. New York, NY: Plenum Press.

Franklin, C. (1988). *Men & Society*. Chicago, IL: Nelson-Hall.

Fullerton, H.N. (1999). Labor force participation: 75 years of change, 1950-98 and 1998-2025. *Monthly Labor Review*, 122(12), 3-10.

Garbarino, J. (1999). *Lost Boys: Why our sons turn violent and how we can save them*. New York, NY: The Free Press.

Ghee, K.L. (1990). Enhancing educational achievement through cultural awareness in young black males. *The Western Journal of Black Studies*, 14(2), 77-89.

Gillian, F. (1999). White males see diversity's other side. *Workforce*, 78(2), 52-55.

Gyekye, K. (1987). *An essay on African philosophical thought: The Akan conceptual scheme*. New York: Cambridge University Press.

Harris, M.B. (1992). Sex and ethnic-differences in past aggressive behaviors. *Journal of Family Violence*, 7(2), 85-102.

Harvey, A.R. & Rauch, J.B. (1997). A comprehensive Afrocentric rites of passage program for black male adolescents. *Health & Social Work*, 22(1), 30-37.

Henderson, E.A. (1995). *Afrocentrism and world politics: Towards a new paradigm.* Westport, CT: Praeger.

Hilliard, A.G. (1989). Kemetic concepts in education. In I.V. Sertima (ed., 3rd printing), *Nile valley civilizations.* Atlanta: Morehouse College.

Holmes, R.M. & Holmes, S.T. (1992). Understanding mass murder: A starting point. *Federal Probation*, 56(1), 53-61.

Horton, R. (1993). *Patterns of thought in Africa and the west: Essays on magic, religion and science.* New York: Cambridge University Press.

Hoyert, D.L., Kochanek, K.D., & Murphy, S.L. (1999). *Deaths: Final data for 1997. National vital statistics report.* Hyattsville, MD: National Center for Health Statistics.

Jansson, B.S. (1997). *The reluctant welfare state: American social welfare policies-past, present, and future (3rd ed.).* Pacific Grove, CA: Brooks/Cole Publishing Company.

Jeff, M. (1994). Afrocentrism and African-American male youths. In R. Mincy, *Nurturing young Black males.* Washington, DC: The Urban Institute Press.

Jimenez, M.A. (1999). A feminist analysis of welfare reform: The personal responsibility act of 1996. *Affilia*, 14(3), 278-293.

Kambon, K. (1992). *The African personality in America: An African centered framework.* Tallahassee, FL: Nubian Nation Publications.

Karenga, M. (1993). *Introduction to black studies* (2nd ed). Los Angles, CA: The University of Sankore Press.

Karenga, M. (1996). The nguzo saba (the seven principles): Their meaning and message. In M.K. Asante & A.S. Abarry (ed.), *African intellectual heritage* (pp. 543-554). Philadelphia, PA: Temple University Press.

Karger, H.J. & Stoesz, D. (1998). *American social welfare policy: A structural analysis (3rd ed.).* New York: Longman.

Khatib, S., Akbar, N., McGee, D. and Nobles, W. (1979). Voodoo or IQ: An introduction to African psychology, in W.D. Smith, K.H. Burlew, M.H. Mosley and W.M. Whitney (Ed.) *Reflections on black psychology.* Washington, DC: University Press of America.

Kingery, P.M., Biafora, F.A., & Zimmerman, R.S. (1996). Risk-factors for violent behaviors among ethnically diverse urban adolescents: Beyond race/ethnicity. *School Psychology International*, 17(2), 171-186.

Lamberg, L. (1998). Preventing school violence: No easy answers. *The Journal of the American Medical Association.* 280(5), 404-409.

Lane, D. (1995). The white race must be saved. In C.P. Cozic (Ed.), *Ethnic conflict*, (pp. 36-39). San Diego, CA: Greenhaven Press.

Lynch, F.R. (1997). *The diversity machine: The drive to change the white male workplace.* New York: The Free Press.

Madhubuti, H. (1990). *Black men: Obsolete, single, dangerous? The African American family in Transition.* Chicago, IL: Third World Press.

Mbiti, J. (1970). *African religions and philosophy.* Garden City, NY: Anchor Books.

Myers, L. (1993). *Understanding an Afrocentric world view: Introduction to an optimal psychology (2nd ed).* Dubuque, IA: Kendall/Hunt Publishing Company.

National Opinion Research Center, (1996). *General social survey cumulative file, 1972-1996*. Chicago, IL: National Opinion Research Center.

Nobles, W.W. (1980). African philosophy: Foundations for black psychology. In R. Jones (3rd ed.) *Black psychology*, (pp. 23-35). New York: Harper and Row.

Nobles, W.W. (1984). Alienation, human transformation and adolescent drug use: Toward a reconceptualization of the problem. *Journal of Drug Issues*, 14(2), 243-252.

Oliver, W. (1989). Black males and social problems: Prevention through Afrocentric socialization. *Journal of Black Studies*, 20(1), 15-39.

Oliver, W. (Forthcoming). The structural-cultural perspective: A theory of black male violence. In D. Hawkins (Ed.), *Violent crimes: The nexus of race, ethnicity, and violence*. New York: Cambridge University Press.

Page, R. & Hammermeister, J. (1997). Weapon-carrying and youth violence. *Adolescence*, 32(127), 505-512.

Paris, P.J. (1995). *The spirituality of African peoples*. Minneapolis, MN: Fortress Press.

Paschall, M.J., Ennett, S.T, & Flewelling, R.L. (1996). Relationships among family characteristics and violent behavior by black and white male adolescents. *Journal of Youth and Adolescence*, 25(2), 177-197.

Pfeil, F. (1997). Sympathy for the devils: Notes on some white guys in the ridiculous class war. In M. Hill (Ed.), *Whiteness: A critical reader* (pp.21-34). New York: New York University Press.

Phillips, F.B. (1990). NTU psychotherapy: An Afrocentric approach. *The Journal of Black Psychology*, 17(1), 55-74.

Price, J.H., Merrill, E.A., & Clause, M.E. (1992). The depiction of guns on prime-time television. *Journal of School Health*, 62(1), 15-18.

Quadagno, J.(1994). *The color of welfare: How racism undermined the war on poverty*. New York: Oxford University Press.

Rifkin, J. (1995). *The end of work: The decline of the global labor force and the dawn of the post-market era*. New York: G.P. Putnam's Sons.

Riley, R.W. (1999, December 17). *Letter to principles on religion and public schools*. Washington, DC: U.S. Department of Education.

Robinson, T.L., & Howard-Hamilton, M.H. (1994). An Afrocentric paradigm: Foundation for a healthy self-image and healthy interpersonal relationships. *Journal of Mental Health Counseling*, 16(3), 327-339.

Rowe, D., & Grills, C. (1993). African-centered drug treatment: An alternative conceptual paradigm for drug counseling with African American clients. *Journal of Psychoactive Drugs*, 25(1), 21-33.

Schiele, J.H. (1996). Afrocentricity: An emerging paradigm in social work practice. *Social Work*. 41(3), 284-294.

Schiele, J.H. (1998). Cultural alignment, African American male youths, and violent crime. *Journal of Human Behavior and the Social Environment*, 1(2/3), 165-181.

Schiele, J.H. (2000). *Human services and the Afrocentric paradigm*. Binghamton, NY: The Haworth Press, Inc.

Shujaa, M. (1994, Ed.). *Too much schooling, too little education*. Lawrenceville, NJ: Africa World Press.

Stewart, R. (1995). Afrocentric Strategies and their promise for solving problems affecting African American males in urban areas. In Koritz et al. *Crossing Boundaries: Collaborative Solutions to Urban Problems*, (pp.239-252). Buffalo, NY: State University of New York College at Buffalo Press.

Thornton, J. (1995). The threat from immigrants. In C.P. Cozic (Ed.), *Ethnic conflict*, (pp.26-35). San Diego, CA: Greenhaven Press.

T'Shaka, O. (1995). *Return to the African mother principle of male female equality.* Oakland, CA: Pan African Publishers and Distributors.

United States Bureau of the Census, (1998). *Current population survey.* Washington, DC: U.S. Government Printing Office.

United States Bureau of the Census, (2001). *Population estimates by age, sex, race, and Hispanic origin, 2000.* Washington, DC: U.S. Government Printing Office.

United States Departments of Education and Justice, (1999). *Annual report on school safety.* Washington, DC: Government Printing Office.

United States Department of Justice, Federal Bureau of Investigation, (1999). *Uniform crime reports for the United States, 1998.* Washington, DC: Government Printing Office.

Unz, R. (1999). California and the end of white America. *Commentary*, 108(4), 17-28.

Walker, M. (1995). America's angry white males. *World Press Review*, 42(7), 28-29.

Ward, J.V. (1995). Cultivating a morality of care in African American adolescents: A culture-based model of violence prevention. *Harvard Educational Review*, 65(2), 175-188.

Welsing, F.C. (1991). *The isis papers: The keys to the colors.* Chicago: Third World Press.

Wilson, A.N. (1992). *Understanding black adolescent male violence: Its remediation and prevention.* New York: African World Infosystems.

Wilson, W.J. (1996). *When work disappears: The world of the new urban poor.* New York: Knopf.

Wood, R., Zalud, G., & Hoag, C. (1996). Opinions of rural mid-western principles toward violence in schools. *Education.* 116(3), 397-402.

Young, I.M. (1990). *Justice and the politics of difference.* Princeton, NJ: Princeton University Press.

Zinn, H. (1999). *A people's history of the United States, 1492-Present.* New York: Harper Collins.

Black Adolescent Females:
An Examination of the Impact
of Violence on Their Lives
and Perceptions of Environmental Supports

Annie Woodley Brown
Ruby Gourdine

SUMMARY. Violence remains a major health problem in the U. S. While teen males are often studied as the victims and perpetrators of violence, there is significant evidence that adolescent females are perpetrators as well as victims of violence; and that both groups are affected by the broader institutional sources of violence. Adolescent girls growing up in inner city neighborhoods are often victimized by exposure to violence, as well as their perceptions of a lack of sustained support from institutions regarded as protective, and nurturing. Survey data and information from focus groups provide insight into their exposure to violence, their fear of violence and coping strategies in neigh-

Annie Woodley Brown, DSW, is Associate Professor and Associate Dean at Howard University School of Social Work, Washington, DC. Dr. Brown received her doctorate degree from Howard and has published in the areas of social welfare history, child welfare and adolescent mental health. She is currently directing a project on violence funded by the Department of Justice.

Ruby Gourdine, DSW, is Associate Professor at Howard University School of Social Work in Washington, DC. She received her PhD from Howard and has published widely in the areas of teenage pregnancy and transracial adoption. Her research interests are in the areas of teenage pregnancy, school social work and child welfare. She served on the District of Columbia panel to monitor services for developmental disabled children ages' birth to three.

[Haworth co-indexing entry note]: "Black Adolescent Females: An Examination of the Impact of Violence on Their Lives and Perceptions of Environmental Supports." Brown, Annie Woodley, and Ruby Gourdine. Co-published simultaneously in *Journal of Human Behavior in the Social Environment* (The Haworth Social Work Practice Press, an imprint of The Haworth Press, Inc.) Vol. 4, No. 4, 2001, pp. 275-298; and: *Violence as Seen Through a Prism of Color* (ed: Letha A. (Lee) See) The Haworth Social Work Practice Press, an imprint of The Haworth Press, Inc., 2001, pp. 275-298. Single or multiple copies of this article are available for a fee from The Haworth Document Delivery Service [1-800-342-9678, 9:00 a.m. - 5:00 p.m. (EST). E-mail address: getinfo@haworthpressinc.com].

borhoods and schools they perceive as unsafe. *[Article copies available for a fee from The Haworth Document Delivery Service: 1-800-342-9678. E-mail address: <getinfo@haworthpressinc.com> Website: <http://www.HaworthPress. com> © 2001 by The Haworth Press, Inc. All rights reserved.]*

KEYWORDS. Black adolescent girls, adolescent violence, exposure to violence

INTRODUCTION

Violence in America is a multifaceted problem that is often described as a major public health concern (Center for Disease Control, 1990; Prothrow-Stith & Spivak, 1992; Bell & Jenkins, 1993). The exposure of children and adolescents to violence as witnesses or victims has profound implications for their social, psychological, and developmental processes in the transition to adulthood. Very troubling is the violence experienced by women and girls, particularly by Black adolescent girls in urban areas in this country, for whom violence may be considered a test of survival in a hostile environment. Cousins and Mabrey (1998) correctly note that the violence experienced by young black girls cannot be understood, explained, or effectively served by using constructs taken from the literature on women, or by applying techniques designed for boys.

Numerous studies have discussed the consequences of children and adolescents exposed to violence in families and communities (Brown & Gourdine, 1997; Guterman & Cameron, 1997; Jenkins & Bell, 1997; Osofsky, Wewers, & Hamn, 1993). In central cities with high rates of homicide and nonlethal shootings and stabbings, children and adolescents are at risk of exposure to violence despite the efforts of their parents to shield them. In a 1990-91 survey sample of Chicago high school students (n = 203), Jenkins and Bell (1994) found that 45% of the students had seen killings. In a similar study of 1,000 middle and high school students in Chicago, Shakoor and Chalmers (1991) found that 23% had seen someone murdered, of whom 40% were family members, friends, or acquaintances. Although there are no substantiated direct cause and effect findings on the effects in children as witnesses or victims of violence, strong correlations exist among several factors. Fitzpatrick and Boldizar (1993), in a study of 221 low-income central-city older children and adolescents, found 27% met the criteria for post-traumatic stress disorder (PTSD). Thus, being victimized and witnessing violence are both associated with PTSD. In the literature on domestic violence and child welfare, exposure to violence and being victimized are strongly associated with intergenerational transmission of violence.

Maslow (1954) identifies safety as one of the basic human needs, yet for many children neither the family, school, nor community appears able to provide the safety needed by their children and adolescents. These institutions, which are expected to socialize, protect, educate, and nurture children, seem unable to meet these basic needs, especially for children living in areas with extreme poverty and community disorganization.

Although a great deal of attention is focused on adolescent males as perpetrators and victims of violence, increasing numbers of adolescent females have been arrested for violent crimes. In a review of literature on female delinquency, Calhoun, Jurgens, and Chen (1993) found that while earlier female delinquency consisted of sexual misconduct, today, increasing numbers of females are involved in armed robbery, gang activity, drug trafficking, burglary, weapon possession, aggravated assault, and prostitution. Durant, Pendergast, and Cadenhead (1994), in a survey of adolescents in 9th through 12th grades, found that 50% of males and 34% of the females surveyed had been in physical fights. However, girls are disproportionately the victims of sexual assault, and such trauma is increasingly evident in mental health assessments of female adolescents and adults.

The purpose of this article is to report a study exploring the impact of violence on Black adolescent females in an urban area where a climate of violence prevails in some neighborhoods. Specifically, the study explores the following: (1) their level of exposure to violence as witnesses, victims, and/or perpetrators; (2) their fear of violence in institutional structures mandated to protect them, instill values, and assist in the transition to adulthood; (3) their future orientation in the midst of the violence they perceived; and, (4) the strategies they employed to cope with the perceived violence in their environments. Two questions are significant for understanding what young Black girls feel about their social environments: What perceptions do young Black girls have of their vulnerability in growing up in unsafe environments? And, how does the issue of violence impact their future orientation? The significance of the questions posed depends on young Black girls' understanding of gender oppression and of the relevance of structured interventions for prevention and treatment.

Defining Violence

Violence does not exist in a vacuum. It is often associated with poverty, family dysfunction, and crime infested neighborhoods. Researchers have observed that "growing up poor in urban America exposes children and adolescents, as well as their parents and guardians to a tremendous amount of violence" (Greene, 1993, p.108). For purposes of this discussion a broad definition of violence is used as any act or situation in which a person injures another, including both direct attacks on a person's physical and psychological integrity and destructive actions that do not involve a direct relationship between the victim and the perpetrators (Bulhan, 1985; Salmi, 1993).

Theoretical Framework

An ecological perspective is especially relevant in analyzing the impact of poverty, violence, social isolation, and discrimination on the adjustment of adolescents and youth of color (Gibbs, 1989). Ecological theory is based on analysis of the interplay of an organism and its environment, the interacting systems in which growth and development occur. The ecological perspective assumes that violence in society undermines institutional structures and diminishes their socializing effectiveness as supports for individuals (in this case Black adolescent girls) in transactions with their environment. Although this view recognizes the contribution of individual personality and intrapsychic factors to situations encountered by individuals, the very nature of the conceptualization precludes blaming the victim without consideration given to environmental factors. Therefore, the ecological perspective provides a contextual understanding of social problems. In the study of adolescents, particularly those growing up in what may be perceived as hostile, violent neighborhoods, it is important to understand some of their behaviors as coping strategies, or as adaptations for survival in an uncertain world.

In examining the relationship of the individual to the environment, it is also important to consider the developmental context of the individual. The successful completion of adolescence supports a successful transition to adulthood. For far too many teenagers, however, childhood is truncated because of adult role responsibilities thrust upon them prematurely by the failure of parents or other adults to assume their roles (Gaudin, Polansky, Kilpatrick, & Shilton, 1993), or because of chronic exposure to violence that robs them of the protective psychological factors of childhood. Because many adolescents rely on their peers for advice, they sometimes inadvertently expose themselves to unnecessary risk in order to fit in and be a part of the group, which is an important aspect of adolescent development. It should be noted, however, that some researchers question reliance on peers in reference to Black girls and contend that this circumstance for many minority girls may be different because of their struggle to survive and make it on their own (Giordano, Cernkovich, & De Maris, 1993; West-Stevens, 1994). Sometimes the desire to have a boyfriend places adolescent girls at risk for violence, including sexual assaults. "Any major life disruption or interruption, temporary or permanent (e.g., victimization), can have a profound effect on an adolescent when it occurs during this critical development phase" (Task Force on Adolescent Assault Victim Needs, 1996, p. 4). The chronic exposure to violence across social systems does impact the normal development of children and adolescents, yet few studies on violence look at developmental issues (Fink, & Thomas, 1995; Children's Defense Fund, 1996). Although youths may be at risk from various aspects of the adolescent development stage, we must understand their behavior within the context of the environment and the interplay between and among other systems that impact them.

Consequences of a Void in Structural Supports: Contributions to the Climate of Violence

It is impossible to analyze the violence experienced by young Black girls without examining the institutions that are so much a part of their lives. Among the underlying causes of the violence that plagues many inner-city neighborhoods and communities are structural racism and economic discrimination. These two social factors shape and define the parameters for families, neighborhoods, and communities. Van Soest and Bryant (1995) note that "violence is deeply embedded in United States culture and is the foundation of revered ideals and institutions" (p. 549). This legacy of violence may have created a climate that condones violence against people because of race or religion.

Racism and the dynamics of the economic system undermine the efficacy of institutions that significantly impact the lives of Black girls. It is necessary to understand the impact of current economic conditions on Black families and the communities and neighborhoods in which they live in order to grasp how they function or fail to function as a viable system (Staples, 1994). In the globalized, post-industrial U.S. economy, the number of unskilled jobs has declined drastically. This has increased the competition for the unskilled jobs that do exist. Furthermore, new requirements for post-high school education has created a mismatch between the existing skills of those youths living in the inner city and the job skills required by industry (Belcher, 1992). Billingsley (1992) describes the technology driven American economy as devastating for African American families and particularly their youth. The high rate of unemployment in the Black community as compared with the overall society may well discourage family formation and increase female-headed households. The structure of the economic system would have to change in order to resolve the problem of persistent poverty in the inner city. The historical record of industrial societies documents the widespread consequences of economic hard times for families and children. Such adverse consequences include a greater risk of marital breakdown, child abuse and neglect, and persistent poverty (Elder, Eccles, Ardelt, & Lord, 1995).

Racism undermines the very fabric of society by destroying the infrastructure of communities and neighborhoods. The historical legacy of discrimination, segregation, and economic oppression has contributed to the disproportionate representation of the Black population by the negative social indicators of unemployment, homelessness, poverty, substance abuse, out-of-home placement of children, and AIDS. Despite the gains of the civil rights movement of the 1960s, race remains a problem in U.S. society, and the society's continued racism remains a barrier to opportunity for many Blacks.

A breakdown in the structure of various institutions is often cited as the reason for many present social ills. Lack of family structure is frequently noted as one reason for teen pregnancy (West-Stevens, 1994) and for juvenile delinquency (National Center for Clinical Programs, 1992; Children's Defense Fund, 1996). Neighborhoods devastated by crime and neglect are physical and mental hazards to residents and often harbor a disproportionate potential for violence. The ability of persons to cope and adapt to their environments depends not only on intrapsychic resources but also on the social supports available to them (Mechanic, 1974). Billingsley (1992) makes the case most profoundly for considering the structural impact of society on individuals and families when he observes that "the family which surrounds and sustains the child is in turn surrounded and sustained by the Black community, and by the wider American society" (p. 76). There are clusters of factors across systems that support/and or mediate opportunities for optimal development (see Table 1).

When institutions that provide the infrastructure for personal development fail, as is the case for so many youth, the consequences have implications for the whole of society. The failure of such institutions or social structures does not occur precipitously as a rule, except in the case of war or other sudden social upheavals. Rather, the failure in institutions occurs subtly, through changes in social policy, realignment of power, or through changes in the perception of who is responsible for social welfare and personal well-being–individuals and families or the government. It is often difficult to determine which events came first. Nevertheless, it is apparent that there are factors that undermine the well-being of many youth in our communities, particularly

TABLE 1. Systemic Structural Supports Necessary for Optimal Development

Individual	Family	Neighborhood	Community	Society
personality	maintenance	quality of life issues	schools	social policy
temperament	safety	condition of housing	police	economic structure
emotional-	appropriate-	availability of affordable	churches	laws/legal
intelligence	development	housing	recreation	framework
genetic make-up	socialization	access to services	social service/	perception of well-
	genetic heritage	(i.e., trash collection/	human service	being
	culture	transportation)	agencies	resources allocation/
	guidance/direction	ongoing maintenance	transportation	opportunity
	love/affection	population density	hospitals/medical	protection/military
	social networks		care	political power
	role definition		employment	international access
			safety	
			political access	

Source: Brown and Gourdine, 1999

adolescent girls. The following is a brief discussion of how failures in social systems that are crucial to the growth and development of adolescents, impact the lives of these children.

Families

Hawkins (1986) observes that "historically Black women and children have been afforded less protection from abuse within the family than any other group within American society" (p. 200). It is estimated that between 3 and 10 million children each year observe violence in the home (Clarke, 1997). Many abusive parents have themselves been abused. O'Keefe, 1996, found that parent-child violence and interparental violence witnessed were significant predictors of both externalizing and internalizing behavior problems for adolescents.

The family is considered the basic building block of a civil society. Many families are vulnerable and are significantly impacted by the negative social indicators of family violence, substance abuse, homelessness, and the acquired immune deficiency syndrome (AIDS). These and other problems, such as poverty, undermine parental effectiveness with grave consequences for the families. The single-parent family structure (vs. the two-parent family) has been identified with several problems–early child bearing for adolescent females (Murray, 1994) and child poverty (Children's Defense Fund, 1996).

Unsafe and unprotected environments often result in children being taken from families and placed in out-of-home care by a child welfare system that is itself in crisis. "From interviews about their community violence experiences, children in child welfare services settings often depict a sense of danger and lonely struggles to survive" (Guterman & Cameron, 1996, p. 497). The largest numbers of children in out-of-home care are African American. They are poor, from poorly educated families, and are disadvantaged in the economic mainstream of the larger society (Brissett-Chapman, 1997). Some suggest that the social stressors and difficulties that many families face increase the risk of child abuse and neglect, while others propose that poor and ethnic minority children and their families are disproportionately reported, labeled, and routinely remanded into the child welfare system by practitioners who are socially and culturally distant from the actual family context (Brissett-Chapman, 1997; Hampton, 1994). Whichever perspective one takes on this issue, the fact remains that poor families are more at risk for entry into the child welfare system. Once there, the consequences of inadequate staff members to provide and plan supportive services to families and children undoubtedly lead to extended stays in the out-of-home care system and delays in family reunification (Brown and Etta, 1997). Substance abuse treatment, adequate housing, and adequate services–the type of structural supports that can assist in family preservation and reunification of children with families–oftentimes do not exist. When children from poor families are reported to the child welfare system, they and their families often have human service needs beyond the capacity of child welfare agencies (Brown & Etta, 1997).

Communities and Neighborhoods

"This is how it's really supposed to be, isn't it?" (Saulny, 1999). These were the words of a youngster from the District of Columbia experiencing for the first time a calm peaceful camping trip to a rural area outside the nation's capital, away from the sounds of gunfire and other disturbing events so much a part of the everyday fabric of the youngster's existence. The crime and violence of many inner-city neighborhoods make it difficult for parents to protect or even to shield their children from violence. Growing up in the poor neighborhoods and communities of urban America exposes children and adolescents, as well as their parents and guardians, to tremendous violence (Greene, 1993). There are abandoned buildings, substandard housing, and sometimes openly sold drugs. Alcohol and drugs are used, and violence erupts periodically. "The knowledge, energy, and passion needed to advocate for change have been drained out of many adults in the affected neighborhoods" (Greene, 1993; p.117). The violence in such neighborhoods makes residents fearful, and the fear decreases their involvement in volunteer associations and informal social control networks essential to the social organization of the neighborhood (Wilson, 1996). Such neighborhoods lose their capacity to provide a kind of–social immunity–for the children and families within its boundaries (Banks, 1993). The violence leads to loss of a sense of safety, to social disintegration of the neighborhoods, and ultimately to loss of the families' capacity to protect their children.

Another important aspect of such neighborhoods is the housing. Housing has important economic, psychological, and symbolic significance for neighborhoods and communities. It has a pervasive effect, beyond the provision of shelter, on the quality of life. Safe, affordable, permanent housing is the key that opens doors to meeting other basic needs. Its location determines personal safety and access to commercial facilities, public and social services, transportation networks, recreational and cultural resources, quality schools, and employment opportunities (Mulroy, 1995; Smizik & Stone, 1988; Mulroy & Ewalt, 1996).

Residential segregation is not a phenomenon of the past or some neutral fact that can be safely ignored (Massey, 1994). Life chances are decisively influenced by where one lives. Segregation is deeply implicated in the perpetuation of Black poverty, and as long as segregation continues, Black poverty will be endemic. Blacks who live in large cities are segregated no matter how much they learn, earn, or achieve. Distressed communities with concentrations of poor people have traditionally been the target of community development. This antipoverty strategy seeks to create new kinds of communities with strong local institutions and residents who are directly involved in planning for local needs (Sullivan, 1993). However, distressed communities are also the target of and the breeding ground for violence because of persistent and consistent neglect and community development that often displaces the people it is intended to help.

Schools

Schools, once a haven for children, have become mini-fortresses in efforts to deal with both internal and external violence. In a study of students from urban neighborhoods, O'Keefe and Sela-Amit (1997) found that 40% of the students reported witnessing a stabbing, and over 30% reported witnessing a shooting during the previous year. The school as a social system reflects the culture and behavior of the environment. Therefore, these students were afflicted with the consequences of crime and violence that occur in families and on the streets (Allen-Meares, Washington, & Welsh, 1996). In many schools, knives and guns have become so commonplace that schools have installed metal detectors to prevent children from taking weapons into class (Alexander & Curtis, 1995; Prothrow-Stith & Spivak, 1991). Nevertheless, an increasing number of students must cope with escalating violence in the school setting. Today, violence in schools is a growing concern. Schools have become dangerous environments where children are victims and witnesses to various types of violence, such as assaults, stabbings, and shootings (Sanchez, 1989). Girls have become targets for sexual harassment and rape in many schools where a climate of violence prevails.

The systems that support families and children are inextricably linked. Failures in one impact functioning in others. The problems in society have become more complex, and there is much overlap in the role of institutions. The expectations are clear, however, that these institutions are necessary for a civil society and for the optimal growth and development of children and adolescents.

METHOD

Design and Procedures

This study was designed to expand an exploratory study conducted by Brown and Gourdine in 1997. The results of the exploratory study provided direction for expanding the scope of this study. In an effort to find out what young Black girls themselves feel about their vulnerability, given the breakdown in structural supports that are supposed to protect them, we conducted an investigation that examines both quantitative and qualitative data related to Black girls and violence. Our interest was also in learning what strategies young Black girls employ to survive in unsafe communities.

Agencies were initially contacted by telephone to solicit their participation. As a follow-up to telephone conversations, packets were sent that contained the following items: (1) a letter requesting their support and a description of the research project; (2) letters of consent for the participants; (3) a copy of the questionnaire and focus group questions; and (4) a copy of the exploratory study previously conducted by these authors. After receipt of the packets, the agencies worked with the researchers to schedule times to administer the questionnaire and conduct the focus groups. The implementation occurred over an intermittent time period that allowed the agencies ample time to recruit girls and obtain appropriate signatures for participation.

The investigators distributed the questionnaire at scheduled group meetings held at agencies' sites. A general orientation on the purpose of the study was given prior to the distribution of the surveys. Once the questionnaires were completed, the girls were allowed to get refreshments as a bridge to the focus group session.

The investigators learned from the pilot study the importance of conducting focus groups in addition to administering questionnaires. Thus, the focus group component for this study was expanded and formalized. The focus group questions consisted of a structured set of eight questions designed to solicit additional data about the girls opinions concerning violence. These focus groups provided an opportunity for the girls to express their attitudes and thoughts about violence and how it affects them in their daily lives. This component proved to be an energetic and engaging part of the research study and provided insight into the semantic and behavioral culture of urban adolescent girls. The young women appeared eager to tell their stories and give their opinions about violence and how it has affected their lives.

A variety of agencies were used, that possibly strengthened the research design because of the diverse pool of participants. To comply with confidentiality issues, specific agency names will not be used. Brief descriptions of representative agencies are as follows:

1. One agency dealt with students with special education needs. The young women were diagnosed as emotionally or behaviorally disturbed, but they were intellectually capable of completing the questionnaire and participating in the focus groups.
2. Several agencies (community-based) provided after-school enrichment activities, such as computer labs, peer discussion groups, field trips, and homework laboratories open to the youth in the community.
3. Several agencies provided substitute living arrangements to girls who were removed from their parental homes for a variety of reasons.

Participants

The sample included 75 African American girls recruited from traditional youth agencies serving this population. All the girls are services at these youth agencies which is the reason for their selection. The girls ranged in age from 13 to 19 years, although three 12 year-old girls were included in the sample since they were considered suitably mature for participation in the groups for adolescents. Fifty percent of the girls were between 14 and 15 years old. The majority of the girls live in two quadrants of the city. Fifty-two percent of the girls lived in female-headed households, while only 15.1% lived in households headed by both parents. For further information about participants, see the demographic characteristics of participants in Table 2.

Measures

The instrument consisted of three components. The first section collected demographic information and solicited information on exposure to violence and fear of violence in the girls neighborhood, school, and home settings. Questions on the research instrument were clustered to produce an exposure to violence scale and a fear of violence scale. Two open-ended questions included statements about positive events in their lives. The first one: if you had 3 wishes question was designed to discover the future orientation of the adolescent girls. The second section of the questionnaire was an adaptation of Kinden's Hopelessness Scale for Children (HSC) designed to determine hopefulness on the part of the adolescent girls. This modified scale consists of 43 items and contains a number of statements with a future orientation (such as, I think about my future often; I think about what I want to do in life; I think about my funeral often) answered according to a Likert type scale: strongly agree, agree, disagree, or strongly disagree.

The present study examines the following variables: (1) exposure to violence; (2) fear of violence/ perceptions of institutional support; (3) the future orientation of the participants; and (4) strategies employed to cope with violence in their perceived environment. Focus groups were structured around discussions of eight questions related to the domains established by the variable selection. The girls all had ample time to complete the questionnaires.

RESULTS

Descriptive statistics were used to examine the level of exposure to violence and the perceived lack of structural support which were expressed as the fear of violence participants perceived in their families, schools, and communities. Pearson product-moment correlations were used to determine relationships between level of

TABLE 2. Demographic Characteristics of Participants

Category	Frequency* N = 75	Percent
Age		
12-13	6	8%
14	22	30%
15	15	20%
16-17	18	24%
18-19		
Living Arrangements+		
With Both Parents	11	15%
With Mother	38	52%
With Dad	6	7%
With Grandmother	10	14%
With Foster	7	10%
With Other (foster family, group homes)	20	26%
Grade		
6th-8th	11	15%
9th	31	44%
10th	6	8%
11th-12th	19	23%
Ever Repeat Grade		
Yes	26	35%
No	47	64%
Ever Suspended from School		
Yes	50	68%
No	24	32%
Suspended for Fighting		
Yes	41	55%
No	10	13%
Not Applicable	23	31%
Have Children		
Yes	16	22%
No	55	76%
Ever Involved with Juvenile Court		
Yes	24	35%
No	45	65%
Ever Had a Job		
Yes	51	72%
No	20	28%

*Frequencies do not always add up to N = 75 because of missing cases.
+Living arrangements were separate categories and some items checked more than once.

exposure to violence and future orientation (hopefulness), and future orientation and fear of violence in the systems that impact the lives of the adolescent girls.

Level of Exposure to Violence

Table 2 presents descriptive information on the types of violence exposure experienced by the adolescent girls in the study. Twenty-two percent of the girls said they had been physically abused, mostly by mothers or fathers, although mothers' boyfriends accounted for 8% of the abusers. Twenty-three percent reported having experienced sexual abuse, and 21% said they had been coerced to have sex. Fifty-five percent of the girls themselves had been suspended from school for fighting. Fifty-four percent had relatives or close friends killed by violent means. On the exposure to violence scale, which included both personal and community violence, 48% of the girls received a score of 3 or more on a scale of 0-8. In addition to violence experienced as victims or loss of a friend or relative, 40% of the girls reported that they themselves had attacked or hurt someone, and 34% had done so within the past year.

Fear of Violence/Perceptions of Institutional Support

Table 3 presents a fear of violence scale based on items from the questionnaire that indicate systems where the girls must interact and whether they were afraid. Thirty-five percent were afraid of violence in the home; 61% were afraid of violence in the school or were afraid of violence in the neighborhood; and 35% were afraid to walk in their neighborhoods.

Future Orientation

Future orientation was measured by a modified Hopelessness Scale for Children (HSC). The score established from this modified scale measures the level of hope felt by the girls. Their scores on the hopefulness scale ranged from 92 to 156. As in the previous exploratory study, the girls are more hopeful than one might anticipate. On one item in the scale, "I look forward

TABLE 3. Items Related to Exposure to Violence

Category	Frequency* N = 75	Percent
Ever Physically Abused?		
Yes	16	22%
No	55	77%
Ever Sexually Abused?		
Yes	17	23%
No	46	61%
Relative or Close Friend Killed by Violence?		
Yes	40	54%
No	33	45%
Ever Attempted Suicide?		
Yes	16	22%
No	56	78%
Know Anyone Who Has Attempted Suicide?		
Yes	40	55%
No	33	45%
Ever Forced to Have Sex?		
Yes	13	21%
No	50	79%

*Frequencies do not always add up to n = 75 because of missing cases

to the future," 95% of the girls strongly agreed and agreed with the statement (see Table 4).

Pearson's product-moment correlation was used to compute the relationship between exposure to violence and hopefulness. Overall, the girls were more hopeful than one might expect under the circumstances. The findings indicate a statistically significant inverse relationship between these variables ($r = -.4828$; $p < .001$). The lower the exposure to violence score, the higher the score on the hopefulness scale. In relation to hopefulness and fear of violence/lack of institutional supports, there was a weak inverse relationship (the lower the level of fear the higher the hopefulness scores) that was not significant ($r = -.2409$; ns)

Focus Groups

Focus groups can be an extremely dynamic addition to quantitative information collected as a part of a study. Focus groups provide an opportunity for researchers to learn about the biographies and life structures of group participants (Berg, 1995). The investigators for this study were particularly interested in the informal interaction of the focus groups that allowed participants to speak about their attitudes, opinions, behaviors, and life structures in relation to violence. The girls in the focus groups were quite expressive,

TABLE 4. Items Related to Fear of Violence in the Environment

Category	Frequency* N = 75	Percent
Fear of Violence		
Within the Family		
Yes	23	35%
No	43	65%
In Neighborhood		
Yes	43	65%
No	23	35%
In School		
Yes	40	61%
No	26	39%
With Friends		
Yes	21	31%
No	46	69%
All of the Above		
Yes	21	32%
No	45	68%
Fear to Walk in Neighborhood		
Yes	26	64%
No	48	35%

*Frequencies do not always add up to n = 75 because of missing cases

revealed very definite opinions about what it means to be a female, and appeared almost eager to talk. The discussion for the focus groups were structured around eight questions that yielded the following thematic categories:

General Understanding and Concern About Violence

How would you define violence? Some people think the concern about violence is exaggerated, what do you think?

The girls generally provided a definition of violence congruent with the generally accepted view–"shooting, stabbing, fighting with the intent to cause harm; killing someone and using weapons." Although all the girls accepted this definition of violence, somewhat unclear initially was the idea that verbal abuse can be considered violence (see, Oliver & Williams, 2001). However, after a vigorous discussion in most of the groups, all but a few of the girls agreed that verbal abuse can be violent and damaging (see, Oliver & Williams, 2001). Two items from the questionnaire supported to some extent the findings from the focus group discussion. On the questionnaire, 85% of the girls agreed that children can be hurt by physical abuse, and 80% responded that verbal abuse can hurt a child. These girls were astute in their view that violence included not only physical harm but emotional and psychological harm as well.

Concerning the exaggeration of violence in poor communities by the media, there was some ambiguity. On the one hand, the girls actually felt that violence in their communities was under reported not exaggerated, and, at the same time, they felt that poor neighborhoods were often targeted for sensational stories on violence. Others felt that violence in the media is exaggerated because teens "do what they see," and that "the media put violence in peoples' heads." The attitude of the girls on this issue reflects the ambivalence in the larger community where the question was hotly debated for years until several recent large-scale studies concluded that exposure to media violence is strongly associated with a child's risk for engaging in aggressive and sometimes violent behavior (APA, 1993; Eron, Gentry, & Schlegel, 1993).

Violence–Community and Personal Safety

The second cluster of questions asked were:

What do you think about violence in your communities? How do you feel about your own safety? What would you like adults to know about young people and violence? Generally, all the girls expressed some level of discomfort with their neighborhoods or nearby neighborhoods. They were candid about the violence in their own neighborhoods but rightly pointed out that violence occurs everywhere, including rural and suburban areas. They did not necessarily see their neighborhoods as more violent but did perceive a lack of community cohesion. They noted that people in their neighborhoods are afraid of violence but do not cooperate with the police to stem the tide of violence. Some of the girls debated whether people who were destructive of their neighborhoods should be allowed to remain in the neighborhood. Interestingly, the girls thought the community bears the responsibility to rehabilitate errant members and report those who cause trouble. Unwittingly, these young girls tapped into constructs that have developed over the years to describe the importance of neighborhood cohesion in stemming the tide of violence–"social immunity" (Banks, 1993) and "neighborhood collective efficacy" (Sampson, Raudenbush & Earls, 1997).

Some of the girls in this study, having been removed from their homes, were in community-based alternative living situations. Some of them questioned the wisdom of government run agencies supposedly helping them by placing them in living situations in neighborhoods the girls perceived as unsafe. In addition to their feeling that institutions that were supposed to care about them often failed to live up to that responsibility, the girls identified other issues in their communities that contributed to the state of their families and communities.

Racial issues were discussed, with some girls believing that Blacks are more violent than Whites; others connected racism and discrimination to the plight of Blacks in deteriorating and violent neighborhoods; and still others grappled with racial distinctions between the types of violence perpetrated in communities and in society at large. At the core of this discussion was the sentiments that many of the girls feel disrespected by the community; that adults are not living up to their responsibilities; and that teens want to be seen as individuals and not as an amorphous, undefined group. These feelings were expressed in statements, such as, "Some adults disrespect children"; "Adults don't respect us"; "Disrespect me, and I'll disrespect you"; and "All teenagers are not the same." Beneath the super confident facade, the apparent self-assurance, was the desire to be liked, to be respected, to be treated like a person of worth.

The girls expressed a great deal of fear based on incidents that occurred in school. They perceived that the fear of their experience was shared by their teachers. Thus, their own fear, and their perception of their teachers' fear did not allow them to rely on adult figures in the schools. They presented school as a scary place.

Gender Issues Related to Violence

On the variable of gender the girls were asked:
What do you think about the idea that males are more violent than fe-

males? Do you think that females are more at risk of being victimized by violence than males? Some young women experience violence in their dating/friendship relationships. Do you have any thoughts on this situation?

"Girls fight." "Girls start more violence." "They worry about their looks–how their hair looks–if their boyfriends like other girls." "Girls will not let anything ride." The girls in the focus groups were emphatic and unequivocal in their opinion that girls are as violent as boys. This perception of gender egalitarianism expressed by the girls in the focus groups reflects the findings by Cousins and Mabrey (1998) that the girls in their study blurred the traditional gender constructs and assumed aggressive and confrontational roles. While they acknowledged that men are physically stronger, and girls sometimes use their feminine wiles to get the better of the men, these girls did not see themselves primarily as victims. They expressed the idea of being able to take care of themselves anyway they had to. The confrontational style also appears to enter into relationships with other girls. They expressed the idea that females usually encourage other females to fight by urging them on or by citing some incident to provoke girls involved in disagreements. And, according to the girls in the focus groups, the conflict among girls was usually about boys.

As for violence in dating relationships, the young women seemed to subscribe to the notion that girls who witness violence in their families, get into violent relationships–"Their mothers and fathers fight"; "Girls marry their fathers"; "Those who witness violence think it is all right." The idea was expressed by the girls in various groups that girls tolerate violence in a dating relationship because they think they cannot get anyone else. Most of the young women admitted they knew girls who were victims of dating violence. However, in their opinion, they thought girls in that situation thought they were in love or that they could control dating violence. It was clear to them that many teen relationships are the precursors of later domestic violence situations.

On gender issues related to violence, the girls discussed the issue of rape and their vulnerability to sexual exploitation by strangers and by members of their own families. A subgroup of the girls (in placement in a treatment facility) described the risky behavior of consensual sex with multiple partners that sometimes leads to rape. Unfortunately, a number of the girls related knowing someone who was pregnant by a father, step-father, brother, or cousin. They appeared to indicate that their gender placed them at risk even in their own families.

Intergenerational Transmission of Violence

The girls were very conversant with the connection between child abuse and violence. They believed there was indeed a connection. They described sexual abuse among children they knew and situations of rape some of them had experienced. Although they acknowledged men's responsibilities for rapes or abuse, they also noted that young boys experiencing sexual abuse might well become perpetrators of violence. The girls identified the boys' violence as stemming from the rage they feel and cannot control. These girls related knowledge of domestic violence in their own homes and communities. The focus groups provided very thoughtful discussions on whether there is a connection between being abused and acting violent toward someone else. Ultimately, the consensus appeared to be that "what a child is taught, they act out"; children who are abused may snap." But there were other voices that raised the issue of the length of time and type of abuse in determining how damaged a child will be from experiencing violence. Another view, although not the prevailing one, was that "if I was beaten as a child, I would not want to beat anyone else–why would you want someone else to go through what you went through?"

Strategies for Coping with Violence

In the focus groups, the girls discussed the strategies they use to overcome the violence they experience in their neighborhoods and the institutions from which they receive services. They made statements, such as, you have to try not to be in the wrong place at the wrong time"; "you have to pay attention to what is going on around you." The weapons some of them carry for protection are scissors, bleach (which can be taken to school in lieu of weapons that can be readily detected), and roach spray (which can be used to deter suspicious characters in their neighborhoods). A particularly innovative technique (and less violent response) was to find a safe-looking person and pretend to be related to the person if they were being followed, or going up to a porch in the neighborhood and calling out to residents as if they were calling a family member to open the door. One factor that presented across the groups is the level of vigilance and awareness the girls must assume as they navigate in their neighborhoods, communities, and schools. Some girls were more spiritual in their responses by noting that their faith in God sustained them and protected them from harm. They acknowledged that God gave them tools to make decisions and that making the right decisions could protect them from some dangerous situations. Fifty percent of the girls identified themselves as religious.

DISCUSSION

Before discussing the implications of the study, some methodological concerns must be addressed. First, although the sample included 75 girls from diverse agencies, it was a convenience sample. The service programs who requested to participate in the research were those contacted by the researchers. Secondly, self-report data must be viewed with caution. The adolescent girls may not accurately recall their experiences, may be reluctant to report the extent of their fears, or may exaggerate their role as perpetrators. Nevertheless, the statistical profile of the present study involving 75 adolescent girls remained very consistent with the profile of the previous exploratory study conducted by the investigators of 30 adolescent girls growing up in an urban environment. The 30 girls from the exploratory study are a part of the present study. Thirdly, the full meaning of this data can be fully realized only when there is a comparison group of adolescent girls from other socioeconomic and geographical backgrounds.

Much of the literature has focused on links between violence and depression (Kozol, 1995; Durant et al., 1994; Elder et al., 1995), violence and anger (Prothrow-Stith & Spivak, 1992), and violence and poverty (Greene, 1993). From this study and others, including the exploratory study by the investigators on Black female adolescents growing up in urban environments, it is clear that Black female adolescents are exposed to violence in their homes, their schools, and communities. Less clear, however, is the impact such exposure has on their aspirations for the future and their general outlook on life. The young women may not feel as hopeless as they are sometimes portrayed. From a study of African American adolescents, both girls and boys, Stevenson (1998) found that girls, especially those who lived in high-risk neighborhoods and had a "realistic fear of calamity," seemed not to be depressed, were more positive in their outlook on life, and were able to "manage hope in an uncertain context." The present study found that although some of the girls had a high level of exposure to violence and fear of violence, less than 30% could be considered despairing in their outlook on life. It should be noted that the expanded exploratory study was consistent with the pilot study. Stevenson (1998) conjectures Black adolescent girls are not hopeless but may suffer from what he calls "hope loss" (that is where institutions give up on youth).

The researchers did not approach the adolescent girls with fixed criteria of what constitutes violence but were interested in hearing from the girls themselves what they thought constituted violence in various systems in which they had interacted. In some studies, African Americans were found to be exposed to the highest levels of violence both in schools and communities. Taking such exposure into consideration, it is remarkable how some adolescents, particularly girls, are able to go on with their lives, remain positive, and have aspirations for themselves and their children. Their wishes are very similar to those expressed by other adolescents–money, success, good jobs, completion of school. But they also revealed a knowledge of a gritty reality of life, "Streets are not like they used to be–children are not going to be like they used to be."

Implications for Interventions with This Population

The impact of violence in communities, neighborhoods and schools suggest a more holistic approach to providing services to children and families. Understanding the impact of violence on the lives of young women can provide earlier identification and more definitive assessments and treatment of trauma associated with violent histories. There is also reason to believe that there is a connection between the violence (especially sexual assault) some adolescent females experience and the sexual acting out that leads to teen pregnancy. Pregnancy prevention programs, therefore, need to include in their intervention methods, strategies and techniques for discerning the impact of trauma. Those in the helping professions need an adequate understanding of the broader institutional sources of violence and its impact on the lives of children and adolescents.

The focus groups provided support for much of what was discerned from the survey. The groups were most helpful in conveying the depth of the girls understanding of the problems in their communities. While the girls were able to articulate the strategies they used to survive in environments they perceived as unsafe, the groups also revealed the girls' perceptions of the lack of neighborhood cohesion and the powerlessness of adults in their environments to effect change. "Adults have to get involved–they have to say we are taking care of you." Some of the young women provided direction for intervention. "When you work with young people, break the group up–see people individually–they really want your help–in a group they are going along with their peers." This suggests the need for interventions that include community-based empowerment strategies, advocacy, and mediation. Violence is a multidimensional phenomenon and requires that efforts to address the issue not only focus on the aggressive behavior of individuals, but also assessment of and changes in the institutions that influence and allow certain conditions to exist.

CONCLUSION

The impact of violence on children and adolescents cannot be addressed by focusing on them as victims. It is clear that the problem of violence in our communities, neighborhoods, and families requires a systemic approach. The issues of violence are interrelated across systems, are multidimensional, and are often concurrent. A broader approach to violence can help identify long-term possibilities for protection from violence, especially for Black adolescent girls. Addressing the problem will require both national and personal commitments. The lack of meaningful employment cannot be underestimated as a factor in the violence experienced by children and adolescents. The high rate of unemployment in inner cities and the loss of jobs have not only affected the stability of neighborhoods but also the relationship between Black males and females. High unemployment has also contributed to "an aura of combat and heightened disparities (and victimization) within urban communities" (Cousins & Mabrey, p. 103).

The climate of violence needs to be changed in the schools and neighborhoods of urban areas, but it is important to know what helps adolescents to survive, particularly Black adolescent females. Although they perceive their schools and neighborhoods as threatening, the real story is that these young girls have developed ways to adapt to their environment and to the structural exigencies of the systems that shape their lives. These systems should provide the support and security that help young people emerge as healthy adults. The adolescent girls in this study exhibit resilience. However, their own resolve and coping strategies should not be the only resources to support their growth and development.

REFERENCES

Alexander, R., & Curtis, C. M. (1995). A critical review of strategies to reduce school violence. *Social Work in Education, 17*(2), 73-82.

Allen-Meares, P., Washington, R. O., & Welsh, B. L. (1996). *Social work services in schools.* Boston: Allyn & Bacon.

American Psychological Association. (1993). *Violence and youth: Psychological response.* Washington, D.C. Author.

Banks, J. (1993). Our Social Immune System: Building Supportive Environments for African American Families in Public Housing. Paper presented at Howard University, Cosby Scholar Lecture Series.

Belcher, J. R. (1992). Poverty, homelessness, and racial exclusion. *Journal of Sociology & Social Welfare, 19* (4), 41-55.

Bell, C. C. & Jenkins, E. J. (1993). Community violence and children on Chicago's south side. *Psychiatry, 56*, 46-54.

Berg, B. L. (1995). *Qualitative Research Methods for the Social Sciences* (2nd ed.). Boston: Allyn & Bacon.

Billingsley, A. (1992). *Climbing Jacobs Ladder: The enduring legacy of African-American families.* New York: Simon & Schuster.

Brissett-Chapman, S. (1997). Child protection risk assessment and African-American children: Cultural ramifications for families and communities. *The Journal of Child Welfare League of America, 85* (1), 45-63.

Brown, A. W., & Baily-Etta, B. (1997). An out-of-home care system in crisis: Implications for African-American children in the child welfare system. *The Journal of Child Welfare League of America, 86* (1), 65-83.

Brown, A. W., & Gourdine, R. M. (1998). Teenage Black girls and violence: Coming of age in an urban environment. In L. L. See (Ed.), *Journal of Human Behavior and the Social Environment, 1* (2-3), 105-124.

Bulhan, H. A. (1985). *Frantz Fanon and the psychology of oppression*. New York: Plenum Press.

Burman,. S., & Allen-Meares, P. (1994). Neglected victims of murder: Children's witness to parental homicide. *Social Work, 39*(1), 29-34.

Calhoun, G., Jurgens, J., & Chen, F. (1993). The neophyte female delinquent: A review of the literature. *Adolescence, 28*(110), 461-471.

Center for Disease Control. (1990). Homicide among young Black males: United States, 1978-1987. *Morbidity and Mortality Weekly Report, 38*, 869-873.

Center for Disease Control [Division of Violence Prevention in the National Center for Injury Prevention and Control]. (1999). Youth violence in the United States. Atlanta: Author. Retrieved from World Wide Web: <http://www.cdc.gov.Ncipc/dvp/yvfacts.html>.

Children's Defense Fund. (1996). *The state of America's children*. Washington, D. C.: Children's Defense Fund.

Clarke, C. (1997). Children exposed to domestic violence. *Understanding domestic violence: A handbook for professionals*. Washington, D.C.: U.S. Department of Justice.

Cousins, L. H., & Mabrey, T. (1998). Re-gendering social work practice and education: The case for African American girls. In L. See (Ed.), *Journal of Human Behavior and the Social Environment, 1* (2-3), 105-124.

Durant, R. H., Pendergast, R. A., & Cadenhead, C. (1994). Exposure to violence and victimization and fighting behavior by urban Black adolescents. *Journal of Adolescence, 15*, 311-318.

Ejigiri, D. (1996). Race in housing and community empowerment: A critical examination. *Community Development Journal, 31*(1), 32-43.

Elder, G. H., Eccles, J., Ardelt, M., & Lord, L. (1995). Inner-city parents under economic pressure: Perspectives of strategies of parenting. *Journal of Marriage and Family, 57*, 771-781.

Erickson, E. H. (1959). *Identity and the life cycle: Psychological issues*. New York: International Universities Press.

Eron, L. D., Gentry, J. A., Schlegel, P. (1993) *Reason to hope: A psychosocial perspective on violence and youth*. Washington, D.C.: American Psychological Association.

Fick, A. C., & Thomas, S. M. (1995). Growing up in a violent environment: Relationship to health-related beliefs and behaviors. *Youth and Society, 27*(2), 136-147.

Fitzpatrick, K. M., & Boldizar, J. P. (1993). The prevalence and consequences of exposure to violence among African-American youth. *Journal of the Academy of Child and Adolescent Psychiatry, 32*(2), 424-430.

Gaudin, J. M., Polansky, N. A., Kilpatrick, A. C., & Shilton, P. (1993). Loneliness, depression, stress, and social supports in neglectful families. *American Journal of Orthopsychiatry Association, 63*(4) 597-605.

Gibbs, J. T. & Huang, L. N. (Eds). (1989). *Children of color: Psychological intervention with minority youth*. San Francisco: Jossey-Bass Publishers.

Giordano, P. C., Cernkovich, S. A., & De Maris, A. (1993). The family and peer relations of Black adolescents. *Journal of Marriage and the Family, 55*, 277-287.

Greene, M. (1987). Chronic exposure to violence and poverty: Interventions that work for youth. *Crime and Delinquency, 39* (1), 106-124.

Guterman, N. B., & Cameron, M. (1997). Assessing the impact of community violence on children and youths. *Social Work, 42* (5), 495-505.

Hampton, R. L. (1994). Race, ethnicity, and child maltreatment: An analysis of cases recognized and reported by hospitals. In Robert Staples (Ed.), *The Black Family: Essays and Studies*. 5th ed. (pp. 174-186). Belmont, CA: Wadsworth Publishing Company.

Hawkins, D. (1986). Devalued lives and racial stereotypes: Ideological barriers to the prevention of family violence among Blacks. In Robert L. Hampton (Ed.), *Violence in the Black family*. MA: D. C. Heath.

Hogan, P. T., & Siu, S. F. (1988 November-December). Minority children and the child welfare system: An historical perspective, *Social Work, 33* (4), 493-498.

Jenkins, E. J., & Bell, C. C. (1997). Exposure and response to community violence among children and adolescents. In J. D. Osofsky (Ed.), *Children in a Violent Society* (pp.9-31). New York: Guilford Press.

Jenkins, E. J., & Bell, C. C. (1994). Violence among inner-city high school students and post-traumatic stress disorder. In S. Friedman (Ed.), *Anxiety disorders in African Americans* (pp. 76-88). New York: Springer.

Kozol, J. (1995). *Amazing grace: The lives of children and the conscience of a nation*. New York: Crown Publishers, Inc.

Maslow, A. (1954) *Motivation and Personality*. New York: Harper.

Massey, D. S. (1994). America's apartheid and urban underclass. *Social Service Review Lecture*, 471-487.

Mechanic, D. (1974). Social structure and adaptations. In George V. Coelho, David A. Hamburg, & John E. Adams (Eds.), *Coping and Adaptation* (pp. 32-46). New York: Basic Books.

Mulroy, E. A. (1995; November 2). *Achieving the systemic neighbor network: The community contact of nonprofit interorganizational collaboration*. Paper presented at the Association for Research on Nonprofit Organizations and Voluntary Action.

Mulroy, E. A., & Ewalt, P. L. (1996). Affordable housing: A basic need and a social issue, *Social Work, 41* (3), 245-249.

Murray, V. M. (1994). Socio-historical study of African American adolescent females' sexuality: Timing of first coitus, 1950s through 1980s. In Robert L. Staples (Ed.), *The Black Family: Essays and Studies*. 5th ed. (pp. 52-65). Belmont, CA: Wadsworth Publishing Company.

National Center for Clinical Infant Programs. (1992, Fall). How community violence affects children, parents and practitioners. *Public Welfare*. 23-35.

O'Keefe, M. (1996). The differential effects of family violence on adolescent adjustment. *Child and Adolescent Social Work Journal, 13*(1), 51-68.

O'Keefe, M., & Sela-Amit, M. (1997). An examination of the effects of race/ethnicity and social class on adolescents exposure to violence. *Journal of Social Service Research, 22*(3), 53-71.

Osofsky, J. D., Wewers, S., Hamn, D. M., & Fick, A. C. (1993). Chronic community violence: What is happening to our children? *Psychiatry, 56*(3) 6-45.

Prothrow-Stith, D. & Spirvak, H. (1992) Homicide and violence: Contemporary health problems for America's Black community. In R.T. Braithwaite & S.E. Taylor (Eds.), *Health Issues in the Black Community* (pp. 132-143). San Francisco: Jossey-Bass.

Prothrow-Stith, D. (1991) *Deadly consequences: How violence is destroying our teenage population and a plan to begin to solve the problem.* New York: Harpers Collins Publishers.

Salmi, J. (1993). *Violence in a democratic society.* London: Zed Books.

Sampson, R. J., Raudenbush, S. W. & Earls, F. (1997). Neighborhood collective efficacy-Does it help reduce violence? *National Institute of Justice: Research Preview.* Washington, D. C.: U. S. Department of Justice.

Sanchez, C. (1989). Four youngsters wounded in NE schoolyard shooting. *The Washington Post.* (1989, March 21).

Saulny, S. (1999, March 25). From the city to a cabin in the woods: Program takes D.C. children camping in a world away from home. *The Washington Post,* pp. B1, B7.

See, L. Williams, O. & Oliver, W. (2001). Domestic violence in African American Families. In L. Rapp Paglicca, A. Roberts, & J.S. Wodarski (Eds). *The Handbook on Violence.* New York: John Wiley & Sons (in press).

Shakoor, B. H. & Chalmers, D. (1991). Co-victimization of African-American children who witness violence: Effects on cognitive, emotional and behavioral development. *Journal of the National Medical Association, 8* (3), 233-238.

Smizik, F., & Stone, M. (1988) Single-parent families and a right to housing. In. E. Mulroy (Ed.), *Women as single-parents: Confronting institutional barriers in the courts, the work place, and housing market.* Westport: CT: Auburn House.

Staples, R. (1994). The family. In R. Staples (Ed.), *The Black family: Essays and studies* (5th ed., pp. 11-19). Belmont, CA: Wadsworth Publishing Company.

Stevenson, H. C. (1998) Raising safe villages: Cultural-ecological factors that influence The emotional adjustment of adolescents. *Journal of Black Psychology 24*(1) 44-60.

Sullivan, M. (1993). *More than housing: How community development corporations go about changing houses and neighborhoods.* New York: Community Development Research Center, Graduate School of Management and Urban Policy, New School of Social Research.

Task Force on Adolescent Assault Victim Needs (1996). Adolescent assault victim needs: A review of issues and a model protocol. Pediatrics, 98, 9991-1001. Retrieved from World Wide Web: <http://www.aap.org/policy/00991.html>.

Van Soest, D., & Bryant, S. (1995). Violence reconceptualized for social work: The urban dilemma. *Social Work, 40*(4), 549-557.

West-Stevens, J. (1994). Adolescent development and adolescent pregnancy among late age African-American female adolescents. *Child and Adolescent Social Work Journal, 11*(6), 433-453.

Wilson, W. J. (1996). *When work disappears: The world of the new urban poor.* New York: Knopf.

SECTION VI:
SYSTEMIC VIOLENCE

Violence in the Black Church

Letha A. (Lee) See

... the hottest places in Hell are reserved for those who, in times of
great moral crisis, maintain their neutrality.

–Dante, Quoted from President John F. Kennedy's book,
Profiles in Courage, p. xv.

SUMMARY. Violence in the Black Church is an issue that is frequently discussed in quiet corners, mainly among church devotees. This article argues that the Black Church is the backbone of the Black community. Moreover, if it becomes secularized, and ensnared with disruptive factionalism, its role may be significantly diminished. Faith-based

Letha A. (Lee) See, EdM, MSW, PhD, is Professor in the School of Social Work at the University of Georgia. She received her PhD from Bryn Mawr College, PA in 1982, and taught at Bryn Mawr, Lincoln University, (PA), Atlanta University, and the University of Arkansas. She has spent many years working in national, state, regional and local social service agencies, and has served as a consultant for major organizations including the U.S. Department of Education.

[Haworth co-indexing entry note]: "Violence in the Black Church." See, (Lee) Letha A. Co-published simultaneously in *Journal of Human Behavior in the Social Environment* (The Haworth Social Work Practice Press, an imprint of The Haworth Press, Inc.) Vol. 4, No. 4, 2001, pp. 299-335; and: *Violence as Seen Through a Prism of Color* (ed: Letha A. (Lee) See) The Haworth Social Work Practice Press, an imprint of The Haworth Press, Inc., 2001, pp. 299-335. Single or multiple copies of this article are available for a fee from The Haworth Document Delivery Service [1-800-342-9678, 9:00 a.m. - 5:00 p.m. (EST). E-mail address: getinfo@haworthpressinc.com].

programs, school vouchers, the role of women in the church, and minis-terial behaviors are among the structural issues giving rise to violence in the Black Church. The paper draws on many sources of data, and is interpreted within the theoretical framework of a systems perspective. *[Article copies available for a fee from The Haworth Document Delivery Service: 1-800-342-9678. E-mail address: <getinfo@haworthpressinc.com> Website: <http://www.HaworthPress.com> © 2001 by The Haworth Press, Inc. All rights reserved.]*

KEYWORDS. Black church, violence, secularization, faith-based pro-grams, vouchers, church women

During the 20th Century, a cadre of distinguished multi-disciplinary scholars compiled a proliferation of research and literature on the Black Church (Bil-lingsley, 1992, 1994, 1998; Billingsley & Caldwell, 1991; Billingsley, Cald-well, & Hill 1991; Billingsley & Rodriguez, 1998; DuBois, 1903; Frazier, 1947, 1957, 1964, 1974; Hill, 1972, 1994; Johnson, O. 2000; Lincoln & Mamiya, 1990; Mays & Nicholson, 1933; Pipes, 1997; Thorpe, 1961; Wash-ington, 1984; Woodson, 1945). Their collective work has yielded a vast body of deeply "grounded," data sufficiently potent to draw from it startling hypotheses to be formulated and tested (Glaser & Strauss, 1967).

Trenchant analysis reveal that 21st Century emerging theoretical and em-pirical focus will concentrate on the problem of homicidal and structural violence in American's well-respected institutions. Since the Black Church is "the" most cherished institution in the Black community, it logically follows that expanding research will examine violence in this dynamic religious organization (Alexander, 1987; Brashears, 1996; Harrison, 1959).

Informal interviews conducted with researchers, social and political scien-tists, reveal that congregants have been grappling with a series of compelling questions such as: Is violence in the Black Church a misnomer, or an issue that warrants examination in an analysis of structural violence? Should a scientific investigation of Black Church violence include non-homicidal acts like grand larceny and emotional skirmishes that do not result in death? Should the Black church become involved in secular enterprises? And, should the behavior of Black clergy remain free from intensive scrutiny? Together, these provocative questions point to some of the fundamental chal-lenges presented to researchers who are anxious to engage in sacred as well as secular research, and have wondered if there is a positive correlation between violence and the behavior of some black Church officials.

Informal observations suggest there is hesitancy on the part of African American social scientists to enter the empirical path of examining Black Church violence. Essentially, the reluctance to engage in such an interrogatory discourse of this ecclesiastical body is owing to the fact that Black scholars find themselves caught on a political tightrope–balancing between making an impartial appraisal, and critical analysis of the sometimes "shoddy" leadership structure, loose "hip pocket," "managerial style," and the subordination of women in the decision-making apparatus in the Black Church; while simultaneously struggling to protect it from unjust criticism hurled against it by antagonistic forces set on destroying its initiatives, efforts, energies, and programs (Billingsley, 1998; Harrison, 1959; Washington, 1984; Younger, 1957; Simpson & Yinger, 1965). Ostensively, there is well-founded fear and legitimate concern among Black social scientists and researchers that no matter how laudable their motives, how delicately disguised their intellectual inquiry, and how obliterated their methodology, delving into Black Church violence can be "messy" business. It requires systematically examining the institution's organizational structure, internal power struggles, and unearthing what See and Khashan (2000), refer to as its "dirty little doings." But, despite the intellectual challenges, Black American scholars have reached a stage of maturity where they no longer rest on their spurious laurels and harbour an abiding fear of the criticism, scrutiny, bitter dissentions, forceful wranglings, and blustering bravado coming from Black apologists. Therefore, they are rejecting imposed moratoriums that contorts facts, and forbids a critique of their leaders, and their moral character (Davis, Daniels & See, 2000; Hare, 1991; Welsing, 1991). In fact, to be utterly frank they realize that violence is an "equal opportunity malady" which is pervasive in both Black and White churches and in other organizations in our society. Moreover, some church-goers believe that concealing the sins and misdeeds committed against any sacred body is itself a "sin," and perpetually insults the integrity of "true believers," striving to live "the life of Christ"–which is a life committed to "casting out devils" from among the children of God.

The purpose of this chapter is to examine from a structural perspective violence in the Black Church. The paper will review the strengths and traditions of this religious body, and analyze two dominant but diametrically opposing perspectives that have been identified as sparking, spewing, and feeding violence into this sacred institution.

Aside from that, the paper will look at secularization in the form of faith-based programs and services managed by the Black Church. Finally, the author will examine the contemporary behavior of ministers and patterns of violence against women. A strategy for assisting the church in maintaining its role of leadership is an objective of this narration.

Data for this writing are drawn from informal interviews with church devotees, plaintive declarations, sermons by active clergy, and the experiences of the author as an active churchgoer. These thick, raw, priceless data will prove to be important in examining patterns of violence in this sacred organization. Given that responses and impressions obtained from interview protocols were scant and not randomly collected, they cannot be universally generalized as conclusive. However, the repetition of the responses gives weight to the evidence that indeed there is violence in the Black Church that deserves to be empirically examined in order to gain more information on the type, extent, depth, intensity, and nature of the conflict.

THE BLACK CHURCH:
DEFINITIONS AND PERSPECTIVES ON VIOLENCE

Violence is an esoteric and a weasel concept and defining it is an intellectual challenge. In a word writers are loath to use the word violence since it is viewed by some as "strong" and "negative"–especially when linked with religious orthodoxy. Buss (1971), defines violence as any behavior that harms or injures others. Expanding on Buss' definition Henderson (1999), observes that professionals who employ the word "violence," seldom mean to imply that any significant type or order does, in fact, prevail. Therefore, the term as applied to the Black Church means intense, furious, and often destructive action or force directed against an individual or group. Accordingly, it refers to vehement feelings, hostility, expressions, and discord that takes place in and around houses of worship. In any case, it is clear that if violence is narrowly and provincially defined, as occur so frequently in philosophical and theoretical discourse, understandably a stretch could be made and an argument presented against associating it with a religious institution. In contrast, if it is broadly defined as evidenced in the social science literature, it will be grounded in the belief that the Black Church is a microcosm of the broader social system. Thus, its officials and members will have the propensity to make inappropriate choices and appraisals, fail to harness their actions, and will exhibit errant behavior in the same manner as do other earthly mortals.

Like the word violence, crafting a definition of "the Black Church" is equally troublesome. This is mainly because discussing this sacred institution can stir a full specter of intense and spirited feelings, emotions and debate. In general for the sake of clarity, the "Black Church" is defined here as an aggregate configuration of members from all affiliations and denominations. Lincoln, (1961,1989, p. 137), a Methodist minister and expert on the Black Muslims, defines the Black Church as a (series) of Black communions or denominations which are independent of White control, resistant to authority hierarchies, and which maintain their own structures of governance, procedural routines finance, ritual, worship, and out-reach.

In this writing the word "Black" is used inexchageably with African American. Both terms refer to people of African descent who have roots and residency in the United States. But before returning to the topic in question the fundamental task of selecting a theoretical framework for guiding this discussion, analysis, and evaluation must be undertaken.

CHURCH VIOLENCE:
THEORETICAL METHOD FOR SYSTEMIC STUDY

Unfortunately of all the multidisciplinary research that has been conducted relevant to the Black Church, seemingly no over-reaching theoretical paradigm has been presented (Lincoln, 1990). So, in the absence of such a perspective, no formulations can offer a better pattern for "bounding" an analytic, empirical, and ethical framework for studying, understanding and explicating Black Church violence than general systems theory. It should be noted that the central tenets, and the imperatives of theoretical construction that contributes to the development of the systems perspective (despite its many shortcomings), have been exhaustively elaborated in the literature (Bertalanffy, 1970; Billingsley & Rodriguez 1998; Churchman, 1968; Daly, 1994; Laszlo, 1972; See, 1999; Wakefield, 1996). Billingsley & Rodriguez (1999) especially explain the systems approach with brevity and clarity. They write:

> Social systems are defined as aggregations of persons or social roles bound together in a pattern of mutual interaction and interrelatedness. Systems have boundaries which enables them to distinguish the internal from the external environment, and they are typically imbedded in a network of social units both larger and smaller than themselves . . .

Systems theory therefore, is the prevailing framework for emphasizing interaction and interrelatedness in order to maintain equilibrium in the totality of any system. Obviously, what must be assumed is that internal and external forces may cause disequilibrium, ideological division, and fragmentation of serious dimensions in the Black Church. In turn, disequilibrium may significantly affect all of the church's accompanying affiliates and society as a whole (See, 1999) (see Figure 1).

As stated, the Black church is not a monolithic organization. Instead, it is fragmented into many different denominations, sects, groups, and cults, each of which sets in motion tensions which frequently culminate into violence. In their long years of study of the Black Church, Lincoln & Mamiya's (1990) delineate six dialectically–related polar tensions that have caused a tangible rift between church members and thus have potentiality for eliciting violence as seen in Table 1.

These models were teased out of data collected when 2,150 Black congregations and 1,894 ministers from seven major Black denominations were studied (Hill, 1999). Since there seems to be fluidity in the Lincoln-Mamiya

FIGURE 1. The Black Church as a Social System

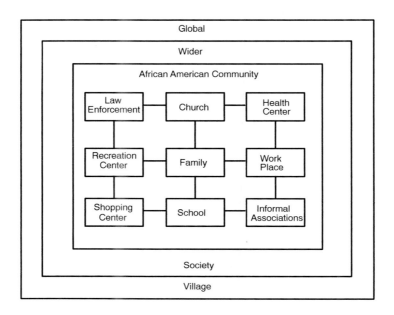

Source: The Billingsley-Rodriguez model of Systems theory as it relates to the Black Church. Cited in *Human Behavior in the Social Environment from an African American Perspective*, L. See (Ed). 2000, The Haworth Press, Inc.

(1990) model this writing has placed all of the Black Church's ideological divisions under one giant umbrella and attached the labels "traditionalists" and "modernists."

TRADITIONALISTS

Traditionalists represent the conservative wing of the Black Church, and its adherents usually consist of an older membership, "the old-timers" (Pipes, 1997). This wing has fond memories of an agrarian era long since passed, when life was simple, community membership smaller, and the weight of words like "love thy neighbor as thyself," were uttered with unmistakable seriousness. Traditionalists have grave misgivings about the forward direction of the Black Church and feel it is succumbing to the pressure of secular life. They believe the church should be faithful to its original role as "soul savers," exhibit a distinctive quality of faith and life, and should mute worldly affairs. According to the traditionalists, indelible

TABLE 1. Dialectically-Related Polar Tensions

Name of Tension	Function
Priestly and Prophetic	Priestly functions involve internal activities such as worship and maintaining the spiritual life of members, while prophetic functions refer to involvement in security matters, such as community uplift, and politics.
Other-Worldly and This-Worldly	An other-worldly orientation is concerned with heaven, eternal life, and after death, while a this-worldly orientation is concerned with improving social and economic conditions in the here and now.
Universalism and Paternalism	Universalism refers to orientation of churches that emphasizes the universalism or "color-blindness" of the gospel rather than focus on the particularism of addressing past and current racism.
Privatistic and Communal	A private orientation refers to churches (and ministers) who believe that their mission is to focus on the religious needs of their members, while a communal orientation refers to churches (and ministers) that believe their mission is to address the social and economic needs of their members and the surrounding communities.
Bureaucratic and Charismatic	Bureaucratic refers to churches (and ministers) who are responsible to bureaucratic authority or hierarchy, while charismatic refers to churches (and ministers) that exercise much autonomy and flexibility.
Accommodation and Resistance	Accommodation refers to orientation of churches (and ministers who view their role as mediators of cultural brokers between the races, while resistance refers to churches and ministers) who are prepared to confront White officials or institutions, when necessary, and are not afraid to affirm their African cultural heritage.

Source: The Lincoln and Mamiya model of tension in the Black Church cited in Robert R. Hill's *The Strengths of African American Families: Twenty-Five Years Later.*

lines between the sacred and secular must not be blurred (Frazier, 1964; Frazier & Lincoln, 1974; Staples, 1978). Traditionalists believe that independence from the state must be diminished and an indispensable prerequisite to decay is set in motion when the Black Church "flirts" with secularization, and refuses to renounce the evil influence of that ideology. It is predicted by the traditionalists that secularization is sure to entice the church to relinquish its role as a "spiritual rock." In a word, this church division insist that the incorporation of secularization into the sacred "house of God" is an abomination–is the devil's work, and Christians must, therefore, "Render unto Caesar the things which are Caesar's and unto God the things that are God's" Matthew 22:21. (Hudson, 1970, p. 10). In short, they predict that with the passing of time perceptible outward signs of moral decay and weakness will surface, spirited debates will enkindle conflict, and hostility, and uncontrolled violence will result–all because secularization has become the church's new master.

THE MODERNIST

The type of intensification to which modernists subscribe is a phenomenon with which most contemporary Black Churches embrace. This group argues that a new tide of "social gospel" has been established with the indispensable responsibility of bringing sinners to Christ. They believe that good Christians must feed the hungry, administer to the sick and the afflicted, the lame and blind, and the widows and orphans–just as the good Samaritan did in the Holy Bible (Cone, 1984; Thomas et al. 1994; Luke 10:33-37). They suggest that the Black Church has a wholehearted obligation to creatively and constructively make peace with the outer world, and seize opportunities for Black people to help shape society in order to eradicate its ills. This means the church must play a pivotal role in eliminating unemployment, poverty, illiteracy, crime, vice, and political corruption (Hudson, 1970 p. 204). After all, says the modernists, Jesus was in the company of saints and sinners like Nicademis (John 3: 1-21) and the woman at the well, (John 4:1-26). Yet, he did not surrender his responsibilities, lose his evangelistic fervor, nor did he lose sight of his mission as the "fisherman of men." Modernists argue that the Black Church must advocate social reform and assist in meeting immediate human needs in service recreation and in the education of children.

Modernists further contend that historically in the Black Church there were no clear lines drawn between the sacred and the secular, and even today the Black Church has missions in secular organization in the broader society. Believing that the Black Church should resort to self-criticism, this sacred institution contends that humility, confession, and self-disclosure are the only methods for keeping its devotees humble (Hudson, 1970, p. 10).

THE ROLE AND TRADITION OF THE BLACK CHURCH

In order to piece together a mosaic of the Black Church, it is important to briefly examine its role and tradition. This masterful institution made up of a collective, complex, and diverse body of human personalities play a vital role in the life space of many black people. It is inherently perceived as a social fortress and masterful enterprise erected to protect oppressed and dispossed African Americans. The Black Church is a repository of tradition, and the influence and "glue" that cements Black people together (Washington, 1984; Woodson, 1945; Peeks, 1971). Despite it's many trials and tribulations, it is as solid as the Rock of Gibraltar, and is allegorically, the "Balm in Gilead" (Wilson, xii). Principally, this institution has been able to endure oppression imposed by a hostile antagonistic society yet, it is still a fearless force with which to reckon. Absorbing fierce blows from all directions, the Black Church has endured the burning of its sanctuaries, and the brutal killing of its children. It has taken risky positions in the service of promoting universal justice and equality, protecting its congregants, and it has sponsored walk-ins, march-ins, kneel-ins, pray-ins, and other acts where danger was forever lurking. Aside from its substantial and enduring role as a fortress for activism, a protectorate of the oppressed and dispossessed, and a cornerstone of Black self-help, and community outreach, the Black Church has taken an unremitting and unrelenting stance against all forces of evil. Today, it has declared war on injustice and stands ready to "do battle" against racism, discrimination and other barriers that exist in the Black diaspora that may lead to the oppression of Black people (Peeks, 1971; West, 1982).

Historically, and even now, during periods of crisis in African American communities it is not only hoped, but expected that the Black Church will overreach its sacred theological orientation of "otherworldliness," and assume an intermediary or social activist role when the rights of Black people are imperiled (Johnson, 1954, 1956). As is apparent the 21st Century finds the Black Church the last visual institutional symbol with the moral presence and authority to remain standing in the gang-infested "hood." In fact, not only does it co-exist with gangs but challenges them without fear. As it happens the Black Church stresses to African Americans in the ghetto the importance of maintaining social cohesion and traditional values even in their insulated piece of geography (Blakemore & Blakemore, 2000).

BLACK CHURCH MEMBERSHIP

With respect to membership, the Black Church has profound and distinctive regulations, and no excessively rigorous inhospitable and inflexible dogma exists in its theological arsenal to prohibit sinners from joining this Christian family. Perhaps, the only religio-political requirement heralded by the Black Church is that the joiner confess his or her sins, read "the word," and believe there is a Great Creator and architect of the universe who is omnipotent, omniscient, and omnipresent. And, that sinners should believe, in the words of Travis (2000), "that God is God, and he's God all by himself."

WORSHIP IN THE BLACK CHURCH

Observers of the Black Church contend that its strength is in its function as a spiritual sanctuary and core refuge to which African Americans go to repair their souls, bond, and receive comfort in time of despair (Cone, 1984; Hill, 1999; Simpson, 1978; West, 1982). It is a succor for the soul, and a mental aberration to be exorcised so that life can be harmonized through devotion (Karenga, 1991). More importantly, the Black Church is a religious institution infused with all the spiritual characteristics with which DuBois (1903) noted must be present to stir the congregation: music (singing gospel music, spirituals, or sacred folk songs); bible-based preaching; shouting (with hand-waving and clapping); and "frenzy," an experience of the Holy Ghost.

In the Black Church there is a systematically contrived hierarchy of power with a Supreme Being, and it is the arena where African Americans go to solicit supernatural help from a power outside the known forces of nature and society (Karenga, 1991). In brief, it is a place where Black people can "take their burdens to the Lord and leave them there." The multitude of sacred and secular functions assumed by the Black Church prompted Mbiti (1970, 1991) to note that the distinction between the Black Church and other areas of American life has been almost imperceptible. No wonder then, that Black Church devotees are pained and repulsed when they observe the spreading, festering violence and corruption that seems to be taking root in their sacred institution.

CHALLENGES FACED IN THE BLACK CHURCH

It is worth mentioning that in multiple interviews held with church devotees all is not well in the Black Church, and an undertow of concerns are verbalized. The essence of the gripes recorded from personal interviews suggests that some members are feeling that the vigor and vitality of the Black Church is in decline, notwithstanding an increase in church attendance. Given it is no longer possible to distinguish between the "Gods of society and the God of the church," some members are experiencing feelings of restlessness, and a depleted source of emptiness. When inquiring about the basis for these expressed feelings, litanies of complaints are articulated. Specifically, one group of members proclaim that their spiritual capital is depleted, they are religiously exhausted, and feel themselves losing spiritual footage. They seemingly are searching for something tangible to hold onto which is not now provided by many Black Churches. Others revealed that their feelings of unrest are stemming from the constant and pervasive "spatting," "squabbling," "fussing," "fighting," and "killing," and the ever present venomous poison of dissention that is causing a loss of spiritual rootage (Hare, 1963). A second complaint is that bitter leadership rivalries, factional disputes, and tests of racial ideology adds to the division in the Church (Peeks, 1971).

With these expressed sentiments and multiple-dimensional criticisms an effort was made to gain a deeper insight into what is being described as violence in the Black Church. Using the personal interview technique (that permits the data to do the talking), questions were posed to some 20 interviewees hailing from several different parts of the country (Needleman and

Needleman, 1973). Some respondents interviewed had assembled in Chicago for family reunions, while others were contacted telephonically in Atlanta, Georgia. The responses of all yielded an array of priceless data on the insidious and destructive violence that is taking place in the Black Church.

IS THERE VIOLENCE IN THE BLACK CHURCH?

The first question posed regarding violence in the Black Church was: Given our definition, does violence, in fact, actually occur in the Black Church? Without hesitation Associate Minister Ramon Harrison of Zion Baptist Church Marietta, Georgia answered the question affirmatively then explained:

> I am from Louisiana, and when I lived there the church was in much confusion. Preachers carried guns to church and it was a bad scene . . . I believe the preachers did not have the love and spirit of God in them, or they would not need guns . . .

Interviews were held with three Associate Women Ministers Reverends Dorie Tuggle, Evelyn Taylor, and Revoydia Rollerson of Zion Baptist Church, Marietta, Georgia. They were also asked if there is violence in The Black Church. In response, all expressed a belief that violence in the Black Church exists both physically and emotionally. However, they made clear that personally neither had been involved in serious violent encounters. On this variable their responses were relatively the same. They explained:

> Although (I), (we) have not personally witnessed physical violence it is discussed in theological circles that ministers in the Greater Atlanta Metro Area have been known to carry a pistol, due to the conflict that existed in his church.

A member of a church in the Atlanta area was interviewed by the author and he confirmed the one Atlanta minster, he knew well, carried a pistol. The respondent explained that the pastor owned a 9mm semiautomatic and a .38-caliber revolver. He said the pastor would use both weapons if necessary since the church had some "mean" members in the congregation.

In a telephone interview with Florence Edna See of Houston, Texas, a devout church worker and retired teacher, the same question was asked: Is there violence in the Black Church? Here is her response:

> Yes, I believe there is violence in the Black Church and it is manifested in more ways than physical encounters. Some violence is connected

with ruining one's influence–and one's good name–spreading untruths about church members, and soiling one's reputation. This violence is more ruinous than fist fighting, which I understand also takes place in some churches.

A telephone interview was held with Dr. Alfrieda Daly, retired college professor at Rutgers University, and author of the best selling book *Workplace Diversity*. When asked if there is violence in the Black Church her response was:

> Most definitely there is violence in the Black Church. When I was at the University of Michigan during the early 1980s, I recall vividly a violent episode that occurred in a storefront church. Seemingly, conflict had erupted between the minister and a church member and the police were called. The White Press was on the scene and T. V. cameras zoomed in on a Black woman walking around with her fist balled-up. The situation was an embarrassment to the city's Black leaders.

> Also, I recall that my father, a minister was almost involved in an episode of violence. Daddy was pastoring a church in Rocky Mountain, North Carolina. I was 10 years old at the time. As an educated man, Daddy attempted to put structure and accountability into the decision-making apparatus of the church. One night at a business meeting one of the deacons had a gun on his person, Daddy thought the deacon may harm him and us (my mother and brother), so he walked out of the church never to return as pastor.

Further testimony of physical as well as emotional violence in the Black Church was revealed in an interview held with Doris Blaine, and Edwina Sanders Lynn, both retired teachers. Both joined in telling a story that affected them deeply:

> When we were girls growing up in Oklahoma, our mother, the daughter of a Methodist minister, was elected church secretary/treasurer of Israel Chapel A. M. E. Church. Mama refused to permit the church's young pastor go into the treasure without proper authorization. Mama's efficiency was irritating to the pastor who at first thought he should have free access to the church treasure. For months he embarrassed, belittled, and harassed Mama, and she made no response. Then, one Monday night at a church conference the minister again embarrassed her. Sobbing, she ran from the meeting, found a brick in the church vestibule, hurled it at the pastor and missed striking him by only a few inches. It is difficult to believe that this beautiful, quiet woman was provoked into committing violence by a minister of the gospel . . .

The same two sisters told this story:

> In the 1940s the A.M.E. Methodist Annual Conference was held in our town. Bishop Tooks was the presiding authority. A power struggle occurred in the church hierarchy, and the bishop was accused of wrong-doing and was not permitted to preside. Ministers carried guns and shots were fired. Fistfights erupted, and as children we were afraid, as the Bishop stayed at our home since hotel accommodations for black people were unavailable in those days. So, you asked if violence occurs in the Black Church, indeed it does.

What is clearly articulated here as the dominant tone, is the general malaise that seems to be promulgated in the Black Church. It all boils down to two types of violence–physical and emotional. In the first, weapons (firearms) are carried when unavoidable clashes occur between the "in" and the "out" groups. Sadly, in this situation, the gravity of the moment is not considered, and the repercussions of ones action is dismissed due to the struggle at that specific moment in time.

The second form of violence is emotional–which is a lethal stressor perpetrated in the form of an unkind word, an arrogant attitude, a cold indifference or a disrespectful gesture (Webb, 1990). The emotional is an extremely serious form of violence as it diminishes human beings and strips them of their personhood. Chiefly, what gives rise to church violence in general is a difference in ideology.

CHURCH VIOLENCE STEMMING
FROM DIFFERENT IDEOLOGIES

Ideology is a set of beliefs which are publicly expressed with the manifest purpose of influencing the orientation and actions of others (Zentner, 1973, p. 75). This definition suggests that a clear difference exists between traditionalist and modernist that has the potential for erupting into violence in the Black Church. On this variable an interview was held with Deacon Harry Bailey of Atlanta. Although unsophisticated by his own description of himself he said:

> You must be a fortune teller cause dar sho'God is two groups in my church. Dar' is us old timers and this new bunch of young folks who come to Atlanta to work for IBM, Georgia Power, and out there at da colleges (Morehouse, Morris Brown, and Clark-Atlanta universities). Our deacons old, but da built this church fo some of these kids wuz born, and now they git no respect. These new folks want to change

everything. They don't lak' da' preacher–saying "he too ignant, too old, too foggy," so dar' is always confusion. Sometimes me, myself, and ma friends jest don't go to church no mo, cause we don't feel welcome in our own church–the one we built with our own hands.

These comments provided an opportunity to ask about the explosion of church attendance, and the overflow crowds of attendees which has recently been an empirical and theoretic subject of discussion among researchers (Hill, 1999). Although interesting, this line of questioning was not pursued. Instead secularization was addressed.

THE SECULARIZATION OF THE BLACK CHURCH

In continuing the probe of ideological differences between traditionalist and modernist in the Black Church seven persons were interviewed at a Chicago family reunion. On this variable questions were asked about the general assertion that the Black Church is becoming too secularized. By definition secularization refers to worldly encounters as distinguished from sacred occurrences, ecclesiastical or religious in nature (Webster's New Collegiate Dictionary, 1965 Edition). To cast light on this issue an interview was held with Reverend Harris T. Travis, Pastor of Zion Baptist Church, Marietta, Georgia. Dr. Travis is a member of the well-educated clergy, holds a PhD degree from Purdue University, and has recently retired as Vice President for Academic Affairs from Southern Polytechnic University (University of Georgia Educational System). When asked specifically if the Black Church was becoming too secular and if secularization was giving rise to violence in the church he responded thusly:

> Let me put it like this, our church has recently constructed a two million dollar annex, and already school officials have been asking us to consider operating several educational programs for children at our new facility. The initiative would bring tremendous revenue to our church. However, administrating such programs is a giant undertaking and would require considerable time, effort and energy. Actually, it is my belief that if I spent large amounts of time on money-making projects, there would be little time left to carry on God's work and minister to members of the church who need me. Therefore, Zion has respectfully declined to participate in these projects, even though we could use the money. I must add that Zion does have outreach programs, and our church is committed to this ministry, but we have no desire to become involved with federal funded projects.

An interview with Will Johnson, a young black Public Accountant and active member of the A. M. E. Methodist Church, Kansas City, Kansas, was asked if secular programs fostered violence in his church. His response represented artful dodging:

> I suppose under the definition you have presented I would say that violence is taking place at our church. Let me explain what I mean. We have an obvious jockeying for power among the new indigenous leadership structure and essentially this is causing friction. The problem is that the new funding we receive from administering several large programs cannot be handled like traditional Sunday offerings, where older deacons took control of the money, counted it, and looted some of it. Today, churches must be multilayered organizations–like corporate America. Money received requires strict accountability, and skillful bookkeeping. Of necessity, the paper work itself is enormous and demands expertise in grantsmanship, management, and organizational behavior. Older members of the church have never wanted us (young professionals) to write grants for our youth programs, nursery, or the "Wee School" programs that we operate. After we wrote the grants and were awarded money to direct these programs, they now want to exert supervisory authority and control the money. We must account for this money so we simply cannot permit them to dictate how the projects will be implemented, and we can't trust them with the money.

A second young deacon from Chicago continued explaining:

> When I, along with other young professionals, try to explain the financial accounting provisions required by the Feds for our programs, these old timers get angry and the conflict begins. They become defensive, they remind us that they were here before we were born, that the church is not a corporation, and we are taking over the church. Right now we are constructing a new wing onto our church with a view of opening a Charter School and a private school that will accept school vouchers, but the older deacons are threatening to block the entire project. This voucher program alone pays from $1,500 to $3,500 per pupil for education. At that rate we can soon get out of debt if we prudently operated these schools. However, last week at our business meeting two deacons almost engaged in a fistfight over this project, and we had to pull them apart. That type action is not healthy for any Christian body.

And, so again it seems as though the Black Church is at a crossroad–whether to continue administering new secular programs like a Fortune 500 company, or accept the criticism that the Black Church has acquiesced from its original mission of responding to the spiritual and social needs of its members. What was likewise revealed is that a generation gap exist which is causing serious conflict, and money is the factor that is causing turmoil–especially with respect to building onto the church to earn money for operating Charter School and accepting vouchers.

ARE BLACK MINISTERS PROMOTING VOUCHERS?

In this series of interviews, the issue of promoting tuition vouchers to make money for the church was discussed. No single issue is causing a greater disconnect between African Americans in the Black community than school vouchers. Interviews with 10 members of the Parks family designed to probe their reaction to controversial subsidies like vouchers and charter schools was undertaken. Family members (at three Chicago family reunion) involved in the discussion were from Illinois, Wisconsin, Virginia, and Texas, and 10 children ages 3-17 were represented in this group. One female member from Illinois around age 25 said:

> This voucher business is the worse form of violence ever concocted against Black children and their families. Now y'all tell me, since when did the Republicans start being concerned about Black kids? Whatever they propose I just right out reject cause I know it's a trick. I don't know what's behind this voucher business, but they'll never get my kids tied up in it.

A second family member from Bay City, Michigan adamant on the subject talked incessantly about the tricks being played on black parents and their children by offering vouchers:

> I believe school vouchers is a sneaky way of closing down Black schools and leaving po' kids "out in the cold" with no education. First these Black preachers talk these crazy Black folks into accepting these vouchers, Then White folks hurry and tear down old Black schools. These Black kids then go to private schools for a week or two with their little vouchers. Then the private schools, not like the public schools will make them "straighten up they act" cause they don't take no shit in these private schools. If Black kids don't "straighten up and fly right," the private schools will kick their asses out. Now the kids are just out in the cold with no place to go to get an education. What's next? They are ready for prison, where White folks "fence them in like cattle," No. Lord! I say to vouchers, "thanks, but no thanks."

A husband-wife couple group from Hampton, Virginia explained their views about vouchers and ministers in these remarks:

I get mad at these Black preachers for urging Black parents to send their kids to private schools just to take advantage of the vouchers. They know full well that private schools don't want these little niggers there. I believe these preachers are "getting their palms greased," they're getting kickbacks, and are "on the hustle" just like me (grin). No stuff! Remember a few years ago in New Jersey–Ed Rollins, Christy Todd Whitman's advisor or something like that admitted he paid Black preachers to urge their members not to vote. Sho' 'nough Blacks registered but didn't vote and Whitman won the election. Now what do we see? We see that Whitman chick doing racial profiling, grinning, and kicking Black men in the ass just like the cops do. That's what Blacks get for putting that Republican chick in office.

The family member from Texas seemingly anxious to top the story about ministers taking kick backs from the voucher issued this statement:

Man! you talking 'bout preachers making some serious bread (money) it's these Texas preachers. I hear Bush is paying a Bishop and other Black preachers and leaders a fortune to round up Black support for him, But you wanted to know about vouchers not politics, right?

Still another family cut in:

I'm like you Bill, I get mad at these preachers for "selling off'" and "pimping off" the Black community. My church right now is planning on opening a private school to get some of that voucher money and they don't know "beans" about operating a school. I asked my friend–who's going to teach these kids, old brother Andrews? (They laughed and explained to the author that old brother Andrews has a 3rd grade education) My church can't even pay the preacher so how in the world will it pay the teachers?

Attention was called to two cousins whispering, laughing, and gesturing. One said:

Had you noticed all these Blacks pushing for vouchers, "they're light, bright, and damn near white?" (laughing hardily) They want to rub shoulders with their white cousins in the private schools.

There was no response to the remark, only a moment of silence. One of the more articulate relatives in this group was from Chicago. She was complimentary of tuition vouchers and her comments were eloquently stated:

I must disagree with all of you in the matter of school vouchers. My Calvin has learned more since attending _____ Academy than he learned in all the years in the public school. He is really getting a good education and there's no way I will ever permit him to attend public school again.

The speaker's cousin, also from Chicago, offered a challenge to the speaker by saying:

Yea! Marie, your Calvin is learning more at that private school because you sit down with him every night and help him with homework–I know, sometimes you get out his homework 'cause you didn't want the White folks to know how dumb he is–When he had a Black teacher and went to public school I never saw you spending all that time with Calvin. You never even set your foot in the schoolhouse–When now every week you doing something at that White school. Now let's hear you deny that–

What was astonishing about these interviews was the opinion among the Parks, the Ashford, and the Cummings family members from several different cities and states was their agreement that vouchers are a trick. Also, that Black ministers are getting kickbacks, and "selling-out" poor Black parents by urging them to send their children to private schools. What was unexpected was the masterful rhetoric and militant rhetoric lodged against vouchers by Black parents from these different states. Unexpectedly, the opinion that Black ministers are "selling out" Black children and their families was not anticipated. Additionally, the view held by the Parks family members is identical with the criticism directed at former Mayor, Andrew Young, of Atlanta, Georgia, also a Black minister. Some Blacks are furious, and frustrated over former Mayor Young's endorsement of school vouchers. Despite constant denial Blacks see the voucher program as a shrewd Republican "risky scheme" cooked up by conservative Think Tanks wrapped in the guise of helping poor Black children escape from bad schools (Knapp et al., 1996). Cynthia Tucker, Editorial Page Editor for the Atlanta Constitution newspaper (August, 2000) wrote that Mayor Young "serves on the board of the Children's Scholarship Fund, a private organization that gives small scholarships to poor families for private school tuition–in essence, he supports tuition vouchers. Some Black leaders are also angry with Colin Powell, Hugh Price, Howard Fuller, and an organization called the Black Alliance for Educational Options (headed by superintendent Fuller) for pushing school vouchers (Tucker, 2000).

What neither the Parks family, Black ministers and Black leaders, advocating vouchers may not know is that reportedly a hidden agenda is behind taking funds from the public schools in order for a few Black students to attend private schools. In effect, it is "sacrificing an advantage for a few, at the expense of many." Knapp, Kronick, Marks, and Vosburgh, (1996, pp. 155-156), write:

> A hidden agenda of the New Right is the protection of the concentration of wealth and power in the upper five percent of our society . . . The New Right intends to reverse the limited patterns of social responsibility that has developed at the national level of government and reverse policies aimed at opening opportunity more widely and easing the burden of poverty on the sick, the disabled, the elderly, and children . . . a platform that advocates tax reductions for the rich and the elimination of safety-net protection for the poor (is the strategy for accomplishing their goal . . .)

The Bell Curve, the New Right Manifesto, makes bold attempts to soften the blow of developing an elitist society by weaving its arguments from appeals to traditional morality couched in humanitarian words, and criticizing the Great Society Programs as being ineffective. In *The Bell Curve*, an argument is made for more elitists and stratified education based on more tracking and market strategies such as vouchers. According to Knapp et al., (1996) if this strategy is enacted it would lead to a permanent isolation of the poor in a cruel authoritarian state.

What has also been revealed in the literature is that during the 1980s under the ultra-conservative administration of Ronald Reagan, a concentrated effort was initiated to slow down the pace of civil rights, eliminate legislation which advocated resource distribution and protect the concentration of wealth in this country (See, 1998). For the past decade the Republican Party has been testing and devising strategies for capturing part of the Black vote which has traditionally been in the democratic column. Finally the party hit upon the issue of vouchers–a market strategy for capturing the Black vote by appealing to parents of Black children. The spin used for pushing faith-based, programs, tuition vouchers, Charter Schools, Christian Schools, faith based schools is that, "the rich already have a choice; why not the poor?" (Carter, 1999).

A number of Black organizations concerned with education feel there is a dangerous threat being imposed on Black people by The New Right. This group is allegedly attempting to use the revered Black Church as the vehicle for disrupting Black progress by neatly tucking away their real intentions which is to fragment Blacks by using Black ministerial leadership as vehicles for that purpose. Thus, The New Right is playing a cynical political game, which will ultimately affect the education of Black children and their families.

BLACK MINISTERS–
THE PERPETRATORS OF VIOLENCE

The mischief of Black ministers articulated with persuasive eloquence seems to flow through the responses of interviews in the Parks family. Neither the "saved" or the "sinners" had faith or respect, or unfaltering loyalty to Black ministers. Unlike the "old time" the respondents as a group felt like modern-day theologians have little commitment to the church, and some have few morals, ethical standards, or family values. One of the most outspoken family members from Chicago laughingly told that preachers were competing with him in sinning and participating in "shady doings and earthly vice." When asked how ministers in their respective churches handle violence a family member from Virginia gave this tort answer:

> How is he handling it? He is causing it. My preacher has divided the church by placing his own little group of deacons in charge of every auxiliary and ignoring other deacons, trustees, and church members. He don't even try to stop the squabbling, but jump on the side of his "Gang of 7." That action makes the other side mad and the violence begins.

One of the two doctors (PhDs) at this reunion commented about remarks consistently made by different ministers directed at professional members. He complained:

> I don't understand why these ministers have such a deep resentment toward educated people. My minister will stand there in the pulpit and make remarks such as, "All you little PhD's, MD's, LLD's, DED's, DDD's, BVD's and all other D's–you may have all that book learning but unless you have "GOD" in your hearts you have nothing, and that little degree is not worth a "hill of Bean" in the eyes of God. This "dumping" on educated members of the church is a direct turn-off for me.

Using the same tone of resentment, a family member from Texas complained about her minister's preaching:

> My preacher reads his sermons. They're probably the ones he wrote in divinity school. He sometimes loses his place and everything gets quiet until he finds his place. He rattles off all those Bible names and most of the time I don't understand what the heck he's saying. He tells us to read along with him in the Bible. Shucks! I can't always find the scriptures and sometimes the other people is done reading before I find a scripture like Nehemiah. To tell the truth I don't want to read the Bible at church. I want to listen to "the word"–like the old fashion preaching

where the preacher is jumping up and down, sweating, kneeling, jumping, kicking, hooping and hallowing. I love that fire and brimstone preaching. I like church where the sisters are shouting, losing their hats, falling and wallowing all on the floor. We use to love watching the sisters on the floor with their drawers and girdles showing. When one fell out on the floor another sister would tip over, with one finger in the air, and pull down the shouter's dress. I like the old fashion hymns Amazing Grace, Precious Lord, Lord, I'm Coming Home. Back then that was church–Today, this "order of service" stuff just don't feel like real church.

The family member from Virginia said that money was a major problem, and is causing most of the violence in the Black Church. He said:

I'm coming from a different place. All I got to say is at least your preacher, talk about the Bible, cause mine only preaches the gospel of St. Money.

Clearly, from the last responses, structuring church service into a "quieter, gentler" direction was not welcomed by some persons interviewed. What was heard is that human beings are the products of their upbringing, as indicated by the subject who longed for old fashion church service.

MONEY–THE ROOT OF ALL EVIL

But according to the group of respondents, money is the problem that stemmed the most violence in the Black Church. Hostility was in the voice of a family member from Chicago who discussed money. He said:

From the time you enter the church until you walk out it's money. You walk in the door and some little kid is selling candy bars for the school, or a rifle for the Boy Scouts. You sit and here comes a note from sister X asking you to "help-out" by buying a ticket to a pie supper. The preacher spends more time talking about tithing than about Jesus, and two or three baskets are passed to you for money. I just wonder how these poor old women whose only income is social security can make it. Even if they gave a dollar every time the basket is passed by the end of the month they would be broke. The preachers don't care about their problem, they just want the money.

Look here, Doc (speaking to the author) I hear there's a preacher in your hometown, Atlanta, Georgia who reviews a person's Income Tax report before accepting him/her for membership in his church. Then he decides how much money must be paid to the church based on the income. Then I understand that he preaches about money not about what "sayth the Lord."

A review of the literature reveals that the many stories about preachers begging for money is congruent with Dr. Nathan Hare's (1991) critique. He wrote:

Many an inexperienced churchgoer has proudly and self-righteously placed a large bill in the first offering, only to be confronted by a multiplicity of subsequent trays for foreign missions, home missions, guest speakers, the pastor and the eternal building fund . . . The quest for conspicuous repute also motivates the programs for the various "Days," where ministers can play at messiahship and otherwise bask in superficial divinity. There are, to name a few: "Appreciation Days," "Anniversaries" (Silver and Gold, although greenbacks always reign supreme), "Institutes," "Women's Day," "Men's Day," "Sister's Day," "Deacon's Day," "May Day," and just about every other kind of "day" short of "Judgement Day."

Inquiring why the church needs so much money the response was provided by a member of a Baptist Church in Atlanta which explained:

These preachers have only two things in mind–competing with each other in building red-carpeted, high ceiling grand sanctuaries as show places, concentrating on money, and trying to be models, (no matter how fat they are). I know a preacher who owns 50 suits all costing over $800 apiece. Some wear $100 dollar shirts, diamond cuff links, and most own a diamond tie tac. My mama use to say, "they wear thousand dollar pins under ten cent chins." Had you noticed Doc, (to the author) preachers love alligator shoes. One preacher I know owns 50 pairs–made out of alligator belly skin, rattle snake skin, lizard skin, and even skin from the testicles of whales (ha! ha! ha!).

Another preacher in my town had the nerve to wear a diamond earring in his ear which, he argued, would lure in young people. But the missionary sisters insisted that he remove that earring. But most preachers love big luxury cars–including black stretch Cadillac limousines. The little "Jack-leg" preachers drive Cadillacs, Mercedes, Lincolns, and Jags. But here of late the "super preachers" drive Royces, and Fiats. I hear a preacher in Atlanta has graduated from cars and now owns a jet airplane, lives in a gated house and has bodyguards. So that's why they need so much money. Then too, those with a sister on the side need MON-EE . . .

THE PREACHERS AND THE SISTERS

One of the most spirited series of interviews examining the Black Church involved preachers "kings of the pulpit," and women who were not their wives. The Cummings family members unanimously agreed that the way ministers conduct themselves these days represents violence against the church, their families, their children, and their friends. The interviewees were implacably hostile, and were harder on "men of the cloth" than on an ordinary layman who committed the same offense. When this difference was called to attention one family member said:

> Acts of mischief by preachers are unforgivable because God told them, "Yield not to Temptation." Then too, those who attended seminaries learned to control and or flèe from all situations that could reflect negatively on them and the church.

An interview on this variable of ministerial behavior was held with Dr. Otis Johnson, from Savannah, Georgia, an expert on the Black Church. In discussing the behavior of ministers he said:

> Approximately a month ago an Associate minister killed the woman he was dating in the church, and it was an ugly scene. This incident literally stunned the Black community in Savannah. So yes, there is definitely violence in the Black Church, and yes, some ministers are exhibiting bad behavior.

A Parks family member from Texas put it bluntly:

> I have lost all respect and feel nothing but disgust for preachers. After Henry Lyons (President of the National Baptist Convention) was caught in that messy business of stealing money from the church to buy a villa in Florida for his girlfriend, Bernice Edwards, I "threw in the towel." He stole over $5 million dollars–can you imagine what Black Churches could have done with all that money, and how many people sacrificed–little old ladies on social security, and even middle class people straining to pay their tithes. I try not to be cynical, but that's how I feel. I know it's not all the preacher's fault, but these preachers need to keep their zippers closed, and these women who tempt preachers need to "get a life." Now what really made me sick was that some members of the Lyons "in-group," still tried to make excuses and retain him as head of the National Baptist Convention–that's disgusting.

A female relative from Michigan with a gift of gab spoke incessantly about Lyons and had the group rolling with laughter. She pranced and talked:

Don't be too hard of Lyons, after all he's a man, and you gotta admit he's got a bad looking woman who I bet is a "cold fish." I understand she was drunk most of the time, so the man had to do something right? No man wants to make love to a drunken woman. On the other hand, I bet old Henry bought the whiskey to keep his wife drunk so he could slip out with that Edwards chick. Me, myself if I had caught my old man with another women, I would have done more than set fire to the house where they were "shacking," I would have put that "Lorena Bobbitt Deal" on him–You remember her right? She was that foreign chick (gesturing and prancing) who whacked off her old man's "thang" with a butcher knife and threw it in a park in Washington, D.C. The police found it and the doctor sewed it back on (Ha! Ha! Ha!). Me, myself I'd have flushed my old man's "thang" right down the toilet stool so the doctor couldn't sew it back on (Ha! Ha! Ha.). See, these men don't mess with the sisters.

The Texas cousin, a handsome male explained:

> Long time ago Black preachers didn't act like they do now. What happened is they now try to act like the White preachers. Don't you remember when Jim Baker was preaching on T. V. prancing, and dancing, and bawling, while all the time he was raking in the money and sleeping with his secretary. My own mama watched him on T. V. and he had her crying and shouting and shit– and we even caught her sending money out of her social security check to him. Then, there was Jimmy Swaggert, that sorry piece of shit–preaching and bawling on T. V. by day and sleeping with whores by night, then calling on the Lord saying, "My Lord, I have sinned" . . . (mimicking). You see doc (to the author) forgive the language, but you said be frank and direct, so I'm being frank and direct. I guess what you hear all of us say is we don't put anything past preachers, as they put the "V" in violence.

A cousin of the speaker, also from Texas made a stunning confession: (Turning to the author) she said:

> Girlfriend, I want you to write my words in your little book. I want you to say Ms. Louise Hester went out partying with a bunch of preachers. One night in the 1990s my friends and me met a bunch of preachers while they were attending a Convention–You talk about partying–"sister girl" these preachers know how to PAR-TEE. They bought plenty food and drinks and they didn't mind spending they money. But you know what? Way down deep I hated these preachers for drinking whiskey with me, and even being with us, cause we were all sinners. When

one of the preachers took off his "hind-parts-before church collar," and looked so drunk, so red eyed, and so ugly I just felt something about that scene was not right. I kept asking myself how can I listen to this man preach when he's been out with me all night? My faith in preachers left that night, and I have not regained it.

In listening to the accounts of ministerial misconduct told in the lexicon of the streets was quite disconcerting. Even long years of experience conducting complex field studies did not prepare me for the data I was retrieving. I suppose I was deeply distressed since my (the author's) grandfather was a minister of the gospel, a professor, and a Christian man in the best tradition of the old theological school. The stories told, some in fun should give today's ministers reason for pause. There is no doubt that many ministers have slid into the world of secularism. The bad news is that some members in their congregation are making no distinction between men of God, and sinners.

The gross criticism lodged against Black ministers prompted the author to ask this question: Do either of you feel all Black pastors are "dress chasing," "money grubbing" sinners who are engaged in violence against their families and God? The most articulate family member from Chicago answered "Lord no!" He then explained:

There's a minister right here in Chicago by the name of Dr. Jeremiah Wright, pastor of Trinity United Church of Christ who is a true servant of God. He is a well educated preacher, a PhD who studied in Africa and other countries, lectured at great universities, has degrees in music, is a linguist, and lived in Africa and all over the world. Dr. Wright not only preaches about God, but he lives the life. He has a big church and operates a so-called "Religious Industrial Complex," but materialism has not affected him as he preaches "the word." Dr. Wright with his depth of knowledge of the Bible, stirs his congregation into a frenzy of handwaving, and some in his church even "speak in tongues." Man–Dr. Wright can "out rap the rappers," he spices his sermons with Black street slang, and he can tickle your "funny bone." Man–I heard him preach a sermon with a text, "Black Woman What Makes You So Strong." The way he put it all together "blew my mind."–rattling off the names of great African Queens like Queen Hatshepset, Queen Ann Nzinga, Queen Cleopatra, Queen Nefertiti, Queen Makeda, the Queen of Sheba, and Queen Hadassah. Then he talked about Black women's "bad hair going back home," and I almost "cracked up." So when you hear me criticizing Black preachers Dr. Wright is not in that number; nor is he in that number of preachers who entered politics to grub money.

POLITICS AND PREACHERS

To obtain a clear view of how pastors are torn between the needs of their members, and the secular building of a Religious Industrial Complex through political connections, interviews were held with three professionals–a college professor from New York (Manhattan), a young Fortune 500 executive, and a master social worker, all from Atlanta, Georgia. During this discussion tensions were heightened as the devious and perilous actions of preacher-politicians got underway for discussion. The author called attention to a church-building boom of Black Churches springing up over the nation and inquired about this phenomenon. The professor responded:

> . . . you have probably observed that many Black preachers like J. C. Watts, and Floyd Flake, quickly enter in, then get out of politics. I argue that these preachers are/were not interested in representing poor people but in the Federal dollars they can grub to build churches. As I understand it, Flake has been awarded so many federal, state, and local dollars until he resigned from Congress to look after his vast empire–or his Religious Industrial Complex. As for J. C. Watts, every time he's seen on T. V. he has that air of indispensableness, and reminds his viewers that "the Congress is not my life." Of course Congress is not his life–money is, but he's not as smart as Flake, and doesn't know how to wield power like Flake. J. C. Watts, a Black Republican, who my grandmother describes as "scarce as hen teeth" in the Congress, is getting a few crumbs, but not the kind of "pork" he should get from the Republican Party that need him to help attract Black votes.

> If you notice, the "money grubbers" don't care which party is in power. If the democrats are in, then they become democrats, and if the Republicans are in power, they become Republicans. I read where J. C. Watts came from a poor family of democrats who live in a little country town in Oklahoma (Eufula) where Republicans were unheard of in the Black community. So how is it that he is a Republican? That goes to show you, he's a politician.

In continuing the interview with the college professor, attention was called to the fact that Congressman Flake had directed the explosive growth of his church from a congregation of 1,400 with an annual budget of $250,000 to a congregation of nearly seven thousand and an annual budget of over $4.5 million. Further, the diverse subsidiaries amassed by Congressman Flake are improving the quality of life for Queen's residents (Simon, 1997; *USA Today*, 8-9-99). Immediately, the professor took issue with my observation and gave a lecture on Rev. Flake's professional career (Flake, 2000). He said:

I can see you are impressed with Congressman Flake, but let me tell you now–I'm not impressed. I teach Policy so I know the history of all the Black Congressmen and women, their voting records and their positions on social issues. I remember when Representative Flake was elected to represent New York's 6th Congressional District (Queens). He never held public office before but with a PhD I believe he figured out a way to use poor Black people in his district as vehicles for building his empire. Flake was placed on the House Committee of Banking and Financial Services and the Committee on Small business. He crafted legislation known as the (Bank Enterprise Act 1994), and the (Community Development Financial Institution Act of 1994). As a member of these powerful committees he was in a position to help pass legislation that was orientated toward business. The professor continued: By sitting on these powerful committees Dr. Flake was in the company of the entire Wall Street, Madison Avenue crowd, so he was in a position to get all the money he needed to build "his" religious empire. Congressman Flake aligned himself with domestic and international bankers, so he was in the " pocket" of the nation's corporate tycoon–most of who are Republicans. I believe his political ties accounts for his "flirting" and even voting with Republicans. With that posture, he lost favor with the Black Caucus as he could not be trusted. Flake speaks in a hoarse, low, modulated voice, and his persona is quiet and pious–just the kind of "Toms" rich White folks love. . . . It is my view now that the ex-Congressman is an empire builder, and his building is for his own ego and edification. So, helping to improve the economic fortunes and growth of urban and undeserved communities is an unintentioned consequence of his deeper motivation, which is to build a monument for himself.

A few months ago he was flirting with the idea of running for either Mayor or Governor of New York. He invited Republicans like Governor Bush and Mayor Giuliani to his church and had them believing he would support Bush for President. I really believe he meant to change from a Democrat to Republican, but his church members came down on him and I understand there was severe conflict at his church, as most members are democrats. I don't trust preachers like Flake, as I said what he is doing is for his own ego, and that's violence against Black people.

The young business executive who listened attentively took strong issue with the professor's analysis and responded angrily:

I don't know why for the life of me you are so forcefully criticizing the brother Congressman. With the many good things he has done for his community how could anyone allege that his intentions are dishonorable. Remember, Congressman Flake has a PhD and could have a good 8 to 5 job making good money. But instead he is getting gray hair dealing with a bunch of ungrateful niggers who do not appreciate what he's doing. This man has been smart and astute enough to "use" the system, and help poor people and still you above all people, an educator like him are not satisfied with his efforts. Would you rather that the people in Queens be left stuck in the ghetto or live in one of the new housing compounds built by Congressman Flake's negotiating with the White power structure? This brother has made employment for 800 poor African American that no one else would probably hire, yet you are finding fault of him. You may as well know this kind of small thinking on the part of people like you, a professor who suppose to be a "big thinker" literally "blows my mind."

The third respondent, the social worker had this to say:

I understand where you both are coming from. But let's analyze Congressman Flakes' effort–if he is doing all this building for the total community and not just for the Methodist Church, then I would feel his intentions are honorable. But the fact that all these projects are under the wing of his church tells me that he may enjoy the feeling of control–and that is "using" Black people and that is violence. Look now, and follow me–Flake recommends vouchers and he welcomes Charter Schools. Most of us don't like these programs because they divide our children into the have's and have-nots. It seems like Rev. Flake could have best used his power to persuade the House of Representatives to appropriate money to build, repair, and improve public schools, and hire more teachers. Also, he could make an effort to support public schools where most teachers are women. But, if women at Congressman Flake's church schools are treated as they are in the larger society, a new and different problem is emerging.

VIOLENCE AGAINST WOMEN
IN THE BLACK CHURCH

Unfortunately, in the Black Church decision-makers have been unable to make a theoretical leap and seriously examine the superiority-inferiority dichotomies between the roles of Black men and women in church management and governance. Indeed, the Black Church hierarchy is seemingly unaware or unwilling to admit that a significant parallel exists between racism, sexism, and oppression that exist in the Black Church the same as it exists in our social system. In other words churchmen assume full power and control over churchwomen, and dismiss their struggle for participation in the decision apparatus of the Black Church. Simply put, Black Church leaders are guilty of imposing the same hostility and transgressions of subordinating and oppressing women that White men have been accused of practicing in the broader society (Cone, 1984; Rodgers-Rose, 1980).

Recent data show that women make up 75% of the Black Church membership, yet 75% of the governance and general decisions are made by men. In most jurisdictions not only are women denied equal access to the pulpit but also are provided few opportunities to serve on Deacon or Trustee Boards. Thus, on any Sunday when communion is administrated to the congregation twelve or more upstanding Black deacons preside over the "body and blood of Christ," as well as all major social and financial functions.

The literature reveals that traditionally Black women often gave Black men an opportunity to be "front and center," since they have been so misused and abused in this society. But, in explaining this practice a church mother said, "no where in the Bible is there any scripture where women are called to preach. When Jesus choose his twelve disciples all were men and none were women as seen in "the word," Mark Chapter 3, Verses 14-15. Verse 14: "And he ordained twelve, that they should be with him, and that he might send them forth to preach. Verse: 15 And to have power to heal sicknesses, and to cast our devils . . ." This church mother's view of a woman's place mirrored the discussion advanced by Cone (1984).

An interview with Rev. Dorie Tuttle, Associate Pastor of Zion Baptist Church helped to explain this issue more succinctly:

> The problem associated with women participating in church governance, and delivering sermons is no issue at my church. Dr. Harris T. Travis, my pastor believes women should have an opportunity to use their God-given talents, and he encourages and supports women ministers and encourages development. Clearly, his view is the exception rather than the rule. But remember, Dr. Travis, is an academically trained theologian and pastor, and his thinking is far more advanced than pastors coming from an older tradition. I don't believe older church members personally dislike women ministers occupying the pulpit but they literally follow "The Word," which places women in subordinate positions of power and influence.

A second testimony regarding the role of women in the church came from Rev. Evelyn Taylor, Associate pastor and Administrative Assistant to Dr. Travis. She said:

> Pastor Travis, believes in promoting women. Initially, there may have been older members of the church who rejected the ideas of women in

the pulpit, and understandably it was not easy for any of us. However, Dr. Travis, has provided wonderful support and church members are getting accustomed to the presence of women ministers.

Again Rev. Tuttle expertly echoed her feeling this way:

In the Black Church I believe there are some Black men who actually believe that women are not cognitively equipped to assume administrative responsibility for church governance. They feel that leadership roles assumed by women collide with the biblical injunction of "wives obeying their husbands" as recorded in the scripture (Ephesians, 5:22 which reads:) Wives, submit yourselves unto your own husbands, as unto the Lord. For the husband is the head of the wife, even as Christ is the head of the Church: and he is the savior of the body.

Seemingly many Black clergy, and even older "mothers of the church" are advocates of women's inferiority. Their passivity reflects the era of their upbringing, which was generally before affirmative action, and women's rights were in vogue. Unfortunately, Black antagonistic ministers use the Holy Scriptures as "the supreme document" to use in arguing their claim of the inferiority of women. But sometimes, it seems they forgot to read the scriptures that condemns the evil of patriarchy (Cone, 1984).

T. D. JAKES–LEADER OF WOMEN

The Parks family members discussed the role of women in the church at quite some length. They were asked why women throughout the world had failed to select a woman leader for their world-wide ministry. Specifically, the author wondered why women choose Bishop T. D. Jakes, (1997), a charismatic "man of the cloth" as the leader of an eight million women's world-wide ministry, instead of selecting one of the great woman preachers as seen in Table 2.
Lisa Lynn, of Oklahoma succinctly answered part of the question:

She said, You know, I never thought about that question. Actually, in the Black Church women have been so accustomed to being left out of leadership positions until we never give thought to the fact that men are leaders in every auxiliary in the church. Now that you mentioned it, I bet there's not a Black man's group in this nation that would accept being led by a woman. The problem is women accept being oppressed.

TABLE 2. Ebony's Greatest Black Women Preachers, 1997 (Rank Order)

Name	Affiliation	City
1. Rev. Prathia Hall Wynn	Mt. Sharon Bapt.	Philadelphia
2. Rev. Vashti M. McKenzie	Payne Mem. A.M.E.	Baltimore
3. Rev. Carolyn A. Knight	ITC	Atlanta
4. Rev. Renita J. Weems	Vanderbilt U.	Nashville
5. Rev Susan J. Cook	Bronx Christian Fellowship	Bronx
6. Rev. Ann Farrar Lightner	Mt. Calvary A.M.E.	Townson, MD
7. Rev. Delores H. Carpenter	Mich. Park Christian	Washington
8. Rev. Caludett A. Copeland	New Creation Fellowship	San Antonio
9. Rev. Jacqueline E. McCullough	Elim Int'l Fellowship Ch.	Brooklyn
10. Rev. Ernestine C. Reems	Center of Hope Comm. Ch.	Oakland, CA
11. Rev. Yvonne Delk	Comm. Renewal Soc. UCC	Chicago
12. Rev. Johnnie Coleman	Christ Universal Temple	Chicago
13. Rev. Ella Pearson Mitchell	ITC	Atlanta
14. Rev. Barbara L. King	Hillside Chapel Truth Center	Atlanta
15. Rev. Jessica K. Ingram	Oak Grove A.M.E	Detroit
16. Rev. Cynthia Hale	Ray of Hope Christian Ch.	Atlanta
17. Rev. Susan Newman	Georgians for Children	Atlanta
18. Rev. Margaret E. Flake	Allen A.M.E.	Jamaica, NY
19. Bishop Barbara Amos	Faith Deliverance Christ Center	Norfolk
20. Rev. Jacqueline Grant-Collier	ITC	Atlanta
21. Rev. Willie T. Barrow	Rainbow/PUSH	Chicago
22. Rev. Bernice King	Greater Rising Star Bapt.	Atlanta
23. Rev. Brenda J. Little	Bethany Bapt.	Evanston
24. Rev. Cecelia W. Bryant	10th District A.M.E.	Dallas
25. Bishop Leontine Kelly	UMC	San Francisco
26. Rev. Joanne Browning	Ebenezer A.M.E.	Ft. Washington, MD
27. Rev. Clarice J. Martin	Colgate Rochester Div.	Rochester
28. Rev. Leah G. Fitchue	Eastern Bapt. Sem.	Wynewood, PA
29. Rev. Susan K. Smith	Advent UCC	Columbus
30. Rev. Martha Simmons	Pilgrim Community UCC	Grand Rapids
31. Rev. Linda Hollies	UMC	Grand Rapids
32. Rev. Iona Locke	Abssinia Interdenom. Ch.	Southfield, MI
33. Rev. Addie Wyatt	Vernon Pk. COGIC	Chicago
34. Bishop Barbara Harris	Episc. Diocese of MA	Boston
35. Rev. Cheryl Sanders	Third St. Church of God	Washington

EBONY'S RUNNER-UP LIST OF GREAT BLACK WOMEN PREACHERS, 1997 (ALPHABETICAL ORDER)

Name	Affiliation	City
Rev. Katie Geneva Cannon	Temple University	Philadelphia
Rev. Delores H. Carpenter	Michigan Park Christian Church	Washington, D.C.
Rev. Johnnie Coleman	Christ Universal Temple	Chicago
Rev. Susan J. Cook	Mariner's Temple Baptist	New York
Rev. Carolyn A. Knight	Philadelphia Baptist	Harlem
Rev. Vashti M. McKenzie	Payne Memorial A.M.E.	Baltimore
Rev. Prathia Hall Wynn	Mt. Sharon Baptist	Philadelphia

Source: *Ebony Magazine* (1997), and Andrew Billingsley, *Mighty Like a River* (1999). New York: Oxford University Press.

Dr. Alfrieda Daly provided a different explanation of the issue:

> Although Black Women do not hold leadership positions, they still have a way of accessing power through their missionary societies, and invisible auxiliaries. In truth, it's not like men wield all the power in church governance; women still give input, but it is exerted in a different way.

What was imparted in these interviews is that women are the backbone, the "workhorses," and the skeletal system of the Black Church paradoxically, have borne the brunt of sexism in this religious organization. Disappointingly, Black men have used scripture and the "patriarchal bad habits of its progenitor" to inhibit Black women's, church participation and have been successful in freezing women into subordinate roles (Cone, 1984).

In some cases typical church women have complained, about the menial chores they are expected to perform in the Black Church which includes preparing wine for Holy Communion, ironing the sacred linen, and beautifying the alter. Except for radical feminists, few have dared question the Church's interpretation of scripture since such inquiries would well be construed as blasphemous or heresy.

But, as we enter the 21st Century, signs are abound that the subordinate role of women in the Black Church is doomed to change. The precipitation of impending change is mainly due to the number of well educated, serious male ministers, and educated congregates who have scoffed at the idea that men can sing, pray, and preach better than women and can better spread the gospel to every living creature. These progressive ministers have therefore given women an opportunity to serve as associates, in order to develop leadership, which will lead to full ordination.

Clearly, the Black Church is duly influenced by the structure of the society which, to this day, continues to be sexist and to impose violence against women by failing to grant them equal access to serve the Lord in any capacity of their choosing.

Already, the first major signs of break through is in progress. In June, 2000, the White Southern Baptist Church made ripples which are sure to have a significant impact on women and the Black Christian community. At its Annual Conference held in Orlando, Florida, the Rev. James Merritt, of Snellville, Georgia, newly elected President of this organization of 15.8 million members, and more than 40,000 churches, announced that women would no longer serve as pastors in the church (Atlanta Constitution, June 25, 2000 p. A-15). The Texas delegation dissatisfied with this backward policy threatened to bolt from the Church. Essentially, the loss of this huge membership contingency will leave a gaping hole in the membership if the Texas threat is carried-out, and will ratchet up violence against women who only wish to serve the Lord. Predictably, this protest will no doubt have a demonstrable consequence in the Black Church unless liberative action is taken to assure the equality in the Black Church.

CONCLUSION

The Black Church is the only institution that represents the "taproot of strength" in the Black community. Unequivocally, it has withstood the test of time, weathered violent storms and protected Black people against an on-slaught of structural oppression by employing the power of Christian religion. But, as we enter the 21st Century, again storm clouds are hovering over the Black Church, which is being subjected to severe criticism due to the violence that has slipped into its sacred body.

The basic forces precipitating violence in the Black Church is seemingly the split between the secular and the sacred divisions. It is ironic that this issue is now emerging since historically the sacred and the secular has always merged with no evidence of polarization. Similarly, self-help, community outreach, and general communalism was promoted. In fact it was the Black Church that favored church-related schools, mutual-aid societies, and fraternal orders and in turn spawned the first Negro insurance companies and banks (Peeks, 1971). The Black Church was even the arena where the seeds of controversy, bitter leadership rivalries, factional disputes, and tests of racial ideology was resolved. However, within the boundary of its system most social, personal, and religious problems were confronted and ultimately solved. Problem-solving then, represented no major hurdle since the Black Church drew from its own history and experience for guidance, and from its rich religious orientation for support.

But that was then, and this is now. Accordingly, significant growth in population, growing secularism and with a more educated and sophisticated church membership, the notion of total self-help is too complex an undertaking for many Black Churches to undertake. Besides, Black Churches in small towns do not have the finances and capital resources to operate independently without the assistance of government. But does that mean that the church must be open to progressive secularization? Indeed it does not for there are alternatives. Church devotees pay heavy taxes, therefore it is incumbent upon the government to fulfill its obligation and provide adequate social and educational resources to the children and adults of church congregants. These services include, but are not limited to adequate schools, social and recreational facilities. The Black Church must be careful about its involvement in "government-run," "faith based," religiously motivated, programs tied to a church. It could be that the government is dropping its social experimentation in the church's arms for a price (Hudson, 1970). Instead, church members may consider pressuring the government to provide societal supports to

Black Church members and their families. Being free of this social burden the church can then ebb back and renew its religious mission of saving souls for Christ.

From the data collected, it is clear that today's church leaders must bear major responsibility for much of the internal dissension, scandalous and tragic behavior and violence observed in the Black Church. Their errant behavior, makes it essential that re-educational facilities be established for wayward ministers of the gospel who, as some ministers would say are humans beings, who have been overcome by sin. These ministers may wish to reorder their lives, and learn new coping skills, so they may continue to help save souls and dedicate their own lives to Christ.

Human service practitioners can assist the Black Church, and subsequently those in need of service by: (1) Engaging in empirical research on many areas of the Black Church, e.g., attendance, secularization, etc.; (2) studying the rich history and legacy of the Black Church; (3) establishing relations with pastors and other church officials, and provide counsel when needed; (4) conducting seminars on conflict resolution for youth and church leaders; (5) distributing literature to church leaders on managing conflict; (6) counseling with pastors on methods of developing leaders for the future; (7) teaching volunteers the fundamentals regarding human behavior in the social environment; (8) holding seminars on anger management and aggression; (9) arranging for activities to be held at Black Churches so youth can interact with college students; and (10) Inviting ministers to attend continuing educational workshops held by social work educators.

These beginning efforts should go a long way in bringing the Black Church together, empowering its leadership, and fostering its "mission of mercy."

REFERENCES

Alexander, B. (1987). The Black Church and community empowerment. In Robert L. Woodson (Ed.) *On the road to economic freedom*. Washington, D.C.: Regency Books. pp. 45-61.

Bailey, H. (Deacon). (1999). Interview. Atlanta, GA.

Bertalanffy, L. (1962). General systems theory: A critical review. *General Systems Yearbook*, 7, 1-20.

Billingsley, A. (1992). Climbing Jacob's Ladder: *The enduring legacy of African-American families*. New York: Simon and Schuster.

Billingsley, A. (1994). The Black Church. *National Journal of Sociology*, 8, (1-2). Double Edition.

Billingsley, A. (1998). *One more river to cross: The Black Church as agent of social reform*. New York: Oxford University Press.

Billingsley, A. (1999). *Mighty like a river*. New York: Oxford.

Billingsley, A., Caldwell, C.H. (1991). The church, the family and the school in the African American community. *Journal of Negro Education* 60(3): 427-440.

Billingsley, A., Caldwell, Hill, R.B. (1991). *Tradition and change: A study of Black Church-operated community outreach programs.* Unpublished manuscript.

Billingsley, A., Rodriguez, B.M. (1998). The black family in the 21st century and the church as an action system: Macro perspective. In L. See (Ed.). *Human Behavior in the Social Environment From an African American Perspective.* Binghamton, NY: The Haworth Press, Inc.

Blaine, D., Lynch, E. (2000). Interview, Poteau, OK.

Blakemore, J., Blakemore, G. (1999). African American street gangs. In *Human Behavior in the Social Environment from an African American Perspective* L. See (Ed.) New York: The Haworth Press, Inc. pp. 203-223.

Brashears, F., Roberts, M. (1996). The Black Church as a resource for change in The black family. Sadye Logan (Ed.). Boulder, CO: Westview Press. pp. 181-192.

Buss, A.H. (1971). Aggression pays. In J.L. Singer (Ed.), *The control of aggression and violence.* New York: Academic Press.

Carter, President Jimmie. (1999). Carter disagrees with Bush, Gore byline: Associate Press, *Atlanta Journal Constitution.*

Churchman, C.W. (1968). *The systems approach.* New York: Dell.

Civil Rights Advocates (1999). Interview. Atlanta, GA.

Cone, J. (1989). Black theology, black churches, and black women. In *black male-female relationships.* D. Aldridge (Ed.). Iowa: Kendall-Hunt Publishers.

Daly, A. (1998). *Workplace diversity.* Washington, D.C.: NASW Press. pp. xi.

Daly, A. (1999). Interview. Richmond, VA.

Davis, Daniels, See. (2000). The psychological effects of skin color on African Americans' self esteem. *In Human Behavior in the Social Environment from an African American Perspective.* L. See (Ed.). New York: The Haworth Press, Inc. pp. 63-91.

DuBois, W.E.B. (Ed.). 1903. *The Negro Church.* Atlanta: Atlanta University Press.

Flake, F. (1997). Major joins Congressman Floyd Flake and Community leaders at Landmark Church. (Press release dedication). *<http://www.ci.nyc.ny.us/html/97/sp546- 97.html>.*

Flake, F. (News Release) Congressman 6th Dist. New York. *http://www.nydems.org/elected/flake.html*

See trying for Black vote GOP looks to heaven. *USA Today.* 8-9-99 (Front page).

School choice and the at-risk child commentaries on current events. CNN News 20/17/2001.

Pastor and former Congressman Floyd Flake preaches action, responsibility. Sermon.

Floyd Flake. (1999). *The way of the boot strapper: Nine action steps for achieving your dreams.* Harper, San Francisco.

Coalition opposing vouchers formed March 19, 1999. *<file:///A/press_02f.htm>.*

Jake Tapper, Oct 8, 1949. George W.'s New York homeboy salon news.

Frazier, E.F. (1964). *The Negro in the Unites States.* New York: The Macmillan Company.

Frazier, E.F. (1974a). The Negro Church in America: New York: Schocken Books.

Frazier, E.F., Lincoln. (1974b). *The Black Church since Frazier.* New York: Schoken Books.

Glaser, B., Strauss, A. (1967). *The discovery of grounded theory*. Chicago: AVC.

Harek, N. (1965). Have Negro ministers failed their roles. *Negro Digest*.

Hare, N. (1991). *The Black Anglo-Saxons*. Illinois: The Third World Press.

Harris, H.R. (1997). *Growing in glory. Emerge*. pp. 49-53.

Harris, T. (Pastor). (1999) Interview. Zion Baptist Church, Marietta, GA.

Harrison, P. (1959). *Authority and power in the free church tradition: A social case study of the American Baptist Convention*. Princeton: Princeton University Press.

Henderson, G. (1999). *Our souls to keep*. Maryland: Intercultural Press, Inc.

Herrnstein, R.J. & Murry, C. (1994). *The bell curve*. New York: Free Press.

Harrison, R. (Minister). (1999). Interview. Zion Baptist Church, Marietta, GA.

Hill, R. (1972). *The strengths of black families*. New York: National Urban League.

Hill, R. (1994). The role of the church in community and economic development activities. *The National Journal of Sociology*. Summer/Winter.

Hill, R. (1999). *The strengths of black families: 25 years later*. New York: University Press of America.

Hudson, W.S. (1970). *The great tradition of the American churches*. MA: Harper & Rowe.

Jakes, T.D. (1997). *Woman, though art loosed!* New York: Inspirational Press.

Johnson, O. (2000). Interview. Savannah, GA.

Johnson, W. (1999). Interview. Kansas City, KS. July 12, 2000.

Johnson. O. (1980). *The social welfare role of the Black Church*. (PhD diss.) Brandeis University.

Johnston, R.F. (1954). *The development of Negro religion*. New York: The Philosophical Library.

Johnston, R.F. (1956). *The religion of Negro protestants*. New York: The Philosophical Library.

Karenga, M. (1991). *Introduction to black studies*. 2nd Ed. Los Angeles: The University of Sankore Press.

Knapp, P., Kronick, J.C., Marks, R.W., Vosburg, M.G. (1996). *The assault on equality*. Westport, CT: Praeger Publishers.

Laszlo, E. (1972). *The systems view of the world*. New York: George Braziller.

Lincoln, C.E. (1961). *The black Muslims in America*. Boston: Beacon Press.

Lincoln, E.E. & Mamiya, L. (1990). *The Black Church in the African American Experience*. Durham: Duke University.

Lincoln, E.E. (1989). *Knowing the black church. What it is and why*. The state of black America, 1989. New York: National Urban League, Inc. pp. 137-151.

Mays, B.E., Nicholson, J.W. (1933). *The Negro's church*. New York: Institute of Social and Religious Research.

Mbiti J. S. (1970). *African religions and philosophy*. Garden City, NY: Doubleday.

Needleman, M., Needleman C. (1974). *Guerrillas in the bureaucracy*. New York: John Wiley & Sons.

Peeks, E. (1971). *The long struggle for black power*. New York: Charles Scribner & Sons.

Rodgers-Rose, L. (1980). *The black woman*. Beverly Hills, CA: Sage Publications, Inc.

Rollerson, R. (Reverend). (1999). Interview. Zion Baptist Church, Marietta, GA.

See, L.A. (Lee). (1998). Diversity in the workplace: Issues and concerns of Africans and Asians. In A. Daly (Ed.) *Workplace diversity issues & perspectives*. Washington, D.C.: NASW Publishers. pp. 354-373.

See, L.A. (Lee), Kashan, N. (2001). Violence in the suites. *Violence as Seen Through a Prism of Color*. L. See (Ed.) New York: The Haworth Press, Inc. In press.

Simon, B.A. (1999). Church schools and public money. *IFA freedom writer*. Jan-Feb 1999. <file:///A/whatischsch.htm>.

Staples, R. (1978). Race, liberalism, conservatism, and premarital sexual permissiveness: A biracial comparison. *Journal of Marriage and Family*. 40: 78-92.

Taylor, E. (Reverend). (1999). Interview. Zion Baptist Church, Marietta, GA.

Thomas, S.S., Quinn, S., Billingsley, A., Caldwell, C. (1984). Community health outreach programs conducted by 635 black churches in the Northern U.S. *American Journal of Public Health*. 84(4):575-579.

Travis, H. (2000). Sermon delivered by Dr. Harris Travis. Zion Baptist Church, December 10, 1999.

Tucker, C. (2000). Vouchers movement: We can't give up on public education. *Atlanta Constitution*. Atlanta, GA: (Editorial).

Tuggle, D. (Reverend). (1999). Interview. Zion Baptist Church, Marietta, GA.

Wakefield, J.C. (1996). Does social work need the eco-system perspective? *Social Service Review*. Pp. 2-30.

Washington, J.R. (1984). *Black religion*. New York: University Press of America.

Washington, J.R. (1984). *Black religion: The Negro and Christianity in the United States*. New York: United Press of America.

Webb, W.J. (1990). *Psychotrauma: The human injustice crisis*. Lima, Ohio: Fairway Press.

Webster's Seventh New Collegiate dictionary. (1965). G&C Merriam Co. Springfield, MA.

Welsing, F.C. (1991). *The Isis papers*: The keys to the colors. Chicago: Third World Press.

West, Cornell. (1982). *Prophecy deliverance!: An Afro American revolutionary Christianity*. Philadelphia: The Westminster Press, 1982.

Wilson, A. (1990). *Black-on-black violence*. New York: African World Infosystems. pp. xiii.

Woodson. C.G. (1992). *The history of the Negro Church*. Washington, D.C.: The Associated Publishers, Inc.

Yinger, J.M., Simpson, G.E. (1965). *Racial and cultural minorities*. New York: Harper & Rowe.

Zentner, J.L. (1973). Organizational ideology. Some functions and problems. *International Preview of History and Political Science*, 10(2): 75-84.

Structural Violence as an Inducement to African American and Hispanic Participation in the Los Angeles Civil Disturbance of 1992

Walter C. Farrell, Jr.
James H. Johnson, Jr.

SUMMARY. This article discusses selected elements of structural violence–unneeded suffering or death resulting from preventable human actions and/or unfair treatment–as contributing factors to the civil disturbance in Los Angeles, California in April and May of 1992. It is argued that structural violence remains firmly and institutionally entrenched in the city and that little has been done to resolve: (1) access to economic opportunity, (2) inter-ethnic minority and majority tensions, (3) police-community conflicts, and (4) to revise government policies

Walter C. Farrell, Jr., PhD, is Professor of Social Work, Public Health, and Public Policy, and Associate Director of the Urban Investment Strategies Center in the Frank Hawkins Kenan Institute of Private Enterprise, Kenan-Flagler Business School, University of North Carolina at Chapel Hill. He received his PhD in Urban-Social Geography from Michigan State University. Previously Dr. Farrell was Professor at the University of Wisconsin at Milwaukee.

James H. Johnson, Jr., PhD, is William Rand Kenan, Jr. Distinguished Professor of Management, Sociology, and Public Policy, and Director of the Urban Investment Strategies Center in the Frank Hawking Kenan Institute of Private Enterprise, Kenan-Flagler Business School, University of North Carolina at Chapel Hill. He received his PhD in Urban-Social Geography from Michigan State University. His current research focuses on the causes and consequences of growing inequality in American society.

[Haworth co-indexing entry note]: "Structural Violence as an Inducement to African-American and Hispanic Participation in the Los Angeles Civil Disturbance of 1992." Farrell, Walter C, Jr., and James H. Johnson, Jr. Co-published simultaneously in *Journal of Human Behavior in the Social Environment* (The Haworth Social Work Practice Press, an imprint of The Haworth Press, Inc.) Vol. 4, No. 4, 2001, pp. 337-359; and: *Violence as Seen Through a Prism of Color* (ed: Letha A. (Lee) See) The Haworth Social Work Practice Press, an imprint of The Haworth Press, Inc., 2001, pp. 337-359. Single or multiple copies of this article are available for a fee from The Haworth Document Delivery Service [1-800-342-9678, 9:00 a.m. - 5:00 p.m. (EST). E-mail address: getinfo@haworthpressinc.com].

to address the needs of poor, ethnic minorities. *[Article copies available for a fee from The Haworth Document Delivery Service: 1-800-342-9678. E-mail address: <getinfo@haworthpressinc.com> Website: <http://www.HaworthPress. com> © 2001 by The Haworth Press, Inc. All rights reserved.]*

KEYWORDS. Civil disturbance, urban rebellion, structural violence, ethnic minority conflicts, police-community relations

INTRODUCTION

Extended joblessness . . . will destroy black American society unless something drastic is done to ease it. The family, everything else will fall apart.

–Sir Arthur Lewis, Nobel Laureate in Economics, Board of Economists, *Black Enterprise*, 1982.

During the past nine years, comprehensive analyses of the causes of and responses to the Los Angeles civil arrest of 1992 have been undertaken. It has been characterized as an urban rebellion, insurrection, civil unrest, civil disorder, urban uprising, conflagration, and/or civil disturbance in a variety of publications (see Johnson, Jones, Farrell, and Oliver, 1992; Johnson, Farrell, and Oliver, 1993; Oliver, Johnson and Farrell, 1993; Johnson and Farrell, 1993; Jackson, Johnson, Farrell, and Jackson, 1994; Jackson, Johnson, and Farrell, 1994; Johnson, Farrell, and Toji, 1997). A reflection on these analyses reveals that the causes of this disturbance can be most properly grouped under the general rubric of structured violence. More recently, in the aftermath of a spate of school shootings and other manifestations of powerlessness and hopelessness, contemporary society is viewed as facilitating violence via its policies and culture (Dionne, 1999, Galtung, 1996).

Borrowing from the definition of Pilisuk (1999), structural violence, in this analysis, is defined as " . . . unneeded suffering or death resulting from preventable human actions" (p. 198). He went on to conclude that "violence is used by the underdogs of society as a way to get out of a 'structural iron cage' of powerlessness and poverty or to get back at the society that put them there" (p. 198). McCord (1998) observes further that "[i]n the United States, the historical record includes persistently discriminatory policies that have isolated poor [B]lacks in cities. Despite the democratic promise of equality, for many American urban [B]lacks discriminatory policies have blocked opportunities for legitimate success. Some urban violence appears to be displayed rage in response to unfair treatment" (p. 79; *Time*, 1992 a & b; *The Wall Street Journal*, 1992 a & b; Stevenson, 1992; *The New Republic*, 1992;

Terry, 1992). It is within this conceptual framework that the research problem is anchored. In an assessment of the genesis of the Watts unrest of 1965, Oliver, Farrell, and Johnson (1990) concluded that Watts (and south-central Los Angeles more generally) "is at more risk today (for civil unrest) than it was 25 years ago. The more things have changed, the worse they have become" (p. B7). They went on to state that "business, government, and the local community . . . must jointly devise strategies to eradicate . . . joblessness, poor education, family disruption, and community divisions" (p. B7).

In concert with these observations, the purpose of this article is to examine, retrospectively, those social, political, and economic arrangements that served to induce the violent outbursts in south-central Los Angeles, California from April 29 through May 4, 1992. Widely affirmed as the worst urban civil unrest in the history of America, the intent here is to document those elements of the social structure that caused largely ethnic minority population groups to express their discontent in violent ways (Whitman, 1993a & b; Duffy, Tharp, and Cooper, 1992; Ellis, 1992; Flannigan, 1992; Institute for Alternative Journalism, 1992; Luttwak, 1992; Rutten, 1992). The specific objectives of this investigation are to examine: (1) joblessness and economic opportunity; (2) demographic change and ethnic minority conflict; (3) government policies; and (4) police-community relations as structural inducements to what is characterized as an urban rebellion.[1] In addition, African-American and Hispanic residents and participants views of the contributing factors are presented. It is hypothesized that the structural violence inherent in the deteriorating urban conditions in the socially and economically distressed communities of south-central Los Angeles induced the violence associated with the civil unrest of 1992.

JOBLESSNESS AND ECONOMIC OPPORTUNITY

From the 1970s to the 1990s, the economic fortunes of residents in south-central Los Angeles, especially those of Black and Hispanic males, declined sharply.[2] The jobless rate for these groups, ages 18 to 35, was nearly 50 percent, while the rate for White men hovered near 10 percent, a five-fold differential (see Fortune, 1992; Moss & Tilly, 1991). During the 1960s, the period of the last rebellion, the disparity in the jobless rate for young minority and majority men, with and without a high school diploma, was not nearly as stark (see Figure 1).

A similar pattern of racial divergence occurred among young women. In the mid-1980s, the jobless rates for all 20-year-old Black women (47.0%), and for 20-year-old Black women with less than a high school education (72.1%), were substantially higher than the rates for their White counterparts (23.6% and 47%, respectively). But in the mid-1960s, the disparities were not as

FIGURE 1. A Comparison of Male Joblessness for U.S. 20-Year-Olds, 1960s and 1980s

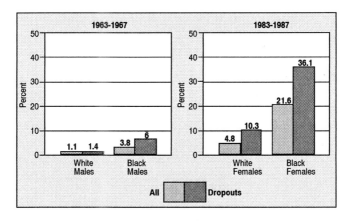

Source: U.S. Census Current Population Survey, 1963-1987.

drastic; in fact, young White women had higher jobless rates than their Black counterparts (see Braddock & McPartland, 1987; Cross, 1990; Culp & Dunson, 1986; Moore, 1981) (see Figure 2). Joblessness was not the only area in which racial divergence had occurred. Also, a disparity in earnings existed along racial lines. Between 1973 and 1992, the earnings of young Black and Hispanic males deteriorated relative to those of White males (Turner, 1991; Moss & Tilly, 1991; Kirschenman & Neckerman, 1991; Turner & Turner, 1981).

Figure 3 shows that south-central Los Angeles had the greatest concentration of job loss and that its most significant negative impact had occurred in Black and Hispanic communities. Meanwhile, job growth in major and minor technopoles was occurring primarily in White and mixed communities. Blacks and Hispanics had been largely abandoned in the post-industrial economy. Between 1978 and 1989, more than 200,000 manufacturing jobs in Los Angeles were lost due to plant closings, and a disproportionate number disappeared in south-central Los Angeles (Johnson, Jones, Farrell, & Oliver, 1992; Oliver, Farrell, & Johnson, 1990; Soja, Morales, & Wolf, 1983).

At the same time that jobs vanished from this area–the traditional industrial core–local employers were seeking alternative sites for their production activities. As a consequence of these seemingly routine decisions, new employment growth nodes emerged in the San Fernando Valley, in the San Gabriel Valley, and in El Segundo near the airport in Los Angeles County, as well as in nearby Orange County (see Figure 4) (Scott, 1988). Historically, these communities had been inaccessible to Blacks due to discrimination in housing, and they remained

FIGURE 2. A Comparison of Female Joblessness for U.S. 20-Year-Olds, 1960s and 1980s

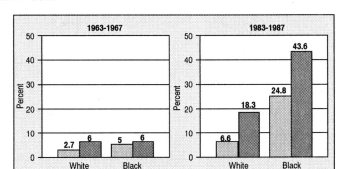

Source: U.S. Census Current Population Survey, 1963-1967 and 1983-1987.

so as a result of the escalation of home prices (Johnson & Roseman, 1990). Collins (1980) documented these patterns of segregation as early as 1940.

It was estimated that over 200 Los Angeles-based firms, including Hughes Aircraft, Northrop, and Rockwell, as well as a host of smaller businesses, participated in this deconcentration process. A number of Los Angeles-based employers also established production facilities in the Mexican border towns of Tijuana, Ensenada, and Tecate. Previous research has shown that in Los Angeles and other U.S. cities, such capital flight, in conjunction with plant closings, essentially has closed off minority access to what were formerly good paying, unionized jobs. This is one of the structural elements of Los Angeles society that gave rise to the 1992 civil disturbance in south-central Los Angeles (Brinkley-Carter, 1974; Bluestone & Harrison, 1982; Johnson, 1992; Johnson & Oliver, 1991; Lichter, 1988; Oliver, Farrell & Johnson, 1990; Castells, 1985; Squires, 1982). And it was closely related to the rapid demographic change in this area.

DEMOGRAPHIC CHANGE
AND ETHNIC MINORITY CONFLICT

Over the past thirty years, the Los Angeles population has become more ethnically diverse (Johnson, Oliver, & Roseman, 1989). In 1960, nearly two-thirds of metropolitan Los Angeles residents were comprised of non-Hispan-

FIGURE 3. Plant Closings in Los Angeles County, 1978-82

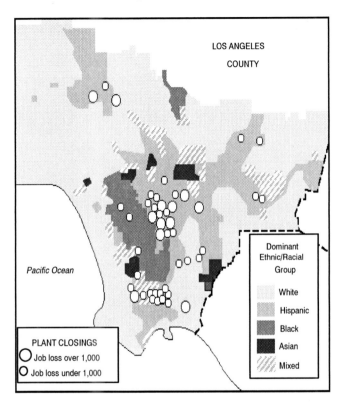

Source: U.S. Census, 1990. Plant Shutdown Directory, 1978-82. U.S. Department of Commerce 1991.

ic Whites. By 1990, largely as a consequence of heightened immigration (both legal and illegal) and the substantial exodus of non-Hispanic Whites, non-White ethnic minority groups (i.e., Asians, Blacks, and Hispanics) numerically had become the majority population of Los Angeles County, accounting for 58% of the total. Approximately one-third was Hispanic; Blacks and Asians each accounted for about 12% (Johnson, Jones, Farrell, & Oliver, 1992). Nowhere was this ethnic change more apparent than in south-central Los Angeles, where the insurrection erupted, and the burning, looting, and violence were most intense (Alter, 1992; Blumenthal, 1992; Johnson, Jones, Farrell, & Oliver, 1992). Two types of ethnic transition had occurred in the formerly all Black south-central Los Angeles communities (Johnson & Oliver, 1989).

FIGURE 4. Location of Craft Specialty Industries and Job Growth Technopoles in Los Angeles County, 1990

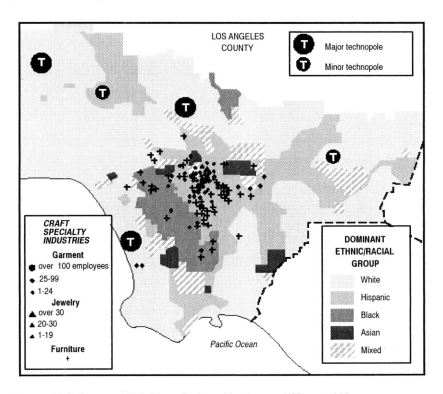

Source: U.S. Census, 1990. Blum, Carlson, Morales, and Wilson, 1992.

The first was a Black-to-Brown population succession in the residential neighborhoods, which began in the 1960s and accelerated in the 1970s and the 1980s. In 1970, an estimated 50,000 Hispanics were residing in south-central Los Angeles neighborhoods, representing 10% of the area's total population. That number had doubled to 100,000, or 21% of the total population, by 1980. Today more than half of the population of south-central Los Angeles is Hispanic (Miles, 1992; Johnson & Oliver, 1989; Grieco and Cassidy, 2001).

Concomitant with this Black-to-Brown residential transition, an ethnic succession also was taking place in the south-central Los Angeles business community. Prior to the Watts uprising of 1965, most of the businesses in the area were owned and operated by Jewish shopkeepers. In the aftermath of that civil disturbance, the Jewish business owners fled the area and were replaced not by Black entrepreneurs, but, rather, by newly arriving Korean immigrants who opened small retail and service establishments (Oliver, Farrell, & Johnson, 1990; Johnson & Oliver, 1989; The 1968 Report of the National Commission on Civil Disorders, 1988).

These transitions in the residential and business communities of south-central Los Angeles have not been particularly smooth. The three ethnic minority groups–Asians, Blacks, and Hispanics–have found themselves in fierce competition and conflict over access to jobs, housing, and other resources, including the political levers of power in the city. The conflict has been most contentious between Blacks and Korean entrepreneurs (Johnson & Oliver, 1989; Chang, 1988; Cleaver, 1987; Cleaver, 1983 a, b, & c). Disadvantaged Blacks in south-central Los Angeles view Korean merchants as "foreigners" who take advantage of them by charging high prices, refusing to hire local Blacks, failing to reinvest any of their profits to otherwise aid the community, and being rude and discourteous in their treatment of Black customers. According to Edward Chang, an expert on Black-Korean relations in Los Angeles, the disrespect that Korean merchants accord Black customers is rooted in Korean stereotypes of Blacks as drug prone, welfare dependent, and lazy. Koreans acquire these stereotypes before they arrive in the United States, Chang contends, through American movies, television shows, and Armed Forces Korean Network Programs (Johnson, Farrell, & Guinn, 1999; Chang, 1988).

Prior to the jury's verdict in the Rodney King police brutality trial, Korean-Black relations in Los Angeles had reached a state of near crisis. Blacks openly questioned how Koreans were able to generate the capital necessary to start or take over businesses in their community, when willing Black entrepreneurs were unable to raise such funds. The *Los Angeles Sentinel*, the city's major Black weekly newspaper, consistently derided Asian shopkeepers for their lack of courteousness to Black customers, reporting both the important and the trivial instances of conflict. However, it was the Latasha Harlins case, in which a Korean merchant killed an unarmed teenage honor student pursuant to a verbal altercation, combined with other Korean insults of Blacks, that escalated the conflict between Black residents and Korean merchants in south-central Los Angeles to crisis proportions (Johnson, Jones, Farrell, & Oliver, 1992; Mydans, 1992a, Oliver, Farrell, & Johnson, 1990; Cleaver, 1987; Cleaver, 1983a, b, & c). That incident preceded the verdict in the Rodney King trial by only a few months.

Assessments of the 1992 civil unrest strongly support the contention that rapidly deteriorating relations between Black residents and Korean merchants of south-central Los Angeles were major elements in the conflagration. As a consequence, Korean businesses were strategically targeted in the burning and the looting. Nearly half of the buildings severely damaged or destroyed during the civil unrest were either Korean-owned or operated (Johnson, Farrell, & Oliver, 1993; Mydans, 1992b & c; Report of the Ad Hoc Committee, 1992).

The King verdict also brought to the fore what apparently was a brewing but previously hidden element of interethnic minority conflict in Los Angeles: antagonisms between Hispanics and Koreans in Koreatown. While often viewed as an ethnic enclave demarcated by Korean control of businesses, Koreatown is actually a residentially mixed community with a large proportion of Hispanics (principally Central American immigrants) as well as Koreans (see Figure 5). It was in this area that Hispanic involvement in the civil unrest was most intense. Post-disturbance surveys and focus group research indicate that Hispanics in this community came in contact with Koreans on multiple levels, and that they experienced hostility at each one. First, on a residential level, Hispanics complained of discrimination by Korean landlords who rented houses and apartments according to racial background. Second, Hispanic customers in Korean establishments complained of disrespectful treatment, similar to that alleged by Black customers. Third, as employees in Korean business establishments, Hispanics expressed concern about exploitation by their Korean employers. Apparently, Hispanics vented their anger and frustration over such discriminatory treatment by looting and destroying a significant number of Korean-owned businesses in Koreatown (Bobo, Oliver, Johnson, & Valenzuela, 2000; Bobo, Johnson, Oliver, Sidanius, & Zubrinsky, 1992; Farrell, Johnson, & Jones, 1992).

Before the civil disorder, local elected officials were well aware that ethnic tensions were potentially explosive among non-White ethnic minority groups in Los Angeles. At both the city and the county levels of government, human relations commissions had long existed to deal with such problems. Traditionally, these agencies had been poorly funded, and they had been delegated limited decision-making power or authority to develop policies to resolve the array of intergroup conflicts that were a part of life in the diverse communities of Los Angeles.

Both the city and the county human relations commissions had directed their activities toward convening hearings on racially, ethnically, and religiously motivated violence and to implementing educational programs that sought to change the stereotypical ways in which the diverse ethnic groups viewed one another. For example, before the civil unrest, the City of Los Angeles Human Relations Commission was instrumental in bringing together south-central Los Angeles Black leaders and Korean entrepreneurs for "prayer breakfasts." These sessions were supposed to offer an opportunity for the two groups to iron out their differences and to promote mutual understanding. Unfortunately, neither this nor any of the other efforts sponsored by

FIGURE 5. Ethnic Change in South Central Los Angeles, 1970-90, and Locations of Korean Businesses, 1987

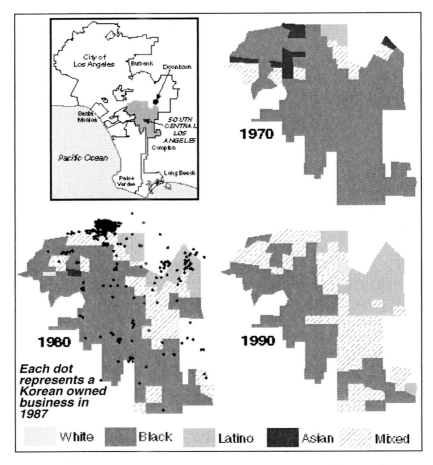

Source: U.S. Bureau of the Census, 1970, 1980, and 1990. *Korean Business Directory, 1987.*

the Human Relations Commission was very successful. In fact, realizing that little progress had been made in reducing the tensions between the two groups, Black and Korean leaders agreed to stop holding such meetings (Farrell, Johnson, & Jones, 1992; Institute for Alternative Journalism, 1992; Cross, 1990; Kim, 1984). The tensions between Blacks, Hispanics, and Koreans continued to escalate–Blacks in conflict with Hispanics over low-wage jobs, Hispanics in conflict with Koreans over condescending and demeaning treatment, Hispanics and Blacks in conflict with Koreans over their stereotypical views and actions toward them, and Black-Hispanic perceptions that Los Angeles' social and economic institutions were more responsive to Korean needs and interests than to theirs (Johnson, Farrell, & Guinn, 1999; Farrell, Johnson, & Jones, 1992). These tensions exploded in the aftermath of the King verdict on April 29, 1992. Meanwhile, government policies at the federal and local levels served, unwittingly perhaps, to exacerbate the situation.

GOVERNMENT POLICIES

Over the past two decades, the federal government has attempted to create a deregulated business environment to increase the competitiveness of U.S. firms in the global marketplace. Changes in antitrust laws and their enforcement have resulted in a growing concentration of large, vertically and horizontally integrated corporations in key sectors of the economy. Due to their economic power and control of markets, these large conglomerates have moved capital quickly and efficiently to select national and international locations to take advantage of cheap labor (Johnson & Oliver, 1992). There is evidence that the federal government, especially during the first Bush Administration, may have used taxpayers' dollars to provide incentives for United States businesses to relocate abroad, primarily to Central American countries (Hinds, 1992).

Furthermore, to facilitate the competitiveness of firms remaining in the United States, the Reagan Administration relaxed environmental regulations and substantially cut both the budgets and staffs of governmental agencies charged with the enforcement of laws governing workplace health, safety, and compensation, as well as hiring, retention, and promotion practices (Palmer & Sawhill, 1984).

This shift toward a *laissez-faire* business climate was partially responsible for the wholesale exodus of manufacturing employment from the nation's urban communities. It also precipitated the emergence of new industrial spaces in the suburbs, exurbs, and nonmetropolitan areas, as well as the movement of manufacturing activities to Third World countries (Johnson & Oliver, 1991). Many of the new industrial spaces on the U.S. landscape have been situated in places where there are few Blacks in the local labor market and few Blacks within reasonable commuting distance (Cole & Deskins, 1988). Nowhere have the effects of these policies been more apparent than in south-central Los Angeles.

Nonetheless, new employment opportunities emerged within or near the traditional industrial core in south-central Los Angeles. Unlike the manufacturing jobs that disappeared from this area, however, the new jobs were in the competitive sector of the economy, including the hospitality services industry (i.e., hotels, motels, restaurants, and entertainment) and such craft specialty industries as clothing, jewelry, and furniture manufacturing (Johnson, Jones, Farrell, & Oliver, 1992). Competitive sector employers survive only to the extent that their prices remain nationally and internationally competitive. To remain competitive, they often hire undocumented workers, offer unattractive working conditions, and pay, at best, minimum wage. Research indicates that newly arriving illegal Hispanic immigrants, who settle in south-central Los Angeles, are often preferred over Blacks in the competitive sector employment market because of their undocumented status and willingness to work for low pay (Levy, 1995 & 1997; Farrell, Johnson, & Jones, 1992; Mueller & Espenshade, 1985).

In part as a consequence of these developments, and partly because of employers' openly negative attitudes toward Black workers, when the Rodney King police brutality verdict was handed down on April 29, 1992, south-central Los Angeles communities were characterized by high concentrations of two disadvantaged populations: the working poor, who were predominantly Hispanic, and the jobless poor, who were predominantly Black (Johnson, Jones, Farrell, & Oliver, 1992; Kirschenman & Neckerman, 1990). Most of the individuals inhabiting these communities had insufficient incomes to maintain a decent standard of living. Both groups–Hispanics and Blacks–were isolated geographically from mainstream employment opportunities that paid livable wages. Intergroup tensions were high as poor Blacks and Hispanics competed for competitive sector jobs and other scarce resources (Luttwak, 1992; Johnson & Oliver, 1989).

Adding to the adverse impacts of a *laissez-faire* business policy on the structure of employment opportunities in south-central Los Angeles, the local government failed to devise and implement a plan to redevelop and revitalize the community. Instead, the city aggressively pursued a policy of downtown and westside redevelopment in an effort to lure international capital (Holcomb & Beauregard, 1981). The "power of the pocketbook" appears to have driven this redevelopment strategy. Research indicated that "[s]ince 1983, Los Angeles city officeholders and candidates received more than $23 million in political contributions, mostly from the Westside, the San Fernando Valley, and Downtown businesses" (Clifford et al., 1992, p. A1). They noted further that "[p]olitical experts and City Hall critics concluded that the contributions made elected officials more attuned to corporate interests and the suburbs than to the city's poorer areas" (p. A1; Labor/Community Strategy Center, 1992).

The transformation of the skylines of downtown and the Wilshire corridor–the twenty mile stretch extending along Wilshire Boulevard from downtown to the Pacific Ocean–is evidence of the success of this redevelopment strategy. A symbol of Los Angeles's emerging transactional economy, this area houses the headquarters of a number of multinational corporations and other advanced service sector employers (Holcomb & Beauregard, 1981). This type of redevelopment, however, has done little to improve the quality of life of the ethnic minority residents of south-central Los Angeles. Jobs in the revitalized downtown area and along the Wilshire corridor typically require high levels of education and technical training–the ability to do "head" work as opposed to "hand" work–that most of the disadvantaged residents of south-central Los Angeles do not possess. The only low-skilled employment opportunities that existed in this area at the time of the insurrection were low-level service and custodial jobs, which were typically filled by newly arrived immigrants (Cross, 1990; Labor/Community Strategy Center, 1992). The pitting of one struggling ethnic minority group against another–Blacks against Hispanics–served to limit economic opportunity and advancement for both and to stimulate discontent. However, each group had equal access to maltreatment by the Los Angeles Police Department (LAPD).

POLICE-COMMUNITY RELATIONS

The use of excessive force against African Americans and Hispanics, males in particular, by LAPD officers has become ingrained in the department's standard operating procedures. Officers who are accused of violence and brutality against citizens expect as a matter of routine that these complaints will be dismissed or that the complainants will be paid off. Thus, there have been repeated incidents of brutality by a core group of officers, causing minority citizens to have little faith that they will receive justice (Farrell, Johnson, & Jones, 1992; Johnson, Jones, Farrell, & Oliver, 1992). Most recently, the "Rampart police scandal," which has resulted in a wide-ranging investigation and a series of indictments, has revealed that Los Angeles police officers have: (1) planted drugs and weapons on suspects; (2) routinely and severely beaten Black and Hispanic males for "sport"; (3) confiscated and resold drugs in drug busts; (4) deported recently arrived Hispanic immigrants on trumped-up charges; (5) coerced witnesses in criminal cases to lie; (6) given false testimony in murder trials; and (7) have committed numerous other felonious and criminal acts, while being shielded by their badges and their fellow officers (Weinstein, 1999; Lait & Glover, 1999; Lait & Glover, 2000a; Lait & Glover, 2000b; Lait & Glover, 2000c; Newton, Lait & Glover, 2000; Cannon, 2000). A federal inquiry into this matter resulted in Los Angeles Mayor Richard Biordan signing of consent decree with the U.S. Department of Justice. He agreed to have an independent outside monitor oversee the LAPD for five years, with powers to investigate the workings of the department (Reuters, 2000; Sterngold, 2000).

Police brutality is so prevalent in south-central Los Angeles that most African-American and Hispanic males have a first- or second-hand story to tell about an incident. As argued elsewhere, "the verdict in the [Rodney King] police brutality trial was merely the straw that 'broke the proverbial camel's back'" (Johnson, Jones, Farrell, & Oliver, 1992, p. 359). The video-taped beating of Rodney King was only the most recent case prior to the insurrection in which serious concerns were raised about the use of excessive force by police to subdue or arrest a Black or Hispanic citizen. For several years, the LAPD has paid out millions of taxpayers' dollars in compensation to local citizens who have been victims of abuse, illegal searches and sei-zures, and property damage (Farrell, Johnson, & Jones, 1992; Davis, 1990). Moreover, Black and Hispanic citizens had been victimized disproportionate-ly by the LAPD's use of the bar arm control and choke holds, outlawed tactics that were formerly employed to subdue suspects perceived to be uncooperative. Between 1975 and 1992, more than sixteen Los Angeles citizens died as a result of LAPD officers' use of these restraint tactics: twelve of them were Black, and most of the remainder were Hispanic (Far-rell, Johnson, & Jones, 1992; Johnson, Jones, Farrell, & Oliver, 1992).

It is interesting to note that most of the urban civil disorders since the 1960s have been sparked by negative incidents between police and/or the larger criminal justice system and the African-American community, espe-cially African-American males. Furthermore, the strongly held perception in Los Angeles' ethnic minority communities, at the time of the insurrection, was that the police had no limits on what they could do to minority citizens (Salholz, 1992; Scheck, 1992; Farrell, Johnson, & Jones, 1992). These views were also confirmed in a study of police brutality commissioned by the U.S. Department of Justice. Begun in 1991, after the videotaped beating of Rodney King, the report investigated police brutality complaints that had been received by the Justice Department from 1984 to 1991. It found that "[t]he jurisdictions generating the highest number of complaints were con-centrated in a geographic band running across the southern part of the United States, with Los Angeles County (the sheriff's department, not the city po-lice) ranking second" (DeParle, 1992, p. A10). However, the Los Angeles Police Department ranked 11th nationally, a ranking that coincided with Afri-can-American perceptions of LAPD misconduct in a *Time Magazine* poll conducted after the civil disorder (Ellis, 1992; Lacayo, 1992). Another dis-turbing trend during the uprising is that 50-60% of those arrested, most by the Los Angeles County Sheriff's Department, had no prior arrest record. It appeared that many were detained by police for simply being Black or Brown (Schatzman, 1992). Personal and anecdotal comments gathered in the immediate aftermath of the disturbance provided additional insights into police-community relations.

VIEWS OF OBSERVER AND PARTICIPANTS

The generally hostile views of the rebellion's observers and participants were formed in a crucible of anger fueled by decades of deep poverty, government neglect, racism, police abuse, joblessness, and interracial and interethnic conflict. Our field analyses–and other post-rebellion assessments–revealed that south-central Los Angeles residents were quite perceptive about their social and economic conditions within the larger local and national context (Farrell, Johnson, & Jones, 1992).

In interviews with Blacks, Whites, and Hispanics in the target area, a number of issues emerged. The nation's rush to send aid to Russia while ignoring the community development and housing needs of south-central Los Angeles residents was roundly assailed. Although many opposed the looting and burning following the Rodney King verdict, they viewed it as a form of outrage against exploitative businesses that came in to take their money, with limited reinvestment in their community in terms of employing residents, purchasing services, and contributing to community programs (Ong & Blumenberg, 1992; Report of the Ad Hoc Committee, 1992; Rule, 1992).

Though this exploitation was not believed to justify the violence, respondents felt it helped to explain it. Several of them indicated that the real looters were the S&L (Savings and Loan) industry bandits whose "total take" had far exceeded the costs of the rebellion. Others saw the conflagration as an excuse by the community's criminal elements to take advantage of an opportunity for self-enrichment and thought that their actions had little to do with the injustice to Rodney King (Zuckerman, 1992; Mydans, 1992b; Mydans, 1992c; Mydans & Marriott, 1992; Matthews, 1992).

In an unprecedented show of unity, the Bloods and the Crips, two violent Los Angeles youth gangs, looted together and then jointly selected a spokesman to tell the political, business, and civic power structure that "no one was listening to or dealing with their concerns about jobs, respect, and fair treatment" (Farrell, Johnson, & Jones, 1992). He expressed anger and hopelessness about the lack of recreational facilities, adequate health care, the quality of public education, and the possibilities for the future. Moreover, the anger and despair in the faces of these young residents were unsettling as they gave graphic examples of the injustices and abuses they had suffered:

- police harassment;
- police brutality (physical assaults for minor offenses (i.e., traffic violations);

- discrimination in applications for employment; and
- consistently unfair treatment in the criminal justice system.

Collectively, they perceived the King verdict as a direct affront to their humanity—"that justice does not apply to people of color in any way, that the law was as lawless as those torching buildings and looting businesses." But this time they were committed to making the system spend money for treating them wrong (Farrell, Johnson, & Jones, 1992).

These responses are a succinct summary of the feelings in the streets of south-central Los Angeles on the eve of the Los Angeles civil disturbance of 1992 and in its immediate aftermath. We must be ever mindful that young people frequently act out the frustrations of a community. In this instance, they were joined by adults across racial lines–Blacks, Whites, and Hispanics –in a virtual rainbow of expressive anger. Moreover, the violence and arson fires were spread out over a large geographic area of poor, working-class, and middle-class communities, ranging from Watts to Hollywood (*Newsweek*, 1992a & b; Rule, 1992; Terry, 1992; *The Washington Post*, 1992a & b; *The New Republic*, 1992; *Time*, 1992a & b).

CONCLUSION

What this analysis has revealed, via primary and secondary sources, is that structural violence–unneeded and preventable suffering, powerlessness, and hopelessness–was firmly anchored and seemingly perpetrated on a continuing basis in south-central Los Angeles for more than half a century. Not only was Watts the focal point of the 1992 civil disorder, but it had experienced a continuing spiral of social and economic decline since the 1940s (Collins, 1981). Earlier, the 1965 predecessor rebellion signaled intense despair in the Los Angeles African-American community (and subsequently in the Hispanic community as it grew in size) (Miles, 1992). Yet, very little was done to ameliorate the aforementioned situations of structural violence leading up to the epochal insurrection of 1992. The structural violence, occasioned by the geography of despair in south-central Los Angeles over an extended time period, is best captured in the eloquent words of the late Senator Robert F. Kennedy (Steel, 1992, p. 17):

> For there is another kind of violence slower, but just as deadly, destructive as the shot of the bomb in the night . . . This is the violence of institutions; indifference and inaction and slow decay. This is the violence that afflicts the poor, that poisons relations between men because their skin has different colors. This is the slow destruction of a child by hunger, and schools without books, and homes without heat in the

winter. When you teach a man to hate and fear his brother, when you teach that he is a lesser man because of his color or his beliefs or the policies he pursues, when you teach that those who differ from you threaten your freedom or your job or your family, then you also learn to confront others not as fellow citizens but as enemies–to be met not with cooperation but with conquest, to be subjugated and mastered.

These findings suggest very strongly that this was the prevailing attitude of those who controlled the social, economic, political, and criminal justice institutions governing the lives of south-central Los Angeles' ethnic minority citizens on the eve of the civil disturbance. As the area became more ethnically and racially diverse, these citizens were institutionally coerced into competition among themselves for increasingly scarce resources in the areas of housing, jobs, and a range of other public sector assets. This structural violence induced anger and hopelessness among south-central Los Angeles residents who struck out via the most effective means–in their view–at their disposal to make their voices heard. Some social policy analysts have condemned this behavior, moralizing that if only the perpetrators had behaved themselves, acted civilized, and brought God into the ghetto, their lives would surely have improved (Bennett, 1992; Loury, 1992; Wilson, 1992). Yet these moralizers fail to acknowledge that the vast majority of the angry (and the passive) members of this community had done just that, to no avail, for an extended time period (Barringer, 1992; Mydans, 1992d).

In other words, the most socially and economically distressed residents in inner cities across this nation are being asked to heal themselves while surrounding institutions brutalized them in all facets of their daily lives. This reality leads to the acceptance of the hypothesis that the 1992 civil disturbance was induced by the structural violence inherent in the deteriorating urban conditions in the socially and economically distressed communities of south-central Los Angeles. The demographic, governmental, economic, and justice issues discussed above remain firmly entrenched in south-central Los Angeles today, buttressed by an ever expanding prison system that is predominantly populated by Black and Hispanic citizens. They have been unable to adjust to the crippling effects of structural violence that they face on an intense and persistent basis (Johnson & Farrell, 1998). This structural violence constitutes "quiet riots" against the poor and disenfranchised in south-central Los Angeles–restricting their economic opportunities, instituting government policies that facilitate interethnic conflict and that tolerate police misconduct, and abandoning the residents to the abyss of hopelessness and despair. A reasonable conclusion is that the "real rioters" were, and are, those who control the levers of power (Harris & Wilkins, 1989).

NOTES

1. This article represents a synthesis of empirical and qualitative research conducted in Los Angeles over the past decade. Here the focus is on the theme–structural violence–that explicates the broader, longitudinal context of the 1992 civil disturbance in Los Angeles. In this paper, the terms urban rebellion, insurrection, civil unrest, civil disturbance, civil disorder, urban uprising, and conflagration are used interchangeably to refer to the rage expressed–often in violent ways–by ethnic minority residents of south-central Los Angeles from April 29 through May 4, 1999 in response to their social, economic, political, and criminal justice environments.

2. The Hispanic males suffering the greatest economic dislocations/unemployment were the most recent immigrants (primarily El Salvadorans) from Central America.

REFERENCES

Alter, J. (1992, May 11). TV and the fireball. *Newsweek*, p. 43.

Barringer, F. (1992, May 15). Census reveals a city of displacement. *The New York Times*, p. A2.

Bennett, W.J. (1992, May 8). The moral origins of the underclass. *The Wall Street Journal*, p. A10.

Black Enterprise. (1992, June). A decade of review. *Black Enterprise*, pp.195-202.

Bluestone, B., and Harrison, B. (1982). *The Deindustrialization of America*. New York: Basic Books.

Blumenthal, S. (1992, May 25). Fireball. *The New Republic*, pp. 11-14.

Bobo, L.D., Oliver, M.L., Johnson, J.H., Jr., and Valenzuela, A. (2000). Analyzing inequality in Los Angeles. In *Prismatic Metropolis: Race, Segregation and Inequaliy in Los Angeles*. Edited by L.D. Bobo, M.L. Oliver, J.H. Johnson, Jr., and A. Valenzuela. New York: Russell Sage, In Press.

Bobo, L., Johnson, J.H., Jr. and Oliver, M.L., Sidanius and Zubrinsky, C. (1992). *Public Opinion Before and After a Spring of Discontent*. (3 CSUP Occasional Working Paper Series). Los Angeles, CA: Center for the Study of Urban Poverty, University of California at Los Angeles.

Braddock, J.M. II, and McPartland, J.M. (1987). How minorities continue to be excluded from equal employment opportunities: Research on labor markets and institutional barriers. *Journal of Social Issues*, Vol. 43, 5-39.

Brinkley-Carter, C. (1979). The impact of the new immigration on native minorities. In R.S. Bryce-LaPorte, editor, *Sourcebook on the New Immigration*. New Brunswick, NJ: Transaction Books.

Cannon, (2000, September 11). One bad cop. *The New York Times Sunday Magazine* <www.nytimes.com/library/magazine/home/2000100/mag-lapd.html>.

Castells, M. (1985). High technology, economic restructuring and the urban regional process in the United States. In M. Castells, editor, *High Technology, Space and Society*. Beverly Hills, CA: Sage Publications.

Chang, E. (1988). *Korean-Black Conflict in Los Angeles: Perceptions and Realities*. (Unpublished paper on file with authors).

Church, G. (1992, May 11). The fire this time. *Time*, pp. 18-25.

Cleaver, J.H. (1987, March 19). One answer to an outcry. *Los Angeles Sentinel*, p. 1.

Cleaver, J.H. (1983a, August 18). Asian attitudes towards Blacks cause raised eyebrows. *Los Angeles Sentinel*, p. 1.

Cleaver, J.H. (1983b, September 1). Citizens air gripes about Asians. *Los Angeles Sentinel*, p. 1.

Cleaver, J.H. (1983c, August 28). Residents complain about alleged Asian problem. *Los Angeles Sentinel*, p. 1.

Clifford, F. et al. (1992, August 30). Leaders lose feel for L.A. *The Los Angeles Times*, p. A1.

Cole, R. E. and Deskins, D. R. (1988). Racial factors in site location and employment patterns of Japanese auto firms. *California Management Review*, 9(13), p. 13.

Collins, K.E. (1980). *Black Los Angeles: The Maturing of the Ghetto, 1940-1950*. Saratoga, CA: Century Twenty One Publishing.

Cross, H. et al. (1990). *Employer Hiring Practices: Differential Treatment of Hispanic and Anglo Job Seekers. Report No. 90-4*. Washington, DC: The Urban Institute Press.

Culp, J., and Dunson, B.H. (1986). Brothers of a different color: A preliminary look at employer treatment of white and black youth. pp. 233-260 in *The Black Youth Employment Crisis*, edited by R.B. Freeman and H.J. Holzer. Chicago: University of Chicago Press.

Davis, M. (1990). *City of Quartz: Excavating the Future of Los Angeles*. New York: Oxford Press.

DeParle, J. (1992, May 20). Year-old study on police abuse is issued by U.S. *The New York Times*, pp. A1 & A10.

Dionne, E.J. (1999, September 27). America the violent. *The Washington Post National Weekly Edition*, p. 26.

Duffy, B., Tharp, M., Streisand, B., Cooper, M., (1992, May 11). Days of rage. *U.S. News & World Report*, pp. 20-26.

Editors. (1992, May 25). Race against time. *The New Republic*, pp. Cover, 7-9.

Ellis, D. (1992, May 11). L.A. lawless. *Time*, pp. 26-29.

Erdman, A. and Ratan, S. (1992, June 1). What we can do now. *Fortune*, pp. 41-48.

Farrell, W.C., Johnson, J.H., and Jones, C.K. (1992). *Field notes from the Rodney King trial and the Los Angeles rebellion*. April, 28 & 29, May 2, 3, & 4. Deerborn, MI: University of Michigan at Dearborn.

Flannigan, J. (1992, May 31). Can L.A. answer cry for economic equality. *The Los Angeles Times*, pp. D1 & D3.

Fortune (1992, June 1). What we can do now. Fortune, pp. 41-48.

Galtung, J. (1996). *Peace by peaceful means: Peace and conflict, development and civilization*. London: Sage.

Grieco, E.M. and Cassidy, R. (2001, March 12) *Querview of Race and Hispanic Origin*. Washington, DC: U.S. Census Bureau.

Harris, F.R. and Wilkins, R.W., eds. (1989). *Quiet Riots*. New York: Pantheon Books.

Hinds, M. (1992, November 11). Survey cited to assail Bush on overseas jobs. *The New York Times*, p. A35.

Holcomb, H.B. and Beauregard, R.A. (1981). *Revitalizing Cities.* (Resource Paper). Washington, DC: Association of American Geographies.

Howlett, D. (1992, May 5). Jobs, skills, most pressing need for cities. *USA Today,* p.13A.

Institute for Alternative Journalism, ed. (1992). *Inside the L.A. Riots.* Los Angeles, CA: Institute for Alternative Journalism.

Jackson, M-R., Johnson, J.H., Jr., and Farrell, W.C. (1994, Spring). After the smoke has cleared: An analysis of selected responses to the Los Angeles civil unrest of 1992. *Contentions,* 3(3), k4-21.

Johnson, J.H., Jr., Jones, C.K., Farrell, W.C., and Oliver, M.L. (1992, November). The Los Angeles Rebellion: A retrospective view. *Economic Development Quarterly,* 6(4), 356-372.

Johnson, J.H., Jr., Farrell, W.C., and Oliver, M.L. (1993, March). Seeds of the Los Angeles rebellion. *International Journal of Urban and Regional Research,* 17(1), 115-119.

Johnson, J.H., Jr., and Farrell, W.C. (1993, June). The fire this time: The genesis of the Los Angeles rebellion of 1992. *North Carolina Law Review,* 71(5), 1403-1420.

Johnson, J.H., Jr., Farrell, W.C., and Jackson, M-R. (1994, February). Los Angeles one year later: A prospective assessment of responses to the 1992 civil unrest. *Economic Development Quarterly,* 8(1), 19-27.

Johnson, J.H., Jr., Farrell, W.C., and Toji, D.S. (1997, August). Assessing the employment impacts of the Los Angeles civil unrest of 1992: Furthering racial divisions. *Economic Development Quarterly,* 11(3), 225-235.

Johnson, J.H., Jr., and Farrell, W.C. (1998). Growing income inequality in American society: A political economy perspective. In *The Inequality Paradox: Growth of Income Disparity.* Edited by J.A. Auerbach and R.S. Belous. Washington, DC: National Policy Association, pp.133-180.

Johnson, J.H., Jr., Farrell, W.C., and Guinn, C. (1999). Immigration reform and the browning of America: Tensions, Conflict, and Community Instability in Metropolitan Los Angeles. In *The Handbook of International Migration.* Edited by C. Hirschman, P. Kasnitz and J. DeWind, pp. 390-415.

Johnson, J.H., Jr. (1992, April 30). The declining economic fortunes of black Americans. Paper presented to the Markle Foundation Seminar on Entrenched Urban Poverty and Racial Strife: Framing the Issues, Spelling Out Choices, and Spotlighting Workable Solutions. New York.

Johnson, J.H., Jr., and Oliver, M. L. (1991). Economic restructuring and black male joblessness in U.S. metropolitan areas. *Urban Geography,* Vol. 12, 542-562.

Johnson, J.H., Jr., Oliver, M.L., and Roseman, C. (1989). Ethnic dilemmas in comparative perspective. *Urban Geography,* 10, pp. 425-433.

Johnson, J.H., Jr., and Oliver, M.L. (1989). Interethnic minority conflict in urban America: The effects of economic and social dislocations. *Urban Geography.* Vol. 10, pp. 449-463.

Johnson, J.H., Jr., and Roseman, C.C. (1990). Increasing black outmigration from Los Angeles: The role of household dynamics and kinship systems. *Annuals of the Association of American Geographers,* Vol. 80, 205-222.

Kennedy, R. (1999, September 13 & 20). Suspect policy. *The New Republic*, pp. 30-35.

Kim, E.H. (1992, May 18). They armed in self-defense. *Newsweek*, p. 10.

Kim, S. (1984, June 8). Seeking a dialogue by Koreans, Blacks. *The Los Angeles Times*, p. 8.

Kirschenman, J., and Neckerman, K. (1991). We'd love to hire them but . . . the meaning of race for employers. pp. 203-324 in *The Urban Underclass*, edited by C. Jencks and P. Peterson. Washington, DC: The Brookings Institution.

Labor/Community Strategy Center (1992). *Reconstructing Los Angeles from the Bottom Up*. Los Angeles, CA; Labor/Community Strategy Center.

Lacayo, R. (1992, May 11). Anatomy of an acquittal. *Time*, pp. 30-32.

Lait, M. and Glover, S. (1999, December 9). Ex-LAPD officer is suspect in rapper's slaying, records show. *The Los Angeles Times*, <latimes.com/news>.

Lait, M. and Glover, S. (2000a, February 10). Police in secret group broke law routinely, transcripts say. *The Los Angeles Times*, latimes.com/news.

Lait, M. and Glover, S. (2000b February 14). Beatings alleged to be routine at Rampart. *The Los Angeles Times*, <latimes.com/news>.

Lait, M. and Glover, S. (2000c, February 24). FBI launches probe into Rampart scandal. *The Los Angeles Times*, <latimes.com/news>.

Levy, F. (1995). Incomes and income equality. In *State of the Union America in the 1990s, Volume I: Economic Trends*. Edited by R. Farley. New York: Russell Sage.

Levy, F. (1987). *Dollars and Dreams: The Changing American Income Distribution*. New York: Russell Sage.

Lichter, D.T. (1988). Racial differences in underemployment in American cities. *American Journal of Sociology*, Vol. 93, 771-792.

Loury, C.C. (1993, February 25). God and the ghetto. *The Wall Street Journal*, p. A14.

Luttwak, E.N. (1992, May 15). The riots: Underclass vs. immigrants. *The New York Times*, p. A15.

Marris, D. (1992, May 20). How social research could reform debate over urban problems. *The Chronicle of Higher Education*, p. A40.

Matthews, T. (1992, May 11). The siege of L.A. *Newsweek*, pp. 30-38.

McCord, J. (1997). Placing urban violence in context. In *Violence and Childhood in the Inner City*. Edited by J. McCord. New York: Cambridge University Press, pp. 78-115.*ek*, pp. 30-38.

Meyer, M. (1992, May 18). Los Angeles will serve itself. *Newsweek*, p. 46.

Miles, J. (1992, October). Blacks vs. Browns. *The Atlantic Monthly*, pp. 41-45, 48, 50-53, 55, 58-60, 62-63, 66-68.

Mitchell, M. (1992). Korean merchants, black gang summit help ease tensions. *Los Angeles Sentinel*. May 28, pp. A1 & A17.

Moore, J. (1981). Minorities in the American class system. *Daedalus*, pp. 110, 275-289.

Morgenthau, T. (1992, May 11). The price of neglect. *Newsweek*, pp. 54-55.

Moss, P., and Tilly, C. (1991). *Why Black Men Are Doing Worse in the Labor Market*. New York: Social Science Research Council.

Mueller, T. and Espenshade, T.J. (1985). *The Fourth Wave*. Washington, DC: The Urban Institute Press.

Mydans, S. (1992a, April 29). Jury acquits Los Angeles policemen in taped beating. *The New York Times*, pp. A1 & A11.

Mydans, S. (1992b, May 7). Revelers facing the music, or the looter as everyman. *The New York Times*, pp. A1 & A11.

Mydans, S. (1992c, May 3). A target of rioters, Koreatown is bitter, armed and determined. *The New York Times*, pp. 1 & 16.

Mydans, S. (1992d, May 15). Riots' ground zero: Street of hopelessness. *The New York Times*, pp. A1 & A12.

Mydans, S. and Marriott, M. (1992, May 18). Riots ruin a business, and a neighborhood suffers. *The New York Times*, pp. A1 and C10.

Newsweek (1992a, May 11). Race: Our dilemma still. *Newsweek*, pp.44-51.

Newsweek (1992b, May 18). Rethinking Race and Crime in America. *Newsweek*, pp. 26-47.

Newton, J., Lait, M. and Glover, S. (2000,March 1). LAPD condemned by its own inquiry into Rampart scandal. *The Los Angeles Times*, <latimes.com/news>.

Oliver, M.L., Farrell, W.C., and Johnson, J.H., Jr. (1990, August 10). A quarter-century of slipping backward. *Los Angeles Times*, p. B7.

Oliver, M.L., Johnson, J.H., and Farrell, W.C. (1993) Anatomy of a rebellion: A political-economic analysis. In *Reading Rodney King*. Edited by Robert Gooding-Williams. New York: Routledge, Inc., pp.117-141.

Oliver, M.L., and Johnson, J.H., Jr. (1984). Interethnic conflict in an urban ghetto: The case of Blacks and Latinos in Los Angeles. *Research in Social Movements, Conflict, and Change*, Vol. 6, 57-94.

Ong, P., and Blumenberg, E. (1992). *Racial and Economic Inequality in Los Angeles*, Los Angeles, CA: Graduate School of Architecture and Urban Planning, University of California at Los Angeles.

Palmer, J.L. and Sawhill, I.V. (1984). *The Reagan Record: An Assessment of America's Changing Priorities*. Washington, DC: The Urban Institute Press.

Pilisuk, M. (1998). The hidden structure of contemporary violence. *Peace and Conflict: Journal of Peace Psychology*, Vol. 4, No. 3, 197-216.

Report of the Ad Hoc Committee on Recovery and Revitalization to the Los Angeles City Council. (1992, October 29).

Reuters (2000, November 22). Los Angeles settles lawsuit against *The New York Times*, <www.nytimes.com/2000/11/national/22ANGE.html>.

Rule, S. (1992). Rappers' words foretold depth of blacks' anger *The New York Times*. May 26, p. B1.

Rutten, T. (1992, June 11). A new kind of riot. *The New York Review of Books*, pp. 52-54.

Salholz, E. (1992, May 11). Blacks and cops: Up against the wall. *Newsweek*, pp. 52-53.

Schatzman, D. (1992, May 28). Fifty to sixty percent of riot arrestees had no prior contact with the law. *The Los Angeles Times*, pp. A1 & A16.

Scheck, B. (1992, May 25). Following orders. *The New Republic*, pp.17-19.

Scott, A.J. (1988). Flexible production systems and regional development: The rise of new industrial spaces in North America and Western Europe. *International Journal of Urban and Regional Research*, 12, 171, 178-182.

Soja, E., Morales, R., and Wolff, G. (1983). Urban restructuring: An analysis of social and spatial change in Los Angeles. *Economic Geography*, Vol. 58, 221-235.

Squires, G.D. (1982). Runaway plants, capital mobility, and black economic rights. pp.62-97 in *Community and Capital in Conflict: Plant Closings and Job Loss*. Edited by J.C. Raines et al. Philadelphia: Temple University Press.

Steel, R. (1992, May 25). The Bobby gap. *The New Republic*, pp.16-17.

Sterngold, J. (2000, November 17). Panel rebukes police leaders in Los Angeles. *The New York Times*, <www.nytimes/2000/11/17/national/17ANGE.html>.

Stevenson, R.W. (1992, April 30). Verdicts in beating case produce anger. *The New York Times*, p. A8.

Terry, D. (1992, May 13). Decades of rage created crucible of violence. *New York Times*, pp. 1 & 17.

The New Republic. (1992, May 25). Race against time. *The New Republic*, pp. 7-9, 11-12, 14-20, & 22-25.

The 1968 Report of the National Commission on Civil Disorders (1988). *The Kerner Report*. New York: Pantheon Books.

Time. (1992a, May 11). Can we all get along? *Time*, pp. 18-41

Time. (1992b, May 18). This is your land . . . *Time*, pp. 28-37.

Turner, C.B., and Turner, B. (1981). Racial discrimination in occupations: Perceived and actual. *Phylon*. 42: 322-34.

Turner, M. et al. (1991). *Opportunities Denied, Opportunities Diminished: Discrimination in Hiring*. Unpublished Project Report. Washington, DC: The Urban Institute Press.

Weinstein, H. (1999, December 15). Rampart probe may now affect 3,000 cases. *The Los Angeles Times*, <latimes.com/news>

Whitman, D. (1993a, May 31). LA riot. *U.S. News and World Report*, pp. 35-57.

Whitman, D. (1993b, May 31). Latinos were prominent as victims and victimizers. *U.S. News and World Report*, p. 55.

Wilson, J.Q. (1992, May 18). How to teach better values in inner cities. *The Wall Street Journal*, p. A14.

Zuckerman, M. (1993, May 31). Los Angeles under the gun. *U.S. News and World Report*, p. 82.

Index

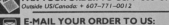
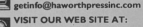

TO ORDER: CALL: 1-800-429-6784 / FAX: 1-800-895-0582 (Outside US/Canada: + 607-771-0012) / E-MAIL: getinfo@haworthpressinc.com

☐ YES, please send me **Survivors Recovering From Sexual Abuse, Addictions, and Compulsive Behaviors**

_____ in hard at $49.95 ISBN: 0-7890-1457-2.

_____ in soft at $34.95 ISBN: 0-7890-1458-0.

- Individual orders outside US, Canada, and Mexico must be prepaid by check or credit card.
- Discounts are not available on 5+ text prices and not available in conjunction with any other discount. • Discount not applicable on books priced under $15.00.
- 5+ text prices are not available for jobbers and wholesalers.
- Postage & handling: In US: $4.00 for first book; $1.50 for each additional book. Outside US: $5.00 for first book; $2.00 for each additional book.
- NY, MN, and OH residents: please add appropriate sales tax after postage & handling. Canadian residents: please add 7% GST after postage & handling. Canadian residents of Newfoundland, Nova Scotia, and New Brunswick, also add 8% for province tax. • Payment in UNESCO coupons welcome.
- If paying in Canadian dollars, use current exchange rate to convert to US dollars.
- Please allow 3-4 weeks for delivery after publication.
- Prices and discounts subject to change without notice.

Signature _____

☐ **BILL ME LATER** ($5 service charge will be added).
(Not available for individuals outside US/Canada/Mexico. Service charge is waived for/to jobbers/wholesalers/booksellers.)

☐ Check here if billing address is different from shipping address and attach purchase order and billing address information.

☐ **PAYMENT ENCLOSED $** _____
(Payment must be in US or Canadian dollars by check or money order drawn on a US or Canadian bank.)

☐ **PLEASE BILL MY CREDIT CARD:**

☐ AmEx ☐ Diners Club ☐ Discover ☐ Eurocard ☐ JCB ☐ Master Card ☐ Visa

Account Number _____

Expiration Date _____

Signature _____

May we open a confidential credit card account for you for possible future purchases? ( ) Yes ( ) No

THE HAWORTH PRESS, INC., 10 Alice Street, Binghamton, NY 13904-1580 USA

Please complete the information below or tape your business card in this area.

NAME _____

INSTITUTION _____

ADDRESS _____

CITY _____

STATE _____ ZIP _____

COUNTRY _____

COUNTY (NY residents only) _____

E-MAIL _____
(type or print clearly!)

May we use your e-mail address for confirmations and other types of information? ( ) **Yes** ( ) **No** We appreciate receiving your e-mail address and fax number. Haworth would like to e-mail or fax special discount offers to you, as a preferred customer. We will never **share, rent, or exchange** your e-mail address or fax number. We regard such actions as an invasion of your privacy.

☐ YES, please send me **Survivors Recovering From Sexual Abuse, Addictions, and Compulsive Behaviors (ISBN: 0-7890-1458-0)** to consider on a 60-day **no risk** examination basis. I understand that I will receive an invoice payable within 60 days, or that **if I decide to adopt the book, my invoice will be cancelled.** I understand that I will be billed at the lowest price. (60-day offer available only to teaching faculty in US, Canada, and Mexico / Outside US/Canada, a proforma invoice will be sent upon receipt of your request and must be paid in advance of shipping. A full refund will be issued with proof of adoption.)

This information is needed to process your examination copy order.

Signature _____

Course Title(s) _____

Current Text(s) _____

Enrollment _____

Semester _____ Decision Date _____

Office Tel _____ Hours _____

(14) (16) (29)   08/01   BIC01